Tolley's Double Taxation Relief

Fourth Edition

by

Alastair Munro BA (OXON) ATII

Members of the LexisNexis Group worldwide

United Kingdom	Butterworths Tolley, a Division of Reed Elsevier (UK) Ltd, Halsbury House, 35 Chancery Lane, London, WC2A 1EL, and 4 Hill Street, EDINBURGH EH2 3JZ
Argentina	Abeledo Perrot, Jurisprudencia Argentina and Depalma, BUENOS AIRES
Australia	Butterworths, a Division of Reed International Books Australia Pty Ltd, CHATSWOOD, New South Wales
Austria	ARD Betriebsdienst and Verlag Orac, VIENNA
Canada	Butterworths Canada Ltd, MARKHAM, Ontario
Chile	Publitecsa and Conosur Ltda, SANTIAGO DE CHILE
Czech Republic	Orac sro, PRAGUE
France	Editions du Juris-Classeur SA, PARIS
Hong Kong	Butterworths Asia (Hong Kong), HONG KONG
Hungary	Hvg Orac, BUDAPEST
India	Butterworths India, NEW DELHI
Ireland	Butterworths (Ireland) Ltd, DUBLIN
Italy	Giuffré, MILAN
Malaysia	Malayan Law Journal Sdn Bhd, KUALA LUMPUR
New Zealand	Butterworths of New Zealand, WELLINGTON
Poland	Wydawnictwa Prawnicze PWN, WARSAW
Singapore	Butterworths Asia, SINGAPORE
South Africa	Butterworths Publishers (Pty) Ltd, DURBAN
Switzerland	Stämpfli Verlag AG, BERNE
USA	LexisNexis, DAYTON, Ohio

A CIP Catalogue record for this book is available from the British Library.

ISBN 0754502619

Typeset by YHT Ltd, London
Printed and bound in Great Britain by The Cromwell Press, Trowbridge, Wiltshire

Visit Butterworths LexisNexis *direct* at www.butterworths.com

Preface to the Fourth Edition

Since Rodney Taylor edited the third edition of this book in 1998, there have been significant and wide-ranging changes to the UK's double tax relief regime. Most notably, the new measures introduced to the UK's domestic rules as part of Finance Act 2000, which brought in the mixer cap restriction and the onshore pooling regime for certain types of foreign dividends, have gone to the heart of the double tax relief planning carried out by many UK multinationals during the 1980s and 1990s.

In the wider sphere of double tax relief both the OECD and the United Nations have recently updated their Model Tax Conventions and the respective commentaries, while the new draft double tax treaty between the UK and the US was published earlier this year. There have also been a number of developments in EU case law. In the context of all these changes, demand for a fourth edition of this book has therefore been extremely high.

Despite the large amount of new material I have included in the fourth edition, most of this book remains the work of Rodney Taylor. Over the last few months, it has been a pleasure for me to follow the path originally beaten by Rodney as the fourth edition has taken shape.

I would like to take this chance to thank my colleagues at KPMG for their expert input into the fourth edition: in particular; Alison Christian (treasury tax), Philip Lewis (insurance), Liz Elsworth (banking), Catherine Shepherd (personal tax) and John Burns (transfer pricing). Special thanks are due to Ruch Pathirana (international tax).

This edition is based on law and agreements in force at 31 August 2001.

Alastair Munro BA (Oxon) ATII
November 2001

Alastair Munro led KPMG's double tax relief specialist group for three years until April 2001. He was involved in the Inland Revenue's review of double tax relief for companies and advises a large number of UK multinationals on double tax relief and controlled foreign companies issues. Alastair is currently a senior manager leading KPMG's energy and national resources tax group in London. He can be contacted on Alastair.Munro@kpmg.co.uk.

Contents

Table of Statutes

Table of Statutes

Table of Cases

Abbreviations and References

ACT	=	Advance corporation tax
CAA	=	Capital Allowances Act 1990
CFC	=	Controlled foreign company
CTT	=	Capital transfer tax
EC	=	European Community
ESC	=	Extra-statutory concession
EU	=	European Union
EUFT	=	Eligible unrelieved foreign tax
FA	=	Finance Act
FICO	=	Financial Intermediaries and Claims Office
FID	=	Foreign income dividend
IHC	=	International headquarters company
IHT	=	Inheritance tax
IHTA	=	Inheritance Tax Act 1984 (formerly Capital Transfer Tax Act)
OECD	=	Organisation for Economic Co-operation and Development
PE	=	Permanent establishment
QFD	=	Qualifying foreign dividend
SI	=	Statutory Instrument
SP	=	Statement of Practice
STC	=	Simon's Tax Cases
TA	=	Income and Corporation Taxes Act 1988
TC	=	Official Reports of Tax Cases
TCGA	=	Taxation of Chargeable Gains Act 1992
TMA	=	Taxes Management Act 1970
UK	=	United Kingdom
UN	=	United Nations
US	=	United States of America

Chapter 1

Introduction to Double Taxation Relief

Introduction

1.1   The potential for double taxation arises in a variety of situations where, under the laws of two or more countries, tax may be levied on the same income, capital gains, transfers of capital or net worth. Where tax is levied in more than one jurisdiction on the same person this is often termed 'juridical double taxation'. Nearly all countries tax economic activity being carried on within their territories, including many which are considered to be tax havens. In addition, many countries tax individuals, companies and other entities which are 'resident' in their territories on their worldwide income or profits. For example, a company which has an overseas branch may be liable to tax both in the country of the head office (on its worldwide profits) and in the country in which the branch is located (on the profits accruing to the branch). Unless there is a mechanism for granting relief, in this case usually in the country of the head office, the result will be double taxation of the profits.

1.2   'Economic' double taxation occurs where more than one person is taxed in respect of the same income. For example, if a parent company manufactures goods and sells them to a subsidiary in a foreign country, both companies will normally file tax returns which include as the transfer value of those goods the price charged by the parent and paid by the subsidiary. However, usually after the submission of tax returns by both companies, the tax authorities of one or both of those countries may seek to adjust the accounts of those companies for tax purposes. The basis of the adjustments may be that the prices charged by the parent to the subsidiary are not those which would have been agreed between the companies if they had been independent parties acting at arm's length. One of the tax authorities (or both of them) may start proceedings to collect additional tax which it considers is due to it from the company within its jurisdiction. As there is usually no mechanism in the domestic tax laws of a country for reducing a tax assessment to take account of additional tax charged on another company in another jurisdiction, the result will be double taxation of the disputed income at the margin.

1.3   The charging of tax more than once on the profits of companies or on the income, capital gains and estates of individuals would act as a significant barrier both to international trade and to movements of people and capital. There is clearly, therefore, a need for mechanisms whereby double taxation is avoided or, at the very least, reduced to tolerable levels.

This book discusses the law and practice of the UK with regard to double taxation relief in its domestic law (unilateral relief) and by its treaty obligations. Historically, those treaty obligations have been principally bilateral double taxation agreements. However, in recent years, the UK as a member of the European Union has entered into a number of important multilateral agreements with other European states.

Examples of double taxation of income

1.4   The following sets out a number of circumstances in which double taxation of income would arise on a source of income in the absence of some form of double taxation relief. The list is not exhaustive.

(*a*)   A UK resident company which has a branch overseas is liable to UK corporation tax on its worldwide profits, including the income of the foreign branch. In addition, it is subject to foreign tax on the branch income in the country in which the branch is situated. The branch profits are therefore liable to be taxed in both jurisdictions.

(*b*)   An overseas incorporated company is resident in the UK because its central management and control is situated in the UK. It is also resident in the country of incorporation under the domestic law of that country. The company is subject to tax on its worldwide profits in both countries.

(*c*)   A UK resident company is undercharging overseas affiliated companies or is being overcharged by them in respect of the supply of goods or services. It is required to compute its taxable profits on the basis that these transactions had been made at an arm's length rate. [*TA 1988, Sch 28AA*].

(*d*)   A UK resident company is overcharging overseas affiliated companies or is being undercharged by them in respect of the supply of goods or services. The profits of the overseas affiliated companies are increased for foreign tax purposes under the transfer pricing legislation of the countries concerned.

(*e*)   An individual who is resident, ordinarily resident and domiciled in the UK and who receives income from abroad including dividends, interest, royalties, pensions and rents may be subject to tax both in the country in which the income arises and in the UK.

(*f*)   An individual may be 'resident' in two (or more) countries at once because, for example, he has homes in both countries and spends part of the year in each home. Such a 'dual resident' individual may be subject to taxation on his worldwide income in both countries.

(*g*)   A UK resident individual who receives remuneration in respect of an employment carried on abroad may be subject to tax in the country in which the duties of the employment are carried out and also in the UK.

(*h*)   The US taxes its citizens on their worldwide income wherever they are resident. Accordingly, US citizens living abroad may be liable to tax on their worldwide income and capital gains both in their country of residence and in the US.

Examples of double taxation of capital gains

1.5   Double taxation of capital gains arises in similar ways. In fact, in many countries there is no separate capital gains tax and gains are included as income in the income tax computation. Accordingly:

(*a*)   a UK resident individual who disposes of assets situated abroad may be liable both to foreign income tax and to UK capital gains tax;

(*b*)   an individual or other person may be resident in more than one country and liable to tax on worldwide gains in both countries.

1.6   Assets situated in the UK which are owned by a person neither resident nor ordinarily resident in the UK are not normally liable to UK tax on the capital gain. However, UK tax is chargeable if:

(*a*)   the assets form part of the business property of a branch or agency in the UK [*TCGA 1992, s 10*];

(*b*)   the provisions of *TA 1988, s 776* (transactions in land: taxation of capital gains) apply; or

(*c*)   a non-UK resident disposes of rights and shares in connection with exploration or exploitation activities in the UK or in a designated area. [*TCGA 1992, s 276*].

(*d*)   from 17 March 1998, where an individual makes a disposal of an asset which he held when he became non-UK resident and he resumes UK residence before five years of assessment have elapsed, any gain is liable to capital gains tax in the year in which he resumes UK residence. [*TCGA 1992, s 10A*].

Examples of double taxation of gifts and inheritances

1.7   Double taxation of gifts and inheritances arises in a number of ways. Again, the list is not exhaustive.

(*a*)   A person domiciled in the UK who makes a gift of a foreign asset may be liable to a foreign gift tax on the disposal and may also be liable to UK inheritance tax (IHT) either immediately or, if the gift is a potentially exempt transfer, on his death within seven years.

(*b*)   A person not domiciled in the UK may be liable to IHT, as well as gift or inheritance tax in his own country, if he dies while owning assets situated in the UK.

(*c*)   A UK domiciled person going abroad to live permanently remains UK domiciled for at least three years under *IHTA 1984, s 267* and therefore remains subject to IHT on his estate wherever it is situated. Should he die during that period he may be liable both to IHT and to foreign gift or estate tax on his worldwide property.

(*d*)   Similarly, under *section 267*, a non-UK domiciled individual who has been resident in the UK for at least 17 of the last 20 years and who goes to live permanently abroad may be deemed to be domiciled in the UK for up to three years following departure. Should he die during this period, his estate may be liable both to IHT and to gift or inheritance taxes in the country in which he has taken up residence.

Chapter 2

Historical Background, Manner of Granting Relief and Administrative Matters

Historical background

2.1   Income tax was first imposed in the UK in 1799, and, although technically it expires at the end of each financial year, effectively became permanent from 1842. Double taxation appears to have become an active issue during the latter half of the nineteenth century primarily because, by that time, countries of the British Empire were beginning to introduce forms of taxation of their own.

Introduction of unilateral relief

2.2   During the early years, concern about double taxation did not meet with a sympathetic reaction from government and for many years no action was taken to provide relief. At that time rates of income tax were relatively low and the burden of double taxation was alleviated somewhat by the fact that many sources of foreign income were taxed on the remittance basis. Double taxation could therefore be avoided in some cases by keeping the income outside the UK.

By 1914 the charge to UK income tax was extended to the whole of an individual's investment income, whether or not remitted to the UK, and with tax rates increasing dramatically during the First World War, the incidence of double taxation began to receive greater consideration by the government. In 1916, unilateral double taxation relief (then known as 'Dominion income tax relief') was introduced. However, it applied only to taxes suffered in countries within the British Empire and was only a partial relief in that it could not reduce the UK tax on income below $17\frac{1}{2}\%$. In 1920 the relief was modified so that, from that time, double taxation relief was given for the full foreign tax suffered, provided that the rate did not exceed 50% of the UK tax rate applicable to the income. If it did exceed this figure, the relief was limited to 50% of the rate of UK tax and was still restricted to taxes of territories within the British Empire.

Early agreements relating to double taxation relief

2.3   A bilateral double taxation agreement was entered into with the Irish Free State in 1926 which adopted the principle of taxation on the basis of the country of residence of the taxpayer rather than the country of the source of the income. This was the only agreement concluded by the UK relating to income generally which adopted this principle, although it still applies in the limited agreements relating to shipping and air transport profits — see 2.20 below.

The end of the Second World War brought major new developments with the conclusion of a comprehensive double taxation agreement with the US in 1945. This can be regarded as the first modern style comprehensive double taxation agreement relating to income entered into by the UK and it was followed shortly afterwards by agreements with most countries of the present Commonwealth.

Many agreements with European countries and other major trading partners followed in the 1950s and 1960s and the UK now has the most extensive network of agreements in the world. This network is still expanding as a result of new agreements with several nations created by the break-up of the Eastern Bloc and with those emerging as major trading nations on the Pacific rim, in the Middle East and in South America. The UK now has well over 100 comprehensive double taxation agreements and this number is growing annually.

Development of unilateral relief

2.4   Unilateral double taxation relief in its present form effectively dates from 1950. Legislation was introduced in that year providing for relief for foreign taxes suffered in countries with which the UK had not concluded a comprehensive agreement. At first, limits similar to those applicable to Dominion income tax relief were laid down, but these restrictions were removed in 1953. From that date the credit for foreign tax was limited, as broadly speaking it is today, to the amount of UK tax charged on the same income.

Model agreements prepared by the OECD and the United Nations

2.5   The Organisation for Economic Co-operation and Development (OECD) was established in 1961. Its members now comprise most Western European countries, Australia, Canada, the Czech Republic, the Slovak Republic, Hungary, Japan, the Republic of Korea, Mexico, New Zealand, Poland, Turkey and the US, and among its functions has been the development of recommendations for the avoidance of double taxation. The Commission of the European Communities also takes part in the work of the OECD under Article 13 of the OECD Convention.

In 1963 the OECD produced its first model double taxation agreement entitled 'Draft Double Taxation Convention on Income and Capital'. Its purpose was to provide a basis for standardisation of double taxation agreements concluded between member countries. While this was not the first such model (since one was produced as early as 1928 by the League of Nations) it was the first to be widely accepted. The 1963 model was superseded by a new model in 1977 containing extensive revisions. The 1977 model was itself replaced by a new model in 1992, although the changes made in the 1992 model were not extensive. The OECD has stated that revising the model has become an ongoing process and that further amendments and updates are to be published regularly without waiting for a complete revision. Minor amendments were made in 1994, 1995, 1997 and 2000. The 1992 OECD model, as subsequently amended, is included as Appendix 1.

In general, the UK has followed many of the articles in the OECD models quite closely, as discussed in Chapters 6, 7 and 8. However, where aspects of the UK or the foreign taxation system differ from that assumed by the model, or where commercial factors dictate otherwise, articles as negotiated in the UK's agreements can be distinctly different from those in the model. For example, the 'dividends' articles in most of the UK's agreements were tailored to the UK's imputation system of corporation tax and the tax credits available on dividends paid by UK companies.

In 1980 the United Nations also published a model double taxation convention which is intended to be a basis for agreements between developed and developing countries. The United Nations has now adopted a revised version of this model which has recently been published. The principal difference between this model and the OECD model is that it tends to be more favourable to the country of source of the income. For example, the 'royalties' article in the UN model allows royalties arising in a territory to be taxed in that territory, increasing the tax revenues of a country which is a net importer of capital.

EC multilateral agreements

2.6   The UK's tax relations with other countries are increasingly being governed by multilateral agreements, particularly those from the European Community. In 1977 a directive on the mutual assistance by the competent authorities of the member states was introduced — see 2.28 below. Two further directives and a convention were approved by member states in July 1990. These were the Parent/Subsidiary Directive (90/435/EEC), the Mergers Directive (90/434/EEC) which is discussed at 3.60 and the Arbitration Convention (90/436/EEC). In addition, a proposal for a Directive to eliminate withholding taxes on interest and royalty payments has been adopted.

The EC Parent/Subsidiary Directive

2.7   The EC Parent/Subsidiary Directive (reproduced as Appendix 7) came into effect on 1 January 1992 with respect to the (then) twelve members of the EC and from 1 January 1995 with respect to Finland, Sweden and Austria under the Act of Accession of those countries. It applies where the parent holds a minimum of 25% of the capital of a company (the 'subsidiary') in another member state. However, the member states have the option, by means of bilateral agreement, of replacing the criterion of a holding in the capital by a holding in voting rights.

The Directive governs three aspects of the payment of a dividend from one member state to another:

(*a*)   a dividend is to be exempt from withholding tax in the country of the paying company;

(*b*)   the country of the recipient is required either to exempt the dividend from tax, or to give credit for the proportion of the subsidiary's corporation tax relating to the dividend; and

(*c*)   the country of the parent is not allowed to charge a withholding tax on the dividend received.

Where the country of the parent applies the exemption method in (*b*) above it is allowed to provide that charges and losses relating to the holding and the dividend are not deductible from the taxable profits of the parent company. If the management costs relating to the shareholding are calculated at a fixed rate, the non-deductible amount may not exceed 5% of the dividend.

Each member state has the option of not applying the Directive in cases where the required shareholding is not maintained for an uninterrupted period of at least two years. This option is applied variously by different countries. Some, such as the UK and Ireland, do not apply such a condition. Others may allow a holding period of less than two years, or may give relief under the Directive before the expiry of the requisite period, subject to guarantees that the shareholding will be maintained for that period.

In *Denkavit Internationaal BV v Bundesamt für Finanzen* [1996] STC 1445 the European Court considered the method of application of a minimum holding period in the Parent/Subsidiary Directive.

The provisions incorporating the Directive into German law stated that 'parent company' meant a company which at the moment when liability to tax arose could show that it had held directly at least one-quarter of the share capital of the subsidiary for an uninterrupted period of at least 12 months. Denkavit Internationaal BV (Denkavit), a Dutch company, had held a direct holding of 25% in its German subsidiary for less than 12 months. When arranging for a distribution of its subsidiary's profits Denkavit requested the German tax authorities to reduce the withholding tax to 5% in accordance with the Directive, giving an undertaking that a 25% holding in the subsidiary would be maintained for an uninterrupted period of at least two years from the date of acquisition. The German tax authorities refused the request on the grounds that the one year minimum holding period under German law had not been complied with at the time of payment of the dividend. The European Court held in favour of Denkavit and said that, in order to qualify for relief under the Directive, the parent company had to maintain the minimum holding in the subsidiary for a certain period of time, but it was not necessary for the period to have elapsed by the time the dividend was paid.

The Directive contains a number of derogations.

(i) Greece was allowed to continue to levy withholding tax on dividends for as long as dividends paid were a deductible item for corporation tax purposes. However, tax reform measures in 1992 abolished the tax deduction for dividends paid and also the withholding tax on dividends, so that the derogation no longer applies.

(ii) As an interim measure, Germany was allowed to retain a 5% withholding tax until 1 July 1996 provided it charged corporation tax on distributed profits at a rate at least 11% lower than the rate applying to distributed profits. From that date no withholding tax may be charged.

(iii)   For budgetary reasons Portugal was allowed to levy a withholding tax for a further period of eight years (i.e. until 31 December 1999), subject to a possible extension. For the first five years the maximum rate of withholding tax was 15% and for the last three years it is 10%.

The term 'withholding tax' does not include an advance payment or prepayment (*précompte*) of corporation tax to the member state of the subsidiary made in connection with a distribution of profits to its parent company. The Directive does not affect in principle arrangements under domestic law or by agreement to eliminate or reduce double taxation of dividends, in particular those relating to the payment of tax credits to the recipients of dividends (see 7.25).

In *IRC v Océ Van Der Grinten NV* [2000] STC 951 it was considered whether, on a dividend by the UK company to a Dutch company, the abatement of the tax credit by 5% of the aggregate of the dividend and the tax credit under the UK/Netherlands agreement was contrary to the EC Parent/Subsidiary Directive. The case has now been referred to the European Court of Justice.

The Directive allows the application of provisions either under domestic law or by agreement for the prevention of fraud or abuse. In particular, anti-abuse provisions may apply in France, Spain, Italy and Germany in cases where the parent company is controlled by non-EC residents.

An amendment to the Directive has been proposed by the European Commission (Com (93) 293). Should this amendment be adopted, the Directive would apply to all companies subject to company tax levied within the European Union regardless of their legal form. In addition, a tax credit would be available for underlying tax paid by second-tier and lower-tier subsidiaries.

The EC Arbitration Convention

2.8   The most significant tax problem faced by many groups of companies which operate internationally is the resolution of transfer pricing disputes with fiscal authorities. While most comprehensive double taxation agreements contain an article setting out a procedure for mutual agreement of such disputes by the tax authorities, this procedure can be lengthy and there is no mechanism whereby the tax authorities can be compelled to reach agreement. However, the EC Arbitration Convention introduced an alternative procedure where the parties to transfer pricing dispute are both countries within the EC. Following a protracted period of ratification by the member states this came into force on 1 January 1995. The new member states of Austria, Finland and Sweden have since acceded to it.

An important aspect of the EC Arbitration Convention is that, unlike bilateral tax treaties, it lays down both a procedure for resolving transfer pricing disputes and time limits within which this must occur. Initially, the tax authorities have two years from the date on which the case was first submitted to one of the tax authorities to reach an agreement which eliminates the double taxation. If they fail to agree, provision is made for a determination by an advisory commission. This comprises a chairman who possesses the qualifications for appointment to the highest judicial offices in his country or is a 'jurisconsult of recognised competence', a maximum of two individuals from each of the tax authorities concerned and an even number of 'independent persons of standing' drawn from a list of persons nominated by member states. The advisory commission is required to reach a decision within six months, and the tax authorities of the countries concerned are then obliged to take steps to eliminate the double taxation within a further six months. They retain the discretion to resolve matters as they see fit provided that any double taxation is eliminated, but, if they cannot agree on the necessary steps to be taken, must abide by the decision of the advisory commission. A number of cases are currently being dealt with through the arbitration convention procedure. However, no cases have yet reached the stage of determination by an advisory commission. It seems likely that the majority of cases will be resolved by the relevant tax authorities within the two years laid down by the Convention and that in only a relatively few instances will an advisory commission be necessary.

Following the introduction of sections 85–87 of the Finance Act 1999, and the Inland Revenue Statement of Practice issued on 31 August 1999, taxpayers may now enter into advance pricing agreements with the Inland Revenue. Such agreements may also be made in conjunction with the Inland Revenue and other relevant tax authorities in connection with a cross-border transaction.

Interest and royalties

2.9   The European Commission proposed a Directive (Com (98) 67 final) on 3 March 1998 which would eliminate withholding taxes on interest and royalty payments between associated companies of different member states where cross shareholdings of at least 25% exist. Interest and royalty payments within the scope of the proposal, would only be taxed in the member state of the recipent company, although Greece and Portugal would continue to be allowed to levy a restricted level of withholding tax in the initial five years.

The Directive forms part of a tax package (which included a savings Directive and measures to eliminate harmful tax competition) which was discussed at the 1999 Helsinki Summit. As no agreement could be reached at the summit, the Directive has not yet come into force. The Commission has recently reiterated that agreement on the tax package should be reached as soon as possible and by no later than the end of 2002.

UK legislative framework

2.10   The legislation covering double taxation relief in respect of income tax and corporation tax is now contained in *Part XVIII* of *TA 1988* which is divided into three chapters. Chapter I of this part, comprising *sections 788* to *791*, introduces the principal reliefs, namely:

(*a*)   relief by agreement with other countries [*s 788*]; and

(*b*)   unilateral relief. [*s 790*].

Chapter I (by *section 789*) also extends agreements made before 1965 so that they apply to corporation tax on income and gains as they previously applied to profits tax. It also gives the Inland Revenue power to make regulations for carrying out the provisions of any double taxation agreement. [*s 791*]. At present two statutory instruments made under this section are in force.

   (i)   *SI 1970 No 488*, which lays down the procedure whereby a person may be authorised to pay certain types of income (including annual interest and UK patent royalties) to a non-resident without deduction of income tax, or after deduction of tax at a lower rate as provided in an agreement. This is reproduced as Appendix 6.

  (ii)   *SI 1993 No 1957*, which enables the payer of a manufactured overseas dividend to make the payment to a non-resident without deduction of UK tax where the beneficial owner is a resident of a territory with which the UK has an agreement containing an 'other income' article (see 7.65).

SI 1973 No 317, which provided procedures for the payment to non-resident shareholders of UK companies of part of the tax credit to which they were entitled under an agreement has now been revoked.

Chapter II [*ss 792–806*] deals with the rules governing credit relief and is sub-divided under four headings.

(A)   General. *Sections 792* to *798* provide definitions of several of the main terms and lay down the principal rules of computation.

(B)   Tax underlying dividends. [*ss 799–803A*]. This is discussed in detail in Chapter 4.

(C)   Miscellaneous rules. This comprises *sections 804* to *806* and deals with a number of areas including the commencement of sources of income of individuals, overseas life assurance business and time limits.

(D)   Foreign dividends: onshore pooling and utilisation of eligible unrelieved foreign tax. This comprises *sections 806A* to *806M* which cover the mechanics of the onshore pooling regime introduced by *FA 2000* and the rules which deal with unrelieved foreign tax in respect of a foreign branch or agency of a UK resident company.

Chapter III, which comprises *sections 807* to *816*, is headed 'Miscellaneous Provisions' and deals with, *inter alia*, the accrued income scheme, thin capitalisation and royalties where there is a special relationship between the payor and payee, relief in respect of the income of discretionary trusts, recovery of tax credits incorrectly paid and disclosure of information under the EC Arbitration Convention.

2.11   The statutory provisions relating to double taxation relief are extended to capital gains tax by *TCGA 1992, s 277*. References to capital gains and capital gains tax are substituted into *Chapters I* and *II* of *Part XVIII* of *TA 1988* in place of references to income and income tax. *Section 277* also provides that an agreement made before the passing of the *FA 1965* (5 August 1965) which refers to relief from UK tax on capital gains is to have effect in relation to capital gains tax.

The provisions concerning double taxation relief in relation to UK inheritance tax (IHT) are contained in *IHTA 1984, ss 158* and *159*. The first of these sections concerns relief by double taxation agreement and the second deals with unilateral relief.

Authority for double taxation agreements

2.12   The Crown may, under *TA 1988, s 788*, declare by Order in Council that a double taxation agreement with a foreign government is to have effect. Such an Order is subject to prior approval by the House of Commons. A similar procedure is laid down for IHT agreements by *IHTA 1984, s 158*. In the UK agreements take their authority from the fact that they are contained in statutory instruments (*CIR v Collco Dealings Ltd (1960) 39 TC 509*).

Unilateral relief

2.13   If foreign tax is charged on overseas income (or gains) which is also liable to UK tax in the hands of a UK resident and there is no agreement between the UK and the other country, unilateral relief will usually be available under *TA 1988, s 790*. This relief can only take the form of a credit for foreign tax paid against the UK tax on the same income or gains.

Unilateral relief is also available even if there is an agreement with the country in question, although unilateral relief may not be claimed if credit for the tax is allowable under the agreement. [*TA 1988, s793A(2)*].

In addition, credit by way of unilateral relief is not allowed where there are express provisions in the relevant agreement to the effect that relief by way of credit is not permitted in such cases as are described in the agreement. [*TA 1988, s 793A(3)*]. Similarly, credit is not allowed uni-laterally for foreign tax which is subject to relief which has not been claimed under an agreement or under foreign law made in consequence of such an assessment. [*TA 1988, s 793A(1)*]. Many countries with which the UK has an agreement have taxes on income which are levied by political subdivisions or local authorities and these taxes may not be covered by the agreement. For example, the current agreements with the US (1975) and Canada (1978) do not cover US state or Canadian pro-vincial income taxes respectively. Credit for these taxes may be claimed under the UK's unilateral relief provisions.

Agreements, arrangements and conventions

2.14   *TA 1988, s 788(1)* refers to 'arrangements ... with the govern-ment of any territory outside the UK', but, strictly, the 'arrangements' may be 'agreements', 'arrangements' or 'conventions' according to the constitutions of the two countries. Arrangements between the UK and Commonwealth countries that have the Queen as Head of State were generally termed 'agreements' or 'amending agreements', although these are now usually termed 'conventions' and 'protocols'. Those between the UK and its dependent territories (e.g. the Isle of Man and the Channel Islands) are termed 'arrangements' and 'amending arrangements' and differ in that because the UK is responsible for the territory's external affairs, there is no signatory on behalf of the UK or the other territory. Those between the UK and other countries are 'conventions', and amendments are 'protocols'. All three categories are commonly referred to as 'treaties' or 'agreements', and in this book the term 'agreement' is used throughout.

Each agreement is unique because it represents the outcome of negotia-tions between the respective governments and refers to the particular taxes of the foreign jurisdiction. It is therefore essential to refer to the particular wording and definitions contained in the relevant agreement.

Signature and ratification of agreements

2.15   Agreements are normally identified by the date on which they are signed. In order for an agreement to come into force both countries must ratify it, i.e. complete the constitutional procedures necessary to give it the force of law in their respective territories. It then enters into force from a date determined by the agreement itself.

The procedure for ratification depends on the laws of the countries concerned. In the UK a draft Order in Council is published as a draft statutory instrument which is laid before the House of Commons. It declares that the arrangements (printed in a schedule to the Order) have been made and that it is expedient that they be given effect. The House then resolves to present an Address to Her Majesty praying that the Order be made. When made, the Order is published as a numbered statutory instrument.

The agreement itself lays down the dates from which it has effect in relation to each tax covered which, because of a prolonged period of negotiation and ratification, may be before the agreement enters into force. There may also be a period in which the taxpayer may rely on the provisions of a previous agreement if that is more favourable.

Relief in the source country under an agreement

2.16   A double taxation agreement may grant relief in the source country, in the country of which the recipient is a resident, or give relief partly in one country and partly in the other. The UK's agreements often grant exemption in the country of source in respect of a number of types of income, including:

(*a*)   trading income which does not arise through a permanent estab-lishment (PE);

(*b*)   interest;

(*c*)   royalties;

(*d*)   remuneration of persons whose stay in the country is of a short duration and whose remuneration is paid by an employer resident outside that country; and

(*e*)   private occupational pensions.

2.17   Alternatively, partial relief may be granted in the source country by reduction of the rate of tax on income of persons resident in the other contracting state. This applies most commonly in the case of dividends, interest and royalties.

Some of the UK's double taxation agreements contain provisions under which relief from tax is granted only to the extent that the income is 'subject to tax' in the other country. The Inland Revenue takes the view that income is subject to tax in the UK where, for example:

• an individual pays no UK tax because of personal allowances and reliefs;

• the income falls out of the charge to income tax because it falls within the penultimate year of a trade, or is chargeable to tax in the transitional year between the prior and the current year bases of assessment (1996/97) on the appropriate percentage of income of a period of more than twelve months;

• the income is covered by capital allowances.

Where the remittance basis applies, only the amount remitted to the UK is considered to be subject to tax. A person is not regarded as subject to tax in the UK if the income in question is exempt from UK tax by statute or extra-statutory concession, e.g. where it is the exempt income of a charity or exempt approved superannuation scheme. However, the Inland Revenue regards UK charities and superannuation schemes as 'liable to tax' in the UK even though they are exempt from tax in some circumstances. They are therefore residents of the UK and are entitled to the benefit of a double taxation agreement on income which is not taxed in the UK (see 3.3), provided there is no requirement in the agreement for the income to be 'subject to tax' in the UK.

Relief by agreement in the recipient's country of residence

2.18   Relief from double taxation of foreign income or gains may be granted in a number of ways in the recipient's country of residence, either under domestic law or by agreement.

(*a*)   By exemption of the income or gains from tax. This method is used by several continental European countries, many of which use the 'exemption with progression' method (see 8.7). The UK exempts foreign income and gains from tax only in very limited circumstances, although, in practice, the remittance basis of taxation for UK resident but non-UK domiciled individuals often means that their foreign source income and gains are not taxed in the UK.

(*b*)   By taxing the net income after deduction of foreign tax. This is only a partial relief and does not fully remove the burden of double taxation as the tax is effectively treated as an expense in computing taxable income — see Example 1 below. This method is used in the UK in some circumstances, e.g.

   (i)   when granting relief for taxes which do not correspond to income tax or corporation tax, such as taxes levied on the basis of payroll, net worth or turnover; or

   (ii)   where there is no UK income tax or corporation tax payable against which to claim a credit, e.g. where the taxpayer has tax losses which are offset against the foreign income.

(*c*)   By granting a credit for foreign tax payable. In this way full relief for foreign tax is given, as the amount of foreign tax paid in the country of source is deducted from the amount of tax payable in the home country.

The amount of the tax credit is usually restricted to the amount of tax in the country of residence on the same income or gains. The total tax burden is therefore the greater of the tax in the source country and the tax in the country of residence. The credit method is used in the UK, Ireland, the US and several Commonwealth countries.

Comparison of relief by deduction and relief by credit

2.19   The following example compares relief for foreign tax by deduction with relief by credit.

Example 1

Minerva Ltd, a UK resident company, receives £100,000 of interest from a non-UK resident from which a foreign withholding tax of 25% has been deducted at source.

	Relief by deduction £	*Relief by credit* £
Gross income	100,000	100,000
Deduct: withholding tax	(25,000)	(25,000)
Net cash received	75,000	75,000
Corporation tax at 30%		
— on £75,000	22,500	
— on £100,000		30,000
Deduct: double taxation relief	—	(25,000)
UK corporation tax payable	22,500	5,000
Net cash retained after tax	£52,500	£70,000

Shipping, air transport and agency profits

2.20   The *Finance Act 1923* and later legislation enabled agreements to be made with foreign governments to grant relief from double taxation in respect of profits from shipping, air transport and agency profits. The first such agreement (covering shipping profits) was made with Iceland in 1928, taking effect from 1923/24. While most of these limited agreements have been superseded by full double taxation agreements, a number of agreements covering these activities alone are still in existence. Joint shipping and air transport agreements are currently in force with Brazil, Jordan, Lebanon, Venezuela and Zaire. Agreements covering air transport only are in force with Algeria, Cameroon, China, Ethiopia, Iran, Kuwait (replaced from 2001 by a new double tax agreement with the UK) and Saudi Arabia. The air transport agreement with the former USSR is currently regarded as being in force with Belarus and the Russian Federation. These agreements broadly provide that profits are exempt from UK tax where they are derived by overseas resident transport enterprises (as defined in each agreement) from international shipping and/or air transport. Similarly, UK transport enterprises covered by the agreement are broadly exempt from tax on their profits (as defined) in the overseas country. A limited shipping agreement with Hong Kong entered into force on 3 May 2001. This will take effect in the UK from 1 April 2002 (for corporation tax) and from 6 April 2002 (for income and capital gains tax).

2.21   Comprehensive double taxation agreements usually contain a 'shipping and air transport' article which provides similar relief (see 7.14). Since air transport agreements were concluded with China and the former USSR, comprehensive double taxation agreements have also been concluded which contain articles which overlap in scope. Relief may be claimed under whichever affords the greater relief in the particular circumstances.

Paying and collecting agents

2.22   UK paying agents are persons in the UK (such as banks and stockbrokers) who are appointed by a foreign government or company to make payments of dividends and interest mainly (but not exclusively) to UK resident individuals and companies who are share or bondholders. Unless it is shown that the recipient of the income is not resident in the UK, they are required to deduct and account for UK income tax on foreign income passing through their hands.

Collecting agents are persons who receive or collect foreign dividends or interest on behalf of the owners of the income. They are normally bankers, but can also be stockbrokers or solicitors. Foreign dividends (including foreign government or public revenue dividends) were, prior to 1 April 2001, subject generally to deduction of tax under the paying and collecting agents provisions formerly contained in *TA 1988, ss 118A* to *118K*. These provisions have now been abolished by *FA 2000, s 111* with effect from 1 April 2001. Under the provisions in what were *TA 1988, ss 118A* to *118K*, the requirement for collecting agents to deduct tax from foreign dividends and interest was limited to circumstances where the agent:

(*a*)   acted as custodian of shares or securities for a UK investor and collected foreign dividends or interest on those shares or securities; or

(*b*)   acted for another person in arranging to collect foreign dividends or interest; or

(*c*)   sold or purchased coupons for foreign dividends or interest for a UK investor.

The requirement for collecting agents to deduct tax did not apply where the agent did no more than arrange for a cheque for foreign dividends or interest to be cleared. Where a collecting agent performed a relevant function and became liable to account for income tax on any chargeable receipt in relation to which it was the collecting agent, it was entitled to be indemnified by the person entitled to the receipt and the amount deducted was treated as income tax of the recipient.

The rate at which UK tax was deducted by paying and collecting agents was the lower rate of income tax. Income tax was not required to be deducted from payments of dividends entrusted for payment to a UK company which had 10% or more of the voting power in the overseas company. This exemption applied for several years as the result of an unpublished concession (the 'Moscow Narodny Concession') which was given statutory authority in *FA 1992* as part of the UK's implementation of the EC Parent/Subsidiary Directive. Certain categories of UK investor, such as charities and exempt approved superannuation schemes, were also entitled to receive foreign dividends and interest without income tax being deducted by agents.

The Financial Intermediaries and Claims Office (FICO) (International), Nottingham produced a list of the countries for which paying and collecting agents could give provisional double tax relief for foreign withholding taxes suffered by treating the amount paid overseas as a credit against the UK tax deductible. For dividends from countries which were not on the Inland Revenue's list, tax was required to be deducted at the full 20% rate on the net cash receipt in the UK after overseas withholding tax had been deducted. Any double taxation relief or refund of excess UK tax deducted then had to be claimed by the recipient of the income from the recipient's tax district.

It should be noted that UK public revenue dividends (i.e. any income from securities which is paid out of the UK or Northern Ireland public revenue but excluding interest on local authority stock which is subject to separate rules) are, from 1 April 2001, payable under deduction of tax. These provisions are subject to any provision to the contrary in the Taxes Acts, e.g. in repect of gilt-edged sercurities. These issues are covered further in *Tolley's Income Tax 2001/02* at 23.3.

2.23   The following example illustrates how the relief operated for overseas withholding taxes and the deduction of UK tax by collecting agents.

Example 2

Prior to 1 April 2001, Angus, a UK resident and domiciled individual, is entitled to a dividend of US$20,000 from Zeta Inc, a US public company in which he is a shareholder. He has appointed Deo Bank in London to act as custodian in respect of the shareholding and has deposited the share certificate with the bank. The rate of US withholding tax on dividends paid to non-US resident individuals is 30%, but under the UK's agreement with the US this is reduced to 15%.

Zeta Inc sends Deo Bank a warrant for $17,000 and accounts to the US Internal Revenue Service for $3,000. As the US is a country listed by FICO (International), Deo Bank allows a provisional credit for the US withholding tax and deducts the sterling equivalent of $1,000 (that is, 20% of the gross dividend less 15% already deducted). It accounts for this to the Inland Revenue as a collecting agent and shows on the dividend voucher which it gives to Angus the gross amount of the dividend and how the amounts of tax have been computed.

If Angus is a higher rate taxpayer he is assessed to higher rate tax on the gross income from Zeta Inc and is able to claim credit both for the 15% US withholding tax and for the UK income tax deducted by Deo Bank.

Claims for double taxation relief

2.24 The Inland Revenue takes the view that the existence of a double taxation agreement exempting a source of income of a non-resident from UK tax (or allowing a reduced rate of tax) does not remove the obligation of the payer of the income to deduct any tax which may be required to be withheld under UK domestic law. Instead, the agreement merely entitles the recipient to make a claim under *TA 1988, s 788(6)* for a refund of tax on demonstrating his entitlement to exemption or reduction in the rate applying. However, under *SI 1970 No 488* (which is reproduced as Appendix 6) the payer may be authorised by the Inland Revenue either not to withhold income tax or to withhold at a reduced rate in accordance with the terms of a double taxation agreement.

Example 3

Mithras Ltd, a UK resident company, has borrowed funds from Prospect (Pty) Ltd, an Australian resident company. It pays annual interest on the loan from which it is required to deduct income tax at the lower rate (currently 20%) under *TA 1988, s 349(2)*. Article 9(1) of the 1967 agreement with Australia limits the UK tax on interest payable to a resident of Australia to 10%. In order to claim the relief to which it is entitled under the agreement, Prospect (Pty) Ltd is required to complete the relevant forms (which are obtainable from FICO (International), Nottingham) giving details of the loan and claiming the relief due. The completed forms are then sent to the Deputy Comissioner of Taxation in the Australian state in which the company is resident who certifies that the company is a resident of Australia. One copy of the form is forwarded by the Deputy Commissioner's office to FICO (International), Nottingham which, on being satisfied that the relief is properly due under the terms of the agreement, arranges the repayment of any tax overpaid by Prospect (Pty) Ltd on past payments of interest, and authorises Mithras Ltd to withhold income tax on future payments at the rate of 10%.

Retrospective relief on claims to pay income gross or at a reduced rate under an agreement may be given, but only from the date on which the claim was received by FICO (International). Where interest (and other income from which there is an obligation to deduct income tax under UK domestic law) is paid before a certified claim has been received, the Inland Revenue expects the payer to meet the statutory obligations and deduct income tax. If the payer does not do so, the Inland Revenue may seek interest under *TMA 1970, s 87* even if, ultimately, no income tax is payable because the recipient is exempt from UK tax under the agreement. If the claim is refused in whole or in part, an assessment is raised for the amount of income tax which should have been deducted and interest is charged on that amount. See Inland Revenue Interpretation No 77 dated August 1994.

2.25 The procedures for a UK resident claiming relief from foreign tax under an agreement vary according to the domestic law of each country. In many cases it is necessary to obtain and complete forms relevant to the country and type of income in question, and in these cases the forms are usually available from FICO (International), Nottingham. The completed forms are then sent to the taxpayer's tax district for appropriate certification by an inspector. The inspector then deals with the forms in accordance with the instructions set out on them.

Some countries, such as the US and the Netherlands, have procedures which allow a UK resident to obtain relief under an agreement at the time of payment of the income. Others, such as Switzerland, require the full rate of withholding tax to be deducted initially and the UK resident later claims a repayment of the excess tax deducted.

2.26   Where the payment of a tax credit on a dividend paid by a UK company is due under an agreement to a resident of another country, the recipient may make a claim to FICO (International). The first claim in respect of a holding of shares must be certified by the tax authorities of the country of residence of the recipient and the procedure is similar to that applying to a claim for a reduction of (or exemption from) UK withholding tax. For subsequent dividends from the same company the form may often be submitted direct by the claimant to FICO (International).

However, there were arrangements (repealed with effect from 6 April 1999) under which, in certain circumstances, the company paying the dividend could pay over the tax credit directly to eligible shareholders resident in a country with an agreement which grants a tax credit. These arrangements (known as the 'G', 'H', 'P' and 'Q' arrangements) were authorised by *SI 1973 No 317* which has now been repealed. On 6 April 1999 the rate of tax credit on dividends from UK companies was reduced to 10/90 of the amount of the dividend. From that date most of the provisions in the UK's agreements for the payment of a tax credit ceased to have practical effect — see 7.20.

The process of obtaining authority to apply the treaty rate of withholding tax can give rise to difficulties and delays in practice. FICO has therefore introduced a Provisional Treaty Relief (PTR) scheme with effect from 1 September 1999. It has published a booklet setting out full details of how the PTR scheme applies in practice. The PTR scheme applies to 'one-to-one' company loans where there is no shareholding relationship or common ownership between the parties to the loans. It also applies to syndicated loans where there is a syndicate manager. Broadly, under the scheme the borrower can approach FICO in the case of a one-to-one company loan for provisional authority to pay interest at the treaty rate of withholding tax as soon as the loan has been advanced, or immediately after the loan has been assigned from one lender to another. For syndicated loans, the Inland Revenue will be prepared to accept a single composite claim for treaty relief made by the syndicate manager on behalf of all the syndicate members eligible to claim the relief, subject to certain conditions, including that the overseas syndicate members should be normal corporate entities and are not transparent entities.

Where authority to apply the treaty rate of withholding tax has already been obtained and the loan is subsequently redenominated from one currency into another (e.g. from sterling to the euro) it should be noted that the borrower is required to notify FICO of the new terms of the loan.

Such terms will include the currency in which the loan is redenominated, the amount of the loan outstanding, the duration of the redenominated loan and the yield or interest on it. Where the loan is between connected persons, the Inland Revenue may require a fresh application to ensure the interest on the redenominated loan without or at a reduced rate of withholding tax if it has concerns that the term of the loan at the time of the redenomination are not as would have been agreed between unconnected parties (Inland Revenue *Tax Bulletin*, February 1999).

Entity classification

2.27   An article in the Inland Revenue *Tax Bulletin* (December 2000, pp 809–812) which is reproduced as Appendix 9 gives details of overseas business entities on whose classification the Inland Revenue has expressed a view. The classification of an entity may often be relevant in establishing the availability of double tax relief under a particular agreement. Where an entity is transparent, it is usually necessary to look to the treaty with the UK of the country in which the persons who hold an interest in the entity are resident.

Claims

2.28   Claims for tax credit relief for foreign taxes are covered by *section 806* and are made to an inspector under *TMA 1970, s 42(2)*. Under self-assessment in the case of indivduals a claim may be made either in a self-assessment return or separately using a claim form. In either case it is not necessary to produce evidence of payment of foreign tax in the form of tax receipts, assessment or tax deduction certificates (see Inland Revenue Tax Bulletin, December 1997). However, such documents may be required to be produced in the event of an enquiry into a self-assessment return or a claim. In such circumstances a translation of documents in a foreign language may be required.

For years of assessment from 1996/97 onwards, claims relating to income tax and capital gains tax must be made not later than the fifth anniversary of the 31 January following the end of the year of assessment. For prior years the limit is six years from the end of the year of assessment. As there are often considerable delays before the amount of foreign tax applying to overseas income is agreed, provisional claims may be accepted by the Inland Revenue and these are adjusted when the amount of overseas tax has been established. Claims relating to corporation tax are required to be made not later than six years after the end of the accounting period in which the overseas income is charged to UK tax (or would be charged if any tax were chargeable) or, if later, not later than one year after the end of the accounting period in which the foreign tax is paid. Where credit given under an agreement is found to be excessive or insufficient because of amendments to the amount of tax payable either in the UK or in the foreign country, any necessary adjustments are made to assessments and claims. Where an adjustment to foreign tax is made by an overseas tax authority on or after 17 March 1998, taxpayers who have claimed relief from foreign tax have a statutory obligation to notify the Inland Revenue within one year of the time of the making of the adjustment if the amount of foreign tax overpaid is adjusted and this results in the claim becoming excessive. [*TA 1988, s 806(3), (4)*]. Under *TA 1988, s 806(2)* there is a six-year time limit for assessments and claims from the date of the final adjustment which gives rise to them. This provision extends to unilateral relief by virtue of *section 790(3)*.

Self-assessments

2.29   For income tax and capital gains tax purposes, credit is claimed in a self-assessment return against UK tax payable in respect of the relevant income or chargeable gain. Where a taxpayer claims relief for foreign tax paid it is necessary to complete the 'Foreign' supplementary pages. For each item of income the following details are entered:

* country of source;

* amount of income (before deducting UK or foreign tax, but after deducting unremittable income);

* amount of UK income tax deducted (e.g. under the paying and collecting agent rules — see 2.22 above);

* amount of foreign tax paid;

* amount of income chargeable to income tax.

A separate tax credit relief working sheet (TCRWS) is completed for each item of foreign income for which the taxpayer has paid foreign tax and claims credit relief. The first TCRWS should relate to the item of income which is subject to the highest rate of foreign tax. The UK tax on this part of the taxpayer's income is calculated (see Example 10 in 3.33) and credit is available for the lower of the foreign tax paid and the UK tax on the same income.

Thereafter, the process is repeated for each source of foreign income beginning with the income which has suffered the next highest rate of foreign tax. In the second (and subsequent) TCRWS, any income on which double credit relief has been claimed in the first (or any previous) TCRWS is excluded from the calculation. This is to ensure that the foreign tax credit claimed on any source of income does not exceed the amount of UK tax on that item of income. Finally, the amount of double tax credit relief from each completed TCRWS is aggregated and entered as a single figure in the 'Foreign' supplementary pages.

There is a similar procedure for calculating credit relief on chargeable gains in the self-assessment return. However, additional information is required, including the period over which the gain accrued for UK and for foreign tax purposes and the amount of gain (in sterling) under foreign tax rules. There is no case law on the method of calculating double tax credit relief on chargeable gains, so that it is open to the taxpayer to challenge the Inland Revenue's method on appeal (see 3.57).

For corporation tax, until the introduction of corporation tax self-assessment (CTSA) with effect from accounting periods ending on or after 1 July 1999, double tax credit relief was normally claimed in corporation tax returns and given in corporation tax assessments. Inland Revenue guidance on the procedures which apply in respect of double tax relief claims under CTSA has yet to be published. Following *FA 1998, Sch 18*, double tax relief is claimed after marginal small companies' relief and corporate venturing scheme investment relief [*FA 1998, Sch 18, para 8 (1)*] in arriving at the corporation tax payable by a company. The amount of the double tax relief claim must be quantified at the time when the claim is made. [*FA 1998, Sch 18, para 54*]. Under CTSA if notice has been given requiring a company to deliver a company tax return for the relevant accounting period, a claim or election by the company which can be made by being included in the return (as originally made or by amendment) must be so made. [*para 57(2)*]. This would in theory impose a two-year time limit on the making of a double tax relief claim since, under CTSA, a return must normally be filed within twelve months of the end of the accounting period and an amendment to a return can broadly be made no more than twelve months after the filing date. [*FA 1998, Sch 18, paras 14, 15*]. This could give rise to problems concerning underlying tax relief claims, in particular where taxpayers can experience delays in obtaining information from overseas or where a foreign tax audit can result in additional underlying tax available for relief in the UK. However, *para 57 (4)(b)* provides that a claim in respect of an accounting period can still be made under *Schedule 1A* to the *Taxes Management Act 1970* if the time limit for amendment of the corporation tax return by the taxpayer has expired, although such a claim must still be made subject to other normal conditions and time limits (*para 60(1)*). Therefore, the time limits in *section 806(2)* prevail.

If foreign tax paid exceeds the UK tax on the income or gain, the excess cannot be deducted from the amount of the income or gain, nor can it be repaid by the Inland Revenue. However, in the case of dividends, the excess tax may give rise to eligible unrelieved foreign tax that can be offset against the UK corporation tax liability on qualifying foreign dividends (see 4.49). In the case of a foreign branch of a UK resident company, the excess foreign tax may be carried back or forward (see 3.43).

TA 1988, ss 788(7) and *790(11)* grant the Inland Revenue the necessary power to raise further assessments in cases where:

(*a*)   it appears that existing assessments to income tax or corporation tax have not been made for the full amount; or

(*b*)   the assessment is incorrect having regard to the credit which is to be given.

In these circumstances any assessments may be made as are necessary to ensure that the total amount of the income or gains is assessed and that the proper credit is given. Where the income is entrusted to any person in the UK for payment, an assessment may be made on the recipient of the income or gains. Such an assessment in respect of income is made under Schedule D Case VI.

Under CTSA, the Inland Revenue may enquire into a company tax re-turn if it gives notice to the company of its intention to do so, broadly, within twelve months of the filing date. Such an enquiry can extend to anything contained in the return or required to be contained in the re-turn, including any claim or election included in the return. Where a claim is not originally included in the return or an amended return, the Inland Revenue has the power to enquire into the claim (under *TMA 1970, Sch 1A, para 5*). It should be noted that under both *FA 1998, Sch 18* and *TMA 1970, Sch 1A* the Inland Revenue has the power to call for documents for the purpose of enquiries. In addition, taxpayers are re-quired to keep documents relating to claims.

Disclosure of information

2.30   Provisions for the disclosure of information to foreign tax au-thorities are contained in *TA 1988, s 816*. Where under a foreign law provision is made for relief for UK income tax or corporation tax against the foreign tax, the obligation of secrecy imposed by the Taxes Acts upon Inland Revenue employees does not prevent the disclosure to the au-thorised officer of the foreign government of such facts as may be ne-cessary to enable the proper reliefs to be given. However, such disclosure may only be made with respect to foreign taxes which correspond to income tax, corporation tax and capital gains tax.

Section 816(2) and *(2A)* allow the Board .of Inland Revenue, or an authorised officer of the Board, to disclose information which is required to be disclosed under an agreement or under the EC Arbitration Con-vention in pursuance of a request made by an advisory commission set up under that Convention. Similar powers are given by *section 816(4)* to provide information under limited agreements concerning shipping and air transport.

It should be noted that the legislation does not permit the Inland Rev-enue to disclose information to other tax authorities in pursuance of an agreement unless the Inland Revenue is satisfied that the other tax au-thorities are bound by rules of confidentially which are as strict as the Inland Revenue's.

2.31   The UK is also a party to the 1977 EC Directive (77/799/EEC) on the mutual assistance by the competent authorities of the member states in the field of direct and indirect taxation. This was given effect in the UK by *FA 1978, s 77*. The Directive applies to taxes on income and capital (which in the UK means income tax, corporation tax, capital gains tax and petroleum revenue tax) and its scope was extended to value added tax (in 1979) and excise duties (1992). Under the Directive the Inland Revenue may disclose information in three circumstances:

(*a*)   on request of the tax authorities of another member state;

(*b*)   automatically, for agreed categories of cases; and

(*c*)   spontaneously, *inter alia*, where it has grounds for supposing that there may be a loss of tax in another member state.

Article 2(2) of the Directive requires the Inland Revenue to initiate enquiries to obtain information not already in its possession. In order to enable it to do so, the Inland Revenue's information powers were extended by *FA 1990, s 125*. It may now call for information under *TMA 1970, s 20* relevant to tax liabilities in other member states where the tax is on income or capital and is covered by the Directive.

The Inland Revenue has set out a statement of its own practice with regard to confidentiality of the information disclosed by it under the Directive in Technical Release 812, as follows.

> 'Confirmation is obtained from other authorities that disclosure by them will be limited to persons directly involved in either the assessment of tax or administrative control of assessment, and to persons directly involved in judicial or administrative proceedings involving sanctions relating to the making or reviewing of the tax assessment. Use of information is also to be limited to taxation purposes, that is the purpose of the particular EC tax covered by the Directive.'

2.32   The UK has not become a signatory to the OECD/Council of Europe Convention for mutual assistance in tax matters which was opened for signature in January 1988. This Convention provides for several forms of assistance including exchange of information, participation in foreign tax examinations, service of documents and assistance in recovery of taxes. Following consultations in 1988 in which UK professional bodies criticised the Convention on the grounds of possible breaches of confidentiality, the UK government announced that the UK would not become a party to it. The reason given was that the UK's network of agreements providing for administrative co-operation made signature unnecessary.

2.33   Where a person beneficially entitled to income from any securities (as defined in *TMA 1970, s 24*) is resident in a country with which the UK has an agreement, a bank may be required to disclose to the Board particulars relating to the income of the overseas resident. The normal protection from disclosure given to a bank under *section 24(3)* does not apply. [*TA 1988, s 816(3)*].

Matters concerning the exchange of information are generally dealt with by the Special Compliance Office (Exchange of Information Unit).

Chapter 3

Double Taxation Relief on Income and Chargeable Gains

Introduction

3.1   This chapter covers the main statutory provisions, case law and practice concerning double taxation relief for income and chargeable gains. It illustrates these with the use of examples showing the computation of relief in various circumstances. However, the statutory provisions, case law and practice relating to underlying tax relief on dividends are considered separately in Chapter 4.

Residence requirement

3.2   With a few exceptions, noted in 3.7 below, a person claiming double tax credit relief in the UK must be resident in the UK during the chargeable period for which UK tax is payable. The statutory authority for this is *TA 1988, s 794(1)* which provides that credit is not to be allowed under any agreement for any chargeable period unless the person is resident in the UK for that period. This is extended to unilateral relief by *section 790(3)* which provides that the same credit relief is to be given as would apply if there were an agreement in force between the UK and the territory for whose tax unilateral relief is being claimed.

The chargeable period for which tax credit relief is granted need not be the period in which the income arose. Generally, a person who is UK resident and is subject to UK tax on income or gains which have suffered foreign tax is entitled to tax credit relief provided he is resident in the UK in the chargeable period in which the income or gains are charged to UK tax.

3.3   Other forms of relief under agreements, such as exemption from or reduction in the rate of tax, are also normally based on the residence status of the person concerned. The 'personal scope' article of most of the UK's agreements limits the benefit of the agreement to residents of one or both of the contracting states, as defined for the purpose of each agreement. Relief in the form of, for example, exemption from foreign tax is available to UK residents and, conversely, relief by exemption from UK tax is available to residents of the other country. However, relief under a double taxation agreement has in some cases been obtained by persons who were not resident in either contracting state, as is illustrated by the cases of *IRC v Commerzbank AG* and *IRC v Banco do Brasil SA [1990] STC 285*. These cases concerned the same point in the 1945 agreement with the US which, unlike more recent agreements, did not contain a 'personal scope' article limiting the scope of the agreement to residents of one or both of the contracting states. The banks, neither of which was resident in the UK or the US, had UK branches which made loans to US corporations and claimed the benefit of the 'interest' article of the 1945 US agreement. This exempted interest paid by a US corporation from UK tax unless the recipient was a UK citizen, resident or corporation. The claims by both banks to exemption from UK tax on the interest paid to their UK branches by US corporations succeeded in the High Court.

The non-discrimination article in the UK's agreements is usually based on the nationality rather than the residence of the person concerned (see 8.11–8.12).

Residence of individuals

3.4   In the UK, the term 'resident' in relation to individuals has been the subject of a number of cases, although case law has been supplemented by a limited amount of statute law. As a result, a body of Inland Revenue practice has built up over a number of years which categorises various fact patterns as indicating either residence or non-residence. This is set out in the current edition (1999) of the Inland Revenue's booklet IR20 *Residents and non-residents — Liability to tax in the United Kingdom*, a copy of which may be obtained from a local tax office or the Inland Revenue's Information Centre at Bush House (see Appendix 8). An individual's UK residence status is a question of fact determined in the light of, *inter alia*, his presence in (or absence from) the UK, his residence history, and the frequency, purpose and regularity of his visits to the UK.

For example, since 6 April 1993 an individual coming to the UK as a visitor has been regarded by the Inland Revenue as resident in the UK for a year of assessment if:

(*a*)   he is present in the UK for more than 182 days or more in the tax year (ending 5 April); or

(*b*)   he visits the UK for an average of 91 days or more per tax year over a period of at least four years.

For these purposes days of arrival in, and departure from, the UK are usually ignored (i.e. are treated as days outside the UK).

For tax years before 1993/94, a person who had a place of abode available to him in the UK and visited the UK even for one day could be treated as UK resident for that tax year. However, from 6 April 1993, *TA 1988, s 336(3)* provides that the question whether a person is in the UK for some temporary purpose only and not with the intention of establishing his residence there is to be decided without regard to any living accommodation available in the UK for his use.

On arrival in the UK for employment or to take up residence, a person may complete a residence questionnaire (Form P86). Similarly, a person leaving the UK following a period of residence may complete a departure questionnaire (Form P85). However, under the self-assessment system individuals self-certify their residence status as part of their income tax return and the Inland Revenue will not normally give a prior ruling. Nevertheless, tax offices are prepared to tell individuals how their residence position has been treated for PAYE coding and repayment purposes. In appropriate cases it may examine an individual's residence status as part of an enquiry into a self-assessment return.

3.5   Each country has its own definition of 'residence' with respect to individuals, and these definitions are often based on factors such as the amount of time spent in a country during a tax year or the place where that person's family normally resides. It is therefore not uncommon for an individual to be a resident of more than one country at the same time under the domestic laws of those countries. Such individuals are often referred to as 'dual residents'. If there is a double taxation agreement between the two countries which contains a 'residence tie-breaker' clause, a dual resident individual is deemed to be resident in one of the countries *for the purposes of the agreement only* following the application of a series of standard tests. These tests are covered in detail in 6.19.

A dual resident individual who is a resident of the other country for the purposes of an agreement remains a resident of the UK for the purposes of UK domestic law and is, for example, subject to the usual requirement to complete UK tax returns. Where necessary, that individual may also claim double tax credit relief under the UK's unilateral provisions in relation to income arising in a third country. Such an individual may, as a UK resident, also claim relief from third country taxes under an agreement between the UK and the third country.

Residence of companies

3.6   Since 15 March 1988, following *FA 1988, s 66*, there have been two criteria for determining whether a company is resident in the UK for the purpose of UK domestic law:

(*a*)   if its central management and control is exercised in the UK; or

(*b*)   if it is incorporated in the UK.

Certain statutory exceptions exist to (*b*), since a company incorporated in the UK which became resident outside the UK following a specific UK Treasury consent prior to 15 March 1988 continues to be treated as non-UK resident so long as its central management and control remains outside the UK and it continues to carry on business. Where a UK incorporated company transferred its central management and control abroad prior to 15 March 1988 as the result of a Treasury general consent, it can remain resident outside the UK provided that it is taxable in another territory. Other companies incorporated in the UK which were non-UK resident at 15 March 1988 and had carried on business before that date became UK resident on 15 March 1993. However, if management and control of these companies moved to the UK prior to that date, they became UK resident from the date when management and control moved to the UK.

A further exception was enacted by *FA 1994, s 249* which provides that a company which is resident in the UK under UK domestic law but is also resident in another country for the purposes of a double taxation agreement is to be treated for all UK tax purposes as not resident in the UK. This provision was enacted to counter a number of devices involving the use of dual resident companies which were effectively managed in another country for the purpose of an agreement. For the purposes of the agreement they were residents of the other country and thereby able to claim exemption from UK tax on certain sources of income.

Exceptional cases

3.7   There are some statutory exceptions to the general rule that tax credit relief may be claimed only by UK residents. Three of these are contained in *TA 1988, s 794(2)* which allows unilateral relief in the following cases.

(*a*)   Isle of Man and Channel Islands tax is eligible for credit if the person in question is resident in the UK, the Isle of Man or any of the Channel Islands in the appropriate chargeable period. Accordingly, where, for example, an individual or company resident in the Channel Islands has UK source income which is liable to UK tax, credit is given in the UK for Channel Islands tax payable on that income.

(*b*)   If the duties of an office or employment are performed wholly or mainly in another country, the tax which that country imposes on the earnings is eligible for credit in the UK if UK tax is chargeable under Schedule E and the person concerned is resident either in the UK or in that other country.

(*c*)   For chargeable periods ending prior to 21 March 2000, where an overseas company carried on a banking business through a UK branch or agency and suffered foreign tax on interest on a foreign loan made through that branch, etc. double tax relief was available as if the UK branch were a UK bank. There were also rules which allowed UK branches of overseas life assurance companies to claim double tax relief for foreign tax paid on the UK branch income or gains. However, tax payable in a country where the overseas company is taxable by reason of its domicile, residence or place of management was excluded from relief. For chargeable periods ending after 20 March 2000, this provision is replaced by a wider relief available on simliar terms to all non-UK resident persons (whether companies or individuals) with UK branches or agencies. [*TA 1988, s 794 (2)(bb)*]. The maximum credit relief available in the UK is limited to that which would be available if the branch or agency had been a person resident in the UK and the income or gains in question had been income or gains of that person.

This change in the legislation occurred mainly as a result of the decision in the European case *Compagnie de Saint-Gobain, Zweinederlausung Deutschland v Finanzamt Aachen-Innerstadt (Case C–307/97 [2000] STC 854.* This case concerned the German branch of a French company which was treated as a German permanent establishment (PE). The German PE was denied double tax relief by the German tax authorities for dividend income received from companies resident in America and Switzerland, although such relief would have been available had the German PE instead been a German company. The European Court of Justice held that this tax treatment was contrary to European law.

For a fuller discussion of UK branches of overseas banks and insurance companies, see Chapter 5.

3.8   As far as persons who are residents of other EU member states are concerned, it may be arguable that the restriction of double tax credit relief to UK residents in respect of accounting periods ending before 21 March 2000 is unlawful discrimination contrary to Articles 52 and 58 of the Treaty of Rome following the decisions of the European Court of Justice in the cases of *R v IRC, ex p Commerzbank AG [1993] STC 605* and *Halliburton Services BV v Staatssecretaris van Financiën [1994] STC 655.*

Source of income — general rules

3.9   It is an essential for the granting of UK tax credit relief that the income on which the relief is being claimed is sourced within the country where the tax is payable. *TA 1988, s 790(4)* refers to 'credit for tax paid under the law of a territory outside the UK and computed by reference to *income arising or any chargeable gain accruing in that territory*'. The determination of the source is based on the principles of UK domestic law which are in many cases overridden by the provisions of double taxation agreements.

In general terms, income or gains derived from property or rights are sourced in a territory if the property or rights from which it derives are located there. For example, income or gains derived from real property are sourced in the country in which that property is situated. Dividends from a company incorporated and resident in a foreign territory would be sourced in that territory. The question of where interest is sourced depends upon a number of factors, including the country of residence of the debtor, the country in which any security is located, and the jurisdiction in which the loan obligation would be enforced — see *Westminster Bank Executor & Trustee Co (Channel Islands) Ltd v National Bank of Greece SA (1970) 46 TC 472.*

TA 1988, s 790(4) deems profits from, or remuneration for, personal or professional services performed in a territory to be income arising in that territory for the purposes of unilateral relief.

The importance of the UK's source rules in relation to a trade is illustrated by the case of *Yates v GCA International Ltd [1991] STC 157,* which was decided on the basis of UK domestic law as there was no double taxation agreement in force at the time between the UK and Venezuela. GCA International Ltd, a UK resident company, carried on the trade of petroleum and natural gas consultants. It entered into a contract with a Venezuelan company under which it received US$161,000 for work carried out in the UK and US$48,300 for work carried out in Venezuela. Venezuelan tax was paid on 90% of the company's total receipts from the contract and the company claimed credit for the Venezuelan tax under the UK's unilateral credit relief provisions. Although it was held that the Venezuelan tax was a creditable tax, it was also held that unilateral relief was due only in respect of the income which arose from the work carried out in Venezuela since the fees it received for the work carried out in the UK were UK source income. Accordingly, only a proportion of the Venezuelan tax paid by the company qualified for tax credit relief.

Where there is an agreement in force, this may specify (usually in the 'elimination of double taxation' article) that profits, income and chargeable gains which may be taxed in the other country are deemed to be sourced there. An example of such a provision is contained in article 22(3) of the agreement with The Netherlands, which provides that profits, income and capital gains owned by a resident of the UK which may be taxed in The Netherlands in accordance with the agreement are deemed to arise from sources in The Netherlands.

Source of income — extra-statutory concessions

3.10   There are two extra-statutory concessions dealing with the source of income. The more important is ESC B8 which covers royalty and know-how receipts. It deals with the situation where a person carrying on a trade in the UK receives, from a non-resident, amounts as consideration for the use of, or for the privilege of using, any copyright, patent, trade mark or similar property in the overseas country. These payments may, in UK law, be UK source, for example because a patent giving rise to royalties is registered in the UK. Under the Concession such income is treated for the purpose of double taxation relief as arising outside the UK. However, the Concession does not apply to consideration received for services (other than merely incidental services) rendered in the UK. In that case, unless a double taxation agreement applies which overrides UK domestic law, the taxpayer may only be able to deduct the tax as a trading expense.

3.11   ESC A12 deals with alimony and maintenance payments where the payer is resident outside the UK. A concession was necessary because payments made under a UK court order or agreement have a UK source under UK domestic law but at the same time may be subject to withholding taxes in the country of residence of the payer. In these circumstances the Concession allows credit to a recipient for the foreign tax paid where:

- the individual making the payments has left the UK and become resident in an overseas country;

- the payments are made out of that individual's income in that country and are subject to tax there;

- any UK income tax, if deducted from the payments, is duly accounted for; and

- the payee is resident in the UK and effectively bears the overseas tax.

This Concession now has limited effect as a result of the changes to maintenance payments rules contained in *FA 1988, s 36* since payments under obligations made (or applied for) after 14 March 1988 are not taxable income of the recipient for UK purposes. In addition payments due after 5 April 2000 under existing obligations no longer form part of the recipient's taxable income.

The 'root income' principle

3.12   Under the unilateral tax credit relief provisions contained in *TA 1988, s 790(4)*, credit for overseas tax paid is to be allowed against any UK income tax or corporation tax 'computed by reference to that income or gain'. This is mirrored in most of the UK's double taxation agreements. For example, the 'elimination of double taxation' article in the 1975 agreement with the US refers to US tax being allowed as a credit against any UK tax computed by reference to 'the same profits or income by reference to which the US tax is computed'.

Example 4

Marcus is a US citizen who has been resident and ordinarily resident in the UK for many years, but is domiciled in the US. In order to meet his UK living expenses, he has remitted to the UK all his income from a US partnership on which he has paid US income taxes. He files US tax returns annually and is assessed to US tax on his share of the partnership profits on the basis of the profits arising in each calendar year. For the year of assessment 1995/96 he was assessed under *Schedule D, Case V* on the amount of his remittances of partnership income during the previous tax year (i.e. during the year ended 5 April 1995). The amount of tax which was creditable during 1995/96 was the amount of US taxes paid on the partnership income for the year 6 April 1994 to 5 April 1995. This was three-quarters of the US tax paid for the year ended 31 December 1994 and one-quarter of the tax paid for the year ended 31 December 1995.

3.13   It is essential in most cases to ensure that in each chargeable period foreign taxes are matched by an equivalent UK liability. This may not always be possible owing to differences between the UK and foreign accounting and tax rules. However, in the case of long-term contracts carried out through, for example, branches of UK companies, the profits are often taxed in the UK and abroad in different chargeable periods. In applying the 'root income' principle in these circumstances, the Inland Revenue accepts that the profits by reference to which the foreign tax is computed are the whole profits of the contract and are not confined to those arising under UK tax principles in individual UK chargeable periods.

Example 5

Dambuilders Ltd, a UK construction company, has a long-term contract in Arcadia and is taxable there on the profits of £2,000,000. Under Arcadian law the anticipated profit is taxed evenly over the life of the contract, whereas under UK accounting and tax principles the profit does not start to be recognised until the attributable profit can be assessed with reasonable certainty. For UK corporation tax purposes the profit is taxed as follows:

Year 1 — Nil
Year 2 — Nil
Year 3 — £400,000
Year 4 — £700,000
Year 5 — £900,000

In applying the root income principle the contract period is considered as a whole. Accordingly, the foreign tax payable over the five years is aggregated and apportioned for credit relief purposes over the accounting periods during which UK tax arises in connection with the contract. Where there are two or more long-term contracts in a territory, each one is considered separately for these purposes.

Definitions

3.14   Several definitions relevant to the double tax credit relief provisions are contained in *TA 1988, s 792* which apply unless the context requires otherwise.

- 'Arrangements' means agreements with the government of a territory outside the UK having effect by virtue of *TA 1988, s 788*.

- 'Foreign tax' means, in relation to any territory with which the UK has a double taxation agreement, any tax charged by that territory for which credit may be allowed under the agreement.

- 'United Kingdom taxes' means income tax and corporation tax and, by extension [*TCGA 1992, s 277*], capital gains tax.

- 'Underlying tax' means, in relation to any dividend, tax which is not chargeable in respect of that dividend directly or by deduction. By inference it is the tax on the profits out of which the dividend is paid. There is a further explanation of the term in *section 799(1)* which refers to 'the foreign tax borne on the relevant profits by the body corporate paying the dividend'.

- 'Unilateral relief' means relief due under *TA 1988, s 790*, which provides for tax credit relief where there is no agreement with the territory concerned, or where there is an agreement but the particular taxes are not covered by it.

- 'Subsidiary' is specially defined for double taxation relief purposes. A company is a subsidiary of another if the other company controls, directly or indirectly, not less than 50% of the voting power. This is an unusual definition since, for this purpose only, the holding of a mere 50% (rather than 50.01%) of the voting power in a company by another company enables it to be treated as a subsidiary.

Other important definitions are contained in *section 799(3)–(7)* (relevant profits) and *section 801(5)* (related companies). These definitions are considered in Chapter 4, along with the key definitions and concepts under the mixer cap and the onshore pooling regime which were introduced by *Finance Act 2000*.

Foreign taxes available for credit

3.15   The foreign taxes which are available for credit relief under an agreement are those taxes which are specified in the relevant agreement. In practice, these are taxes based on income or gains, whether paid by an individual or a company. They are usually specified at the beginning of the agreement, often in a separate 'taxes covered' article, although this list is in some cases modified by the 'elimination of double taxation' article which may exclude some of the taxes covered by the agreement from the credit relief provisions.

As far as unilateral tax credit relief is concerned, *TA 1988, s 790(12)* provides that references to tax payable or paid under the law of a territory outside the UK include only references to:

(*a*)   taxes which are charged on income and which correspond to UK income tax; and

(*b*)   taxes which are charged on income or chargeable gains and which correspond to UK corporation tax.

Unilateral tax credit relief is extended to capital gains tax by *TCGA 1992, s 277* which substitutes into *section 790* references to 'capital gains' and 'capital gains tax' for 'income' and 'income tax'.

3.16   The issue of whether a tax corresponded to UK income tax or corporation tax was one of two points decided in the case of *Yates v GCA International Ltd [1991] STC 157* — see 3.9 above. The company suffered Venezuelan tax which was levied on 90% of its gross receipts from a contract with a Venezuelan company at the rate of 25%. The Inland Revenue argued that the Venezuelan tax did not correspond to UK income tax or corporation tax since it was levied on such a high percentage of gross receipts. In its view the tax was not levied on income but, in effect, on turnover. However, it was held in the High Court by Scott J that it was necessary to consider whether the tax in question had the same function as UK income or corporation taxes. Although the Venezuelan tax was computed on the basis that only 10% of the gross income was deductible, it was intended to be a tax on profits rather than on turnover. Accordingly, he held that the Venezuelan tax corresponded to income or corporation tax and was therefore creditable.

As a result of the *GCA International* case the Inland Revenue issued a Statement of Practice (SP 7/91) revising its previous interpretation of a 'corresponding' tax. The relevant part of SP 7/91 reads:

'In future the question of whether or not a foreign tax is admissible for unilateral relief under *s 790 ICTA 1988* will be determined by examining the tax within its legislative context in the foreign territory and deciding whether it serves the same function as income and corporation tax serve in the UK in relation to the profits of the business. Turnover taxes, as such, are not therefore affected by the revised interpretation and will continue to be inadmissible for relief'.

3.17   Taxes which are payable under the law of a province, state or other part of a country or are levied by or on behalf of a municipality or other local body may also be treated as corresponding to income tax and corporation tax by virtue of *section 790(12)*. This is of importance in relation to a number of countries whose local authorities or political subdivisions levy income taxes not covered by an agreement. Among these countries are the US — US state and city income taxes are not covered in the 1975 agreement (nor are they covered in the revised draft agreement) and therefore relief for such taxes is available only unilaterally — and Canada.

The Inland Revenue published a revised booklet 146 containing a list of admissible (creditable) and inadmissible (non-creditable) taxes in March 1995. However, no further editions of IR146 have been published. Instead, further revisions to the list are published periodically in the Inland Revenue Double Taxation Relief Manual. The current list of admissible and inadmissible taxes is included as Appendix 4.

3.18   An illustration of the taxes available for credit both by agreement and unilaterally can be given by considering taxes in Germany, a country with which the UK has an agreement, and Brazil with which there is no agreement. In the 1964 agreement with Germany, the German taxes which are the subject of the agreement are as follows.

(*a*)   The income tax (*Einkommensteuer*), including the surcharge (*Ergänzungsabgabe*) thereon. This is charged at a maximum rate of 48.5% and there is a solidarity surcharge equal to 5.5% of the tax charged.

(*b*)   The corporation tax (*Körperschaftsteuer*), including the surcharge (*Ergänzungsabgabe*). Under the new corporate income tax system this is charged at 25% together with a 5.5% surcharge as for income tax.

(*c*)   The capital tax (*Vermögensteuer*). This was abolished effective 1 January 1997 but was charged on the worldwide net worth of German resident individuals, companies and certain other entities and on certain properties in Germany owned by non-resident individuals and entities.

(*d*)   The trade tax (*Gewerbesteuer*). This is a local tax charged on the basis of both income and capital at rates up to about 20% on income and 0.2% on capital.

(*e*)   Identical or substantially similar taxes imposed after the date of signature of the agreement in addition to, or in place of, the existing taxes. Therefore, for example, the current solidarity surcharge is available for credit under the agreement.

However, the 'elimination of double taxation' article excludes capital tax (*Vermögensteuer*) from credit relief, and also trade tax (*Gewerbesteuer*) to the extent that it is computed on a basis other than profits.

3.19   The Inland Revenue's list of admissible and inadmissible taxes includes as admissible taxes in Germany:

(*a*)   the income tax (*Einkommensteuer*) which includes wages tax (*Lohnsteuer*), capital yields tax (*Kapitalertragsteuer*) and director's tax (*Aufsichtsratsteuer*);

(*b*)   the corporation tax (*Körperschaftsteuer*), including the solidarity surcharge (*Ergänzungsabgabe/Solidaritätszuschlag*); and

(*c*)   the trade tax (*Gewerbesteuer*) to the extent that it is computed by reference to trading profits (*Gewerbeertrag*).

3.20   German taxes which are considered by the Inland Revenue to be inadmissible are:

(*a*)   value added tax (*Umsatzsteuer*);

(*b*)   wealth or net worth tax (*Vermögensteuer*);

(*c*)   trade tax on capital employed (*Gewerbekapital*), which is part of the trade tax (*Gewerbesteuer*);

(*d*)   inheritance tax (*Erbschaftsteuer*);

(*e*)   fire protection tax (*Feuerschutzsteuer*);

(*f*)   church tax (*Kirchensteuer*).

3.21   The UK Inland Revenue currently lists several Brazilian taxes as being available for unilateral credit relief and a number which are not creditable. The admissible taxes are:

(*a*)   income tax (*imposto de renda*);

(*b*)   state income taxes (*imposto de renda estadual*);

(*c*)   corporate income tax (*imposto de renda das pessoas jurídicas*);

(*d*)   withholding tax imposed on income, including tax charged on gross receipts, interest, royalties or dividends and the supplementary tax charged on dividends remitted abroad in excess of 12% registered capital;

(*e*)   payments to the development funds *Programa de Integração Nacional* (**PIN**) and *Fundação Movimento Brasiliero de Alfabetização* (**MOBRAL**); and (*f*)   social contributions tax (*contribuição social*).

3.22   In February 1995 the Inland Revenue issued Interpretation No 98 setting out its position on the creditability of California unitary tax. This followed the decision of the US Supreme Court in June 1994 in *Barclays Bank plc v Franchise Tax Board of California* to uphold California's right to impose its corporate franchise tax using a unitary method, i.e. based on a formulary apportionment of worldwide profits of a unitary business. Its view is that where a UK resident company has a branch which pays Californian Franchise tax, unilateral relief is available for the lesser of:

(*a*)   the actual California tax paid; or

(*b*)   the amount of the tax that would have been paid on the basis of the profits of the branch which arise in the US and (where relevant) the US profits of any affiliated companies to the extent that these are brought into calculation of the tax as members of the unitary group or following a 'water's edge' election.

Similar relief for California tax is allowed with respect to underlying tax (see 4.25).

No double relief and minimum foreign tax rule

3.23   For double tax relief claims made after 20 March 2000 a new provision takes effect [*TA 1988, s 793A*] which denies credit relief for foreign tax in respect of which relief may be allowed under an agreement or under the local law of the foreign country as a result of such an agreement. The purpose of this provision is to ensure that taxpayers make full use of the UK's double tax treaty network to reduce their foreign tax bills. Similarly, unilateral relief is denied for foreign tax where relief for the foreign tax against a UK tax liability is provided for by the relevant agreement. In addition, where there is an express provision in an agreement which prohibits relief for foreign tax in cases or circumstances that are specified in the agreement, unilateral relief is denied.

The long-standing Inland Revenue practice of the minimum foreign tax rule has now been put onto a statutory basis in *TA 1988, s 795A* with effect for claims for credit made after 20 March 2000. As a result of this rule, credit is allowed in the UK, whether under an agreement or unilaterally, only for the minimum foreign tax which is payable under the foreign country's laws. Where there is an agreement between the foreign country and the UK which provides for a reduction in the tax in question, credit is given only for the minimum amount of tax which is payable under the agreement. The legislation requires the recipient of the income to take all reasonable steps to minimise the foreign tax liabilities.

Such steps include claiming, or otherwise securing the benefit of, reliefs, deductions, reductions or allowances and making elections for tax purposes. In ascertaining whether reasonable steps have been taken by the tax payer to minimise the relevant foreign tax liability, it is necessary to consider what the taxpayer would reasonably be expected to do in the absence of any double tax relief being available in the UK.

Example 6

Dubris Ltd, a UK resident company, owns 40% of the voting shares in a Swiss company. It receives a dividend from the Swiss company of £50,000 (gross) from which, under Swiss domestic law, a withholding tax of 35% (£17,500) is deducted. Dubris Ltd omits to file a repayment claim with the Swiss tax authorities under the 1977 agreement with Switzerland, but instead submits a UK corporation tax return claiming relief for the full Swiss tax deducted of £17,500.

Under article 10(1) of the agreement with Switzerland, where a UK resident company is the beneficial owner of the dividend and controls at least 25% of the voting power in the Swiss company paying it, Swiss dividend withholding tax is limited to 5%. The legislation limits the double tax relief claim for the withholding tax to 5% of £50,000 (i.e. £2,500) and no relief (either by credit or deduction) is given for the excess Swiss tax deducted.

The Inland Revenue has also published some guidance on how the new legislation may be interpreted in practice, which is reproduced below.

'Minimisation Of Foreign Tax

A new Section 795A states that all reasonable steps must be taken to minimise the amount of foreign tax paid.

We expect companies to claim the normal reliefs and allowances available to all entities under the standard tax regime for the territory concerned.

Some guidance was published in the March 2000 paper "Double Taxation Relief for Companies: Outcome of the Review". The following examples were given of situations where the Revenue considers the provision would apply:

- Acceptance of an estimated tax assessment in the other country which is likely to be excessive;
- Not claiming an allowance or relief (e.g. capital allowances or losses) which is generally known to be available;
- Where the other country's domestic law or the relevant double taxation agreement provides for alternative bases of taxation, not choosing the basis which would produce the lowest tax bill.

At Committee Stage for the Finance Bill some further guidance was given by the PMG:

"Subsection (3) of the new section refers to what a taxpayer might reasonably be expected to have done if he had not been able to obtain credit for the tax in the United Kingdom. In such cases, the taxpayer might have tried to keep his foreign tax bill down, having

regard to the amount of time, effort and expense involved in dis-
cussing his case with the Foreign tax authorities on the one hand
and the amount of the expected reduction on the other.

... Examples of situations in which the provision would not apply
include not claiming a relief, the availability of which is uncertain,
when disproportionate expenditure would have to be incurred in
researching the other country's law to pursue the claim ... claiming
that a loss incurred in another country should be carried forwards
and not backwards or vice versa, and the case of underlying tax
paid by a subsidiary company when the United Kingdom company,
which claims the relief for that tax, is not in a position to influence
the amount of tax paid."

In some countries there are regimes which are wholly or partly ring-
fenced from residents, or from transactions with residents, and which
provide for lower tax rates than those which are generally applying. A
case in point is the "designer rate" regimes in some territories. This
provision does not compel or even encourage companies to exploit
such special niches, as we consider this is outside the compass of
"reasonable steps". We will therefore give relief, subject to any other
provisions, for normal rate tax suffered in these territories.'

3.24   An inspector will refer to International Division (Double
Taxation) any case where:

- the taxpayer makes a claim to relief from foreign tax to the foreign
  tax authority but the claim is refused for procedural reasons, e.g.
  failure to observe time limits, or the foreign tax authority does not
  respond to or act upon the claim; or

- the foreign country imposes tax on income which does not arise in
  that country.

The foreign tax allowable for credit is the final liability, not the tax paid
on account. It excludes interest or penalties paid in respect of the foreign
tax.

Identification and quantification of income

3.25   As indicated in 3.9 above, in order to claim tax credit relief it is
necessary for the income or gains to be foreign sourced. This principle is
applied by the Inland Revenue to dividend withholding taxes paid by
dual resident companies.

A US company managed and controlled in the UK is resident both in the
US (which applies the incorporation test for residence) and in the UK.
When it pays a dividend to its UK parent company a 5% withholding tax
is applied under US domestic law as modified by the 1975 agreement with
the US. However, because the company is also UK resident, the Inland

Revenue considers that the dividend is UK source income and there is nothing in the agreement which deems the income to be from a US source. No credit is allowed in the UK for US withholding tax paid on the dividend, although credit is allowed for US taxes payable on, for example, US source trading income of the dual resident company.

3.26   The case of *George Wimpey International Ltd v Rolfe [1989] STC 609* illustrates that, in order to claim credit relief, there must be UK tax charged in respect of the same income as that on which foreign tax is paid. The taxpayer was a UK resident company which had a single worldwide trade of construction and civil engineering. In 1984 it had worldwide trading losses (as adjusted for UK tax purposes) of £2.5 million, but this figure included profits totalling almost £3.9 million arising in Hong Kong, Gabon and Jordan on which it had paid foreign tax of approximately £1.2 million. The company also had non-trading income with the result that it had a UK tax liability on which it claimed double tax credit relief for the foreign taxes suffered.

Hoffman J held that it was a basic principle of UK tax law that tax was charged on various kinds of income identified by reference to its source under the appropriate Schedules and Cases. When *TA 1988, s 793* refers to UK tax chargeable 'in respect of income' it means, in relation to income tax, the tax chargeable by virtue of one of the Cases in the Schedules. Each Case gives rise to a separate computation of income and consequently of tax. Corporation tax is assessed in accordance with the principles of income tax and the fact that trading income and non-trading income are aggregated for corporation tax purposes and tax is charged on the total profits was immaterial. He held that the company was not chargeable to any UK tax computed by reference to income on which the foreign tax had been paid as required by *section 790(4)*, and no credit was therefore allowed.

3.27   The statutory rules relating to the quantification of income on which credit relief is available are contained in *TA 1988, s 795*. Where income is assessed to UK tax on a remittance basis the amount of overseas income or gains is calculated for credit purposes by adding the net amount of the income received in the UK to the amount of the foreign tax (i.e. overseas tax for which a credit is allowed) in respect of the income. In the case of a partial remittance the UK assessable income is the amount remitted plus the overseas tax proportionate to the remitted income.

Example 7

Maurice, a doctor who is resident but not domiciled in the UK, is a partner in a practice in France. His earnings from the practice are £40,000 on which he pays French tax of £15,000. He remits to the UK 50% of his post-tax earnings from the partnership. His marginal rate of tax in the UK is 40% and this applies to the whole of his overseas income.

	£
Income remitted to the UK	12,500
Add: 50% of overseas tax	7,500
UK assessable income	20,000

The double taxation relief computation would then proceed as follows:

	£
UK income tax at 40% on £20,000	8,000
Deduct: credit for French tax	(7,500)
UK income tax payable	500

3.28 Where the foreign income is liable to UK tax on the amount arising, rather than on the amount remitted to the UK, in computing the amount of income or gain for the purpose of income or corporation tax, no deduction is made for foreign tax, whether in respect of the same or any other income or gains. In the case of a dividend, the general rule is that any qualifying underlying tax is to be added to the amount of the income (see Chapter 4).

Example 8

Transiton Ltd, a UK resident company, has a branch in Arcadia which has made pre-tax profits of £620,000. A local church tax of £20,000 is payable based on the company's net worth which is deductible for Arcadian corporation tax purposes but is inadmissible for unilateral relief. The rate of Arcadian corporation tax is 26% and a branch profits tax of 5% of the net profit is also payable. There is no agreement between the UK and Arcadia. The company is liable to UK corporation tax at the rate of 30%. The Arcadian tax computation is as follows.

	£	£
Profit before taxes		620,000
Deduct: church tax		(20,000)
		600,000
Arcadian corporation tax	156,000	
Branch profits tax	22,200	
		(178,200)
Net profit after Arcadian tax		421,800

The UK corporation tax computation is as follows.

	£
UK corporation tax at 30% on £600,000	180,000
Deduct credit for overseas taxes	(178,200)
UK corporation tax payable	1,800

3.29 Where the foreign income is 'pure income profit' in the hands of a UK resident recipient, e.g. it is a royalty on a patent held as an investment or is interest earned otherwise than by a bank or financial trader, credit relief is available against UK tax chargeable on the full amount of the income. Where the foreign income is not pure income profit, e.g. it arises as part of a trade, the Inland Revenue will often argue that credit is given for UK tax on the income after deduction of related expenses. So that, for example, if a UK resident receives fees in the course of a trade in respect of a contract to provide know-how and technical services in a foreign country and a foreign tax is charged on the gross payments which is available for tax credit relief, in determining the measure of UK income on which credit relief is available, a deduction should be made from the gross income for expenses and capital allowances relating to the contract.

It should be noted that there are technical arguments in certain instances for claiming double tax relief by reference to the UK tax on the gross income. For example, as a matter of statutory construction, double tax treaties and the unilateral relief provisions (except in the case of financial institutions and insurance companies) do not generally expressly provide that relief must be given after expenses, etc.

3.30   The measure of foreign branch profits liable to UK tax on which a credit for foreign tax is available is usually the amount calculated in accordance with UK tax principles, and not that as computed for foreign tax or accounting purposes. Accordingly, for UK purposes adjustments (where material) are required to be made for such items as depreciation of fixed assets, entertaining, capital allowances and general provisions. However, historically, in some cases the Inland Revenue has accepted the foreign accounting profits as being equal to the profits for UK tax purposes and has applied the rate of UK income or corporation tax to that amount, provided that this approach has been adopted consistently. This basis has no longer been accepted in new cases for a number of years, although it is understood that existing cases where this has been employed are not being disturbed.

However, there is some flexibility in computing the branch profits for UK tax purposes. The effect of the different capital allowance systems may be to produce an overseas tax charge significantly different from the UK tax charge for the same accounting period, causing a loss of double taxation relief. Claims to capital allowances can be reduced, where advantageous, under *CAA 2001, s 56(5)* — see Example 9 below.

As an alternative to not claiming capital allowances in this situation, it is now possible to obtain relief for the excess foreign tax by carrying it forward for offset against the UK tax payable on profits from the same branch or agency (see 3.43 below).

Example 9

Vectis Ltd, a UK resident company, trades wholly overseas through a branch in Illyria. Its profits for the purpose of Illyria corporation tax are £2,750,000 on which it pays tax at 34% (£935,000). The profits of the company as adjusted for UK corporation tax purposes are £2,700,000 after deduction of UK plant and machinery allowances of £500,000. If the company claims the capital allowances in full, the UK corporation tax computation is as follows.

	£
Schedule D Case I profit	2,700,000
UK corporation tax at 30%	810,000

Less: double tax relief	935,000	
Limited to UK tax payable		(810,000)
UK corporation tax liability		Nil
Double tax relief unutilised (£935,000 − £810,000)		125,000

However, if the company limits its claim to capital allowances to £83,333, the computation becomes:

		£
Taxable profit after full capital allowances		2,700,000
Add: allowances not claimed		416,667
Schedule D Case I profit		3,116,667
UK corporation tax at 30%		935,000
Less: double tax relief (not restricted)	935,000	
		(935,000)
UK corporation tax liability		Nil
Double tax relief unutilised		Nil

The unclaimed plant and machinery allowances remain in the pool of allowances and increase allowances available (or reduce balancing charges) in subsequent years.

Limitation and quantification of credit

3.31   In accordance with the 'root income' principle discussed at 3.12 above, relief is given for foreign tax against UK tax computed by reference to the same income or gain, irrespective of the year or period for which it is assessed in the UK. The tax credit available in the UK is equal to the full amount of the overseas tax borne, limited to the UK tax liability on the same income or gain. Credit is therefore given for the lower of the overseas and UK taxes payable.

For the purpose of calculating tax credit relief, foreign tax paid either directly by the taxpayer or by withholding from income is converted into sterling at the rate of exchange ruling on the date the tax becomes payable. In practice, this is often taken to be the date when the tax is paid or, in the case of taxes withheld, the date when the relevant income is paid. If, however, the taxpayer objects to this treatment or there is a substantial amount of tax involved, the exchange rate ruling on that date when the tax became payable will be applied. If a different basis for conversion of tax has been applied and accepted by the Inland Revenue in a particular case, this basis may be continued if it is reasonable and the taxpayer agrees to apply it consistently.

3.32   There is no requirement that the person assessed in the foreign country be the same person as is assessed in the UK. For example, income from a trust may be assessed abroad on the settlor or on the trustees, and the same income may be liable to UK income tax in the hands of a UK resident beneficiary. In these circumstances credit may be given to the UK resident beneficiary for the foreign tax paid by the settlor or trustees.

The Inland Revenue also allows credit relief where overseas directors' fees are treated as income of a partnership or of a company under ESC A37, even though the foreign tax may have been suffered by the director — see the Inland Revenue's Double Taxation Relief Manual paragraph 507.

However, credit for the foreign tax paid by another person cannot be claimed where the nature of the income has changed. It is common practice for an entertainer, for example, to contract his services to a 'loan out' company which is wholly owned by him and for that company to pay him a salary equal to a percentage of the gross receipts from the services performed. If the entertainer performs abroad and the foreign country requires tax to be deducted from performance fees payable to the loan out company, the Inland Revenue's view is that the foreign tax is not creditable against UK income tax due under Schedule E on the entertainer's salary. Since the loan out company has paid a salary to the entertainer its own corporation tax liability may be substantially less than the foreign tax paid, resulting in a loss of double tax credit relief.

Where income is assessed on an individual under *TA 1988, s 739* (transfer of assets abroad), in computing the liability to income tax the same deductions and reliefs (including double tax credit relief) are allowed as would have been allowed if the income had actually been received by the individual concerned. [*s 743(2)*]. However, relief is not available where an individual receives a benefit which is liable to income tax under *section 740*.

3.33   The limitation on the credit available for income tax purposes is contained in *TA 1988, s 796*. This provides that the amount of such credit allowed to a person for any year of assessment under any arrangement is not to exceed the difference between income tax which would be borne by him for the year if:

(a)   he were charged to tax on his total income for the year computed in accordance with *section 795* (see 3.27 and 3.28 above); and

(b)   he were charged to tax on the same income but excluding the foreign income on which credit is to be allowed.

Example 10

Georgio is domiciled and resident in the UK. His assessable income for 2000/01 comprises a salary of £23,000 and dividends from a foreign company of £12,000 from which foreign withholding tax of 30% has been deducted.

Computation for 2000/01 including foreign income.

			£
Schedule E			23,000
Schedule D Case V			12,000
			35,000
Personal allowance			(4,385)
			30,615

	£		£
Tax on:	1,520	at 10%	152
	17,095	at 22%	3,761
	9,785	at 10%	979
	2,215	at 32.5%	720
	30,615		5,612

Computation for 2000/01 excluding foreign income.

	£
Schedule E	23,000
Personal allowance	(4,385)
	18,615

	£		£
Tax on:	1,520	at 10%	152
	17,095	at 22%	3,761
	15,955		3,913

The maximum double tax credit relief is therefore £1,699 (i.e £5,612 − £3,913), an effective rate of approximately 14.2%.

Where an individual has foreign income from more than one source on which tax credit relief is claimed, this procedure is applied to each source of income in succession. The taxpayer may choose the order in which the sources of income are taken and it will normally be advantageous to apply the procedure to the source which has suffered the highest rate of foreign tax first, since credit will then be given against the person's highest UK marginal rate.

TA 1988, s 796(3) provides that the total credit for foreign tax for any year of assessment is not to exceed the total income tax payable by the claimant for that year of assessment after deduction of tax retained by him on annual charges.

3.34   Where an individual incurs a loss in a trade (either alone or in partnership) claims may be made under *TA 1988, s 380 or 381* to offset the loss against other income. A claim may also be made under *FA 1991, s 72* to offset the loss against capital gains where a claim has been made under *section 380*. *Section 381* applies to the opening years of a business, allowing a carry-back of losses for three years, whereas *section 380* applies to losses incurred at any stage in the life of a business. A claim under *section 380* may be made against the income of the year of the loss and the subsequent year where the prior year basis of assessment applies, and against the income of the year of the loss and the previous year under the current year basis. Claims under these sections are inflexible since relief is given for the lower of the amount of income for the relevant year of assessment and the amount of the loss available for relief. Where a claim under these sections reduces income which has suffered foreign tax to nil for UK purposes, credit relief is not available, but relief is available by deduction under *TA 1988, s 811* (see 3.42 below).

Where the amount of income for the relevant year of assessment exceeds the amount of the loss, so that some income remains chargeable to tax, the losses may be allocated to different sources of income in order to maximise double tax credit relief. The loss is therefore set against UK source income and foreign untaxed income first and the balance of the loss can be split and set against different sources of foreign taxed income to the taxpayer's best advantage.

3.35   The limitation of credit as it applies to corporation tax is contained in *section 797*. The amount of the credit for foreign tax which under any arrangement is to be allowed against UK corporation tax in respect of any income or gain is not to exceed the corporation tax attributable to the relevant income or gain.

The amount of corporation tax for the company as a whole is calculated (before deduction of any credit relief) and the limit of credit is equal to the company's average corporation tax rate for that accounting period multiplied by the foreign income or gain to which the credit applies. There is therefore no 'top-slicing' calculation for each source of foreign income as set out above in relation to income tax. If the amount of foreign tax exceeds the limit of credit calculated above, the excess may, subject to certain conditions, represent eligible unrelieved foreign tax where it has arisen in respect of foreign dividend income (see 4.49). Where it has arisen in repect of foreign branch income taxable under Schedule D Case I, it may be eligible for carry-forward or carry-back against the UK tax liability on income from the same foreign branch (see 3.43 below).

Where in the relevant accounting period there is any deduction to be made for charges on income, management expenses or other amounts (including group relief) which can be deducted from, set against, or treated as reducing profits of more than one description, *section 797(3)* allows the company to allocate the deduction in such amounts and to such of its profits as it thinks fit. In making the allocation, each source of income is considered separately and income from each foreign branch is treated as arising from a separate source.

Example 11

During the year ended 31 December 2000 Vester Ltd, a UK resident company, had UK trading income, branch profits from Germany which had suffered foreign tax at 40% and interest from Australia which had suffered 10% withholding tax. It had charges on income of £60,000 for the year and a group relief claim of £40,000. The company is liable to UK corporation tax at the rate of 30%.

	UK Case I	Germany Case I	Australia Case III	Total
Foreign tax rate		40%	10%	
	£	£	£	£
Income from each source	50,000	200,000	100,000	350,000

Charges on income	(50,000)	–	(10,000)	(60,000)
Group relief	–	–	(40,000)	(40,000)
Income chargeable to corporation tax	Nil	200,000	50,000	250,000
UK corporation tax at 30%	–	60,000	15,000	75,000
Double taxation relief (limited to UK tax)	–	(60,000)	(10,000)	(70,000)
UK corporation tax payable	–	Nil	5,000	5,000

Excess foreign tax credit of £20,000 (£80,000 − £60,000) in respect of the German profits is not available for relief in the current period but may be carried forward for relief against the UK corporation tax liability on future profits from the same branch.

3.36   Where a company which has a single trade has trading losses brought forward, these may be allocated first against profits arising in the UK, even when these arose in a foreign branch, and the balance is allocated to the foreign branches so that the maximum double tax credit relief is given.

Example 12

Electron Ltd, a UK resident company, trades in the UK and through branches in Sweden and Hong Kong. At 31 December 1999 it had trading losses brought forward under *TA 1988, s 393(1)* of £350,000. During the year ended 31 December 2000 it made profits of £750,000, of which £250,000 arose in Sweden and £375,000 in Hong Kong. Tax of £50,000 was paid in Sweden and £60,000 in Hong Kong. The company is liable to UK corporation tax at the rate of 30%.

	UK Case I £	Hong Kong Case I £	Sweden Case I £	Total £
Income from each source	125,000	375,000	250,000	750,000
Deduct: losses brought forward [*s 393(1)*]	(125,000)	(175,000)	(50,000)	(350,000)
Profits chargeable to corporation tax	Nil	200,000	200,000	400,000
UK corporation tax at 30%	–	60,000	60,000	120,000
Double tax relief	–	(60,000)	(50,000)	(110,000)
UK corporation tax payable	–	Nil	10,000	10,000

3.37   In *Commercial Union Assurance Co plc v Shaw [1998] STC 386*, the company received foreign dividends which had suffered foreign withholding tax. Some relief for underlying tax was also available (see Chapter 4). The company also had charges on income (loan interest) which it sought to set off under *section 797(3)* in such a way that they exceeded the amount of UK source profits to which they were allocated. The company's aim was to increase the amount of UK tax on foreign dividend income on which double tax relief was available and to produce excess charges on income within *TA 1988, s 393(9)*. Harman J held that under *section 797(3)(a)* the company was entitled to allocate a sum of charges on income to any category of profits up to (but not exceeding) the amount of those profits. The deduction to be made for charges on income may not be greater than the profits from which those charges are deductible. The scope of *section 797(3)(a)* is restricted to the allocation of a deduction of charges on income, etc. for the purposes of that section and does not operate to create a loss under *section 393(9)*. This case is largely superseded following the introduction of the rules regarding company loan relationship set out in 3.38 below.

Company loan relationships

3.38   Under the company loan relationships legislation which was introduced in *FA 1996* and took effect from 1 April 1996, profits and gains (including interest, discounts and premiums) arising to a company on its loan relationships are generally chargeable to tax as income. To the extent that a company is a party to a loan relationship for the purposes of its trade, profits or gains (credits) arising from the relationship are brought into account in computing the profits and gains of the trade. Corresponding expenses or losses (debits) in connection with a loan relationship entered into for the purposes of a trade are expenses of that trade and are deductible in computing the profits or gains of that trade. [*s 82(2)*]. Profits or gains from loan relationships of a company which are not for trade purposes (non-trading credits) are chargeable to tax under Schedule D Case III, even where the loan has a foreign source. Expenses and losses incurred from such loan relationships (non-trading debits) are automatically deducted from non-trading credits in computing either the amount chargeable under Schedule D Case III or, if the debits exceed the credits, the 'non-trading deficit' for the accounting period. [*s 82(3)* and *(4)*].

3.39   Where there is a non-trading deficit on a company's loan relationships the company may make a claim for the whole or any part of the deficit to be treated in any of the following ways [*s 83(2)*]:

(*a*)   to be set off against any profits of the company (of whatever description) for the period;

(*b*)   to be group relieved;

(*c*)   to be carried back to be set off against Schedule D Case III profits arising from the company's loan relationships of earlier accounting periods, including non-trading foreign exchange and financial instruments profits; or

(*d*)   to be carried forward and set against non-trading profits for the next accounting period.

The amount available for group relief under (*b*) is the amount which would be allowed as group relief under *TA 1988, s 403(1)* if it were a trading loss incurred in the deficit period. [*Sch 8, para 2*]. This is more favourable than if the amount were treated as a charge on income, since the group relief claim is not restricted to the excess over the company's income for the period as it would be under *section 403(3)*. For deficit periods ending on or after 2 July 1997 the carry back under (*c*) is allowed within a 'permitted period' of twelve months immediately preceding the period in which the deficit arose. The deficit is set off against profits of a later period before profits of an earlier period. [*Sch 8, para 3(3)*]. Claims must be made within two years of the end of the 'relevant period', or such longer period as the Board may allow. Where the claim is made under (*a*) to (*c*) above, the relevant period is the period in which the deficit arises. In relation to a claim under (*d*), it is the accounting period following the deficit period. [*s 83(6)* and *(7)*]. The profits against which the non-trading deficit is to be set off are identified in the claim and those profits are to be reduced accordingly. Where the set off of the deficit is against trading profits of the deficit period the reduction is made after deduction of brought forward trading losses, but before relief for losses under *section 393A(1)*. A current year deficit takes precedence over a deficit carried back from a subsequent accounting period. [*Sch 8, para 1(3)*]. There are also rules to identify the order of set-off where there is a claim to carry back a deficit to a previous accounting period. [*Sch 8, para 3(6)*].

The amount which is still unused becomes 'a carried forward debit' for the accounting period immediately following the deficit period and can be offset only against non-trading profits of the company in that and future accounting periods. [*s 83(3)* and *(4)*]. Non-trading profits are profits of the company which are not trading income for the purposes of *TA 1988, s 393A*. [*Sch 8, para 4(3)*].

3.40   The deduction for any non-trading debit is determined solely by the provisions of *FA 1996*, but some of the debits may be allowed to be offset differently for double tax relief purposes. Where there is no foreign source interest for the period on which tax credit relief is available, the allocation of the non-trading deficit for the period for the purpose of double tax credit relief falls within *TA 1988, s 797*, as amended by *FA 1996, Sch 14, para 42*. A new *subsection 3A* provides that, where a claim has been made for a non-trading loan deficit to be set against current year profits (or in accordance with special rules for insurance companies), the deficit can be allocated for the purpose of *section 797(3)* to profits of any description, but only to those profits against which it is set off in pursuance of the claim. Where a non-trading deficit is carried forward (whether in pursuance of a claim or not), for the purpose of *section 797(3)* it must be allocated to non-trading profits of the later period (so far as they are sufficient) and cannot be allocated to any other profits. [*section 797(3B)*].

3.41   Where any foreign source interest is chargeable to tax in an accounting period and credit relief is available for that tax, *TA 1988, s 797A* applies. Under *section 797A(2)* it is assumed that tax is chargeable under Schedule D Case III on the non-trading credits without the automatic deduction of any non-trading debits. This enables the foreign source interest to be left chargeable to UK corporation tax so that credit relief is available in principle.

Section 797A(3) provides that *section 797(3)* is to have effect as if for the accounting period there were an amount equal to the 'adjusted amount of the non-trading debits' to be brought into account. This amount can be offset for the purposes of double tax relief against such profits of the company for the period as it chooses. The 'adjusted amount of a company's non-trading debits' for an accounting period is the total non-trading debits given for that period for the purposes of the loan re-lationships legislation less the aggregate of the following:

(*a*)   the amount of the non-trading deficit for the applicable accounting period which is claimed for group relief, carry-back of deficits and carry-forward to the next accounting period;

(*b*)   the amount of the non-trading deficit which falls to be carried forward to a subsequent period; and

(*c*)   the amount of any deficit carried forward to the applicable ac-counting period in pursuance of a claim.

In the operation of *section 797(3)* the amount in (*c*) above is to be allocated only against non-trading profits. Where the company has a non-trading deficit for the applicable accounting period which exceeds the total of (*a*) to (*c*) and, in pursuance of a claim for the deficit to be set against current year profits that excess is set off against profits of any description, the allocation under *section 797(3)* follows the claim.

Example 13

Veritas Ltd, a UK resident company, has the following items of income and expenditure for the years ended 31 March 1999 and 31 March 2000. It is a member of a group for the purposes of group relief and another group company has profits of £50,000 in each year which may be group relieved.

	Year ended 31 March 1999		Year ended 31 March 2000	
	£	Foreign tax £	£	Foreign tax £
Trading profits (UK) before interest	150,000		250,000	
Trading profits (foreign)	50,000	10,000	80,000	20,000
Interest — non-trading (US)	150,000		100,000	
Interest — non-trading (Canada)			50,000	5,000
Loan relationship debits				
— trading	100,000		100,000	
— non-trading	400,000		400,000	
Dividend from foreign subsidiary	200,000	40,000	150,000	35,000

Year ended 31 March 1999

Non-trading deficit
Non-trading debits	400,000
Non-trading credits	(150,000)
Non-trading deficit	250,000

Claim under section 83

For group relief [*(2)(b)*]	50,000
For set off against trading profits [*(2)(a)*]	67,742
For set off against foreign dividend [*(2)(a)*]	70,968
For offset against non-trading profits of following year [*(2)(d)*]	
Schedule D Case V	33,333
Schedule D Case III	27,957
	250,000

	Case I UK	Case I Foreign	Case III	Case V	Total
	150,000	50,000	150,000	200,000	550,000
Loan relationship debits — trading	(100,000)	–	–	–	(100,000)
Non-trading debits [*s 82(3)* and *(4)*]	–	–	(150,000)	–	(150,000)
Non-trading debits (claim under *section 83(2)(a)*)	(50,000)	(17,742)	–	(70,968)	(138,710)
	–	32,258	–	129,032	161,290
Corporation tax at 31%			50,000		
Double taxation relief					
— Schedule D Case I		(10,000)			
— Schedule D Case V		(40,000)			
			(50,000)		
Corporation tax payable			Nil		

Year ended 31 March 2000

	Case I UK	Case I Foreign	Case III US	Case III Canada	Case V	Total
	250,000	80,000	100,000	50,000	150,000	630,000
Loan relationship debits — trading	(100,000)	–	–	–	–	(100,000)
Loan relationship debits — non-trading						
From previous year [*s 83(2)(d)*]	–	–	(27,957)	–	(33,333)	(61,290)
Set off in current year	–	–	(72,043)	(33,334)	–	(105,377)
Claim under *section 83(2)(a)*	(150,000)	(13,333)	–	–	–	(163,333)
Chargeable to corporation tax	Nil	66,667	Nil	16,666	116,667	200,000
Corporation tax at 30%			60,000			
Double taxation relief						
— Schedule D Case I		20,000				
— Schedule D Case III		5,000				
— Schedule D Case V		35,000				
			(60,000)			
Corporation tax payable			Nil			

Deduction of foreign tax where no credit is allowable

3.42   Under *TA 1988, s 811*, foreign tax paid, instead of being claimed as a credit, may be treated as reducing the foreign income assessable to UK tax. This applies only in cases where the income is assessed on the arising, and not the remittance, basis. *Section 805* allows a taxpayer to make an election that credit is not to be allowed in respect of particular income or gains.

There were a number of circumstances where it may have been necessary or advantageous to take foreign tax as a deduction rather than as a tax credit, including:

● where, because of losses or charges on income deducted from the foreign income before it was assessed to UK tax, there was no (or insufficient) UK tax on the foreign income against which the foreign tax could be credited; and

● where the person who had borne the foreign tax was not resident in the UK, e.g. if the foreign income had arisen in connection with the UK branch of a foreign company.

It should be noted that following the introduction of *TA 1988, s 806L* in respect of accounting periods ending after 31 March 2000, UK resident companies may now carry forward or carry back foreign tax in respect of Schedule D Case I trading income arising from an overseas branch or agency for offset against the UK corporation tax liability on income from the same source. This is discussed in further detail at 3.46 below.

In the case of non-UK residents with a UK branch or agency, unilateral relief is now available under *section 794(2)(bb)* with effect for chargeable periods ending after 20 March 2000, broadly as if the UK branch or agency were a UK resident company.

Example 14

Ambrose Ltd, a UK resident company, trades in the UK and through a branch in Germany. In the year ended 31 December 1997 it made branch profits in Germany of £200,000 on which tax of £105,000 was payable. However, in the UK it made trading losses of £150,000. It has no associated companies.

	UK Case I £	Germany Case I £	Total Case I £
Income from each source	(150,000)	200,000	50,000
UK corporation tax at 21.75%			10,875
Double taxation relief (limited to UK tax payable)			(10,875)
UK corporation tax payable			Nil

There are no losses available to carry forward under *TA 1988, s 393(1)*, or back under *s 393A(1)(b)*.

If, instead, the company deducts the German tax paid on the German branch profits as an expense the Schedule D Case I computation becomes:

	UK Case I £	Germany Case I £	Total Case I £
Income from each source	(150,000)	200,000	50,000
German tax expensed		(105,000)	(105,000)
	(150,000)	95,000	(55,000)

Ambrose Ltd has £55,000 of trading losses available for carry-forward under *TA 1988, s 393(1)*, or back under *s 393A(1)(b)*.

Where relief by deduction of the foreign tax is given, new provisions apply [*TA 1988, s 811 (4)–(10)* and *TCGA 1992, s 278*] where there is an adjustment of the amount of foreign tax paid which takes the form of a repayment of all or part of that tax. In this situation, the amount of the expense relief previously allowed will become excessive. Therefore, the normal time limit for adjusting the amount of the expense relief previously allowed is extended. As a result, nothing in the Taxes Acts limiting the time for the making of assessments shall apply to any assessment to which the adjustment gives rise, provided that the assessment is made not later than six years from the time when the other country repaid the foreign tax.

In addition, the requirement is imposed on taxpayers to inform the Inland Revenue within one year of an adjustment taking place to the foreign tax paid. Failure to comply with this requirement will result in a penalty of an amount up to the additional UK tax payable as a result of the adjustment.

Carry-back or carry-forward of unrelieved foreign tax

3.43   For accounting periods ending after 31 March 2000 *TA 1988, s 806L* applies where in an accounting period of a UK tax resident company, an amount of unrelieved foreign tax arises in respect of any of the company's qualifying income from an overseas branch or agency of the company. Qualifying income is defined as the Schedule D Case I profits of an overseas branch or agency or profits which are included in the profits of life reinsurance business or overseas life assurance business chargeable under Schedule D Case VI by virtue of *TA 1988, s 439B* or *441.* [*TA 1988, s 806L(5)*]. An amount of unrelieved foreign tax is treated as arising where the amount of the credit for foreign tax which would be allowable, apart from *section 797*, against the UK corporation tax liability on that income exceeds the amount of credit for foreign tax which is actually allowed against the UK corporation tax liability on that income. For example, unrelieved foreign tax can arise where the rate of foreign tax exceeds the UK tax rate or the UK measure of taxable profits is less than the foreign measure. It can also arise where the Schedule D Case I trade is loss-making overall.

Any unrelieved foreign tax can generally only be credited against profits from the same overseas branch or agency that has given rise to the unrelieved foreign tax. However, it is possible to offset the unrelieved foreign tax arising in respect of one overseas branch against the UK corporation tax arising or the profits of another overseas branch which is in the same territory. [*s 806M(4)*].

3.44   Unrelieved foreign tax can generally be carried forward indefinitely for future offset unless the branch or agency that gave rise to the unrelieved foreign tax ceases to exist [*s 806M (2)*]. If, at a later date, a new branch or agency is opened in the same territory as the old one they will generally be treated as separate entities for the purposes of these rules. Therefore, unrelieved foreign tax that arose in respect of the defunct branch cannot be carried forward for offset against UK tax on the profits of the new branch.

The carry-back of unrelieved foreign tax is permitted in respect of accounting periods beginning not more than three years before the accounting period in which the unrelieved foreign tax arises. [*s 806L (2)*]. It should be noted that unrelieved foreign tax may be partly carried back and partly carried forward if necessary. Where unrelieved foreign tax is carried back to previous accounting periods, relief is given on a 'last in, first out' basis, i.e. the carry-back is to a later accounting period in priority to an earlier one. In addition, credit is first given for foreign tax of that accounting period and second to unrelieved foreign tax brought forward from an earlier accounting period before credit is given for unrelieved foreign tax carried back. Unrelieved foreign tax may not be carried back to accounting periods ending before 1 April 2000.

3.45   For unrelieved foreign tax to be utilised it is necessary to make a claim. Such a claim must specify the amount of unrelieved foreign tax to be carried forward, or back, for offset. Claims must be made within six years of the accounting period in which the unrelieved foreign tax arises or, if later, one year after the end of the accounting period in which the foreign tax is paid.

It could be argued that the relief available under *s 806L* for the foreign tax paid in respect of foreign branches is more restrictive than the onshore pooling regime that applies to certain foreign dividend income. In particular, under the onshore pooling regime, eligible unrelieved foreign tax arising on dividends from one company can be set off against qualifying foreign dividends from other companies. Companies wishing to offset unrelieved foreign tax from one overseas branch against the UK tax liability on the profits of a foreign branch in another country should consider the technical arguments for this under the EU principle of the freedom of establishment (i.e. that branches should not be treated less favourably than companies), where both branches are EU resident, or under the non-discrimination article of the relevant double tax treaty in other cases.

Tax credit relief planning for groups of companies

3.46   The *George Wimpey International* case (see 3.26 above) illustrates that, where a company carries on a single trade in a number of countries, in determining the limit of credit relief the profits and losses of the trade are aggregated. Accordingly, losses incurred in the UK or unprofitable branches may be set automatically against the profits of other foreign branches which have suffered foreign tax, thereby limiting the amount of credit relief available. While the new rules in *section 806L-M* (see 3.43 above) can alleviate this situation to a certain extent, it can be avoided by placing the trading activities of profitable foreign branches in one or more separate members of the UK group, in order to isolate these activities.

If such companies have a residual UK corporation tax liability (because overseas tax has been paid at a rate lower than the rate of UK corporation tax or the measure of profits for foreign tax purposes is lower than the UK measure) and there are losses or other amounts available for group relief from another group company, a claim may be made for the exact amount of group relief necessary to reduce the UK corporation tax liability to the amount of the foreign tax credit.

3.47   Similar considerations apply in relation to the holding of shares in foreign subsidiaries paying dividends which have borne foreign tax. If these dividends are received by a UK company which has trading losses, charges on income or excess management expenses, the UK's loss relief rules may result in the reduction in the foreign income which is charged to UK tax and hence the amount of double tax credit relief available. For example, where a company receiving taxed foreign dividends makes a claim for the offset of trading losses against its other profits under *TA 1988, s 393A(1)* and there are insufficient UK or untaxed foreign profits to set against the loss, the balance of the loss is offset against the foreign dividend income. In consequence the UK tax on that foreign income (and therefore the limit of foreign tax credit) is correspondingly reduced. However, it should be noted that for foreign dividends paid to the UK after 30 March 2001, the excess foreign tax may represent eligible unrelieved foreign tax (see 4.49). Therefore, credit for the foreign tax that cannot be relieved may not be entirely lost. While trading losses (and also non-trading loan deficits) may be group relieved in the current year, this is possible only if there is a company in the group with taxable profits. If the company receiving the foreign dividends has charges on income or management expenses, these may be surrendered as group relief only to the extent that they exceed the current year profits of the company, including taxed foreign income. [*TA 1988, s 403(3)*].

Prior to the introduction of the loan relationships legislation in 1996, shares in foreign subsidiaries were usually held in a separate company (often referred to as a '*Case V* trap') used solely for the purpose of receiving taxed foreign income. If such a company had a residual UK corporation tax liability and there were losses elsewhere in the group available for group relief, the exact amount of group relief could be surrendered to the company in order to reduce its corporation tax liability so that it matched the foreign tax credit.

3.48 The introduction of the loan relationships legislation changed the position concerning the holding of shares in a Case V trap company since there is significantly more flexibility in dealing with non-trading loan relationship debits than with charges on income — see Example 13 above. In particular, non-trading deficits may be group relieved as if they are trading losses and there is additional flexibility over the carry forward and carry back of loan relationship deficits. Nevertheless, the ownership of foreign subsidiaries is still usually maintained in a separate company, but for reasons connected with the foreign exchange provisions in *FA 1993*. A UK group may wish to borrow in the foreign currency of the overseas subsidiary in order to hedge its currency exposure on the investment. For tax purposes an election may be made to match the monetary liability with the investment in shares as provided by *FA 1993, Sch 15, para 4* and the subsequent regulations. [*SI 1994 No 3227*]. The election allows taxation of the exchange difference on the borrowing to be deferred until the shares are sold, at which time they are taken into account in calculating the capital gains position on the shares.

In applying the concept of matching to groups of companies, the election may be made only if the asset and liability are in the same company. Since a matching election is intended to be permanent, but external finance for the group is subject to fluctuation, a separate UK company can be used to hold shares in foreign subsidiaries so that the loan which is used in the matching election is intra-group. In this way, external finance may be arranged in accordance with the commercial requirements of the group without affecting the matching election. Following the introduction of the onshore pooling rules, to the extent that eligible unrelieved foreign tax

Example 15

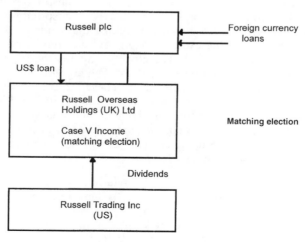

arises in the 'Case V trap' company it can be surrendered to other group companies (see 4.65).

3.49   Since the introduction of the loan relationships legislation a new device, the 'Case III trap' company, has emerged. This is used where interest is earned on a loan denominated in a foreign currency and foreign tax is payable on the interest. If the loan gives rise to an exchange loss, such a loss is set off automatically against interest income. [*FA 1993, s 130*]. In those circumstances the foreign Case III income is reduced by the exchange loss, thereby restricting the double taxation relief claim.

The solution is for the currency exposure to be hedged by way of a currency swap between the Case III trap company and another company within the group, so that any exchange loss on the loan is balanced by a profit on the swap, ensuring that the foreign Case III income remains fully chargeable to corporation tax.

Example 16

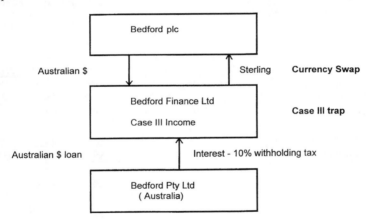

Interaction with advance corporation tax

3.50   Prior to the case of *Collard v Mining and Industrial Holdings Ltd* which ultimately reached the House of Lords at *[1989] STC 384*, it was the view of the Inland Revenue under what was then *FA 1972, s 100(6)* that advance corporation tax (ACT) should be allocated pro rata to the corporation tax attributable to the various sources of income. According to that view, ACT was set off against corporation tax in priority to double tax relief. However, the House of Lords decided that on the existing legislation credit relief for foreign tax was available in priority to ACT.

In 1984, in response to the judgment of the High Court, amendments were made to the legislation which were contained in *TA 1988, s 797(4)* and *(5)*. These provided that where any ACT falls to be set against the company's liability to corporation tax on its profits for the relevant accounting period:

(*a*)   the corporation tax liability is reduced by the amount of the credit for foreign tax attributable to the income or gain; and

(*b*)   the amount of ACT is then set off against the corporation tax liability, subject to the lower of the two following limits, which are:

    (i)   the normal limit which would apply to ACT on the income under what was *TA 1988, s 239(2)*; or

    (ii)   the amount of corporation tax on the income or gain after deduction of the foreign tax credit.

Example 17

Nectar Plc, a UK resident company, has a UK trade and has branches in France and Belgium. In the year ended 31 December 1997 it made profits in the UK of £1,600,000 and its branches in France and Belgium made profits of £300,000 and £400,000 and paid tax of £90,000 and £160,000 respectively. The company also had interest income of £100,000 from loans made abroad which were subject to a withholding tax of 15%. In 1997 the company paid dividends of £2,000,000 on which it paid ACT of £500,000.

	UK Case I	France Case I	Belgium Case I	Case I	Case III	Total
	£	£	£	£	£	£
UK profits chargeable to CT	1,600,000	300,000	400,000	100,000	2,400,000
UK CT at 31.5%	504,000	94,500	126,000	31,500	756,000
Double tax relief	–	(90,000)	(126,000)	(15,000)	(231,000)
CT before deduction of ACT	504,000	4,500	Nil	16,500	525,000
ACT set-off (max 20%)	(320,000)	(4,500)	–	(16,500)	(341,000)
Mainstream CT payable	184,000	Nil	Nil	Nil	184,000

The company has surplus ACT of £159,000 (i.e. £500,000–£341,000) for the year.

With effect for accounting periods ending after 5 April 1999 in respect pf which ACT has been abolished, *section 797(4) and (5)* have been repealed. Companies which have surplus ACT carried forward after this date will need to consider the shadow ACT regulations [*SI 1999 No 358*] to establish the amount of surplus ACT carried forward that can be offset in subsequent accounting periods.

Foreign income dividends and international headquarters companies

3.51   Surplus ACT due to insufficient UK corporation tax capacity has been a problem for UK multinational groups since the introduction of the UK's imputation system of corporation tax in 1973. Following representations over several years from many such groups of companies and associations representing them, in his March 1993 Budget speech the

Chancellor of the Exchequer, Norman Lamont, proposed the introduction of a 'foreign income dividend' (FID) scheme. Legislation was included in *FA 1994* and introduced *TA 1988, ss 246A to 246Y*. This took effect with respect to dividends paid from 1 July 1994 and to foreign source profits arising in accounting periods beginning after 1 July 1993. The FID scheme was abolished at the same date as the abolition of ACT, i.e. from 6 April 1999.

Until that date where a company elected for a dividend to be treated as a FID, ACT was payable on the dividend in the normal way; but where the FID was shown to have been paid out of foreign source profits, any surplus ACT in respect of the FID was repayable to the company at the earliest on the normal due date for payment of the company's corporation tax liability (i.e. nine months after the end of the company's accounting period).

The company paying a FID needed to match FIDs paid by it during an accounting period with:

(*a*)   its own distributable foreign profits of that accounting period and the immediately preceding accounting period; and

(*b*)   the distributable foreign profit of any 51% subsidiary for any such accounting period (or that part of the subsidiary's accounting period which coincides with it).

3.52   *Section 246D* provided that individual shareholders receiving a FID were treated as receiving income of an amount which, if reduced by income tax at the lower rate, would equal the amount of the dividend. They were treated as having paid tax on the dividend at the lower rate, but were not entitled to a repayment of income tax. Nor did the dividend constitute franked investment income, although a company receiving a FID could itself pay a FID without paying ACT in respect of that amount.

Where the shareholder receiving a FID was a resident of a country which had an agreement with the UK which would normally entitle the recipient to payment of part of the UK tax credit, those provisions in the agreement did not apply with respect to the FID. This is because agreements give the foreign shareholder an entitlement to a tax credit based on the tax credit to which an individual resident in the UK would have been entitled had he been the recipient of the dividend. As a UK individual was not entitled to a tax credit in respect of a FID, neither was the foreign shareholder.

There are a number of circumstances in which a FID election could not be made:

(*a*)   where a company's dividends were 'streamed' (i.e. FIDs and non-FIDs could not be paid to different shareholders or on different classes of shares);

(*b*)   where it was open to the shareholder to choose the form of the dividend (e.g. where there is a scrip alternative).

3.53   *FA 1994* also introduced legislation concerning international headquarters companies (IHCs). An IHC could pay an FID without accounting for ACT, which avoided the cash flow disadvantage and administrative inconvenience of the FID scheme as it applied to other companies. However, there was an adjustment mechanism for the payment of ACT (plus interest) if later it transpired that ACT would have arisen on an FID paid by it. The IHC legislation was also repealed with effect from 6 April 1999.

Briefly, with effect from accounting periods ending after 28 November 1995, an IHC was a company which was in the accounting period in which the dividend was paid and was, in the immediately preceding accounting period (if any):

(*a*)   a 100% subsidiary [*TA 1988, s 838*] of a non-UK resident company whose shares were quoted (and whose shares were dealt in) on a recognised stock exchange outside the UK. This condition had to be met for the whole of the accounting period and the twelve months immediately preceding it; or

(*b*)   a wholly owned subsidiary of a 'foreign held company', (i.e. a company at least 80% of the shares of which were owned by non-UK resident persons, or which was a wholly owned subsidiary of a company which was so owned) and not more than 20% of the ordinary share capital was ultimately owned by UK resident persons, other than companies; or

(*c*)   not less than 80% of its share capital was owned by non-UK resident persons (other than companies) and/or by foreign held companies each of which owned at least 5% of the share capital. In addition, not more than 20% of the ordinary share capital could ultimately be owned by UK resident persons, other than companies.

Tax sparing relief

3.54   Several countries, mainly in the developing world, have instituted forms of tax relief in order to stimulate certain parts of their economy and to make them more attractive to foreign investors. In some countries this is referred to as 'pioneer relief'. Examples of such relief include:

●   accelerated depreciation allowances may be given for tax purposes on certain fixed assets;

●   profits may be free from tax in the early years of an investment;

●   the effective rate of tax on the profits may be reduced for a certain period;

●   tax may be forgiven by reference to the percentage of goods manufactured within the country which are subsequently exported;

- a reduction may be given on withholding taxes on interest and royalties paid to non-residents in respect of an approved investment.

When a UK company operates through a foreign branch which qualifies for pioneer relief the profits of the branch are also taxed in the UK in the same accounting period. Without some additional form of relief in the UK, the UK corporation tax liability would simply be increased, often by the full amount of the tax relief given by the developing country, and the benefit of the pioneer relief would be lost.

3.55   As a result, what is now *TA 1988, s 788(5)* allows credit under double taxation agreements for the foreign tax which would have been payable but for certain reliefs which are specified in the agreement. This credit is generally referred to as 'tax sparing relief'. The result is that the amount of overseas tax which would be payable under a foreign country's laws but for the relief specified in the agreement is treated as if it had been paid and credit is given against UK tax for that amount. Countries whose agreements with the UK currently provide for such relief include Kenya, the Gambia, Zambia, Singapore, Malaysia, Sri Lanka and India. Tax sparing relief is not available unilaterally. *Section 788(5)* applies only to tax which would have been payable under the law of a foreign country but for a specific tax relief, which is:

(*a*)   relief of a type given with a view to promoting industrial, commercial, scientific, educational or other development overseas, being a relief for which provision is made in the double taxation agreement; and

(*b*)   any relief given in accordance with an agreement, provided the agreement expressly contemplates that relief is to fall within *section 788(5)*.

Please refer to 4.27 and 4.28 for a discussion of the technical position where the tax spared is at the level of a second or lower tier foreign subsiduary.

Although the amount of overseas tax spared is treated as paid, no part of it is added back in computing the amount of income assessable to income tax or corporation tax by virtue of *TA 1988, s 795(3)*.

3.56   The following example illustrates the operation of tax sparing relief where the activity qualifying for the pioneer relief is carried out through an overseas branch of a UK company.

Example 18

Hibernia Ltd is a UK resident company which has a branch in Freedonia carrying out infrastructure development work. The activity qualifies for a special pioneer relief under which the standard rate of Freedonia tax is reduced by 70%. In 2000 the Freedonia branch made profits of £500,000 and the standard rate of corporation tax in Freedonia was 40%. There is an agreement in force between the UK and Freedonia under which the UK gives credit for tax spared under the Freedonia pioneer relief provisions. The Freedonia corporation tax computation is as follows.

	£	£
Profit liable to Freedonia corporation tax		500,000
Corporation tax at 40%	(200,000)	
Tax spared	140,000	
Freedonia corporation tax paid		(60,000)
Profit after Freedonia tax		440,000

UK corporation tax computation

	£	£
Profit assessable to UK corporation tax		500,000
UK corporation tax at 30%		150,000
Double tax relief:		
Freedonia corporation tax paid	60,000	
Freedonia corporation tax spared	140,000	
	200,000	
Limited to UK corporation tax		(150,000)
UK corporation tax payable		Nil

If the foreign income which qualifies for pioneer relief is interest or royalties, the tax sparing relief is limited to the withholding tax rates provided by the agreement. For a discussion of tax sparing relief in relation to credit for underlying tax on dividends, see 4.27.

In November 1997, the UK government indicated that it was its policy to phase out tax sparing relief. As indicated above, a number of agreements still contain tax sparing provisions although in certain cases tax sparing relief is only given for a limited number of years as specified in the particular treaty.

Double taxation relief on chargeable gains

3.57   As indicated earlier, the statutory provisions relating to double taxation relief, both by agreement and unilaterally, are extended to capital gains tax (CGT) by *TCGA 1992, s 277*. This section also provides that agreements made before the passing of the *Finance Act 1965* which refer to relief from UK tax chargeable on capital gains have effect in relation to CGT. Foreign tax chargeable on the disposal of an asset which is borne by the person making the disposal and is not claimed as a credit is allowable as a deduction in computing the gain under *section 278*.

The general requirement for tax credit relief under an agreement is that tax payable under the law of the foreign country on gains from sources within that country is allowed as a credit against any UK tax computed by reference to the same gains by reference to which the foreign tax is computed. *TA 1988, s 790* (as extended by *section 277*) applies similar rules for the purposes of unilateral relief. There is no requirement that the respective tax liabilities should arise at the same time or that they should be charged on the same person.

The principles applying to the computation of double tax credit relief in relation to CGT are similar to those which apply for income tax. Where CGT is chargeable on the arising basis the full amount of the gain is assessed without deduction of the foreign tax. Where an individual is assessed on the remittance basis, the amount to be assessed is the amount remitted to the UK together with the amount of creditable foreign tax attributable to the remitted gain, as for income tax (see Example 7 above).

In calculating the amount of foreign tax credit relief available, the Inland Revenue takes the view that if the period of ownership considered in arriving at the foreign taxable amount is longer than the period over which the UK chargeable gain has accrued, the foreign tax eligible for credit is restricted to:

$$\frac{\text{UK period}}{\text{Foreign period}} \times \text{Foreign tax paid}$$

Similarly, if the amount of UK taxable gain is less than the sterling amount of foreign assessable gain, its view is that the foreign tax eligible for credit is restricted to:

$$\frac{\text{UK gain}}{\text{Foreign gain}} \times \text{Foreign tax paid}$$

However, there has been no case law on the method of calculating double tax credit relief in relation to chargeable gains, so that the Inland Revenue's practice in this area is open to challenge on appeal.

The amount of the credit for foreign tax may not exceed the lesser of the foreign tax paid and the UK CGT charged at the taxpayer's marginal rate. The amount of credit must be calculated separately for each gain and any excess foreign tax may not be credited against UK tax on another foreign gain or on the gain on disposal of a UK asset. Capital losses and the annual CGT exemption may be set against gains on UK assets first, enabling the tax credit relief to be maximised.

Example 19

Henry is a UK resident and domiciled individual whose marginal rate of tax is 40%. In 2000/01 he had the following capital gains.

	Capital gain	*Foreign tax*
UK	£10,000	–
France	£5,000	£1,000
Belgium	£15,000	£3,000

He also had capital losses brought forward from 1996/97 of £8,000.

	UK	*France*	*Belgium*	*Total*
	£	£	£	£
Capital gains	10,000	5,000	15,000	30,000
Capital losses	(8,000)	–	–	(8,000)

65

	2,000	5,000	15,000	22,000
Annual exemption	(2,000)	(2,500)	(2,700)	(7,200)
Chargeable to CGT	Nil	2,500	12,300	14,800
CGT at 40%	–	1,000	4,920	5,920
Double taxation relief	–	(1,000)	(3,000)	(4,000)
UK CGT payable	–	Nil	1,920	1,920

In order to claim credit relief the taxpayer is normally required to be resident in the UK. However, persons who are not resident but who are ordinarily resident in the UK may, exceptionally, be granted relief. Cases where such a person claims credit relief are referred to International Division (Double Taxation).

3.58   Statement of Practice SP 6/88 sets out a number of circumstances in which a credit is available for foreign tax payable against UK CGT or corporation tax on chargeable gains.

*   The overseas country charges capital gains as income.

*   Overseas tax is payable on a disposal which falls within *TCGA 1992, s 171* (transfer between companies in the same group treated as taking place at no gain/no loss) and a liability to UK tax arises on a subsequent disposal.

*   An overseas trade carried on through a branch or agency is transferred to a local subsidiary and relief is given under *TCGA 1992, s 140* so that any chargeable gain is postponed for UK tax purposes. However, the transfer may give rise to an immediate tax charge in the foreign country. If there is a subsequent disposal of the shares in the local subsidiary (or the subsidiary disposes of the assets within six years of the transfer) and a liability to UK corporation tax arises at that time, any foreign tax paid in relation to the earlier transfer of assets may be credited against UK corporation tax on that disposal.

*   Overseas tax is payable by reference to increases in the value of assets although there is no disposal. On a subsequent disposal giving rise to a UK tax liability the foreign tax paid on the increase in value may be credited against the UK tax.

However, SP 6/88 indicates that the relief is conditional on the subject of the overseas tax being identified with the gains on which the UK liability arises. Therefore, where gains giving rise to a foreign tax liability are 'rolled over' under *TCGA 1992, s 152*, no tax credit relief is given because no UK liability arises on the disposal of the old asset. The gain on the new asset is considered to be a gain separate from that realised on the old asset, even though the gain may in fact have arisen entirely as a result of the increase in value of the old asset. No tax credit relief is allowed, although the overseas tax may be deducted from the gain under *TCGA 1992, s 278* in computing the rollover relief.

3.59   Where, under *TCGA 1992, s 13*, a UK shareholder in a non-UK resident company which would be a close company if resident in the UK is chargeable to CGT on a proportion of the capital gain accruing to that company, tax credit relief may be given against UK capital gains tax on the appropriate proportion of the overseas tax payable in respect of the gain by the company in the country in which it is resident. Alternatively, the appropriate proportion of the overseas tax may be deducted in computing the shareholder's gain (SP D/23). Where the gain arises in a company which is a resident of a country with which the UK has a double taxation agreement, the Inland Revenue accepts that the terms of the 'capital gains' article in the agreement may prevent assessment of the gain order *s 13* on a UK resident participator — see Inland Revenue's Double Taxation Relief Manual paragraph 1506.

For chargeable gains accruing after 6 March 2001, where a tax charge arises under *TCGA 1992, s 13* and an amount in respect of the chargeable gain is distributed (either by way of dividend or distribution of capital or on the dissolution of the foreign company) the amount of tax on the earlier gain can be applied for reducing or extinguishing any tax liability arising in respect of the distribution. [*TCGA 1992, s 13(5A)–(5B)*]. For this relief to apply, the distribution must take place within three years of the end of the period for which the company makes up its accounts in which the chargeable gain arose or four years from when the gain arose, if earlier (for chargeable gains accruing before 7 March 2001, the distribution had to take place within two years of the chargeable gain accruing for this relief to be available). Relief under *section 13(5A)–(5B)* does not apply if the CGT has been reimbursed by the non-resident company or allowed as a deduction in computing the gain on a disposal of an interest in the non-resident company.

Transfer of a non-UK trade

3.60   The EC Mergers Directive (90/434/EEC), which took effect from 1 January 1992, applies to the transfer of assets of a permanent establishment (PE) which a UK company has in another member state to a company resident in another member state in exchange for shares in that company. Where the Directive applies, the country in which the PE is situated is not permitted to tax any capital gain arising on the transfer. However, where the state of the transferring company applies a worldwide system of taxation (as the UK does) article 10(2) of the Directive allows that state to tax any profits or capital gains of the PE resulting from a merger, division or transfer of assets (as defined in the Directive). This is conditional on the state of the transferring company giving relief for the tax which would, but for the provisions of the Directive, have been charged on those profits or capital gains ('notional tax') in the member state in which the PE is situated ('the relevant member state') as if that tax had actually been charged and paid.

This relief was introduced in the UK in *FA 1992* and is now contained in *TCGA 1992, s 140C* and *TA 1988, s 815A*. Where the conditions laid down in *section 140C* are satisfied, a credit against UK corporation tax is given for notional tax in the relevant member state. In respect of accounting periods ending on or after 1 July 1999 the UK company is responsible for calculating the notional tax for which relief is given and to claim relief in its return under self-assessment. For prior accounting periods the UK company is required to produce to the inspector an 'appropriate certificate' from the tax authorities of that state. Where the company has been unable to obtain an appropriate certificate it makes a claim to the Board and provides it with such information as is required. The Board then determines the amount which in its opinion would have been payable under the law of the relevant member state in respect of the gains and gives credit for it as if it were tax payable under the laws of that state.

In many circumstances a transfer of the assets of a PE in another EC member state qualifies for relief under both *TCGA 1992, s 140* (postponement of charge on transfer of assets to a non-resident company) and *s 140C*. However, claims cannot be made under both *sections 140* and *140C* in respect of the same transfer of assets.

Controlled foreign companies

3.61   When an apportionment of a controlled foreign company's (CFC's) chargeable profits is made, an apportionment of any creditable tax attributable for that period is also made under *TA 1988, s 747(3)* and this is taken as a credit against the tax payable under the CFC legislation.

'Creditable tax' (as defined by *section 751(6)*) is the total of:

(*a*)   the amount of relief from corporation tax (including underlying tax relief) in respect of the CFC's income which would be given to the company under the double taxation relief provisions [*TA 1988, Part XVIII*] for foreign tax attributable to any income brought into account in determining its chargeable profits under the CFC legislation;

(*b*)   any UK income tax deducted at source which could be offset against the CFC's corporation tax liability under *TA 1988, s 7(2)*; and

(*c*)   the amount of UK income and corporation tax actually charged (and not repaid or repayable) in respect of the CFC's chargeable profits for that accounting period.

In determining the amount of relief available under (*a*) and (*b*), assumptions are made as set out in *TA 1988, Sch 24*. The principal assumption is that the CFC became resident in the UK at the beginning of the first accounting period in respect of which a direction is given (or which, from 28 November 1995 is an 'ADP [acceptable distribution policy] exempt period') and continued to be UK resident until it ceased to be controlled by persons resident in the UK.

The Inland Revenue stated in its explanatory notes to the CFC legislation that, where the CFC has benefited from tax sparing provisions and the UK's agreement with the country in question allows tax sparing relief, the computation of creditable taxes takes into account a credit for the foreign taxes spared. Double tax credit relief is available under the terms of the relevant agreement against corporation tax on income as if the CFC were resident in the UK.

For an analysis of the underlying tax position where a CFC pays an acceptable distribution policy to the UK, please refer to 4.66.

3.62   In *Bricom Holdings Ltd v IRC [1997] STC 1179* the Court of Appeal considered the interaction between the CFC legislation and double taxation agreements. Bricom Holdings Limited (Bricom) was a UK resident company which held 100% of the shares in Spinneys International BV (Spinneys), a company resident in the Netherlands. Spinneys received interest from a UK resident company which was exempt from UK tax under the 'interest' article of the agreement with the Netherlands. However, the Inland Revenue applied the CFC legislation and issued assessments on Bricom for a sum equal to corporation tax on Spinneys' chargeable profits.

The Court of Appeal held that the agreement with the Netherlands did not prevent a CFC charge arising on the shareholders of Spinneys. The interest received by Spinneys merely provided a measure by which a notional sum was calculated which could be apportioned to its UK corporate shareholders. Accordingly, Spinneys' chargeable profits were ascertained on the basis that it was resident in the United Kingdom without reference to the double taxation agreement and the notional sum was apportioned to Bricom under the CFC legislation.

Income tax — special rules for years of commencement and cessation

3.63   In *Imperial Chemical Industries Ltd v Caro (1960) 39 TC 374* the Court of Appeal held that once a foreign tax credit had been used in respect of a particular year no further tax credit was available, even though in the opening years of a business the same income could be used as the basis of assessment for more than one tax year. As a result, what is now *TA 1988, s 804* was enacted, the purpose of which was to allow additional tax credit in the opening years of a source of income, but to ensure that this additional relief could be clawed back in the closing years, if necessary, when income fell out of the charge to UK tax. *Section 804* has been amended with respect to sources of income commencing after 5 April 1994 to reflect the changes in the basis of assessment for such new sources. However, it also continues to apply the closing year rules, with transitional provisions contained in *FA 1994, Sch 20*, with respect to sources of income which commenced before that date.

The current year basis applies immediately to trades, professions and foreign sources of income assessable under Schedule D Case IV or V which commence on or after 6 April 1994. However, unless the taxpayer's accounting year coincides with the tax year, basis periods for trades and professions overlap in the opening years, with the result that some income (the 'overlap profit') is included in the basis of computation in two successive years of assessment. *Section 804(1)* allows additional double tax credit relief to be obtained when the same income is being charged to UK tax for more than one year of assessment.

3.64   *Section 804* provides that credit for overseas tax paid in respect of any income which is an overlap profit is to be allowed against UK income tax chargeable for any year of assessment in respect of that income where it would have been allowed except that it has already been allowed against UK income tax chargeable on that income for an earlier year of assessment. In effect, the double taxation relief is increased proportionately to take account of the use of the income as the basis of assessment for UK purposes more than once. The credit to be allowed [*s 804(2)*] in any one year is not to exceed the difference between:

(*a*)   the total credit in respect of that income (including under *section 804*) for all years of assessment for which credit is allowable; and

(*b*)   the credit which has been allowed in respect of that income for any earlier year of assessment.

Credit is given for the overseas tax charged on that income, adjusted where the number of UK assessment periods exceeds the number of foreign assessment periods in the proportion that the UK assessment period bears to the overseas assessment period. Periods for which only part of the income is chargeable to tax are treated for this purpose as fractions of a period. [*s 804(3)*]. Where the income charged to UK tax has been charged to different foreign taxes for different foreign assessment periods the calculations for arriving at the total credit allowable under these provisions are to be made separately for each overseas tax. [*s 804(4)*].

Example 20

Gloria commences a trade on 1 July 1994 and carries it on partly through a branch in Australia which is liable to Australian income tax, making up accounts to 30 June annually. Her Australian profits for the year to 30 June 1995 are £40,000 on which Australian tax of £12,000 is payable and she is liable to UK income tax at the higher rate of 40% on this income.

The basis of assessment under Schedule D Case I for 1994/95 is the profits for the period 1 July 1994 to 5 April 1995 (£30,000) and for 1995/96 is the year ended 30 June 1995 (£40,000).

Accordingly, the profits for the period 1 July 1994 to 5 April 1995 are overlap profits, being assessed in the UK in both years.

In accordance with *section 804(3)*, the amount of credit for Australian tax is increased by three quarters to £21,000. Relief up to the maximum due in accordance with the normal rules (i.e. £9,000) is available in 1994/95 and the balance (£12,000) is given in 1995/96.

3.65   In a subsequent year the overlap profit (or part of it) may be deducted from profits chargeable to UK income tax because either the business ceases or the accounting date is changed to a date later in the tax year. Where such overlap relief occurs *section 804(5)* to *(5B)* provides that the additional double taxation relief originally given on the overlap profits is recovered either by restricting the tax credit relief in the year in which the overlap relief is given, or, if this is insufficient, by charging an amount under Schedule D Case VI at the basic rate so that the over-deduction of double tax credit is recovered.

Example 21

The facts are the same as in Example 20 above. Gloria ceases to trade on 30 June 2007 and the Australian income assessable in the year of cessation (2007/08) is £12,000 on which Australian tax payable is £2,000. This is compared with the £9,000 additional tax credit relief allowed in respect of the overlap profit in 1994/95 and 1995/96.

No tax credit relief is allowed for 2007/08, and Gloria is assessed to tax under Schedule D Case VI on an amount such that tax at the basic rate equals the balance of relief unrecovered (£7,000). Assuming a basic rate of income tax in 2007/08 of 20%, the assessment will be on £35,000 of notional income. This will not form part of Gloria's income for any other purpose.

3.66   Similar rules apply in relation to years of commencement of a trade, profession or source of foreign income which was in existence at 6 April 1994. Where in the commencement years certain profits have been used as the basis of assessment for UK purposes in more than one year of assessment the foreign tax credit relief is increased by applying the formula:

$$\frac{\text{Number of UK years of assessment}}{\text{Number of foreign years of assessment}}$$

Where only part of the income has been assessed in either a foreign or UK year of assessment, only the relevant proportion of that year is counted in the formula.

Where a trade or other profession or other source of foreign income commenced before 6 April 1994 and ceases before 6 April 1998 (or, in the case of trades and professions, 6 April 1999), some income will (or may) fall out of the charge to UK tax under the old cessation rules or the transitional provisions. In these circumstances, if foreign tax has been paid on this income, no credit is allowed in the UK where the income is assessable on the 'root income' principle because the income has not been charged to UK tax.

Section 804(5) as it applies to trades in existence at 5 April 1994 ensures that excessive credit is not given in years of cessation where income falls out of assessment to UK income tax. It provides that, in cases where additional credit has been given in years of commencement under *section 804(1)* and subsequently, as a result of the rules for the cessation of a business, income arising from the same source as the original income is not assessed to UK income tax, the total credit which has been allowed in the years of commencement on the original income is not to exceed the aggregate of the following amounts:

(a)   the amount of the credit against income tax which would have been allowed in the years of commencement on the original income without the enhancement in *section 804(1)*; and

(b)   the amount of overseas tax for which credit would have been allowed against income tax in respect of income which arises in a 'non-basis period' (i.e. a period which falls outside a basis period of assessment on cessation).

Where additional tax credit relief has been obtained under this section in the commencement years of a business and the amount of the additional relief exceeds the foreign tax paid in respect of a non-basis period under the cessation rules, an assessment under Schedule D Case VI is raised at the basic rate of income tax in order to recover the benefit of this extra relief. However, the taxpayer does not obtain any further relief where the foreign tax paid in respect of the non-basis period exceeds the additional relief given in the commencement years.

Example 22

Frederick opened a foreign bank account in 1989/90 and received interest on which a 10% withholding tax was deducted. The account was closed during 1995/96. The interest received and foreign tax deducted was as follows.

Year of assessment £	Interest received £	Foreign tax
1989/90	10,000	1,000
1990/91	25,000	2,500
1991/92	30,000	3,000
1992/93	28,000	2,800
1993/94	15,000	1,500
1994/95	12,000	1,200
1995/96	5,000	500

Under the commencement rules for sources of income which began prior to 6 April 1994, the income of 1990/91 has been used as the basis of assessment for 1990/91 (current year basis) and 1991/92 (prior year basis). In accordance with *section 804(1)*, the total tax credit allowed for the two years was £5,000 (i.e. 2 2 £2,500).

The interest received in 1994/95 does not form the basis of an assessment to income tax and is therefore income of a 'non-basis period'. In accordance with *section 804(5)* (as it applies to sources of income which commenced prior to 6 April 1994) the extra credit allowed in 1990/91 and 1991/92 is withdrawn as follows.

	£
Credit given in 1990/91 and 1991/92	5,000
Less: foreign tax actually paid	(2,500)
	2,500
Less: foreign tax on income of non-basis period	(1,200)
Excess foreign tax credit given	£1,300

An assessment is raised under Schedule D Case VI on an amount such that income tax at the basic rate equals the excess foreign tax credit given.

3.67 Where a trade, profession or other source of income commences before 6 April 1994 and continues until after 5 April 1998 (or 6 April 1999 for a trade or profession), 1996/97 is the transitional year between the prior year and the current year basis. The assessment for the year is based on a twelve-month average (referred to in *FA 1994, Sch 20* as 'the appropriate percentage') of profits and foreign tax credit of a period longer than twelve months. Unless (in the case of a trade or profession) there has been a change of accounting date, the appropriate percentage is 50%. The tax credit which falls out of account in the transitional year is taken into account in computing any recovery of additional tax credit given under *section 804(1)* when the source eventually ceases. [*FA 1994, Sch 20, para 11*].

Example 23

Stephen and Matilda are UK residents who have been in partnership since 1984. The partnership has traded partly through a branch in the US, and has made up accounts to 31 December annually. It continues trading beyond 6 April 1999. Its US branch profits and US tax liabilities from 1994 to 1997 are as follows.

Year ended 31 December	US profits	US tax paid
£	£	
1994	40,000	12,000
1995	50,000	16,000
1996	70,000	25,000
1997	60,000	18,000

The basis periods, foreign profits and attributable foreign tax for 1995/96 to 1997/98 are as follows.

Year of assessment	Basis of assessment	Foreign profits	Attributable foreign tax
		£	£
1995/96			
Prior year basis	Year ended 31 December 1994	40,000	12,000
1996/97			
Transitional year	Year ended 31 December 1995	50,000	16,000
	Year ended 31 December 1996	70,000	25,000
		120,000	41,000
	Average	60,000	20,500
1997/98			
Current year basis	Year ended 31 December 1997	60,000	18,000

The balance of tax unrelieved (£20,500) from the two-year period ended 31 December 1996 cannot be relieved against UK tax in any other way, but it is taken into account in computing the amount of any recovery of additional tax credit relief previously allowed under *section 804(1)* when the source eventually ceases.

If a trade or profession which commenced before 6 April 1994 ceases before 5 April 1999 and the basis of assessment for 1996/97 is the actual profits for the year rather than the twelve-month average, credit relief is given for the foreign tax paid on the profits arising in the basis period and there is no averaging of the tax credit relief. [*FA 1994, Sch 20, para 12*].

3.68   Under *section 804(7)* as amended by *FA 1996, Sch 21, para 22*, from 1996/97 claims for relief under *section 804* must be made by the fifth anniversary of 31 January following the year of assessment for which relief is claimed or by the fifth anniversary of 31 January following the later year where there is more than one relevant year of assessment. For years of assessment prior to 1996/97, the limit is six years from the end of the year of assessment, or six years from the end of the later year where there is more than one relevant year of assessment.

Provisions concerning accrued interest

3.69   Double taxation relief in relation to the accrued income scheme is dealt with in *TA 1988, s 807*. With effect from the introduction of the loan relationships legislation contained in *FA 1996*, it applies for the purposes of income tax only. The section applies where:

- a person is treated as receiving annual profits or gains on the day an interest period ends; and

- assuming that, in the chargeable period in which the day falls, he were to become entitled to any interest on the securities concerned, he would be chargeable under Schedule D Case IV or V; and

- he is liable to foreign tax in respect of the interest (or would be liable to foreign tax if he were entitled to such interest).

In these circumstances credit of an amount equal to the relevant proportion of the profits or gains is allowed against any UK income tax (and, prior to 1 April 1996, corporation tax) computed by reference to the profits or gains. The 'relevant proportion' is the rate of foreign tax which would apply to the income and is treated for these purposes as if it were allowed under the unilateral relief provisions of *section 790(4)*.

When the interest payable on the overseas security is actually received the amount of double taxation relief is reduced on a pro-rata basis in accordance with the formula:

$$\frac{I - R}{I}$$

where: I = the amount of the interest, and
R = the amount by which it is treated as reduced for UK tax purposes.

Similar principles apply where relief is given by deduction rather than by credit under *section 807(4)*.

Example 24

Claire bought Australian corporate bonds in January 1996 which she sold in August 1998. Interest was received in January and July each year and was subject to a 10% withholding tax in Australia.

The amount of interest received in each tax year and the withholding tax deducted were as follows:

	Interest Received	Withholding Tax
	£	£
1996/97	Nil	Nil
1997/98	180,000	18,000
1998/99	90,000	9,000

However, the following amounts were chargeable to income tax under Schedule D Case V or VI:

	£
	£
1996/97	45,000
1997/98	180,000
1998/99	75,000

The double tax credit available in each year is 10% of the amount assessed to income tax, as follows:

	£
	£
1996/97	4,500
1997/98	18,000
1998/99	7,500

3.70   *FA 1996* inserted *TA 1988, s 807A* which applies to corporation tax under the loan relationships legislation and took effect from 1 April 1996. *Section 807A(1)* excludes from double taxation relief (whether by credit or by deduction) foreign tax attributable to interest accruing under a loan relationship and certain payments under financial instruments at a time when the company is not a party to the relationship or instrument. However, *section 807A(3)* gives unilateral tax credit relief in circumstances where:

(*a*)   any non-trading credit relating to interest under a loan relationship is brought into account for the purposes of the loan relationship legislation; and

(*b*)   the interest falls, as a result of any related transaction (other than the initial transfer under or in accordance with any 'repo' (sale and repurchase agreement) or stock lending arrangements), to be paid to a person other than the company; and

(*c*)   had the company been entitled, at the time of the transaction, to receive a payment of the interest, the company would have been liable to foreign tax in respect of the interest received.

Credit is allowed under the unilateral relief provisions as if that foreign tax were paid in respect of the interest.

The term 'related transaction' means any disposal or acquisition (in whole or in part) of rights or liabilities under that relationship.

Section 807A does not apply if,

- at the time the interest accrues the company has ceased to be a party to a loan relationship because it has made the initial transfer under or in accordance with any 'repo' (sale and repurchase agreement) or stock lending arrangements relating to that relationship; and

- those arrangements are in effect at that time. [*s 807A(2A)*]

Double taxation relief in respect of discretionary trusts

3.71   *TA 1988, s 687* applies where trustees of a discretionary trust make a payment in any year of assessment to any person as a result of exercising their discretionary powers and such payment is treated as income of the person to whom it is made. The payment is treated as a net sum after deduction of tax at the rate applicable to trusts (currently 34%) which applies for the year of payment. [*s 687(2)*]. If the payment to the UK beneficiary has included income which had suffered overseas tax, without some relieving provision, double taxation of the income will result.

If the beneficiary were to receive the income directly double taxation relief would be available. Accordingly, *TA 1988, s 809* provides that the person to whom the payment is made may claim that, up to the amount certified by the trustees, the payment is to be treated as income received by him directly from the overseas source in the year of payment. For this purpose, the trustees must certify that:

(*a*)   the income out of which the payment was made was (or included an amount of) taxed overseas income as specified in the certificate, and

(*b*)   that amount arose to the trust not earlier than six years before the end of the year of assessment in which the payment was made.

3.72   In addition ESC B18 allows a 'look through' approach when a non-UK resident beneficiary receives income from a UK discretionary trust. It applies to a beneficiary of a UK resident discretionary trust where a payment is made out of income of the trustees in respect of which, had he received it directly, the beneficiary:

- would have been entitled to relief under *TA 1988, ss 47, 48* or *123* (exemption from UK tax on certain UK government securities held by persons not ordinarily resident in the UK and on overseas securities held by persons not resident in the UK); or

- would have been entitled to relief under the terms of a double taxation agreement; or

- would not have been chargeable to UK tax.

The beneficiary may claim those reliefs or, where he would not have been chargeable, repayment of the tax treated as deducted from the payment (or a proportion of it). Relief is granted to the extent that payment is out of income which arose to the trustees not more than six years before the end of the year of assessment in which the payment was made, provided that the trustees have made trust returns for each year which are supported by the relevant income tax certificates giving details of all sources of trust income and payments to the beneficiaries. A similar concession applies where a beneficiary receives a payment from a non-resident discretionary trust which has suffered UK income tax.

3.73   Statement of Practice SP 3/86 explains how relief from UK tax under double taxation agreements is given to non-residents in respect of payments out of a UK discretionary trust or a UK estate. Where the beneficiary of a UK resident discretionary trust is resident in a country with which the UK has a double taxation agreement relief may be given on the 'look through' principle. For example, where the withholding tax rate on interest is 15% under the agreement and interest liable to UK tax formed part of the trust income which had suffered tax at 34% (i.e. the rate applicable to trusts), the beneficiary is repaid the difference of 19%. The same principles apply to payments to non-UK resident residuary beneficiaries out of UK estates during the administration period.

Where the relevant agreement contains an 'other income' article which gives sole taxing rights in respect of the beneficiary's income arising from the trust to the beneficiary's country of residence, it used to be the practice of the Inland Revenue to apply the 'look through' basis as above and to refuse claims to full repayment of tax under the 'other income' article. However, following a review of its practice, the Inland Revenue no longer consider that the 'look through' principle is appropriate in these cases. Accordingly, tax paid by the trustees in respect of the discretionary payment is now repaid to the beneficiary provided that any conditions set out in the 'other income' article are met.

Chapter 4

Dividends and Relief for Underlying Tax

Introduction

4.1   The *Finance Act 2000* introduced a number of significant changes to the UK's existing double tax relief rules. The key changes were the introduction of the so-called mixer cap, which, broadly, restricts the underlying tax rate to 30% on any dividend paid through a chain of foreign companies to the UK, and the onshore pooling provisions which relax the source-by-source principle and allow excess foreign tax to be offset against the UK tax on certain low tax dividends, as if they were a single pool of income. The mixer cap will have a fundamental effect on the existing tax planning carried out by many major UK multinational groups going forward, since it is likely to render largely ineffective the use of offshore holding companies to mix high and low tax dividend income.

While the onshore pooling rules will allow foreign taxes in excess of 30% to be offset to a certain degree against the residual UK tax liability on dividend income with an underlying tax rate of less than 30%, it may be necessary for many groups to restructure to take full advantage of these rules. As well as looking at the basic underlying tax provisions, this chapter considers the Finance Act 2000 changes in detail and their impact on the original underlying tax relief rules.

Basic requirements for underlying tax relief

4.2   In nearly all jurisdictions, dividends paid by a company represent the distribution of its post-tax profits. Where the company paying the dividends is resident outside the UK and has paid foreign tax on its profits, the taxation of the dividends in the hands of the UK shareholder results in double taxation of those profits. Accordingly, as detailed below, credit is allowed against UK tax not only for foreign tax paid directly on a dividend (i.e. dividend withholding tax), but also for taxes paid on the profits out of which the dividend is paid (underlying tax). With certain exceptions noted below, relief for underlying tax is available only to 'direct investors' (i.e. companies owning at least 10% of the voting power in the foreign company paying the dividend). Other investors ('portfolio investors') do not normally qualify for underlying tax relief.

Chapter 3 set out the general rules for computing double tax credit relief (see 3.31 ff). In the case of dividend income, credit relief may be available for the income or corporation taxes suffered by the company paying the dividend. The basic legislation covering unilateral relief for underlying tax is contained in *TA 1988, s 790(6)–(10C)* while *sections 799–801C* define and extend the relief which is available under agreements. *Sections 799–801C* also apply to unilateral relief by virtue of the general extension contained in *section 790(3)*. The new onshore pooling rules introduced by *Finance Act 2000* are found in *sections 806A–806M*.

4.3   The 'elimination of double taxation' article in most of the UK's agreements provides that where a dividend is paid by a company resident in the other country to a UK resident company which controls directly or indirectly at least 10% of the voting power in the company paying the dividend, credit is to take into account the tax of that country payable by the company in respect of the profits out of which the dividend is paid. However, some old agreements gave underlying tax relief to all UK resident shareholders of the foreign resident company, including individuals and companies owning less than 10% of the voting power. Only two such agreements remain in force, namely those with Myanmar (formerly Burma) and St Christopher (St Kitts) and Nevis.

4.4   Where relief under an agreement is not available, the circumstances in which credit is to be allowed unilaterally for underlying tax on a dividend paid by an overseas company are set out in *TA 1988, s 790(6)*. The most common case is where the dividend is paid by an overseas resident company to a UK resident company which is 'related' to it.

A company is 'related' to another company if that other company:

(*a*)   controls directly or indirectly; or

(*b*)   is a subsidiary of a company which controls directly or indirectly, not less than 10% of the voting power in the first-mentioned company.

Although, strictly the term 'related' as defined in *section 801(5)* applies only for the purposes of that section, the same concept appears elsewhere in the underlying tax legislation, including *sections 790, 800* and *806C*. A company is a 'subsidiary' of another if the other company controls, directly or indirectly, not less than 50% of its voting power. [*TA 1988, s 792(2)*].

4.5   There are limited circumstances in which a company which controls less than 10% of the voting power in the company paying the dividend may claim unilateral relief for underlying tax. These are where the voting power in the company paying the dividend:

(*a*)   has been reduced below 10% on or after 1 April 1972; or

(*b*)   the shareholding has been acquired on or after 1 April 1972 in exchange for voting power in another company in respect of which underlying tax relief was due prior to the exchange.

However, further conditions have to be satisfied, as set out in *section 790(7)*:

(i)   the reduction below the 10% limit (and any further reduction) or the exchange (and any reduction thereafter) could not have been prevented by any reasonable endeavours on the part of the company receiving the dividend; and

(ii)   it was due to a cause (or causes) not reasonably foreseeable by it when control of the relevant voting power was acquired; and

(iii)   no reasonable endeavours on the part of that company could have restored or increased the voting power to at least 10%.

4.6   *Section 790(8)* provides that these conditions need to be satisfied not only by the company receiving the dividend, but also by any company of which that company is a subsidiary; and where, prior to the reduction or exchange, control of 10% of the voting power by that company was indirect, each other company relevant for determining whether the necessary 10% of the voting power was controlled as required by *section 790(6)*.

Example 25

For many years Mining Investments Plc owned directly a 15% interest in Nullarbor Minerals Pty Ltd, a mining company resident in Freedonia. In 1990 Nullarbor Minerals Pty Ltd made a one-for-one rights issue in order to develop a newly discovered source of mineral deposits. Owing to laws in Freedonia requiring local participation in new mineral projects, Mining Investments Plc was unable to take up any of its shares in the rights issue and, in consequence, its shareholding in Nullarbor Minerals Pty Ltd fell to 7.5%.

Mining Investments Plc may continue to claim underlying tax relief unilaterally on dividends paid by Nullarbor Minerals Pty Ltd provided that it can show that it met (and, where appropriate, continues to meet) all the conditions contained in *section 790(7)* as set out in 4.5 above.

Where unilateral relief for underlying taxes is available to a company which controls less than 10% of the voting power by virtue of *section 790*, relief is available for any tax which would be available for relief under *section 801* if the company paying the dividend and the company receiving it were related to each other. [*s 790(10)*].

Extension of underlying tax relief

4.7   Underlying tax credit relief provided by agreements is quite limited since it applies only to tax paid in the territory which is the other party to the agreement. It does not include taxes paid in third territories or underlying tax paid by companies which have themselves paid dividends to the first-tier foreign company. Accordingly, the basic relief provided under agreements is extended by statutory provisions.

TA 1988, s 801(1) extends the relief to tax paid both in the UK and in third countries (i.e. any territory other than the UK and the country of residence). It provides that, where an overseas company pays a dividend to a company resident in the UK and the overseas company is related to the UK company (see 4.3 above) then, for the purpose of allowing credit under an agreement against corporation tax in respect of the dividend, there is to be taken into account as if it were tax payable under the laws of the territory in which the overseas company is resident:

(*a*)   any UK income or corporation tax payable by the overseas company in respect of its profits; and

(*b*)   any tax which, under the laws of any other territory, is payable by the overseas company in respect of its profits.

4.8   *Dividends and Relief for Underlying Tax*

The following example illustrates the extension of underlying tax credit relief to UK and third country taxes under *TA 1988, s 801*.

Example 26

Etona Plc owns 75% of the voting shares of Etona SA, a Belgian company. For the year ended 31 December 1996 Etona SA paid Belgian tax of BF17,000,000 on its profits. It owned a property in the UK on which it received rental income and paid UK income tax of £35,000.

Etona SA also had a branch in Switzerland and paid Swiss federal and cantonal income taxes of SwFr80,000. Overall, the company's accounts showed a profit for the year of BF42,500,000 available for distribution to shareholders on which it had paid Belgian, UK and Swiss tax totalling the equivalent of BF20,100,000. During 2000 it paid a dividend of BF21,000,000 out of the profits for 1996. Under the EC Parent/Subsidiary Directive no dividend withholding tax was payable. The rate of underlying tax is as follows.

	BF'000
Creditable tax paid by the company for the period	20,100
Relevant profits	42,500

In accordance with the formula the rate of underlying tax on the profits is:

$$\frac{20,100}{62,600} = 32.11\%$$

UK corporation tax computation of Etona Plc	BF'000
Dividend received (BF21,000,000 × 0.75)	15,750
	£
Dividend converted to sterling: £1 = BF60	262,500
Grossed up for underlying tax (at 32.11%)	124,500
Schedule D Case V income	386,655
UK corporation tax at 30%	115,997
Less: double tax relief (limited to UK tax)	(115,997)
UK corporation tax payable	Nil

4.8   Where the foreign company paying the dividend has received a dividend from a third company to which it is related, a credit is available for underlying tax paid by that company. *Section 801(2)* provides that any underlying tax paid by the third company is to be treated as if it were paid by the foreign company to the extent that it would be taken into account if the dividend had been paid by a company resident outside the UK to a company resident in the UK. This extension of relief is subject to a number of restrictions. The key limitation is that, for dividends paid to the UK on or after 31 March 2001, the rate of underlying tax at each stage in the chain is in most circumstances limited to 30%. This point is dealt with in further detail at 4.36 below. In addition:

(a)   no tax is to be taken into account in respect of a dividend paid by a company resident in the UK except (subject to certain deeming provisions discussed at 4.70 below) UK corporation tax and any other tax for which that company would be entitled to credit relief under the double tax credit relief provisions; and

(b)   no tax is to be taken into account in respect of a dividend paid by a non-UK resident company to another non-UK resident company unless it could have been taken into account if the dividend had been paid to a UK company.

Relief for underlying tax extends as far down the corporate chain as is necessary, provided that each company in the chain is related to the one above it. [*s 801(3)*]. The definition of 'related' for this purpose is the same as that used for first-tier foreign companies.

Examples of the application of underlying tax relief

4.9   For the purpose of the following examples it is assumed that the shares mentioned are voting shares which entitle the holder to the relevant percentage of the voting power in the company.

Example 27

Shares held directly. A UK resident company, Albam Ltd, has a direct interest in the shares of a Netherlands company, Albam BV, as follows:

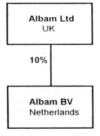

As Albam Ltd has direct control of 10% of the voting power of Albam BV it qualifies for underlying tax relief in respect of the dividends paid by that company.

Example 28

Shares held indirectly. The facts are the same as in Example 27 except that Albam BV has shareholdings in two other companies, Albam Inc (US resident) and Albam AB (Swedish resident) of 10% and 5% respectively.

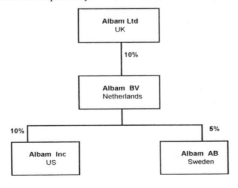

4.9 Dividends and Relief for Underlying Tax

Albam Ltd does not control directly or indirectly 10% of the voting power of either Albam Inc or Albam AB. However, Albam Inc (but not Albam AB) is related to Albam BV under *section 801(5)* and therefore in computing the underlying tax available to Albam Ltd on dividends paid by Albam BV, any underlying tax attributable to dividends paid by Albam Inc to Albam BV is taken into account. [*s 801(2)*].

Example 29

Exorna Ltd, a UK resident company, owns directly 6% of the shares of Exorna Gmbh and 40% of the shares of a French company, Exorna Sarl. Exorna Sarl itself owns 25% of the shares of Exorna Gmbh.

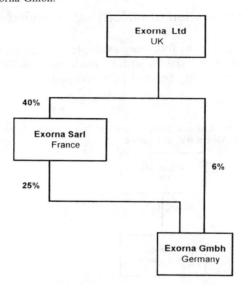

Since it does not have control of Exorna Sarl, the shareholding which that company has in Exorna Gmbh is not taken into account in determining whether Exorna Ltd controls directly or indirectly 10% of the voting power of Exorna Gmbh. Accordingly, no underlying tax relief is available on the 6% of Exorna Gmbh held directly by Exorna Ltd. However, as Exorna Sarl owns at least 10% of the voting power in Exorna Gmbh the companies are related under *section 801(2)* and Exorna Ltd may claim underlying tax relief on the dividends paid by Exorna Gmbh to Exorna Sarl when Exorna Sarl pays these by way of dividend to Exorna Ltd.

Example 30

The facts are the same as in Example 29 except that Exorna Ltd now owns 51% of the shares in Exorna Sarl.

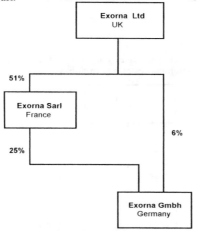

In this case Exorna Ltd controls indirectly the shares which Exorna Sarl holds in Exorna Gmbh. The shareholdings are aggregated, so that Exorna Ltd's control (direct and indirect) of Exorna Gmbh is 31%. Accordingly, Exorna Ltd may now also claim underlying tax relief on dividends it receives from Exorna Gmbh on its 6% direct shareholding.

4.10   In the following examples shares are held by a subsidiary.

Example 31

Soli Ltd is a UK resident company which has a 50% interest in another UK resident company, Soli Overseas Investments Ltd. Soli Ltd and Soli Overseas Investments Ltd have direct shareholdings in Soli SA, a Spanish company, of 15% and 5% respectively.

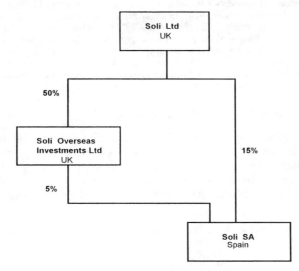

Soli Ltd can claim underlying relief on dividends it receives from Soli SA. Although Soli Overseas Investments Ltd does not itself control 10% of Soli SA, it is a subsidiary of Soli Ltd (which does) and therefore qualifies for underlying tax relief under *section 790(6)*. Accordingly, it may claim credit for underlying tax on dividends received in respect of its own 5% shareholding.

Example 32

The facts are the same as in Example 31, except that both Soli Ltd and Soli Overseas Investments Ltd have direct shareholdings of 5% in Soli SA.

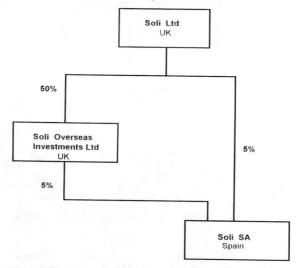

In this example underlying tax relief can be claimed only if Soli Ltd controls the shares which Soli Overseas Investments Ltd holds in Soli SA. Soli Overseas Investments Ltd is a 'subsidiary' of Soli Ltd as it controls not less than 50% of the voting power – see 4.3 above. Although the 50% shareholding does not necessarily give control within the *TA 1988, s 840* definition, the Inland Revenue accepts that the shareholdings of the subsidiary are aggregated with those of the parent in determining the percentage of voting power held in the foreign subsidiary. (see the Inland Revenue's *Double Taxation Relief* manual, para 1393). Accordingly, both Soli Ltd and Soli Overseas Investments Ltd would be granted underlying tax relief on dividends paid by Soli SA.

The identification of 'relevant profits'

4.11   *TA 1998, s 799(1)* provides that underlying tax is the amount of foreign tax borne on the 'relevant profits' of the company paying the dividend which is properly attributable to the proportion of the relevant profits represented by the dividend. In the case of dividends paid to the UK on or before 30 March 2001, *section 799(3)* defines 'relevant' profits as follows:

(*a*)   if the dividend is paid for a specific period, the profits of that period;

(*b*)   if the dividend is not paid for a specified period, but is paid out of specified profits, those profits;

(*c*) if the dividend is paid neither for a specified period nor out of specified profits, the profits of the last period for which accounts of the company were made up which ended before the dividend became payable.

The company paying the dividend may or may not have identified the profits out of which the dividend is paid. The identification may be simply that the profits distributed are the profits of a particular period, e.g. an interim or final dividend from the profits of the year ended 31 March 1999. This falls within *subsection 3(a)* and the relevant profits are the profits of that period.

Alternatively, the company paying the dividend may specify that it is paid out of particular (i.e. 'specified') profits, e.g. out of a dividend received from another company or out of trading profits of a particular period in *subsection 3(b)*. If no particular profits or period is specified, then the dividend will be taken to be paid out of the profits of the last accounting period to have ended before the dividend became payable.

4.12   In the case of dividends paid to the UK on or after 31 March 2001, *section 799(3)(b)* has been repealed so that it is no longer possible to specify the profits out of which a dividend is paid although it is still possible to specify the profits of a particular accounting period as the source of a dividend.

This new restriction is likely to make it more difficult to manage the underlying tax rate of foreign dividends. In particular, before *section 799(3)(b)* was repealed, it was common practice to specify dividends out of pools of profit that had suffered tax at an underlying rate sufficient to ensure that there would be little or no residual UK corporation tax liability.

4.13   *Section 799(4)* provides that if, under (*a*) or (*c*), the total dividend exceeds the profits available for distribution of the period, the 'relevant profits' are to be the profits of that period plus undistributed profits available from previous periods. For these purposes a 'last in, first out' rule is applied so that the profits of earlier accounting periods are then also treated as relevant profits, latest period first, until sufficient relevant profits have been identified. Profits treated as relevant profits in relation to an earlier dividend are excluded from consideration.

Normally, the profits out of which the dividend is being paid are specified by means of a dividend resolution of the company paying the dividend. As the form of the dividend resolution for this purpose will be prepared in order to secure the optimum UK tax position, it is important to obtain confirmation from local advisers that it is appropriate for the purposes of company and tax law in the country of residence of the foreign subsidiary.

Example 33

Newby Holdings BV is a wholly owned Dutch resident subsidiary of Newby Ltd, a UK resident company. It has accounting profits as follows:

Year ended 30 June 2000

	NLG	Tax NLG	Total after tax NLG
Trading profits (before tax)	100,000	35,000	65,000
Capital gains (before tax)	40,000	Nil	40,000
			105,000

Year ended 30 June 2001

	NLG	Tax NLG	Total after tax NLG
Trading profits (before tax)	140,000	49,000	91,000

Newby Holdings BV wishes to pay a dividend of NLG 49,000 to its UK parent on 1 July 2001 with an underlying tax rate equal to 30%. Under the old rules contained in *s 799(3)(b)* it could have achieved this result by specifying the profits of the dividend as follows:

	NLG	Tax NLG
Year ended 30 June 2000 trading profit	39,000	21,000
Year ended 30 June 2000 capital gains	10,000	Nil
	49,000	21,000

Underlying tax rate on dividend: 30%

However, now that *s 799(3)(b)* has been repealed, it is only possible to pay a dividend out of the total relevant profits of a company for a given accounting period. The underlying tax rate on the relevant profits for Newby Holdings BV's year ended 30 June 2000 is 25%. Therefore, if a dividend of NLG49,000 is paid out of that year's relevant profits, there would be a residual UK corporation tax liability. The new onshore pooling rules which are discussed in further detail at 4.43–4.65 allow this liability to be sheltered if two separate dividends totalling NLG49,000 are paid by Newby Holdings BV out of its profits for the years ended 30 June 2000 and 2001 (see below).

Dividend 1 (specified out of year ended 30 June 2000)

	NLG
Dividend	26,250
Add: underlying tax	8,750
Schedule D Case V	35,000
UK corporation tax @ 30%	10,500
Less: double tax relief	(8,750)
	1,750
Less: eligible unrelieved foreign tax (dividend 2)	(1,750)
UK corporation tax payable	Nil

Dividend 2 (specified out of the year ended 30 June 2001)

	NLG
Dividend	22,750
Add: underlying tax	12,250
Schedule D Case V	35,000
UK corporation tax @ 30%	10,500
Less: double tax relief	12,250
Eligible unrelieved foreign tax	1,750

4.14   In some countries, such as the United States, it is not necessarily typical for dividend resolutions to specify the profits or the year out of which the dividends are paid. In these circumstances the Inland Revenue has indicated that it treats quarterly or interim dividends as paid out of the profits for the year in which the dividends are declared. Otherwise, where the profits used for the dividend have not been specified, dividends are treated as being paid out of the profits of the last period for which the company's accounts were made up which ended prior to the payment of the dividend. [*s 799(3)(c)*]. However, dependent on the facts, it may be preferable to arrange for an appropriate dividend resolution to be passed which both meets local company law requirements and specifies profits out of a particular accounting period in accordance with *section 799(3)(a)*.

Example 34

Overmoon Ltd, a UK resident company has a US resident subsidiary, Underweather Inc. Underweather Inc's historical relevant profits are as follows. It wishes to pay a dividend of US$500,000 to its UK parent on 30 June 2001.

Year ended 30 June	Relevant profit	Tax	Underlying tax rate
	US$	US$	
2001	750,000	250,000	25%
2000	600,000	400,000	40%
1999	550,000	450,000	45%
1998	700,000	300,000	30%

If Underweather Inc specifies the dividend as sourced from the relevant profit of its year ended 30 June 1998 this should ensure no residual UK tax liability will arise and that no foreign tax credits would potentially be wasted.

The *Bowater* case and its application

4.15   Although the term 'relevant profits' is originally described in *section 799*, it was not clear from the original legislation whether the word 'profits' meant 'accounting profits' of the company concerned or 'profits as adjusted for the purposes of the foreign tax computation'. The issue was considered by the House of Lords in the case of *Bowater Paper Corporation v Murgatroyd (1969) 46 TC 52*. It should be noted that *FA 2000* has now introduced a statutory definition of relevant profits which can be found in *section 799(5)–(7)* and is discussed at 4.18 below.

The *Bowater* case involved a UK resident company, which received dividends from a Canadian subsidiary which, in turn, received dividends from Canadian and US sub-subsidiaries. The point in dispute was whether the 'relevant profits' were the profits as computed for the purposes of foreign taxes (the company's contention) or whether they were the 'gross divisible profits' shown in the accounts after various deductions which did not rank as appropriations of profit (the Inland Revenue's contention). The House of Lords agreed with the Inland Revenue and held that the term 'relevant profits' meant the distributable profits as shown by the accounts of each company and not the profits assessed to foreign tax.

4.16   The formula for calculating the underlying tax rate on profits was therefore established as:

$$\frac{A}{A+B}$$

where: A = creditable taxes paid by the company on its profits for the period; and

B = the company's relevant profits for the period.

In establishing the relevant profits for a period, transfers of profits to legal reserves (i.e. non-distributable reserves required to be maintained under the company law of the relevant foreign jurisdiction) are not included, i.e. such transfers are deductible in arriving at the relevant profits but only up to the minimum statutory requirements under the relevant foreign company law.

ICAEW Technical Release 362, October 1979, discussed the treatment of gains on exchange differences (both realised and unrealised) on the calculation of the underlying tax rate. Unrealised gains were provisionally treated as not available for distribution for the purposes of *section 799* unless in fact used for a dividend or put to a reserve of a general nature which is considered distributable or left in the retained earnings account. Realised gains are regarded as available for distribution.

TR 362 also discussed the position of realised capital profits credited directly to capital reserves. The Inland Revenue's view was that it is of no significance whether a capital profit is taken in the accounts directly to capital reserves or is first credited to the profit and loss account. The question is whether such a profit is available for distribution to shareholders. If it is, it formed part of the relevant profits under the principles in the *Bowater* case.

4.17   In some countries, such as Saudi Arabia, local nationals are not subject to tax. Moreover, where a national of the country is a shareholder in a company which is partly owned by foreigners, tax is levied only on the proportion of the profits which relates to the foreign shareholding. Where a UK company is a shareholder in such a company and qualifies for underlying tax relief under the normal rules, for the purpose of determining 'relevant profits' in accordance with the *Bowater* principle, only that proportion of the profits which is liable to tax is taken into account.

Finance Act 2000 definition of relevant profits

4.18   In *FA 2000*, the definition of 'relevant profits' was put onto a statutory basis. According to *section 799(5)–(7)*, the relevant profits for a dividend paid after 20 March 2000 by a company resident outside the UK to a company resident in the UK are the profits of any period shown as available for distribution in the accounts of the company which pays the dividend. Those accounts must be drawn up in accordance with the law of the company's home state and making no provision for reserves, bad debts or contingencies other than such as is required to be made under that law. It is understood that this new statutory definition of relevant profits should not generally affect most of the practices set out in the Inland Revenue's leaflets referred to at 4.35 below.

While the legislation defines 'home state' as the country or territory under the law of which the company is incorporated or formed, it does not define what it means by the law of a company's home state. It is assumed that this must refer to the company law of the relevant territory but it could also be interpreted as referring to accounting law. Such accounting law may contain a prudence concept which requires certain provisions to be made. In the author's view, such provisions should be allowed in arriving at the relevant profits of a company. However, it is not clear how, in practice, the Inland Revenue would deal with the situation where the relevant foreign accounting law would permit more than one method of arriving at the distributable profits and where this would produce a different result in each case.

4.19   The method of calculating relevant profits of a company may depend on its country of residence. For example, in some territories, companies are required under local law to make a transfer out of their annual profits to a legal reserve up to a certain proportion of their share capital, e.g. 10%. The Inland Revenue regards this as being deductible in arriving at the relevant profits of the company. However, transfers in excess of the minimum requirements under the relevant local law would not be deductible. The specific practices which the Inland Revenue applies in relation to individual countries are set out in a series of leaflets published by the Inland Revenue underlying tax group, Nottingham (again, see 4.35 below).

4.20   In addition to provisions for reserves and contingencies, etc. other movements to reserves can give rise to difficulties in practice in establishing the relevant profits of a company. The Inland Revenue provides some guidance on this area in its leaflet FD (Rates) 1 (page 4) which is reproduced below. The Underlying Tax leaflet is reproduced in full at Appendix 5).

'Profit appropriation and prior year adjustments.

● **General**

S 799(4) ICTA 1988 provides for dividend deficiencies to be taken from earlier years' profits on a LIFO basis. The legislation is silent on the treatment of other items of appropriation and amounts deductible in arriving at relevant profits, although there is a presumption that the allocation should also be on a LIFO basis.

Bowater v Murgatroyd (46 TC 37) decided that relevant profits meant profits available for distribution as shown in the accounts. The accounting treatment of any item is therefore of paramount importance. If the accounts show it to have been deducted from a particular part of the profits, that treatment must be followed. Where the accounting treatment is ambiguous, then any reasonable allocation LIFO or FIFO, is acceptable.

● **Capitalisation of profits**

The source of profits capitalised (e.g. bonus issues) is determined as above. Since the capitalisation is an appropriation of profits, not a diminution, it has no effect on the underlying tax rate computation.

● **Prior year adjustments/changes of accounting policy**.

a)   Increases are regarded as relevant profit for the year in which the adjustment is made. The accounts for the period show an amount of distributable profit and it follows from *Bowater* that that amount is relevant profit for the period.

b)   Decreases, such as losses, are deductible in arriving at relevant profit. The allocation of the decrease is determined as above. In particular, if the accounts show a loss deducted from prior years' profits in the reserves, rather than from the current year profit and loss account profits, that treatment must be followed. Prior year adjustments, which are deductible, may increase the underlying tax rates for earlier years but only in respect of dividends declared payable after the date of the accounting adjustments.'

4.21   An illustration of how this guidance might be applied in practice is set out below.

Example 35

Kelly BV's accounting profits and losses after tax, tax paid and dividend payments to its UK parent are as follows:

Year ended 30 June	2001 NLG	2002 NLG	2003 NLG	2004 NLG
Accounting profit/(loss) after tax	100,000	100,000	(100,000)	300,000
Less: dividend	(100,000)	(100,000)	(100,000)	(100,000)
Profit (loss) after tax/dividend	Nil	Nil	(200,000)	200,000
Retained reserves b/f	Nil	Nil	Nil	(200,000)
Retained reserves c/f	Nil	Nil	(200,000)	Nil
Foreign tax paid	50,000	50,000	Nil	150,000

In the above example, the relevant profits for the dividend of NLG100,000 paid in year 3 would be the profits of year 4, since there are no other profits out of which this dividend can be sourced. This is supported by the accounting treatment, i.e. the dividend payment is reflected in the negative reserves brought forward at the start of year 4 which the accounts show as set off against year 4's profits. The relevant profits for this dividend would therefore be computed as follows:

	NLG
Accounting profits for the year after tax	300,000
Less: retained loss b/f	(100,000)
Relevant profits	200,000

The underlying tax attributable to the above relevant profits is NLG150,000. Therefore the dividend of NLG100,000 paid in year 3 would carry underlying tax of NLG75,000, i.e. the effect of deducting the loss brought forward from year 4's profits is to increase the underlying tax rate on those profits

Example 36

Lilac BV's accounting profits and losses, tax paid and dividend payments to the UK parent are as follows:

Year ended 30 June	2001	2002	2003
	NLG	NLG	NLG
Accounting profit/(loss) after tax	300,000	300,000	(100,000)
Less: dividend	(100,000)	(100,000)	(100,000)
Profit/(loss) after tax/dividend	200,000	200,000	(200,000)
Retained reserves b/f	Nil	200,000	400,000
Retained reserves c/f	200,000	400,000	200,000
Foreign tax paid	150,000	150,000	Nil

In the above example, the accounting loss in year 3 could reduce the relevant profits of the prior years, either on a first in, first out or on a last in, first out basis because, again, this is how the accounts of the foreign company deal with the loss, i.e. the accounts show the loss as deducted from profits brought forward generally at the start of year 3 so it is up to the taxpayer to decide whether to deduct the loss on a LIFO or a FIFO basis. Therefore, assuming a LIFO basis is applied, the relevant profits of year 2 would become NLG200,000.

However, the Inland Revenue takes the view that the loss at the end of year 3 cannot affect the relevant profit for the year 2 dividend, if the year 2 dividend was specified as sourced out of year 2 profits. In this situation, the relevant profits for the year 2 dividend would continue to be NLG300,000 and the underlying tax NLG50,000. As far as the year 3 dividend is concerned, this would also be treated as sourced out of year 2 unless otherwise specified. The relevant profits for the year 3 dividend would be NLG100,000 being the profit of year 2 of NLG300,000 less the year 2 dividend of NLG100,000 and the year 3 loss of NLG100,000. Those relevant profits of NLG100,000 for the year 2 dividend would carry underlying tax of NLG100,000 being the remaining underlying tax in respect of year 2.

4.22   Dividends and Relief for Underlying Tax

Example 37

Tulip BV's accounting profits and losses, tax paid and dividend payments to its UK parent are as follows:

Year ended 30 June	2001 NLG	2002 NLG	2003 NLG	2004 NLG
Accounting profit/(loss) after tax	100,000	100,000	(200,000)	200,000
Less: dividend	—	—	—	(200,000)
Profit/(loss) after tax/dividend	100,000	100,000	(200,000)	Nil
Retained reserves b/f	Nil	100,000	200,000	Nil
Retained reserves c/f	100,000	200,000	Nil	Nil
Foreign tax paid	50,000	50,000	Nil	Nil

In the above example, it is current Inland Revenue practice to treat the profits of year 1 and 2 as being extinguished by the losses in year 3 so that they could not be accessed for the purposes of dividends. The underlying tax attributable to these profits would therefore be lost and the dividend in year 4 would need to be treated as sourced from year 4's profits, which have not borne any underlying tax. If there were no profits in year 4 and a dividend of 200,000 were paid, it would be treated as sourced out of the next accounting period(s) in the future where relevant profits arise on a first in, first out basis.

4.22   The Inland Revenue accepts that this treatment can operate unfairly in the sense that genuine payments of foreign tax can become ineligible for underlying tax relief where losses arise. There are also concerns that underlying tax relief claims could be left open indefinitely until relevant profits arise in a future accounting period. As a result the Inland Revenue produced a draft statement of practice at the time of the 2000 Budget, which would allow relevant profits from earlier periods to be accessed, but only where a company has cumulative losses. The relevant extracts from the text of this are set out below. It is understood that this has not yet come into force as it is still to be finalised. It is therefore subject to change.

'B: Losses

Where the foreign company that pays a dividend has accumulated losses, the Inland Revenue's view is that the relevant profits are the undistributed profits of the most recent period available at the time that the dividend was paid.

Example

The accounts for a foreign company show the following results.

	Year 1	Year 2	Year 3
Profits/(losses)	1000	(3000)	1500
Accumulated profits/(losses)	1000	(2000)	(500)

At the end of Year 3 it pays a dividend of 2000.

The relevant profits are 1500, Year 3 and 500, Year 1.'

In the meantime, it is understood that the Inland Revenue will ignore cumulative losses where a dividend is paid out of current year profits before the end of the current year so that relief for the tax paid on the current year profits can be claimed.

The draft statement of practice also deals with the situation where a split rate tax system can apply in a particular jurisdiction (notable examples of this are Germany, prior to the recent introduction of a classical system of taxation, and South Africa). The current practice in the case of these two countries differs from that in the draft statement of practice. In the case of Germany, a tax rebate may arise on the distribution of taxed profits. There is currently no fixed method of dealing with this rebate and it can lead to anomalies in calculating the underlying tax rate on relevant profits. In the case of South Africa, the Inland Revenue currently treats the secondary tax on companies as attributable to the relevant profits of a period as a whole and not purely to the amount of those profits which is distributed. The relevant extracts from the draft statement of practice are set out below.

'Under some foreign tax systems the amount of tax charged on company profits depends on how much of the profits are distributed. The Inland Revenue's view is that in such circumstances the amount of tax to be taken into account in respect of a particular dividend is the actual tax charged on the proportion of the profits that the dividend represents. The amount of underlying tax taken into account will therefore reflect the rate charged on the distributed profits and not the average rate of tax paid at that point on all of the relevant profits.

A foreign company has profits of 1000. These profits are taxed at 20% unless they are distributed, in which case they are taxed at 30%. The company pays a dividend of 500 to a United Kingdom resident company.

Profits   1000
Foreign tax   250 (500 @ 20% + 500 @ 30%)
Relevant profits   750

The amount of underlying tax to be taken into account in respect of the dividend of 500 is 214 [(500 + 214) @ 30%].

A foreign company has profits of 1000. These profits are taxed at 40% unless they are distributed, in which case they are taxed at 25%. The company pays a dividend of 600 to a United Kingdom company.

Profits   1000
Foreign tax   310 (400 @ 40% + 600 @ 25%)
Relevant profits   690

The amount of underlying tax to be taken into account in respect of the dividend of 600 is 200 [(600 + 200) @ 25%].'

Effect of imputation tax credits under agreements

4.23   *TA 1988, s 799(2)* applies in circumstances where a corporate shareholder claiming underlying tax relief is entitled to an imputation tax credit under one of the UK's agreements. It provides that, where under a foreign tax law the dividend paid by a company is increased for tax purposes by a tax credit which may be offset against the shareholder's liability to foreign tax (or, if it exceeds his liability to foreign tax, paid to the shareholder), the amount of underlying tax relief is to be reduced by that amount.

A few of the UK's agreements, including those with Italy (1988) and Denmark (1980), have allowed imputation tax credits to UK corporate shareholders. In the case of Denmark, the tax credit was, until 31 December 1997, available to corporate shareholders owning less than 25% of the capital in the Danish company paying the dividends.

Example 38

Osiris Ltd, a UK resident company, owns 20%, of the share capital of a Danish company, Lindelse A/S. In 1996 it received a dividend of £100,000 paid out of the 1995 profits of Lindelse A/S on which the rate of underlying tax was 35%.

	£	£
Dividend received		100,000
Danish tax credit		25,000
		125,000
Underlying tax (100,000 × 35/(100−35))	53,846	
Less: Danish tax credit	(25,000)	
		28,846
Schedule D Case V income		153,846
UK corporation tax @ 33%		50,769
Double taxation relief:		
Withholding tax (125,000 × 15%)	18,750	
Underlying tax	28,846	
		(47,596)
UK corporation tax liability		3,173

4.24   Statement of Practice SP 12/93 applies to dividends received from a number of countries which apply a 'company tax deducted' system. When a dividend is paid, tax is accounted for at the standard rate of tax applicable to the company's profits. The tax represents a payment on account of the company's liability to corporation tax on its own profits and, if the tax deducted on the dividend exceeds the company's own liability, the balance of the tax may, in some cases, be repaid. Systems of this kind operate in Jersey, Guernsey, Belize, the Gambia, Malaysia, Malta and Singapore.

Prior to 27 July 1993 it was the practice of the Inland Revenue to allow credit at the rate of 'company tax deducted' or at the actual underlying rate of tax on the company's profits, whichever was the greater. Usually this would have been the amount shown as deducted on a dividend voucher received by the shareholder. However, following a review of this practice, it was decided that, from 27 July 1993, credit would be granted only for the actual underlying tax paid by the company on the profits out of which the dividend was paid. This is determined in the usual way by examination of the overseas company's accounts and tax assessments.

4.25   In accordance with Inland Revenue Interpretation No 98, issued in February 1995 (see 3.22) relief is allowed where California unitary tax is paid by a company resident outside the UK which pays a dividend to a UK company and the companies are related to each other under *TA 1988, s 801*. In these circumstances the Inland Revenue regards as eligible for inclusion in the calculation of underlying tax the lesser of:

(*a*)   the actual California tax paid by the overseas company; and

(*b*)   the California tax which it would have paid on the basis of its profits arising in the US and (where relevant) on the US profits of affiliated companies, to the extent that the profits of affiliated companies are brought into the calculation of the tax as members of the unitary group or following a 'water's edge' election (which limits the base of unitary tax to activities within the US).

Extra-statutory concession — portfolio shareholders

4.26   ESC C1(*a*) applies to those few cases where a double taxation agreement still grants underlying tax relief to portfolio shareholders. The agreements in force with Myanmar (formerly Burma) dating from 1950 and St Christopher (St Kitts) and Nevis (1947) are the only agreements still in force which allow such relief.

Where there is an agreement providing for underlying relief for portfolio shareholders and a UK resident receives a dividend from a company in the overseas country, the credit available against the UK tax chargeable on the dividend would, under the agreement, include only the underlying tax payable on the company's profits in the country which is party to the agreement. The concession extends this relief in the two remaining cases to:

(*a*)   any UK tax or foreign tax in a third country payable by the overseas company on its income; and,

(*b*)   where the overseas company's profits include dividends from a second company resident in that or another overseas country, to both the direct tax charged on the dividend and the underlying tax payable on the profits of the second company. Relief is also given for similar taxes relating to dividends and profits further down the chain of shareholdings.

Tax sparing relief

4.27   The general outline of tax sparing provisions (pioneer relief) in certain overseas countries and UK tax sparing relief is discussed at 3.54. The country granting pioneer relief may make it a condition of obtaining the relief that the investment is made through a locally incorporated subsidiary. In the case of a UK group of companies investing through such a vehicle, the profits will be subject to UK corporation tax either when dividends are paid to the UK or when the profits are taxed under the UK's controlled foreign company legislation. When the company paying the dividend has benefited from pioneer relief for which tax sparing relief is available under the relevant agreement with the UK, *section 788(5)* provides that the spared tax is to be treated as if it were tax payable. However, the dividend is not grossed up for UK corporation tax purposes by the amount of the spared tax. If only part of the underlying tax is spared tax, the dividend is grossed up by the underlying tax actually borne (as in a normal underlying tax relief calculation), but tax credit relief is available both for the tax paid and the tax spared.

Example 39

Caledonia Ltd is a UK resident company and has a wholly-owned subsidiary in Freedonia, Caledonia Pte Ltd, which carries out infrastructure development projects. The activity qualifies for a pioneer relief under which the standard rate of Freedonia tax is reduced by 60%. In 1997 Caledonia Pte Ltd made profits of £500,000 and the standard rate of corporation tax in Freedonia was 30%. There is an agreement in force between the UK and Freedonia under which the UK gives credit for tax spared under the Freedonia pioneer relief provisions.

In 2000 Caledonia Pte Ltd paid a dividend equal to 50% of its 1997 post-tax profits to Caledonia Ltd, the maximum allowed under the Freedonia pioneer relief provisions. The dividend resolution specified that the dividend was payable out of the profits for 1997. Freedonia does not levy a dividend withholding tax.

The Freedonia corporation tax computation is as follows:

	£	£
Profit liable to Freedonia corporation tax		500,000
Freedonia corporation tax at 30%	(150,000)	
Freedonia tax spared	90,000	
Freedonia corporation tax paid		(60,000)
Profit after Freedonia tax		440,000
Dividend paid to the UK (50%) — £220,000		
UK corporation tax computation:		
Dividend received from Caledonia Pte Ltd		220,000
Add: underlying tax (50% of Freedonia tax paid)		30,000
Profit assessable to UK corporation tax		250,000
UK corporation tax at 30%		75,000
Relief for underlying tax:		
Freedonia corporation tax paid (above)	30,000	
Freedonia corporation tax spared (50%)	45,000	
	75,000	
Limited to UK corporation tax		(75,000)
UK corporation tax payable		Nil

4.28   Tax sparing relief is not available under the UK's unilateral relief provisions. Accordingly, in order for the relief to be available there must be an agreement between the UK and the country giving the pioneer relief, and that agreement must specify that the relief claimed is available.

In the past, it has been maintained that, if there is an intermediate foreign holding company interposed between the country granting the relief and the UK, the benefit of the tax sparing relief provisions may still be retained under the extension provisions contained in *TA 1988, s 801*. The credit under *section 801(2)* for tax paid by a third company is limited under *section 801(4)(b)* to tax which could have been taken into account had the company receiving the dividend been resident in the UK. In applying this limitation it was argued that it was possible to take into account any tax sparing relief provisions in an agreement between the UK and the country giving pioneer relief.

In recent years, the Inland Revenue indicated that its practice of allowing tax sparing relief in those circumstances was under review. Subsequently, *section 790(10A)–(10C)* was introduced in respect of dividends paid after 20 March 2000 by a company resident outside the UK to a company resident in the UK. The effect of these new provisions is only to allow credit for tax spared in relation to the third company where the intermediate holding company between the third company and the UK is resident in the same territory as the third company. There is a further requirement that, were the intermediate company resident in the UK, it would be entitled under arrangements between the UK and its country of residence to relief for the tax spared under *section 788(5)*.

Dividend mixing companies

4.29   Prior to *FA 2000* each dividend paid to a company resident in the UK was treated as a separate source of income and the attributable underlying tax relief was calculated on that dividend. This caused a potential problem for UK groups of companies with subsidiaries in several countries, particularly if some profits arose in subsidiaries in countries where the combined rate of underlying and withholding taxes was lower than the UK rate of corporation tax while others arose in high-tax jurisdictions, as in Example 40(a) below.

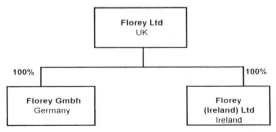

In the year ended 31 December 2000 Florey (Ireland) Ltd made profits after tax of Ir£500,000 after paying Irish corporation tax of Ir£50,000. In the same year Florey Gmbh made profits after tax of DM400,000 on which it had paid German corporation taxes of DM350,000. In January 2001 Florey (Ireland) Ltd and Florey Gmbh paid dividends of Ir£400,000 and DM300,000 respectively to their UK parent company, Florey Ltd. On the date of payment of the dividends, the exchange rates applicable were £1 = Ir£1.20 and £1 = DM3.

Example 40(a)

Rate of underlying tax on Irish dividend.

$$\frac{50,000}{50,000 + 500,000} = 9.09\%$$

Rate of underlying tax on German dividend:

$$\frac{350,000}{400,000 + 350,000} = 46.67\%$$

UK corporation tax computation of Florey Ltd for the year ended 31 December 2000:

	Dividend currency	Conversion rate	Dividend	Under- lying tax rate	Under- lying tax	Dividend and under- lying tax
			£		£	£
Irish dividend	400,000	1.20	333,333	9.09%	33,333	366,666
German dividend	300,000	3.00	100,000	46.67%	87,500	187,500
Total			433,333		120,833	554,166

Schedule D Case V income	554,166
UK corporation tax at 30%	166,250
Less: double taxation relief	
Ireland	33,333
Germany (limited to £187,500 × 30%)	56,250 (89,583)
UK corporation tax payable	76,667

Additional UK tax was therefore payable on the dividend from Ireland which carried a low rate of underlying tax and excess double taxation relief (which could not be utilised in any way) arose on the dividend from Germany which carried a high rate of underlying tax.

4.30   As relief is allowed by the extension provisions of *TA 1988, s 801(2)* for underlying tax on dividends received from related third companies, prior to *FA 2000* this position could usually be improved by interposing an appropriate foreign holding company. Most commonly a Netherlands holding company was used for this purpose, but sometimes a company incorporated and resident in, for example, Switzerland, France, Luxembourg, Singapore or a tax haven could be beneficial, depending upon the circumstances.

Example 40(b)

The facts are the same as for Example 40(a), except that Florey (Ireland) Ltd and Florey Gmbh are held by a Netherlands holding company, Florey BV.

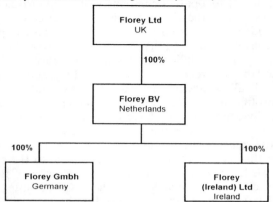

In 1998, Florey (Ireland) Ltd and Florey Gmbh paid dividends to Florey BV out of which it subsequently, in January 2001, paid a dividend of the same amount to Florey Ltd. The dividends are not taxable in The Netherlands as the Dutch 'participation exemption' applies. The rate of underlying tax applicable to the dividend from Florey BV is equal to the total underlying tax on the two dividends received, except that the limitation of the underlying rate to the rate of UK corporation tax (30%) applies only to the dividend received from Florey BV and not to each dividend from the sub-subsidiaries.

	Dividend	*Underlying tax rate*	*Underlying tax*	*Dividend and underlying tax*
	£		£	£
Irish dividend	333,333	9.09%	33,333	366,666
German dividend	100,000	46.67%	87,500	187,500
Total	433,333		120,833	554,166
Dividend from Florey BV		433,333	120,833	554,166
Schedule D Case V income			554,166	
UK corporation tax at 30%			166,250	
Less: double taxation relief				
Combined Irish and				
Germany tax (above)			(120,833)	
UK corporation tax payable			45,417	

Therefore, the UK corporation tax saving over the position in Example 40(a) without the dividend mixing company is £31,250 (£76,667 − £45,417). In effect, the high underlying tax rate on the dividend from Germany is used to cover part of the additional UK liability which would otherwise arise on the dividend from Ireland which has suffered a low rate of underlying tax.

Problem areas prior to Finance Act 2000

4.31   There are a number of problem areas associated with the claiming of underlying tax relief on dividends.

(*a*)   Company law in certain countries, including the US and the Netherlands, allows dividends to be paid out of the consolidated reserves of a group of companies, so that the payment of dividends from a subsidiary to a parent company in its own jurisdiction is not always necessary. As the UK system is mainly based on the premise that dividends are paid from reserves of individual companies and not from consolidated or equity accounted reserves, this can cause considerable practical difficulties in claiming double taxation relief on tax paid by a foreign sub-subsidiary. In practice, the Inland Revenue will allow underlying relief for tax paid on equity accounted profits in the accounts of a company in circumstances where the dividend can only have come out of equity accounted reserves. However, where the dividends have been paid out of consolidated reserves of a group of companies, the Inland Revenue may argue that no underlying relief is available to the extent that the dividends have not been paid out of the reserves of the holding company itself. For dividends paid to the UK on or after 31 March 2001 relief is now given automatically for the tax paid on equity accounted profits (*TA 1988, s 801B*).

(*b*)   In many countries (e.g. the US and the Netherlands) a single tax return is filed for all the companies within a consolidated tax group, whereas the UK gives credit for tax borne by individual companies. In these circumstances the tax paid in respect of the consolidated return needs to be allocated amongst the companies within the consolidated tax group and credit relief is given in the UK for the tax allocated to each company (examples of how the Inland Revenue has dealt with this in practice can be found in the leaflets produced by it in respect of the US and the Netherlands — broadly, the allocation is made by reference to the taxable profits of the companies). An allocation would not be acceptable if, for example, a full tax charge were to be allocated to profit making companies and a negative tax charge to loss making companies, since this would enable the group to claim underlying tax relief for more tax than has actually been paid by the group. Instead, no tax is allocated to the loss making companies, which reduces the amount of tax allocated to each profit making company in the group. It should be noted that the above practices have now been replaced by the provisions contained in *section 803A* (see 4.71 below).

(*c*)   If tax is paid by (or, in the case of a consolidated tax group, allocated to) a company which has losses for accounting purposes there are no 'relevant profits' which can be distributed. The effect is that the tax paid by (or allocated to) such companies is effectively lost for the purposes of underlying tax relief.

(*d*)   Underlying tax relief is available only if the company which has borne the tax pays dividends to its parent company. If a foreign company is dissolved or put into liquidation, subsequent distributions may not be considered to be dividends, but capital distributions and, consequently, no underlying relief may be available.

(e)   It is permissible under the company law of some jurisdictions for a parent and subsidiary to merge their businesses and assets so that, following the merger, the subsidiary ceases to exist. In that case any underlying tax which was available in the subsidiary prior to the merger may be lost, since the company paying the dividend has not borne the tax as required by *section 799(1)*. This problem is discussed in the Inland Revenue Tax Bulletin of October 1997 at page 473. A merger took place under the laws of New Jersey between two corporations, X and Y, corporation Y being the 'surviving corporation'. It was accepted that the effect of the New Jersey law was that X continued to exist after the merger with Y, albeit in altered form. As a result, the Inland Revenue agreed that the tax paid by X before the merger in respect of profits that were distributed by Y after the merger could be regarded as tax paid by Y for the purposes of a claim to relief for underlying tax. In practice, the Inland Revenue has also been known to allow relief where it can be demonstrated that the surviving company remains liable for the historic tax liabilities of the merged company, e.g. if these tax liabilities had not been paid. Therefore, it may not be necessary to demonstrate the concept of the merged company continuing to exist in the surviving entity for relief for tax paid by the merged company to be available. For dividends paid to the UK on or after 31 March 2001, relief is now given automatically for the tax paid on merged profits under *TA 1988, s 801B*.

(f)   Where a new foreign holding company is inserted into an international structure, company law and accounting principles of that jurisdiction may require that dividends received from the newly acquired subsidiaries out of pre-acquisition profits be deducted from the cost of acquisition. Underlying tax paid on those profits by the subsidiaries may be trapped in the local holding company since they cannot be distributed as dividends to the UK parent.

(g)   If a foreign subsidiary has a deficit on its distributable reserves and subsequently makes profits on which it pays foreign tax, the UK tax treatment depends upon the position in local company law. Where the deficit has arisen through over-distribution of profits in prior years, local company law may require that the deficit is made good before further dividend distributions are made. This may trap the underlying tax on the profits in the foreign subsidiary, although the underlying tax attributable to the profits required to make good the deficit may be able to be taken into account in respect of an earlier dividend (see also Example 37 above).

(h)   Where a merger occurs between two foreign subsidiaries which results in increases to distributable reserves in an accounting period, such increases may be treated as relevant profits in accordance with the principles of the *Bowater* case. The effect of this may be to dilute or increase underlying tax rates on dividends relating to that accounting period.

(*i*)   Where the UK shareholder owns a minority of the shares of the overseas company paying the dividends, the paying company may be reluctant to supply details of its tax assessments and other necessary information to enable a claim for credit relief to be agreed. In such circumstances, the Inland Revenue may be prepared to approach the relevant foreign tax authority for this information and calculate the underlying tax rate on behalf of the UK taxpayer.

(*j*)   A UK corporate shareholder may receive a distribution of profits from a US limited liability company (LLC). Generally speaking, US federal income tax is charged on the profits of LLCs on the basis that they are fiscally transparent, i.e. tax is imposed on the members of the LLC and not on the LLC itself. However, for UK tax purposes the Inland Revenue takes the view that LLCs should generally be considered as taxable entities and not as fiscally transparent. As a result, a UK member of an LLC is taxed by reference to distribution of profits made by the LLC and not by reference to the income of the LLC as it arises. If tax is paid in the US on the profit of the LLC, the Inland Revenue regards that tax as underlying tax and credit relief is available for it if the UK company which controls, directly or indirectly, at least 10% of the voting power in the LLC (Inland Revenue Tax Bulletin, June 1997).

The *Memec* case

4.32   In *Memec plc v IRC [1998] STC 754* the taxpayer (Memec) was a company resident in the UK which held (directly or indirectly) the entire share capital of the company incorporated in Germany (GmbH). GmbH was the holding company of two German trading subsidiaries. In 1985 GmbH and Memec entered into a silent partnership under which, in return for a capital contribution to GmbH, Memec obtained a contractual right to payment of 87.84% of the annual profits of the partnership whose income comprised dividends from the two subsidiaries. Under German law, GmbH remained the owner of the subsidiaries and of the income from them and Memec, as the silent partner, had no proprietary interest in them.

The Court of Appeal, confirming the judgment of Robert Walker J, held first that the source of Memec's income was right under the silent partnership (which was held not to be 'tax transparent') and not dividends from the German trading subsidiaries. Secondly, the expression 'dividends' in the UK's double taxation relief provisions (both unilateral and under the 'elimination of double taxation' article of the agreement with Germany) did not include a distribution of profits made by a silent partnership, despite a contrary definition under the 'dividends' article of the agreement. Accordingly, credit relief for underlying tax paid by the subsidiaries was held not to be available to the UK parent company.

Anti-avoidance

4.33   An anti-avoidance section, inserted as *TA 1988, s 801A*, was introduced to counter schemes for claiming what were termed 'bought-in' foreign tax credits. It has effect for dividends paid to a company resident in the UK on or after 26 November 1996 (it should be noted that, following the introduction of the mixer cap (see 4.36 below), for dividends paid to the UK on or after 31 March 2001, *section* 801A will be largely redundant).

The Inland Revenue was concerned that UK groups of companies had entered into schemes under which they acquired for a specified period a stream of highly taxed foreign income (such as dividends paid by a previously unconnected company out of its highly taxed profits). These were then to be mixed in a non-UK intermediate holding company (see 4.29 and 4.30 above) with other income on which little or no foreign tax had been paid. Relief was then to be claimed in the UK for all the underlying tax. The tax that had been 'bought-in' would, in effect, shelter from UK tax the lowly taxed income which was being brought into the UK as part of the dividend. Where *section 801A* applies, relief for the bought-in foreign tax is limited to the rate of UK corporation tax in force when the dividend was paid ('the relievable rate').

The section applies where:

(*a*)   a company resident in the UK ('the UK company') makes a claim for double tax credit relief;

(*b*)   the claim relates to underlying tax on a dividend paid to that company by a non-UK resident company ('the overseas company');

(*c*)   that underlying tax is (or includes) an amount in respect of tax ('the high rate tax') payable by:

● the overseas company or,

● a third, fourth (or lower) tier foreign related subsidiary,

at a rate in excess of the relievable rate of corporation tax; and

(*d*)   the whole (or any part) of the amount of the high rate tax would not be included in the underlying tax but for an avoidance scheme.

An 'avoidance scheme' is defined in *section 801A(6)* and *(7)* as meaning any scheme or arrangement which includes as parties both the UK company, a company related to that company or a person connected with the UK company and a person who was not under the control of the UK company at any time before the doing of anything as part of (or in pursuance of) the scheme or arrangement and, in addition, has the purpose (or one of the main purposes) of having an amount of underlying tax taken into account in a double tax credit relief claim.

For the purposes of *section 801A* a person who is a party to a scheme or arrangement is taken to have been under the 'control' of the UK company at the following times:

(*a*)   at any time when the UK company would have had control of the person under *TA 1988, s 416*;

(*b*)   any time when the UK company would have had control if that section applied (with the necessary modifications) in the case of partnerships and unincorporated associations; and

(*c*)   any time when that person acted in relation to the scheme or arrangement (or any proposal for it) either directly or indirectly under the direction of the UK company.

4.34   *Section 801A* was criticised for the potential breadth of its application, if the Inland Revenue were to seek to apply it widely. It could, for example, potentially have affected any acquisition of a foreign company which has highly taxed reserves which were at some stage to be paid to the UK via a 'mixer' company. The Tax Bulletin of June 1997 (page 411) contains an interpretation concerning the scope of *section 801A*, the relevant part of which is as follows:

> 'Concerns have been expressed about the application of s 801A (7). We can confirm that we would not regard a company acquired 'off the shelf' as not having been under the control of a UK company at any time by reason only of the fact that it was owned by a company formation agent throughout the period between its incorporation and its acquisition by the UK company. Also generally speaking, we accept that a company is not caught if there was a time before the doing of anything as part of, or in pursuance of, the avoidance scheme when it was under the control of the UK company. However, we will not necessarily be bound to adopt that approach in a case involving a company that was under the control of the UK company in the past, which then ceased to be so and in which an interest is subsequently acquired as part of, or in pursuance of, an avoidance scheme.

> The simple introduction of a new 'mixer' company into an existing group would not of itself trigger the new legislation, assuming that it does not form part of an avoidance scheme within s 801A. Equally, the new rules will not apply in cases where the acquisition of an interest in a highly-taxed company is not, or is not part of, a scheme or arrangement having as its purpose, or as one of its main purposes, obtaining relief for underlying tax, even though the interest may, at the time of acquisition or later as a result of an intra-group reorganisation, be held through a 'mixer' company.

> Of course, each case must be examined by reference to its own particular facts. We may also have to reassess the position if new schemes come to light which are designed to circumvent s 801A, especially if they seek to take advantage of our practice as set out above. We will publish any new or revised approach to the application of s 801A.'

Information required for claiming underlying tax relief

4.35 A number of information leaflets are published by the Underlying Tax Group, Nottingham, (now part of Inland Revenue International Division) which give guidance both generally on the information required to agree an underlying tax relief claim and on specific information required with respect to tax paid in each country.

The general leaflet covering all countries is reproduced as Appendix 5. The documentation required depends on the amount of the dividend and the country from which it is received. However, in general, the following are required:

(a) a notice of assessment to tax, or, where the tax is self-assessed, the first page of the tax return;

(b) if the dividend resolution specifies the profits from which the dividend has been paid, a copy of the dividend resolution;

(c) a copy of the parts of the company's (non-consolidated) accounts for the relevant period(s) showing:

　(i) the profit and loss account and liabilities section of the balance sheet prepared under the foreign country's accounting standards (comparative figures in the following year's accounts are acceptable);

　(ii) any notes to the accounts affecting profits and reserves;

　(iii) details of how the profits have been appropriated;

　(iv) details of dividends received (if underlying tax relief is claimed in respect of them).

There are also leaflets covering the information requirements and other points relating to more than 70 countries which are available from the Underlying Tax Group, Nottingham. These currently include those listed below. It is understood that some information in certain of these leaflets is now obsolete following the new rules in *FA 2000*. The relevant leaflets are currently being updated by the Inland Revenue.

Argentina	Brunei	Finland	Indonesia
Australia	Cameroon	France	Ireland
Austria	Canada	Gambia	Isle of Man
Bahamas	Cayman Islands	Germany	Israel
Bangladesh	Chile	Ghana	Italy
Barbados	Colombia	Greece	Ivory Coast
Belgium	Cyprus	Guernsey	Jamaica
Belize	Denmark	Guyana	Japan
Bermuda	Ecuador	Hong Kong	Jersey
Botswana	Egypt	Iceland	Kenya
Brazil	Ethiopia	India	Korea

Liberia	New Zealand	Sierra Leone	Thailand
Luxembourg	Nigeria	Singapore	Trinidad and Tobago
Malaysia	Norway	South Africa	Uganda
Malawi	Pakistan	Spain	United States
Malta	Peru	Sri Lanka	Venezuela
Mauritius	Philippines	Swaziland	Zaire
Mexico	Portugal	Sweden	Zambia
Namibia	Saudi Arabia	Switzerland	Zimbabwe
Netherlands	Senegal	Taiwan	

The mixer cap

4.36   Paragraphs 4.29–4.30 above illustrated how UK companies with overseas subsidiaries have historically used mixer companies to reduce UK taxes payable on low taxed dividend income.

FA 2000 introduced the mixer cap concept to limit offshore mixing by imposing restrictions on the availability of underlying tax relief. The mixer cap is based on the concept originally contained in the anti-avoidance provisions in *section 801A*. The following paragraphs cover the mixer cap provisions in detail. While some tax planning involving mixer companies will remain possible following these changes, it is now severely limited. However, some of the remaining planning concepts are discussed at 4.42 and 4.48 below.

Before considering in detail the mixer cap issues, it is useful to comment on the interaction between these new restrictions and the new onshore pooling provisions. The calculations to establish any underlying tax restrictions on the payment of a foreign dividend to the UK form a part of the initial calculations to ascertain whether there is a potential liability to UK tax. The new onshore pooling provisions then operate to identify whether a taxable foreign dividend can be pooled with other foreign dividends. These rules also establish whether it is possible to utilise any unrelieved foreign tax that has arisen as a result of the mixer cap. The detailed rules as to how the onshore pooling provisions work are dealt with in 4.43–4.48 below.

4.37   The restrictions on underlying tax are calculated by applying the mixer cap which ensures that the creditable underlying tax on any dividend does not exceed a maximum amount given by the following formula [*s 799(1A)*]:

$$(D + U) \times M$$

where: D = the amount of the dividend,
   U = the actual underlying tax attributable to the dividend, and
   M = the ordinary rate of corporation tax

This formula applies to dividends paid on or after 31 March 2001 by companies resident outside the UK to companies resident in the UK. However, underlying tax relief claims made on or after 31 March 2001 in respect of dividends paid to the UK before that date are not affected by the mixer cap. For the purpose of the examples in the remainder of this chapter, it is assumed that M is 30%, being the rate of corporation tax in force for the financial year 2001.

The mixer cap applies at each level in a dividend chain. While the creditable tax is restricted by the mixer cap formula, when calculating the amount of income to be treated as Schedule D Case V taxable profits, it is still necessary to gross up the dividend by the actual underlying tax attributable to the dividend — see Example 41 below.

Example 41

Rushmore Plc, a UK resident company, has a wholly owned Dutch subsidiary, Rushmore BV. On 30 June 2001 Rushmore BV distributed in full its after-tax profits for the year to its UK parent. The UK corporation tax computation (ignoring the calculation of eligible unrelieved foreign tax) is as follows:

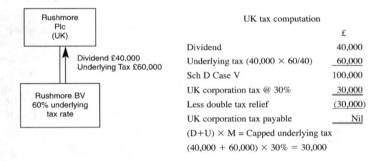

UK tax computation	
	£
Dividend	40,000
Underlying tax (40,000 × 60/40)	60,000
Sch D Case V	100,000
UK corporation tax @ 30%	30,000
Less double tax relief	(30,000)
UK corporation tax payable	Nil

(D+U) × M = Capped underlying tax

(40,000 + 60,000) × 30% = 30,000

4.38   Although the above result appears to be no different from the position before 31 March 2001, the effect of the mixer cap becomes clear when looking at offshore mixer company structures. Here it can be seen that where high and low tax dividends are paid through a mixer company, the excess foreign tax on the high tax dividends may no longer be utilised against the effective UK tax payable on the low tax dividends (see Example 42 below).

Example 42

A UK parent company Blurton Plc holds the shares in an offshore mixer company Blurton BV. The mixer company holds two overseas subsidiaries, a high tax subsidiary with a 60% underlying tax rate Blurton SPA and a nil tax subsidiary, Blurton SA. The high tax subsidiary pays a dividend of £40,000 to the mixer company and the low tax subsidiary pays a dividend of £100,000. The dividends are paid out of the profits of the two companies for the period ended 30 June 2000. On 30 June 2000, the mixer company pays a dividend of £140,000 to the UK out of the dividends received.

Prior to the introduction of the mixer cap the UK tax computation would have been as follows:

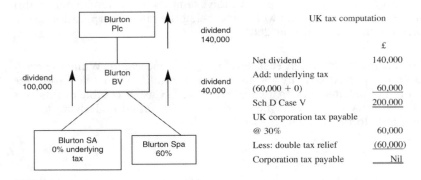

UK tax computation	
	£
Net dividend	140,000
Add: underlying tax	
(60,000 + 0)	60,000
Sch D Case V	200,000
UK corporation tax payable	
@ 30%	60,000
Less: double tax relief	(60,000)
Corporation tax payable	Nil

However, if the dividends had instead been paid on 30 June 2001, following the introduction of the mixer cap, the position would be:

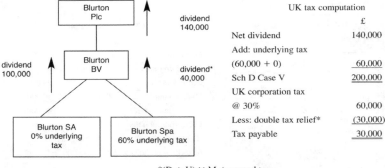

UK tax computation	
	£
Net dividend	140,000
Add: underlying tax	
(60,000 + 0)	60,000
Sch D Case V	200,000
UK corporation tax	
@ 30%	60,000
Less: double tax relief*	(30,000)
Tax payable	30,000

*(D + U) × M + capped tax
Cap on underlying tax (40,000 + 60,000) × 30% = 30,000

There is no underlying tax to restrict on the nil tax dividend paid to the mixer company but the creditable underlying tax on the high tax dividend is restricted to £30,000. The mixer cap formula does not come into operation on the mixer company dividend of £140,000 to restrict the underlying taxes further. As can be seen, a substantial additional tax liability arises as a result of the mixer cap changes.

4.39   The mixer cap restriction applies to dividends paid directly to the UK as well as dividends paid between two overseas companies in a dividend chain. One important exception to this rule is that the restriction does not apply to dividends paid between companies resident in the same territory. [*s 801(2A)(a)*]. It is therefore possible to continue to mix dividends within a single country where there is a common holding company in that country. The Inland Revenue does, however, have the power to bring in further restrictions on in-country mixing in the form of regulations. [*s 801(2A)(b)*]. In this respect, regulations [*SI 2001 No 1156*] have been introduced to prevent certain dual resident companies from obtaining the benefit of in-country mixing. Essentially, these rules apply the same test as the controlled foreign companies rules for establishing the residence status of a dual resident company.

4.40   It should be noted that the mixer cap only applies to underlying taxes. It is possible that a dividend paid to the UK suffers foreign taxes in excess of 30% due to the underlying tax being below 30% and there being additional withholding taxes. In these circumstances the mixer cap does not apply. However, withholding taxes arising on dividends between foreign companies in a chain of companies are treated as part of the underlying tax charge within the respective recipient companies. [*s 801(1)(b)*]. Therefore, withholding tax can lead to the application of the mixer cap higher up the dividend chain.

In addition, the expenses of an offshore holding company may affect the underlying tax rate, causing the mixer cap to apply, since the relevant profits of the holding company are reduced by its expenses. This can increase the effective underlying tax rates of dividends paid through the holding company.

4.41   The mixer cap restrictions apply to dividends paid to the UK after 30 March 2001. Where a dividend is paid by an offshore holding company after 30 March 2001 from dividends received prior to 31 March 2001, the underlying tax restriction will still apply to all lower tier dividends. For dividends paid to the UK prior to 31 March 2001, the mixer cap restrictions do not apply. Therefore, taxpayers still need to apply the old rules when making claims in respect of double tax relief on dividends paid before 31 March 2001.

Capping at more than one level

4.42   Set out below is an example of the mixer cap applying at more than one level in a chain of overseas companies, A, B and C which are owned ultimately by a UK company. It is assumed that the dividends are paid on 30 June 2001, which is also the accounting year end of each of the companies.

Example 43 (see diagram overleaf)

The mixer cap is calculated in respect of the total dividends at each level. In addition, the amount of underlying tax available as a credit takes into account capped underlying tax at lower levels.

It is assumed that the dividend from overseas company C is exempt from tax in overseas company B, and that the dividend from overseas company B is exempt from tax in overseas company A. Overseas company B has also generated after-tax profits of its own of 12,000 on which underlying tax was paid of 8,000. The dividend from overseas company B of 25,000 is subject to a mixer cap of 12,000, i.e. 30% of the dividend itself and the total actual underlying tax incurred by overseas company B and overseas company C of 15,000. Effectively the underlying tax on overseas company B's own profits has been restricted to 6,000.

Overseas company A's dividend of 41,000 paid to the UK includes its own after-tax profits of 16,000 as well as the dividend from overseas company B of 25,000. The underlying tax on

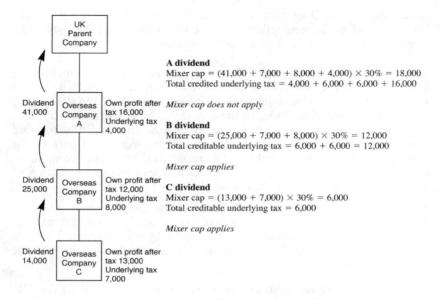

overseas company A's own profits amounts to 4,000. The total underlying tax allowed as a credit against UK corporation tax is 4,000 plus the capped tax of 12,000 on the dividend from overseas company B, i.e. 16,000.

The mixer cap limit on the underlying tax in relation to the dividend from overseas company A is 18,000, i.e. 30% of the dividend of 41,000 and the total actual cumulative underlying tax of 19,000. However, this amount is greater than the total credit available of 18,000 which takes into account the mixer capped amounts in relation to the dividends from overseas company B and overseas company C. Therefore, the mixer cap does not apply to the dividend from overseas company A to the UK parent company.

The UK corporation tax computation is as follows:

Dividend	41,000
Add: unrestricted underlying tax	19,000
Sch D Case V	60,000
UK corporation tax @ 30%	18,000
Less: double tax relief	(16,000)
Corporation tax payable	2,000

It should be noted that the UK tax position would differ if overseas company A were owned by company B, so that the low taxed profits of overseas company A are distributed to a company with highly taxed profits. Again, this is on the assumption that the dividend from overseas company A to overseas company B would have been exempt from tax in overseas company B and that the dividend is not an acceptable distribution for the purposes of the UK controlled foreign companies legislation. It is also assumed that each of the above dividends is paid on 30 June 2001 and that this is also the accounting year end of each of the companies. An example is set out below.

Example 44

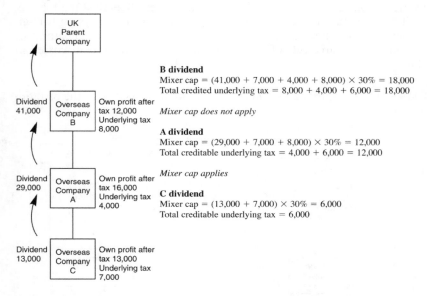

B dividend
Mixer cap = (41,000 + 7,000 + 4,000 + 8,000) × 30% = 18,000
Total credited underlying tax = 8,000 + 4,000 + 6,000 = 18,000

Mixer cap does not apply

A dividend
Mixer cap = (29,000 + 7,000 + 8,000) × 30% = 12,000
Total creditable underlying tax = 4,000 + 6,000 = 12,000

Mixer cap applies

C dividend
Mixer cap = (13,000 + 7,000) × 30% = 6,000
Total creditable underlying tax = 6,000

In this revised structure the creditable tax is increased to 18,000 and there is no UK tax to pay. The mixer cap only applies on the dividend of 13,000 from overseas company C. The creditable underlying tax is restricted to 6,000 at this level.

There is no mixer cap restriction on the dividend paid by overseas company A because the creditable tax is 10,000, being the underlying tax of 4,000 incurred by overseas company A in relation to its own profits and the restricted underlying tax of 6,000 on the dividend from overseas company A. This is less than the potential mixer cap of 12,000 at this level.

The dividend from overseas company B to the UK is subject to a mixer cap of 18,000. However, as the creditable tax is exactly 18,000 the mixer cap does not apply. Moreover, the underlying tax of 8,000 incurred by overseas company B on its own profits is now fully creditable. This is due to the low taxed profits generated by overseas company A being brought into the dividend chain at a lower level and thereby creating greater capacity at the higher level to credit tax on higher taxed profits.

In summary, the above example shows that it is possible to mix low tax profits into high tax profits following the *FA 2000* changes although to a much lesser extent than under the old rules.

Overview of onshore pooling

4.43   The onshore pooling regime was introduced as a late amendment to *FA 2000* as a result of significant lobbying by UK multinationals and their professional advisers. It was intended to alleviate to an extent the additional tax liabilities many UK multinationals faced as a result of the introduction of the mixing restrictions.

In overview, under the onshore pooling regime, eligible unrelieved foreign tax arising on certain high tax dividends can be set off against the UK tax liability on certain low tax dividends which are called qualifying foreign dividends. This extension of double tax relief represents a relaxation of the source-by-source rule of UK taxation of foreign income discussed in Chapter 3.

4.44   The diagram below illustrates the broad workings of the onshore pooling regime.

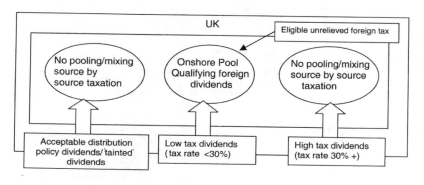

The key features of this regime are as follows:

- High tax dividends, i.e. dividends with an underlying tax rate in excess of 30% and which remain taxed on a source-by-source basis, can give rise to eligible unrelieved foreign tax.

- Certain foreign dividends are now classified as qualifying foreign dividends. These are, broadly, low tax dividends (subject to certain exceptions) against which eligible unrelieved foreign tax can be set off.

- Some foreign dividends will be outside the onshore pooling regime. They will either not be qualifying foreign dividends or will not give rise to eligible unrelieved foreign tax or both. Acceptable distribution policy dividends and what are termed 'tainted' dividends fall into this category. Tainted dividends are dividends carrying a low underlying tax rate but which give rise to eligible unrelieved foreign tax at a lower level in the dividend chain. The classic mixer company dividend made up of high and low tax lower level dividends will often be a tainted dividend.

The principles of onshore pooling are straightforward but the detailed rules mean that in practice the operation of the system is very complicated. While the regime was introduced in response to lobbying, many multinationals with existing mixer company structures are likely to find that the regime is of limited benefit to them and that they need to re-

structure their groups to take full advantage of the new rules. In particular, the effect of the *FA 2000* changes is to encourage UK multinationals to hold their overseas subsidiaries directly from the UK as
opposed to using offshore holding companies.

Qualifying foreign dividends

4.45   Qualifying foreign dividends are those dividends against which
eligible unrelieved foreign tax can be offset. Qualifying foreign dividends
are all Schedule D Case V dividends [*s 806C(1)*] other than the following:

- Dividends which represent an acceptable distribution policy dividend paid directly to a UK company by a controlled foreign
  company.

- Any dividend representing an acceptable distribution policy cannot
  be a qualifying foreign dividend. This exclusion deals with the
  situation where a controlled foreign company is held through an
  offshore holding company and the acceptable distribution policy
  dividend paid by the lower tier controlled foreign company is paid
  up though the holding company in the UK. There are special rules
  to identify acceptable distribution policy dividends in this situation (see 4.66–4.68 below).

- Any dividend on which eligible unrelieved foreign tax arises cannot
  be a qualifying foreign dividend. These dividends are termed
  'tainted' dividends. This exclusion is a major pitfall in the onshore
  pooling regime and may well mean that, for the majority of UK
  companies holding subsidiaries through mixer companies, the onshore pooling regime leads to higher UK tax liabilities than under
  the pre-*FA 2000* rules unless restructuring is carried out.

- Any dividend which is excluded from generating eligible unrelieved
  foreign tax (see *s 806A(2)*) cannot be a qualifying foreign divided
  (see 4.49 below).

4.46   As a general rule, underlying tax can only be claimed where the
UK company receiving the overseas dividend owns 10% or more of the
overseas company's voting power directly or indirectly. This rule is preserved in the onshore pooling regime. Eligible unrelieved foreign tax that
arises from underlying tax cannot be offset against the tax liability on
qualifying foreign dividends from companies in which the UK recipient
company has less than 10% of the voting power.

As a result, qualifying foreign dividends are categorised as related or
unrelated qualifying foreign dividends. Related qualifying foreign dividends are those received from companies in which the UK recipient holds
at least 10% of the voting power. [*s 806C(2)(a)*]. Unrelated qualifying
foreign dividends are those received from companies in which the UK
recipient controls less than 10% of the voting power. [*s 806C(2)(b)*].

The following steps are required to compute the Schedule D Case V tax liability on qualifying foreign dividends, before any eligible unrelieved tax can be offset.

- All the related qualifying foreign dividends in a period are aggregated and treated as a single source called the 'single related dividend'. [*s 806C(3)(a), (4)(b)*].

- All the unrelated qualifying foreign dividends in a period are also aggregated and treated as single source called the 'single unrelated dividend'. [*s 806C(3)(b), (4)(b)*].

- All the underlying tax on the related qualifying foreign dividends is aggregated and forms the 'aggregated underlying tax'. [*s 806C(3)(c)*]. The underlying tax on the qualifying foreign dividends in a period will only arise from the related qualifying foreign dividends. Therefore, the underlying tax is treated as the underlying tax of the single related dividend.

- All the withholding tax suffered on both the related and unrelated qualifying foreign dividends is aggregated and forms the 'aggregated withholding tax'. [*s 806C(4)(d)*]. The aggregated withholding tax can be allocated as the claimant company sees fit, e.g. partly to the single related dividend and partly to the single unrelated dividend, provided that the allocation does not give rise to eligible unrelieved foreign tax. [*s 806D(6)*].

For an example of the computation of the UK corporation tax liability on qualifying foreign dividends, please refer to Example 59 at 4.64 below.

Tainted dividends

4.47 A dividend on which eligible unrelieved foreign tax arises cannot be a qualifying foreign dividend. It is possible to have situations in which eligible unrelieved foreign tax arises on a dividend and there is a residual UK tax liability on the dividend, e.g. in the case of dividends paid through a holding company made up of high and low tax lower level dividends. These dividends are 'tainted' dividends for the purposes of the onshore pooling regime (see Example 45 below). As can be seen from this a residual UK tax liability arises in this situation. In particular, overseas company B's dividend is not a qualifying foreign dividend because it includes a dividend from overseas company D to which the mixer cap has applied.

Example 45

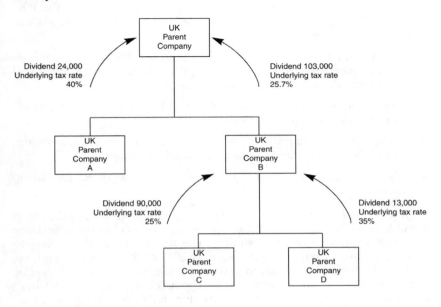

UK corporation tax computation	Overseas Company A	Overseas Company B*
Dividend	24,000	103,000
Underlying tax	16,000	37,000
Schedule D Case V	40,000	140,000
UK corporation tax at 30%	12,000	42,000
Double tax relief		
— overseas company A	(6,000)	
— overseas company B		
* dividend from overseas company C		(30,000)
* dividend from overseas company D**		(6,000)
UK corporation tax payable	Nil	6,000

Eligible unrelieved foreign tax calculation	Overseas Company A	Overseas Company B
Upper amounts		
— company A	16,000	—
— company D	—	7,000
— company C	—	30,000
	16,000	37,000
Tax actually credited	(12,000)	(36,000)
Eligible unrelieved foreign tax	4,000	1,000

* The mixer cap applies to restrict the underlying tax to 6,000 i.e. (13,000 + 7,000) × 30% = 6,000.

** As the dividend from overseas company B is not a qualifying foreign dividend, eligible unrelieved foreign tax arising on the overseas company A and overseas company D dividends cannot be utilised against the residual tax liability on the dividend from overseas company B.

4.48   Dividend tainting is likely to be a major problem for any company that does not hold its overseas subsidiaries directly from the UK. However, there are a number of possible solutions to this problem which include the following.

- Part of the foreign tax need not be claimed [*s 799(1B)*] so that high tax dividends do not give rise to eligible unrelieved foreign tax and therefore do not taint low tax dividends.

- Dividend flows can be alternated so that high and low tax dividends are paid up as separate dividends.

- The group can be restructured so that high and low tax subsidiaries are held through separate overseas holding companies.

- The overseas subsidiaries can be transferred to direct ownership from the UK.

Section 799(1B) which was introduced by *FA 2001* means that it is possible to exclude any amount of foreign tax on a claim for underlying tax relief to avoid dividend tainting. The mechanics of this provision involve claiming foreign tax equal to only 30% of the gross dividend, i.e. 30% of the sum of the dividend and total underlying taxes. It should be noted that the foreign tax which is not claimed is permanently lost both for normal credit purposes and for eligible unrelieved foreign tax purposes. However, any dividend in respect of which an amount of foreign tax has not been claimed must still be grossed up for the tax which is not claimed in the Schedule D Case V calculation. In arriving at the decision as to whether foreign tax should not be claimed, it will be necessary to compare the UK tax payable on a tainted dividend with the potential eligible unrelieved foreign tax lost as a result and any possibility for utilising the eligible unrelieved foreign tax in other periods.

If in Example 45, 1,000 of underlying tax is not claimed on the dividend from overseas company D, overseas company B's dividend will no longer be tainted and it will represent a qualifying foreign dividend (see below).

Example 46

UK corporation tax computation is as follows	*Overseas Company A*	*Overseas Company B*
Dividend	24,000	103,000
Underlying tax	16,000	37,000
Schedule D Case V	40,000	140,000
UK corporation tax at 30%	12,000	42,000
Double tax relief		
— overseas company A	(12,000)	
— overseas company B		
* dividend from overseas company C		(30,000)
* dividend from overseas company D	—	(6,000)
		6,000
Eligible unrelieved foreign tax	—	(4,000)
UK corporation tax payable	Nil	2,000

118

Eligible unrelieved foreign tax calculation	Overseas Company A	Overseas Company B
Upper amounts		
— overseas company A	16,000	—
— overseas company B	—	6,000
— overseas company C	—	30,000
	16,000	36,000
Tax actually credited	(12,000)	(36,000)
Eligible unrelieved foreign tax	4,000	Nil

As a result of underlying tax of 1,000 not being claimed in respect of the total underlying tax of 7,000 on overseas company D's dividend, eligible unrelieved foreign tax no longer arises on overseas company D's dividend so that overseas company B's dividend can represent a qualifying foreign dividend. Although foreign tax of 1,000 has been lost, eligible unrelieved foreign tax of 4,000 on overseas company A's dividend can be utilised to offset the residual UK tax liability on overseas company B's dividend.

As mentioned above, another method of avoiding dividend tainting is alternating high and low tax dividend flows through an offshore holding company (see Example 47 below).

Example 47

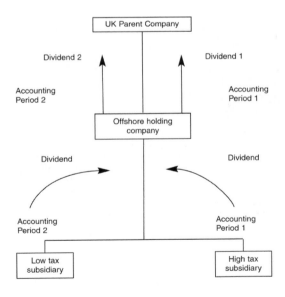

In accounting period 1 the high tax subsidiary pays a dividend to the offshore holding company, while the low tax subsidiary pays a dividend to the offshore holding company in accounting period 2. The offshore holding company pays separate dividends out of accounting period 1 and accounting period 2 to the UK company. Dividend 1 is paid out of accounting period 1, and this represents purely the dividend received from the high tax subsidiary. This dividend generates eligible unrelieved foreign tax and suffers no further UK tax liability, since the underlying tax rate is in excess of 30%.

Dividend 2 paid by the offshore holding company is paid purely out of accounting period 2's profit. This is the dividend received from the low tax subsidiary. Dividend 2 will be a qualifying foreign dividend, since it is not a tainted dividend. The eligible unrelieved foreign tax generated on dividend 1 can be offset against the UK tax liability on dividend 2.

It should be noted that, for this structure to work, the offshore holding company must have control over the dividend flows from its high and low tax subsidiaries.

Companies may also consider demerging their group structures so that high and low tax subsidiaries currently held under one holding company for mixing purposes are held under two or more separate holding companies (see Example 48 below).

Example 48

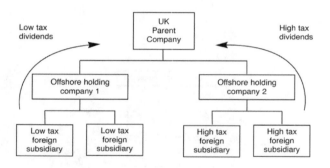

Offshore holding company 1 holds purely low tax subsidiaries, and offshore holding company 2 holds purely high tax subsidiaries. Dividends paid up through the offshore holding company 1 chain should be low tax dividends and represent qualifying foreign dividends assuming that none of these dividends is an acceptable distribution policy dividend from a controlled foreign company. Dividends paid up through the offshore holding company 2 structure are high tax dividends which will generate eligible unrelieved foreign tax. Eligible unrelieved foreign tax arising on offshore holding company 2 dividends can then be offset against the residual UK tax liability or qualifying foreign dividends from offshore holding company 1.

It will be necessary to consider whether any reduction in UK tax associated with this structure outweighs any overseas restructuring costs. In addition, many companies may not find it simple commercially to reorganise their group structures on the basis of underlying tax rates rather than geographical structures. It should also be noted that those subsidiaries which are low tax subsidiaries may well become high tax subsidiaries and vice versa due to timing differences and permanent differences in their tax computations.

Eligible unrelieved foreign tax — overview

4.49   Eligible unrelieved foreign tax can be described as unrelieved foreign tax arising on certain foreign dividends that can be used to credit the residual UK tax liability on qualifying foreign dividends. It is important to bear in mind that not all excess foreign taxes qualify as eligible unrelieved foreign tax and not all high tax dividends generate eligible unrelieved foreign tax. In particular, the following types of dividends do not generate eligible unrelieved foreign tax [*s 806A(2)*]:

• dividends which are taxed as trading income;

• dividends falling within *section 801A* (this is an anti-avoidance provision designed to prevent companies from buying high tax dividend streams as part of a scheme of tax avoidance (see 4.33 above);

• dividends falling within *section 803* (this is a specific restriction which broadly applies to financial institutions and limits underlying tax relief to the extent that the underlying tax represents lower level withholding tax suffered on interest income); and

• any dividend in respect of which foreign tax has been expensed.

4.50   Unrelieved foreign tax, where foreign tax paid exceeds the tax credited, can arise in the following two circumstances for the purposes of the onshore pooling regime.

• The UK tax payable on a dividend is lower than the creditable foreign taxes. This refers back to the general limitation in *section 797(2)* in that credit relief is restricted to the lower of UK tax payable and foreign taxes paid. This situation is called Case A. [*s 806B(2)*].

• Unrelieved foreign taxes can also arise where the mixer cap has applied. This is where the underlying tax paid is more than 30% of the dividend plus any associated underlying tax. This situation is called Case B. [*s 806B(3)*].

In both Case A and Case B, the amount of unrelieved foreign tax that is eligible for offset against qualifying foreign dividends is subject to an upper limit. In a Case A situation, the amount of eligible unrelieved foreign tax is the amount of foreign tax that would have been available for credit had UK tax been charged at 45% less the credit actually given for foreign tax in the UK tax computation. In a Case B, or mixer cap, situation, the amount of foreign tax that is eligible unrelieved foreign tax is the amount of underlying tax that would have been available for credit had the mixer cap been at 45% less the amount creditable at 30%. In both cases an upper limit of 45% is imposed on the taxes which will generate eligible unrelieved foreign tax. If the actual taxes are less than this figure, it should broadly be the actual tax that is taken as the figure from which the tax credited will be deducted to arrive at the amount of eligible unrelieved foreign tax.

4.51   The following examples illustrate how Case A and Case B eligible unrelieved foreign tax are calculated. It is assumed that each of the dividends in these examples is paid on 30 June 2001 and that this is the accounting year end of each of the companies.

Example 49

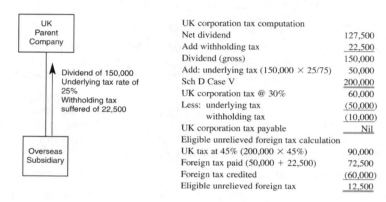

Case A eligible unrelieved foreign tax

UK corporation tax computation	
Net dividend	127,500
Add withholding tax	22,500
Dividend (gross)	150,000
Add: underlying tax (150,000 × 25/75)	50,000
Sch D Case V	200,000
UK corporation tax @ 30%	60,000
Less: underlying tax	(50,000)
withholding tax	(10,000)
UK corporation tax payable	Nil
Eligible unrelieved foreign tax calculation	
UK tax at 45% (200,000 × 45%)	90,000
Foreign tax paid (50,000 + 22,500)	72,500
Foreign tax credited	(60,000)
Eligible unrelieved foreign tax	12,500

Diagram labels:
- UK Parent Company
- Dividend of 150,000 Underlying tax rate of 25% Withholding tax suffered of 22,500
- Overseas Subsidiary

Case A eligible unrelieved foreign tax arises where the UK tax payable on a dividend is less than the foreign taxes credited on that dividend, but not as a result of the mixer cap. This can arise where the creditable foreign underlying and withholding taxes exceed the UK tax payable. In this example the overseas company pays a dividend of 150,000 to the UK parent. The dividend carries an underlying tax rate of 25% and also suffers withholding tax of 22,500. The underlying tax rate on this dividend is less than 30% and it is not therefore subject to a mixer cap.

The foreign tax suffered on the dividend is 72,500, being underlying tax of 50,000 and withholding tax of 22,500. The credit given for foreign tax is restricted to 60,000. Under the onshore pooling rules, where credit is available for both underlying tax and withholding tax, the underlying tax will be treated as credited first. [*s 806F*]. Therefore, in this example, the whole of the underlying tax of 50,000 is credited and withholding tax of 10,000 is credited, leaving withholding tax of 12,500 unrelieved.

To arrive at the amount of the unrelieved withholding tax that represents eligible unrelieved foreign tax it is necessary to calculate the amount of foreign tax that would be creditable were the UK rate of corporation tax 45%. The maximum creditable amount based on a 45% tax rate would be the Schedule D Case V income of 200,000 times 45% which is 90,000. However, the foreign tax actually paid is only 72,500. Since credit is not available for more tax than actually paid the lower figure is taken. Taking the total foreign tax paid of 72,500 and deducting the foreign tax actually credited of 60,000 the eligible unrelieved foreign tax is 12,500. In this case, the eligible unrelieved foreign tax is all withholding tax.

Case A eligible unrelieved foreign tax can also arise when losses in the UK company reduce the profits chargeable to corporation tax (see Example 50 below).

Example 50

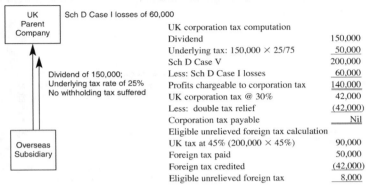

Case A eligible unrelieved foreign tax

UK corporation tax computation

Dividend	150,000
Underlying tax: 150,000 × 25/75	50,000
Sch D Case V	200,000
Less: Sch D Case I losses	60,000
Profits chargeable to corporation tax	140,000
UK corporation tax @ 30%	42,000
Less: double tax relief	(42,000)
Corporation tax payable	Nil

Eligible unrelieved foreign tax calculation

UK tax at 45% (200,000 × 45%)	90,000
Foreign tax paid	50,000
Foreign tax credited	(42,000)
Eligible unrelieved foreign tax	8,000

It is unclear from the legislation whether the calculation of the eligible unrelieved foreign tax at 45% should be by reference to the gross amount of income, i.e. Schedule D Case V income of 200,000 or the profit chargeable to corporation tax of 140,000 (in this case). In this example, the point is not strictly relevant since the actual tax of 50,000 is less than 45% of 140,000. However, the Inland Revenue has confirmed that in practice the 45% calculation would be based on the Schedule D Case V income of 200,000 in this example.

Example 51 below shows the calculation of eligible unrelieved foreign tax where there are underlying taxes, withholding taxes and losses.

Example 51

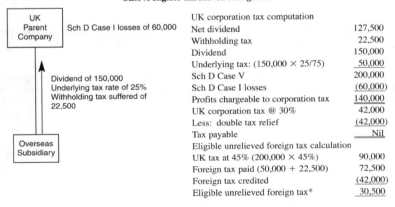

Case A eligible unrelieved foreign tax

UK corporation tax computation

Net dividend	127,500
Withholding tax	22,500
Dividend	150,000
Underlying tax: (150,000 × 25/75)	50,000
Sch D Case V	200,000
Sch D Case I losses	(60,000)
Profits chargeable to corporation tax	140,000
UK corporation tax @ 30%	42,000
Less: double tax relief	(42,000)
Tax payable	Nil

Eligible unrelieved foreign tax calculation

UK tax at 45% (200,000 × 45%)	90,000
Foreign tax paid (50,000 + 22,500)	72,500
Foreign tax credited	(42,000)
Eligible unrelieved foreign tax*	30,500

* Eligible unrelieved foreign tax is 22,500 withholding tax and 8,000 underlying tax

The eligible unrelieved foreign tax of 30,500 represents withholding tax of 22,500 and underlying tax of 8,000. This is because *section 806F(1)(a)* requires credit to be given first in the UK corporation tax computation of the UK parent company for underlying tax before foreign tax other than underlying tax. This means that the amount of foreign tax remaining that can be treated as eligible unrelieved foreign tax is mainly withholding tax.

4.52   Example 52 below shows a calculation of Case B eligible un-relieved foreign tax. Case B only applies if there is mixer cap restriction. As the mixer cap only restricts underlying tax, Case B eligible unrelieved foreign tax is always underlying tax.

Example 52

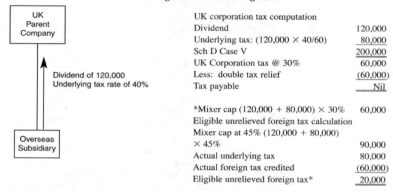

Case B eligible unrelieved foreign tax

UK
Parent
Company

Dividend of 120,000
Underlying tax rate of 40%

Overseas
Subsidiary

UK corporation tax computation	
Dividend	120,000
Underlying tax: (120,000 × 40/60)	80,000
Sch D Case V	200,000
UK Corporation tax @ 30%	60,000
Less: double tax relief	(60,000)
Tax payable	Nil
*Mixer cap (120,000 + 80,000) × 30%	60,000
Eligible unrelieved foreign tax calculation	
Mixer cap at 45% (120,000 + 80,000)	
× 45%	90,000
Actual underlying tax	80,000
Actual foreign tax credited	(60,000)
Eligible unrelieved foreign tax*	20,000

The amount of the Case B eligible unrelieved foreign tax is the creditable amount of un-derlying tax if the mixer cap had been applied at 45% less the creditable amount of 30%.

In this example, if the mixer cap were at 45% the maximum creditable underlying tax would be 90,000. The actual underlying tax is only 80,000. Taking this lower amount and deducting the tax credited of 60,000, results in eligible unrelieved foreign tax of 20,000. This is all eligible unrelieved foreign tax that is to be treated as if it were underlying tax.

4.53   Example 53 below shows the calculation of Case A and Case B eligible unrelieved foreign tax on the same dividend.

The overseas company pays a dividend of 130,000 with underlying tax of 70,000. The dividend also suffers withholding tax of 32,500. The total foreign tax suffered on the dividend is 102,500.

The dividend is subject to a mixer cap so that creditable underlying tax is restricted to 60,000. The Schedule D Case V amount is 200,000. The UK corporation tax payable is 60,000 and this is fully covered by the restricted underlying tax (again, underlying tax is credited in priority to the withholding tax).

Example 53

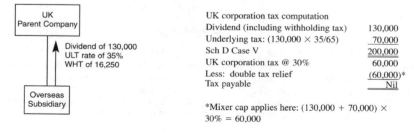

Case A and Case B eligible unrelieved foreign tax

UK
Parent Company

Dividend of 130,000
ULT rate of 35%
WHT of 16,250

Overseas
Subsidiary

UK corporation tax computation	
Dividend (including withholding tax)	130,000
Underlying tax: (130,000 × 35/65)	70,000
Sch D Case V	200,000
UK corporation tax @ 30%	60,000
Less: double tax relief	(60,000)*
Tax payable	Nil

*Mixer cap applies here: (130,000 + 70,000) × 30% = 60,000

Case A eligible unrelieved foreign tax

Maximum creditable tax (200,000 × 45%)	90,000
Actual creditable tax 45% (restricted underlying tax and withholding tax)	76,250
Tax credited (underlying tax)	(60,000)
Case A eligible unrelieved foreign tax (all withholding tax)	16,250

Case B eligible unrelieved foreign tax calculation

Mixer cap @ 45% (200,000 × 45%)	90,000
Actual underlying tax	70,000
Creditable underlying tax @ 30%	(60,000)
Case B eligible unrelieved foreign tax (underlying tax)	10,000

4.54   Example 54 below looks at a Case A and a Case B calculation of eligible unrelieved foreign tax on the same dividend where it is necessary to consider both withholding tax and underlying tax in the Case A calculation.

Example 54

Case A and Case B eligible unrelieved foreign tax

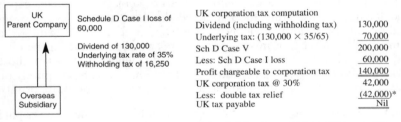

UK Parent Company

Schedule D Case I loss of 60,000

Dividend of 130,000
Underlying tax rate of 35%
Withholding tax of 16,250

Overseas Subsidiary

UK corporation tax computation

Dividend (including withholding tax)	130,000
Underlying tax: (130,000 × 35/65)	70,000
Sch D Case V	200,000
Less: Sch D Case I loss	60,000
Profit chargeable to corporation tax	140,000
UK corporation tax @ 30%	42,000
Less: double tax relief	(42,000)*
UK tax payable	Nil

*All underlying tax – restricted to UK tax payable.

Case A eligible unrelieved foreign tax calculation

Maximum creditable tax 45% (200,000* 45%)	90,000
Actual creditable tax (withholding tax and capped underlying tax)	76,250
Tax credited (underlying tax)	42,000
Case A eligible unrelieved foreign tax (withholding tax of 16,250 and underlying tax of 18,000)	(34,250)

Case B eligible unrelieved foreign tax calculation

Mixer cap @ 45% (200,000* 45%)	90,000
Actual underlying tax	70,000
Creditable underlying tax @ 30%	60,000
Case B eligible unrelieved foreign tax (underlying tax)	10,000

Calculation of eligible unrelieved foreign tax in a dividend chain

4.55   Since the mixer cap can potentially apply at any level in a dividend chain, Case B eligible unrelieved foreign tax can also arise at any level in the dividend chain where the mixer cap applies.

For dividends paid directly to the UK both Case A and Case B eligible unrelieved foreign tax can arise. However, only Case B eligible unrelieved foreign tax can arise in respect of dividends lower down the chain. It must be remembered here that the mixer cap and calculation of eligible unrelieved foreign tax are two entirely separate calculations.

Where a number of dividends are paid through a chain of companies, the Case B eligible unrelieved foreign tax arising on the Schedule D Case V dividend is established by calculating the aggregate of the upper limit amounts at each level in the dividend chain and deducting from this aggregate figure the restricted tax which is creditable against the UK tax liability on the Schedule D Case V dividend. [*s 806B(3)–(10)*]. It is therefore necessary to consider the dividend included at each level including all lower level dividends unless the mixer cap applies.

4.56   There are certain restrictions to prevent the generation of eligible unrelieved foreign taxes in excess of 45%. Specifically, it is necessary to calculate the upper limit amount at each level in the dividend chain. The upper limit amount on a dividend that is not subject to a mixer cap is calculated by considering the combined dividend at that level, i.e. including all lower level dividends. However, if a dividend paid by a company is subject to a mixer cap, the upper limit amount on the dividend is calculated by ignoring all lower level dividends and taxes on those dividends [*s 806B(4),(5)*], i.e. the upper limit amount is based purely on that company's own profits and the underlying tax paid on those profits.

The purpose of the legislation is to prevent double counting of taxes paid in a dividend chain. Broadly, in calculating eligible unrelieved foreign tax, all lower level taxes are ignored to the extent that they are included in another calculation of an upper limit amount. An example of the calculation of the upper limit amount is set out below (Example 55).

4.57   There are two different sets of rules for the calculation of the upper limit amount. The first applies to Schedule D Case V dividends, i.e. dividends paid directly to the UK. The second set of rules applies to lower level dividends. In particular it should be noted that a Schedule D Case V dividend can carry a deemed underlying tax credit in relation to dividends from UK companies lower down the chain which are held by an intermediate offshore holding company. The treatment of UK companies in dividend chains is covered in further detail at 4.70 below. If a mixer cap does not apply to the Schedule D Case V dividend, the upper limit is the actual amount of underlying tax attaching to the dividend. [*s 806B(4)(a)*].

Where the mixer cap applies to the Schedule D Case V dividend, the upper limit is calculated by applying a rate of 45% to the dividend after deducting from the Schedule D Case V dividend all lower level dividends and taxes on those dividends. This means that only the profits and taxes arising at the level of the company immediately below the UK company that is paying the dividend are considered in calculating the upper limit. [*s 806B(4)(b)*].

Where the dividend is a lower level dividend and the mixer cap does not apply to that dividend, the upper limit is the tax on that dividend. [*s 806B(5)(a)*]. If the mixer cap applies to a lower level dividend, the upper limit amount is calculated by applying a rate of 45% to the dividend after deducting from that dividend all lower level dividends and taxes on those dividends. [*s 806B(5)(c)*].

If the lower level dividend subject to a mixer cap is a UK dividend, the upper limit amount is the restricted amount of underlying tax on the dividend, i.e. a 30% underlying tax rate is assumed on the UK dividend. [*s 806B(5)(b)*]. This means that high UK underlying tax rates will not generate eligible unrelieved foreign tax.

Example 55 below sets out how upper limit amounts of eligible unrelieved foreign tax are calculated. Again, it is assumed that the dividends in this example are each paid on 30 June 2001 and that this is also the accounting year end of each of the companies.

Example 55

Eligible unrelieved foreign tax – upper limit amounts

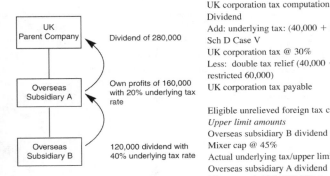

UK corporation tax computation	
Dividend	280,000
Add: underlying tax: (40,000 + 80,000)	120,000
Sch D Case V	400,000
UK corporation tax @ 30%	120,000
Less: double tax relief (40,000 + restricted 60,000)	(100,000)
UK corporation tax payable	20,000
Eligible unrelieved foreign tax calculation	
Upper limit amounts	
Overseas subsidiary B dividend	
Mixer cap @ 45%	90,000
Actual underlying tax/upper limit	80,000
Overseas subsidiary A dividend	
Mixer cap @ 45% (280,000 + 120,000) × 45%	180,000
Actual underlying tax	120,000
Less: B dividend upper limit	(80,000)
A dividend upper limit	40,000
Aggregate upper limits	120,000
Less: tax credited	(100,000)
Eligible unrelieved foreign tax	20,000

(Diagram labels: UK Parent Company; Dividend of 280,000; Overseas Subsidiary A; Own profits of 160,000 with 20% underlying tax rate; Overseas Subsidiary B; 120,000 dividend with 40% underlying tax rate)

The underlying tax rate on the overseas company B dividend is 40% and it is therefore subject to a mixer cap. The upper limit amount is the creditable tax if the mixer cap were applied at 45% and this is the actual underlying tax of 80,000.

The overseas company A dividend is not subject to a mixer cap. Therefore the upper limit amount is the underlying tax on the dividend. This is the 40,000 from overseas company A and the 80,000 from overseas company B. Because the upper limit amount of 80,000 from overseas company B is already included in overseas company B's upper limit amount, A's upper limit amount must be reduced by 80,000.

The total upper limit amounts are therefore 120,000. The creditable tax on the Schedule D Case V dividend is 100,000 (being 40,000 from A and the restricted 60,000 from B). Therefore, the eligible unrelieved foreign tax is 20,000.

4.58   In Example 56 below, overseas company B pays a dividend of 150,000 with underlying tax of 50,000 to overseas company A. Overseas company A has its own profits of 100,000 with underlying tax of 50,000. Overseas company A pays a combined dividend of 250,000 to the UK. This dividend carries an underlying tax rate of 37.5% and a mixer cap will apply at the level of overseas company A. Again, it is assumed in Examples 56 and 57 below that the dividends are each paid on 30 June 2001 and that this is also the accounting year end of each of the companies.

Example 56

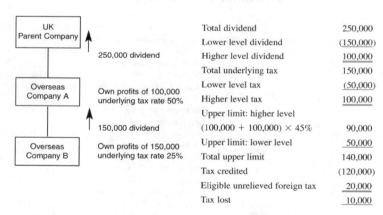

Eligible unrelieved foreign tax calculation

Total dividend	250,000
Lower level dividend	(150,000)
Higher level dividend	100,000
Total underlying tax	150,000
Lower level tax	(50,000)
Higher level tax	100,000
Upper limit: higher level	
(100,000 + 100,000) × 45%	90,000
Upper limit: lower level	50,000
Total upper limit	140,000
Tax credited	(120,000)
Eligible unrelieved foreign tax	20,000
Tax lost	10,000

In calculating the upper limit amount on the overseas company A dividend, the 45% limit is applied to overseas company A's dividend after deducting all lower level dividends and underlying taxes on those dividends. This means deducting the 150,000 dividend from overseas company B leaving profits of 100,000. Taking the total tax on the overseas company A dividend and deducting the underlying tax attributable to the overseas company B dividend leaves 100,000 being the tax attributable to overseas company A's own profits. Applying the mixer cap at 45% to the sum of the two amounts (i.e. 100,000 + 100,000), the upper limit amount is 90,000.

The aggregated upper limit amount on the dividend to the UK is the 90,000 arising at the level of overseas company A and the 50,000 arising at the level of overseas company B giving a total of 140,000. The creditable tax on the dividend is 120,000 with eligible unrelieved foreign tax of 20,000. Therefore, of 150,000 tax paid on the dividend, credit has been given for 120,000, eligible unrelieved foreign tax of 20,000 has been generated and 10,000 is lost.

The above example illustrates the principle that taxes in excess of 45% should not generally give rise to eligible unrelieved foreign tax. In particular, reducing the tax rate on a combined dividend below 45% by paying a low tax dividend into a high tax company will not allow eligible unrelieved tax to be generated on taxes in excess of 45%. However, this kind of structure can still achieve a form of mixing of underlying tax rates following the *FA 2000* changes (see Example 44).

4.59   The application of the upper limit can result in loss of relief for foreign tax even where the effective rate of foreign tax is less than 45% (see Example 57 below).

Example 57

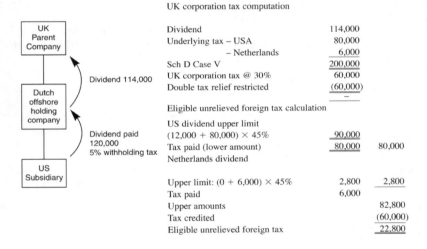

UK corporation tax computation

Dividend	114,000
Underlying tax – USA	80,000
– Netherlands	6,000
Sch D Case V	200,000
UK corporation tax @ 30%	60,000
Double tax relief restricted	(60,000)
	–

Eligible unrelieved foreign tax calculation

US dividend upper limit

(12,000 + 80,000) × 45%	90,000	
Tax paid (lower amount)	80,000	80,000
Netherlands dividend		
Upper limit: (0 + 6,000) × 45%	2,800	2,800
Tax paid	6,000	
Upper amounts		82,800
Tax credited		(60,000)
Eligible unrelieved foreign tax		22,800

Diagram labels: UK Parent Company; Dutch offshore holding company; US Subsidiary. Dividend 114,000. Dividend paid 120,000 5% withholding tax.

In this example, a US company pays a dividend of 12,000 with an underlying tax rate of 40% to a Dutch company. The dividend is subject to 5% withholding tax (the tax charged is 6,000). This withholding tax suffered is treated as underlying tax in the Dutch company under *section 801(1)(b)*. The US dividend is subject to a mixer cap. The Dutch dividend is also subject to a mixer cap. The underlying tax rate on the Dutch dividend paid of 114,000 is 43%, i.e. less than 45%. The underlying tax on the dividend is the 80,000 in the US dividend and the 6,000 suffered by the Dutch company in the form of US withholding tax.

In calculating the upper limit amount at the level of the Dutch company, lower level dividends and taxes must be ignored. The Dutch profits are nil after deducting the US dividend which is a lower level dividend. After deducting the US underlying tax of 80,000 the underlying tax of the Dutch company is 6,000. Applying the mixer cap formula to the amount of Dutch profits of nil and underlying tax of 6,000 results in an upper limit amount of 2,800 (i.e. 6,000 × 45%). Although the Dutch tax is 6,000 it is necessary to take the lower figure as the upper limit amount.

The aggregate of the upper limit amounts is 82,800 being 80,000 from the US and 2,800 at the Dutch level. The actual tax creditable in the UK is 60,000 and therefore eligible unrelieved foreign tax is 122,800. Of the total foreign tax paid of 86,000 in total, 3,200 has been lost completely, i.e. although the overall tax rate on the dividend is only 43% (i.e. less than 45% credit for foreign tax is still lost).

4.60   The previous examples all assume that there is full distribution of dividends up a chain. However, this may not necessarily occur in practice. If eligible unrelieved foreign tax arises on a lower level dividend and only a part of that dividend is paid up by the next company up the dividend chain, not all of the eligible unrelieved foreign tax on the lower level dividend will crystallise. Instead the actual eligible unrelieved foreign tax arising on the dividend paid to the UK will be the appropriate portion of the total eligible unrelieved foreign tax on the lower level dividend.

The appropriate portion is found by multiplying the total eligible unrelieved foreign tax by the reducing fractions at the stages of each of the higher-level dividends. [s 806B(6)]. The reducing fraction represents the dividend paid by the higher level company over the total relevant profits in that company. [s 806B(7)]. An example of this is set out below. Again, it is assumed that each of the dividends is paid on 30 June 2001 and that this is the accounting year end of each of the companies

Example 58

Reducing fractions – example

			Reducing fractions
Dividend income	200,000		
Own income	400,000		A Dividend = 240,000/480,000
Tax	(120,000)		B Dividend = 200,000/280,000
Profit after tax	480,000		
Dividend paid	240,000		Eligible unrelieved foreign tax on
			C dividend = 20,000
Dividend income	120,000		
Own income	200,000		Eligible unrelieved foreign tax
Tax	(400,000)		arising on dividend to UK:
Profit after tax	280,000		C dividend eligible unrelieved
			foreign tax of 20,000*
Dividend paid	200,000		200,000/280,000*
			240,000/480,000 = 12,000
Profits of 120,000			
With 40% underlying tax			
Dividend paid	120,000		

In this example, there is a high tax dividend of 120,000 paid by overseas company C on which eligible unrelieved foreign tax of 20,000 arises. (The calculation of eligible unrelieved foreign tax is not shown here but should be clear from previous examples.) The dividend is paid to overseas company B which has relevant profits of 280,000. Overseas company B pays a dividend of 200,000 to overseas company A, which has relevant profits of 480,000. Overseas company A pays a dividend of 240,000 to the UK. The overseas company A and B dividends are not subject to a mixer cap.

As neither overseas company A nor overseas company B fully distribute their profits in the period, not all of the lower level overseas C dividend is paid to the UK. Therefore, not all of the eligible unrelieved foreign tax arising on the C dividend can be realised in the UK.

The reducing fraction at the level of overseas company A is the dividend paid of 240,000 over relevant profits of 480,000. The reducing fraction at the level of overseas company B is the dividend paid of 100 over the relevant profits of 280,000. Multiplying the total eligible unrelieved foreign tax of 20,000 on the overseas company C dividend by these fractions results in eligible unrelieved foreign tax of 12,000.

Where eligible unrelieved foreign tax arises at more than one level in the dividend chain, it will be necessary to apply the reducing fractions on each higher level dividend to the upper limit amounts calculated at each level in the dividend chain. Whilst this is straightforward in principle, calculations where a large number of companies or eligible unrelieved foreign tax calculations are involved are likely to prove onerous in practice.

Eligible unrelieved foreign tax — computational issues

4.61   Eligible unrelieved foreign tax that has arisen from underlying tax can be set off only against related qualifying foreign dividends. Eligible unrelieved foreign tax must therefore be categorised either as 're-lievable underlying tax' or 'relievable withholding tax'. When calculating eligible unrelieved foreign tax in an accounting period it is therefore necessary to separate the amounts arising into underlying tax and with-holding tax before aggregating these amounts into eligible unrelieved foreign tax that is underlying tax and eligible unrelieved foreign tax that is withholding tax.

Eligible unrelieved foreign tax arising under Case B will always be un-derlying tax. However, Case A eligible unrelieved foreign tax can be either withholding tax or underlying tax. For example, underlying tax eligible unrelieved foreign tax that is underlying tax can arise under Case A if a UK company receiving a dividend with, for example, a 30% un-derlying tax rate has offset its tax trading losses against the Schedule D Case V dividend income.

'Relievable underlying tax' can only be set off against the UK tax arising on a 'single related dividend' (see 4.46 above) whereas 'relievable with-holding tax' can be utilised against both 'single related dividends' and 'single unrelated dividends'. [*s 806D(5)*].

In both cases, the set-off can be made against the UK tax liability in the single related (or unrelated) dividend in the same accounting period, accounting periods beginning in the three years prior to the accounting period in which the eligible unrelieved foreign tax arises [*s 806E(2)*] or carried forward indefinitely into future accounting periods.

4.62   The set-off of eligible unrelieved foreign tax against a single re-lated (or unrelated) dividend must not itself cause eligible unrelieved foreign tax to arise. [*s 806D(6)*]. Therefore, the aggregated foreign tax that has been allocated to the single related (and unrelated) dividends must be set off before any eligible unrelieved foreign tax. It should be remembered here that the single related or unrelated dividend may comprise a number of dividends none of which themselves would nor-mally give rise to eligible unrelieved foreign tax since they represent qualifying foreign dividends.

Where eligible unrelieved foreign tax is utilised in the case of a single related dividend under the onshore pooling regime, eligible unrelieved foreign tax that is underlying tax must be used in priority to eligible unrelieved foreign tax that is withholding tax. [*s 806F(1)(c)*]. This rule is beneficial to taxpayers because relievable withholding tax, which can be credited against either single related or unrelated dividends, is preserved.

4.63   If eligible unrelieved foreign tax is carried back, it must be set off in a later accounting period before an earlier one, i.e. on a 'last in first out' basis. For example, eligible unrelieved foreign tax arising in 2004 would be carried back first to 2003 and then to 2002. [*s 806E(3)*].

Where eligible unrelieved foreign tax has arisen over a number of periods, eligible unrelieved foreign tax from the earliest period must be used first, i.e. on a first in first out basis. However, before any amount of eligible unrelieved foreign tax is utilised in respect of a single related or unrelated dividend, credit must always be claimed for the aggregated foreign tax on the single dividend. [*s 806F(1)(a)* and *(b)*].

4.64   To utilise eligible unrelieved foreign tax, a claim must be made specifying the amount of tax to be utilised within six years of the end of the accounting period in which the eligible unrelieved foreign tax arises, or within one year after the end of the accounting period in which the foreign tax is paid, if later. [*s 806G*].

Some examples of the utilisation of eligible unrelieved foreign tax are set out below. It is assumed that all dividends are paid on 30 June 2001 and that this is the accounting year end of each of the companies unless otherwise stated.

Example 59

The UK parent company above has three wholly owned overseas subsidiaries, A, B and C. As a result, any qualifying foreign dividends from these companies will be related dividends. The UK company owns only 8% of the voting power in overseas company D. Therefore any dividends received from overseas company D will be unrelated. It is assumed that none of the overseas companies is a controlled foreign company.

Current year utilisation of eligible unrelieved foreign tax

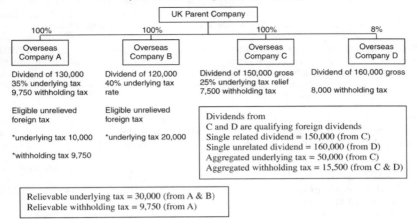

Relievable underlying tax = 30,000 (from A & B)
Relievable withholding tax = 9,750 (from A)

Each of the dividends from overseas companies A, B and C will give rise to Schedule D Case V income of 200,000 when grossed up for underlying tax. This means that the mixer cap in the case of each of these three dividends will be 200,000 at 30%, i.e. 60,000. No underlying tax can be taken into account on the unrelated dividend from overseas company D. Therefore, the mixer cap is not applicable to that dividend.

For overseas company A's dividend the underlying tax is 70,000 and the withholding tax is 9,750. Therefore, Case B eligible unrelieved foreign tax of 10,000 will arise when the mixer cap of 60,000 is applied. As the capped underlying tax is sufficient to offset the UK tax liability, the withholding tax of 9,750 will give rise to Case A eligible unrelieved foreign tax. The total eligible unrelieved foreign tax on overseas company A's dividend is therefore 19,750 which comprises 10,000 of relievable underlying tax and 9,750 of relievable withholding tax.

The dividend from overseas company B carries underlying tax of 80,000. Therefore, it will give rise to Case B eligible unrelieved foreign tax of 20,000 when the mixer cap of 60,000 is applied. The whole of this 20,000 is relievable underlying tax.

The dividend from overseas company C only suffers underlying tax of 50,000. Therefore, the mixer cap does not apply and there is no Case B eligible unrelieved foreign tax. The withholding tax of 7,500 can be fully offset against the UK corporation tax liability on the single unrelated dividend from overseas company D (see below). Therefore, all of the overseas tax suffered on this dividend has been credited and there is no Case A eligible unrelieved foreign tax. Because no eligible unrelieved foreign tax has arisen on C's dividend, it is a qualifying foreign dividend. Overseas company C is 100% owned so its dividend is a related qualifying foreign dividend.

Overseas company D is an unrelated company. Therefore, no underlying tax can be taken into account for UK double tax relief purposes and the dividend from overseas company D cannot give rise to Case B eligible unrelieved foreign tax. The withholding tax of 8,000 is fully offset against the UK tax liability on overseas company D's dividend so there is also no Case A eligible unrelieved foreign tax. As overseas company D's dividend does not give rise to eligible unrelieved foreign tax, the dividend is an unrelated qualifying foreign dividend.

The eligible unrelieved foreign tax arising in the period is aggregated into relievable underlying tax of 30,000 (being 10,000 from overseas company A and 20,000 from overseas company B) and relievable withholding tax of 9,750 (all from overseas company A).

4.65   Dividends and Relief for Underlying Tax

There is one related qualifying foreign dividend of 150,000 from overseas company C which has underlying tax of 50,000 and one unrelated qualifying foreign dividend of 160,000 from overseas company D. The related qualifying foreign dividend is the single related dividend and the unrelated qualifying foreign dividend is the single unrelated dividend.

The aggregated withholding tax is 15,500 (being 7,500 from overseas company C and 8,000 from overseas company D). Any amount of this can be allocated between the single related dividend and the single unrelated dividend at the choice of the taxpayer. In this example, it is more tax efficient to allocate the aggregated withholding tax to the single unrelated dividend as this results in the lowest overall corporation tax charge.

It is then necessary to consider how the eligible unrelieved foreign tax from the overseas company A and overseas company B dividends should be offset against the qualifying foreign dividends from overseas company C and overseas company D.

	Single related dividend	Single unrelated dividend
Single dividend (gross of withholding tax)	150,000	160,000
Aggregated underlying tax	50,000	–
Sch D Case V income	200,000	160,000
UK corporation tax @ 30%	60,000	48,000
Less: Aggregated underlying tax	(50,000)	
Aggregated withholding tax	–	(15,500)
Relievable underlying tax	(10,000)	–
Relievable withholding tax	–	(9,750)
Tax payable	–	22,750

Eligible unrelieved foreign tax (relievable underlying tax) carried forward 20,000

There is no underlying tax to offset against the UK tax liability on the single unrelated dividend, while it is not possible to utilise any relievable underlying tax from the eligible unrelieved foreign tax pool. However, the whole of the aggregated withholding tax of 15,500 that has arisen from qualifying foreign dividends in the year can be credited against the UK tax on the single unrelated dividend along with the relievable withholding tax of 9,750 leaving a residual UK tax liability of 22,750. The remaining relievable underlying tax of 20,000 cannot be used in this period.

4.65   Example 60 below illustrates the order of set-off when eligible unrelieved foreign tax is carried back.

Example 60

Eligible unrelieved foreign tax carried back

Year ended 30 June	2001	2002	2003	2004	2005
Relievable underlying tax	–	–	(14,000)	(4,000)	(50,000)
Relievable withholding tax	–	–	(10,000)	(8,000)	–
Tax on single related dividend	36,000	40,000	–	–	–
Set-off of eligible unrelieved foreign tax					
(1) Accounting period 3 underlying tax	–	(14,000)	14,000	–	–
(2) Accounting period 4 underlying tax	–	(4,000)	–	4,000	–
(3) Accounting period 5 underlying tax (restricted carried back)	–	(22,000)	–	–	22,000
(4) Accounting period 3 withholding tax	(10,000)	–	10,000	–	–
(5) Accounting period 4 withholding tax	(8,000)	–	–	8,000	–
Corporation tax liability/(eligible unrelieved foreign tax)	18,000	–	–	–	(28,000)

In accounting periods one and two, UK corporation tax of 36,000 and 40,000 is payable on the single related dividend for those periods respectively. Eligible unrelieved foreign tax has arisen in accounting periods three, four and five. There is relievable underlying tax of 14,000, 4,000 and 50,000 in accounting periods three, four and five respectively and relievable withholding tax of 10,000 and 8,000 in accounting periods three and four respectively.

The two key rules that this example illustrates are:

- eligible unrelieved foreign tax that arises from underlying tax must be used before eligible unrelieved foreign tax that arises from withholding tax [*s 806F(1),(c)*]; and

- where eligible unrelieved foreign tax is utilised, it is eligible unrelieved foreign tax that arises in the earliest period which is used first. [*s 806E(4)(b)*].

Therefore, the eligible unrelieved foreign tax to be offset first is the relievable underlying tax of 14,000 in accounting period three. The carry-back to prior years is on a 'last in, first out' basis and the set-off is against the tax liability of 40,000 in accounting period two. The relievable underlying tax which next arises is in accounting period four and this is also offset against the tax liability of accounting period two.

In accounting period five there is relievable underlying tax of 50,000, which can be carried back a maximum of three years to accounting period two. However, after offsetting the relievable underlying tax from accounting periods three and four, the remaining tax liability in accounting period two is only 22,000. Therefore, the excess relievable underlying tax of 28,000 must be carried forward for offset in accounting periods following accounting period five.

As far as relievable withholding tax is concerned, it is again necessary to start with accounting period three which has relievable withholding tax of 10,000. The carry-back for relievable withholding tax is also on a 'last in, first out' basis. Therefore, relievable withholding tax is carried back to the later accounting periods before the earlier ones. There is no UK tax liability remaining in accounting period two so it is necessary to consider accounting period one.

The relievable withholding tax in accounting periods three and four can be carried back to accounting period one. The overall result is a tax liability of 18,000 in accounting period one and unused eligible unrelieved foreign tax that is relievable underlying tax of 28,000 in accounting period five.

4.65   In addition to being carried forward and carried back, eligible unrelieved foreign tax can also be surrendered from one UK company to another within a qualifying group. The rules for surrender of eligible unrelieved foreign tax are dealt with in regulations (*SI 2001 No 1163*) that came into force on 31 March 2001 in respect of dividends paid to UK resident companies on or after that date. The definition of a group is broadly the same as for group relief, although consortium companies are excluded.

The amount of eligible unrelieved foreign tax that can be surrendered is the amount remaining after all possible current year and prior year set-offs (even if the claims are not actually made). Therefore, in practical terms, a surrender of eligible unrelieved foreign tax is only possible if the only alternative is to carry it forward.

The claimant company treats the eligible unrelieved foreign tax surrendered as if it had arisen in that company in that accounting period.

Therefore the claimant company can carry the surrendered eligible un-relieved foreign tax back and forward subject to the usual rules.

A claim to surrender eligible unrelieved foreign tax can be made at any time within six years from the end of the accounting period in which the eligible unrelieved foreign tax arose or within one year of the end of the accounting period in which the foreign tax is paid, if later. The surrendering and claimant company must be members of the same group throughout the surrendering company's accounting period in which the eligible unrelieved foreign tax actually arose.

It should be noted that two or more claimant companies may make claims relating to the same surrendering company and to the same accounting period of that surrendering company. Payments for group relief can be made up to the amount surrendered without the payment being treated as taxable in the hands of the recipient. Eligible unrelieved foreign tax cannot be surrendered by a company which is a dual resident investment company as defined by *TA 1988, s 404*, nor can relief be given more than once in respect of the same amount of eligible unrelieved foreign tax. In addition, there are special rules dealing with life assurance companies.

Acceptable distribution policy dividends paid by controlled foreign companies

4.66   By way of background, a controlled foreign company is an overseas resident company controlled by UK residents, the overseas tax paid on the profits of which is less than three-quarters of the UK tax it would have paid had the company been UK tax resident.

Broadly, a UK company that controls at least 25% of a controlled foreign company is subject to an apportionment on the controlled foreign company's profits unless one of the controlled foreign company exemptions applies. Such an apportionment results in the UK company paying corporation tax on its share of the controlled foreign company's profits.

An example of one of the exemptions mentioned above is where the overseas subsidiary pays at least 90% of its net chargeable taxable profits back to the UK as a dividend. This is known as the acceptable distribution policy. This dividend is then taxed in the UK as Schedule D Case V income (with credit for any attributable underlying tax).

4.67   Under the pre-*FA 2000* double tax relief rules, groups could arrange for acceptable distribution policy dividends to be paid through an offshore mixer company and mix the low tax acceptable distribution policy dividend with high taxed dividends. The purpose of this was to increase the underlying tax rate on the acceptable distribution policy dividend when it was paid up to the UK. The controlled foreign company could satisfy the acceptable distribution policy without giving rise to a significant UK tax charge as long as the dividend paid by the offshore holding company was sufficient to ensure that at least 90% of the controlled foreign company's net chargeable profits reached the UK.

To prevent this mixing occurring onshore under the new rules [*s 801C*] where an acceptable distribution policy dividend is paid directly to the UK, that dividend will not be a qualifying foreign dividend and therefore any residual UK tax liability on the dividend cannot be offset by eligible unrelieved foreign tax.

Where the acceptable distribution policy dividend is paid to the UK via an offshore holding company, the amount of the holding company's dividend that represents the acceptable distribution policy dividend will be ring-fenced and treated as a separate source of Schedule D Case V income. This amount of the dividend will not be a qualifying foreign dividend. In effect the acceptable distribution policy streaming rules effectively identify and ring-fence acceptable distribution policy dividends paid through offshore holding companies. The balance of the dividend paid by the offshore holding company may represent a qualify-ing foreign dividend subject to the normal rules.

It should be noted that *section 801C* only applies in the context of acceptable distribution policy dividends. Where a controlled foreign company pays a dividend that does not satisfy the acceptable distribution policy test, *section 801C* is not in point.

4.68   An acceptable distribution policy paid by a controlled foreign company to an offshore holding company is called an 'initial dividend'. The offshore holding company is called an 'intermediate company'. If the intermediate company is treated as paying a dividend out of an initial dividend, that dividend is called an 'intermediate dividend'. Dividends which are not in any part onward payments of initial dividends are called 'independent dividends'.

For the dividend paid by the intermediate company to represent an acceptable distribution policy from its controlled foreign company subsidiaries, the intermediate company may need to specify that its dividend represents the dividend it has received. This will be particularly relevant where the intermediate company does not distribute all of its profits. Care therefore needs to be taken with the specification in the dividend resolution of the intermediate company to ensure that the acceptable distribution policy is met. Although it is no longer possible to specify the profits out of which a dividend is paid for double tax relief purposes following the repeal of *section 799(3)(b)* the Inland Revenue has confirmed that it will continue to allow dividends from intermediate companies to be specified as sourced out of dividends received from lower tier companies that are controlled foreign companies, to enable the latter companies to satisfy an acceptable distribution policy for the purposes of *Schedule 25, paragraph 3(5)*.

Where the intermediate dividend which is specified as representing the initial dividend is less than or equal to the initial dividend, the whole of the intermediate dividend is treated as a separate acceptable distribution policy dividend. Where such an intermediate dividend is greater than the initial dividend received, it is treated as two separate dividends: an acceptable distribution policy dividend equal to the amount of the initial dividend specified by the intermediate company and a residual dividend.

The acceptable distribution policy dividend is treated as if it were paid by a separate company the relevant profits of which consist of the amount of acceptable distribution policy dividend and the tax on the profits of which is the tax paid by the controlled foreign company on its initial dividend (or the appropriate proportion of that tax). Mixing of high taxes in the intermediate holding company with the initial dividend received from the controlled foreign company is therefore restricted. This treatment of an acceptable controlled policy dividend as a separate dividend paid by a separate company is applied through any number of intermediate holding companies until the acceptable distribution policy dividend reaches the UK.

For the purposes of giving double tax relief in relation to the non-acceptable distribution policy dividend income in the intermediate company (i.e. on residual and independent dividends), the intermediate company's relevant profits are broadly its profits after deducting the initial dividends received. The creditable overseas tax is the taxes suffered on those profits alone.

If the intermediate company is itself a controlled foreign company and that company also receives an acceptable distribution policy dividend from a lower level controlled foreign company, then the profits and underlying tax of the intermediate company are also kept separate for double tax relief purposes from the acceptable distribution policy dividend which it receives. Again, care may be required to ensure the appropriate specification in the wording of the intermediate company's dividend resolution to ensure that it too can satisfy the acceptance distribution policy test.

4.69   An example of the application of *section 801C* is set out below.

Example 61

In this example, the intermediate foreign company is not a controlled foreign company. It is assumed that dividend 1 and the controlled foreign company's dividend are paid on 30 June 2001 and that this is the accounting year end of each of the companies. The controlled foreign company's dividend is paid in respect of the year ended 30 June 2001. Dividends 2 and 3 are paid on 30 July and 31 August 2001 respectively.

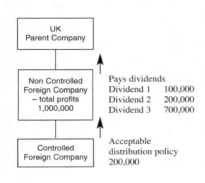

Dividend 1: Separate acceptable distribution policy dividend	100,000
Dividend 2: Separate acceptable distribution policy dividend	100,000
Residual dividend	100,000
Dividend 3: Independent dividend	700,000
Relevant profits of intermediate company are:	
Dividend 1: Separate company 1	100,000
Dividend 2: 'Separate' company 1	100,000
'Separate' company 2	100,000
Dividend 3: Residual and independent dividend	700,000

Next to the diagram:

Pays dividends
Dividend 1   100,000
Dividend 2   200,000
Dividend 3   700,000

Acceptable distribution policy
200,000

The intermediate offshore company specifies that its dividend of 100,000 paid on 30 June 2001 is paid out of the acceptable distribution policy dividend received from the controlled foreign company. This dividend of 100,000 is not sufficient to allow the controlled foreign company to satisfy the acceptable distribution policy as 90% of its net chargeable profits have not been paid up to the UK. Therefore, when the intermediate offshore company pays dividend 2 to the UK it specifies that 100,000 of the dividend represents the remainder of the dividend of 200,000 which it received from the controlled foreign company.

For double tax relief purposes, dividend 1 and 100,000 of dividend 2 will be treated as if they were paid to the UK by a separate company the relevant profits of which comprise the dividend received from the controlled foreign company. This means that the dividend from the controlled foreign company cannot be mixed with other profits (e.g. high tax profits) within the intermediate offshore company. The underlying tax rate on the remainder of dividend 2 (which is not specified as being paid out of the dividend received from the controlled foreign company) and/or dividend 3 is based on the remainder of the relevant profits within the offshore holding company. The remainder of dividend 2 and 3 may represent qualifying foreign dividends if they satisfy the normal conditions.

Effect of a UK company in the dividend chain

4.70   Where a UK company pays a dividend to an overseas company and the overseas company then pays the dividend to the UK, the dividend will be taxed as Schedule D Case V income.

Prior to *FA 2001*, double tax relief in this situation was calculated in the normal way by comparing the relevant profits of the UK subsidiary with the UK corporation tax which it had paid. Although it would be natural for the underlying tax rate to be 30% in this situation, because it was calculated by reference to the tax paid and accounting profits, it could be above or below 30%. This could result in further UK tax becoming payable despite the fact that the underlying profits of the UK subsidiary had already been taxed in the UK.

To prevent this, new provisions have been introduced [*s 801(4A)–(4B)*] which deem the underlying tax rate of a dividend which has been paid by a UK tax resident company to be 30% in spite of the actual underlying tax rate.

Therefore, if the actual underlying tax rate is below 30%, an additional deemed credit is given to increase the underlying tax rate to 30% (see Example 62 below). However, this additional deemed credit is not used to gross up the dividend for the purposes of arriving at the measure of the Schedule D Case V income and is ignored in calculating any eligible unrelieved foreign tax arising on other dividends which may be mixed with the UK dividend in a chain of companies. [s 806B(4)(a)].

If the underlying tax rate is above 30%, the mixer cap will apply limiting the rate to 30%. The excess will not give rise to any eligible unrelieved foreign tax [s 806B(5)(b)] — see Example 63 below. However, although the mixer cap will apply to the UK dividend, if it is mixed with low tax dividends, the overall dividend will not be tainted. This is because a dividend is only tainted if eligible unrelieved foreign tax has arisen on that dividend at any point in the dividend chain and no eligible unrelieved foreign tax arises on UK dividends with high underlying tax rates.

Example 62

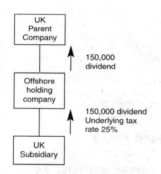

UK corporation tax computation		
Dividend		150,000
Underlying tax		50,000
Sch D Case V		200,000
UK corporation tax @ 30%		60,000
Double tax relief	– actual	(50,000)
	– deemed	10,000
UK corporation tax payable		Nil
Deemed credit:		
Mixer cap amount (150,000		
+ 50,000) × 30%		60,000
Actual underlying tax		(50,000)
Excess = deemed credit		10,000

Diagram labels: UK Parent Company; 150,000 dividend; Offshore holding company; 150,000 dividend Underlying tax rate 25%; UK Subsidiary.

Example 63

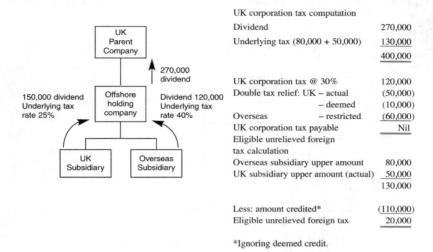

UK corporation tax computation

Dividend	270,000
Underlying tax (80,000 + 50,000)	130,000
	400,000

UK corporation tax @ 30%	120,000
Double tax relief: UK – actual	(50,000)
– deemed	(10,000)
Overseas – restricted	(60,000)
UK corporation tax payable	Nil
Eligible unrelieved foreign	
tax calculation	
Overseas subsidiary upper amount	80,000
UK subsidiary upper amount (actual)	50,000
	130,000
Less: amount credited*	(110,000)
Eligible unrelieved foreign tax	20,000

*Ignoring deemed credit.

A key point to note in Example 63 is that when calculating the amount of Case B eligible unrelieved foreign tax that arises on the dividend from the offshore holding company to the UK, it is necessary to aggregate the upper amounts arising from the UK subsidiary and overseas subsidiary dividends (50,000 plus 80,000 is 130,000) and subtract the double tax relief credited in the UK from this amount. For this purpose the deemed credit of 10,000 on the UK dividend is ignored and only the actual amounts of underlying tax credited (i.e. 110,000 is deducted). Therefore, there is Case B eligible unrelieved foreign tax of 20,000 rather than 10,000.

Foreign taxation of a group as a single entity

4.71   In some countries, e.g. the US and the Netherlands, groups of companies may pay tax on a consolidated basis. In this situation, the profits and losses of group companies are aggregated and the tax is paid by a nominated company in the group on the aggregated profits. Prior to *FA 2000*, the double tax relief legislation [*ss 790(6)* and *s 799(1)*] implied that underlying tax relief was available where the company paying the dividend had also paid the tax on the profits out of which the dividend was paid. In countries where tax consolidations existed this could have potentially given rise to severe restrictions in the relief that could be claimed since in many cases the company that paid the tax was not necessarily the same as the company that paid the dividend. However, in practice the Inland Revenue allowed the tax paid by the nominated company to be allocated to individual companies in the tax consolidation in proportion to their taxable profits. Therefore, each company in the group had an amount of tax allocated to it which was treated as the tax paid by that company on its own profits (see Example 64 below).

Example 64

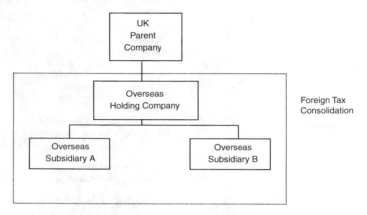

	Overseas holding company	*Overseas subsidiary A*	*Overseas subsidiary B*	*Total*
Total taxable profit/(loss)	(100,000)	200,000	150,000	250,000
Foreign corporate tax @ 30%			75,000	75,000
Local taxes paid		10,000	5,000	15,000
Total foreign tax				90,000
Accounting profit after tax	50,000	150,000	175,000	375,000
Underlying tax				
— corporate tax*	Nil	42,857	32,143	
— local tax	Nil	10,000	5,000	
	Nil	52,857	37,143	
Underlying tax rate	Nil	26.06%	17.51%	

* The foreign corporate tax is allocated based on the ratio of taxable profits (ignoring loss making companies). Therefore, tax is allocated between overseas subsidiaries A and B respectively in the ratio 200,000:150,000.

FA 2000 introduced a new treatment for tax consolidated groups, which is set out in *section 803A*. The rules apply to dividends paid to the UK on or after 21 March 2000 although certain transitional practices apply (see 4.72 below). Companies in a tax consolidation are now treated as a single entity for double tax relief purposes. In calculating relevant profits and underlying tax rates, all relevant profits and losses of the individual companies for the year are aggregated and taken as the relevant profits of the single entity. The taxes paid both at group and individual company levels are aggregated and taken as the tax paid on the single entity's profits. This results in a group underlying tax rate for an accounting period which applies to the relevant profits of each individual company in the group.

Therefore, applying the new rules to Example 64 above would give a group underlying tax rate of 19.35%, i.e. it would be necessary to compare total tax paid in the group of 90,000 with the total relevant profits of 375,000 so that the tax would be allocated as follows:

	Overseas holding company	Overseas subsidiary A	Overseas subsidiary B	Total
Relevant profits	50,000	150,000	175,000	375,000
Tax	12,000	36,000	42,000	90,000
Underlying tax rate				19.35%

It should be noted that *section 803A* only applies where a single company resident in the same territory as the other companies in the overseas tax group pays the tax on behalf of the group and a consolidated tax return is filed so that the companies in the group are treated as if they were a single entity for the purposes of the relevant foreign tax law. Therefore, *section 803A* will not apply to foreign groups which do not pay tax on such a basis or file a consolidated tax return, even if the same result is effectively achieved in practice by the surrender of tax attributes among group companies.

Section 803A problem areas

4.72   A number of complications can arise when applying *section 803A* in practice. Most of these are dealt with in Issue 54 of the Inland Revenue *Tax Bulletin* but some of the key points are highlighted below.

Where a group acquires a new company, the Inland Revenue takes the view that it is necessary to adjust the single entity's relevant profits and taxes for the profits or losses of the company acquired and the tax paid on these profits on a year-by-year basis. Similarly where a company leaves a group, it will be necessary to adjust the single entity's relevant profit of the profits of the disposed company which are no longer in the group again, on a year-by-year basis.

In both cases, it is necessary to allocate tax to the profits of the company acquired or sold. The allocation of tax on an acquisition or disposal is straightforward in situations where there are no losses in any of the group companies, i.e. the Inland Revenue takes the view that the allocation should be done by comparing the relevant profits of the company acquired or sold with the total relevant profits of the single entity. However, if there is a company in the group with a loss, the Inland Revenue considers that a different approach is necessary which involves allocating taxes to individual companies on the basis of taxable profits as opposed to relevant profits to establish the tax attributable to the profits of the company that has been acquired or sold. This approach is broadly the same as that used for allocating tax in a consolidated group prior to the introduction of *section 803A*.

Another complication that can arise in practice is that the rules only apply to corporate entities resident in the same territory. If the tax consolidation includes as its 'parent' entity a non-corporate entity like a partnership or a branch of a company resident in another territory, the profits and tax of such entities need to be excluded from the single entity. If the non-corporate entity company pays the tax on behalf of the foreign tax group, the tax consolidated group treatment does not apply at all and it will be necessary to continue to allocate taxes to individual entities on the basis of taxable profits.

Section 803A is framed so that only companies that are resident as a matter of fact in the country concerned may be included in the calculations of relevant profits and foreign tax for the deemed single entity. Therefore, a dual resident company is only included in the calculation of underlying tax for the group as a single entity, if it satisfies the criteria for inclusion as set out in SI 2001/1156.

4.73   The new rules apply to dividends paid to the UK after 21 March 2000, but the Inland Revenue allowed taxpayers to continue to apply the old basis for dividends paid to the UK before 31 March 2001 in order to give taxpayers time to get to grips with the new rules. The Inland Revenue has also indicated that where the underlying tax rate for a particular accounting period has been previously calculated under the individual company basis, to avoid the costs of recalculating underlying tax rates, they may allow the old basis to be used until all the profits of the relevant accounting period have been paid up to the UK including post-30 March 2001. However, it will be necessary to agree this treatment with the Inland Revenue on a case-by-case basis.

Foreign mergers

4.74   In many countries, a legal merger can occur whereby one company is merged into another company leaving a single surviving company. The profits of the merging company may become the profits of the surviving company and the surviving company may be able to distribute those profits as dividends. Prior to *FA 2000*, the Inland Revenue took the position that the surviving company which distributed the profits had not paid the tax on those profits and therefore no double tax relief was available. In some circumstances, where it was shown that the merged company continued to exist within the surviving company or where the surviving company was liable for the taxes on the profits of the merged company, the Inland Revenue was prepared to give double tax relief although there was no strict statutory mechanism for this.

FA 2000 introduced a rule contained in *section 801B* allowing double tax relief in cases where the profits of one company become the profits of another company other than by way of payment of a dividend. This rule is intended to deal, among other things, with foreign mergers. The calculation of the underlying tax rate within a German *Organshaft* and on profits accounted for on an equity basis may also fall within *section 801B* (see below).

In the case of a merger, it is assumed that the profits of the merged company were transferred by way of a dividend. As a result, the taxes paid on the transferred profits are treated as taxes paid by the surviving entity. Since it is assumed for the purposes of *section 801B* that a dividend has been paid to the surviving company by the merged company, the mixer cap will apply to limit credit relief for underlying taxes to 30% to the extent that the transfer of profits is cross-border. However, the mixer cap should not normally apply where the merger is between two companies resident in the same territory.

Section 801B applies to dividends paid to the UK out of transferred profits on or after 21 March 2000. Therefore, the new rules will still apply even if the merger took place before this date.

4.75   The Inland Revenue has confirmed that *section 801B* is also intended to deal with the calculation of underlying tax in the case of equity accounted profits. For example, some countries, most notably the Netherlands, allow distributions to be made by a holding company out of equity accounted profits of its subsidiaries rather than the holding company's actual realised profits. If this is the case, the equity accounted profits of the subsidiaries are treated for the purposes of *section 801B* as if they have become the profits of the holding company through the payment of dividends (again, the mixer cap may apply here). Therefore, in calculating the underlying tax rate on a dividend paid by the holding company it will be necessary to calculate the underlying tax rates applicable to the profits of all of its subsidiaries for which the holding company accounts on an equity basis. This may well lead to a significant compliance burden as well as complications with dividend tainting under the onshore pooling regime. Therefore, holding companies with a large number of equity accounted subsidiaries may wish to consider changing their method of accounting to a non-equity basis of accounting if this is permitted under the relevant foreign accounting law.

Extension of relief to UK branches of foreign companies

4.76   *Section 794(2)(bb)* extends underlying tax relief to dividends received by UK branches or agencies of foreign resident companies. This new relief takes effect for chargeable periods ending after 20 March 2000. It should be noted that the amount of relief claimed cannot exceed the amount available had the UK branch or agency instead been a UK resident company.

The future of the UK double tax relief system

4.77   The European Court of Justice has ruled that the Netherlands' restriction of an exemption from Dutch income tax for dividends to dividends (up to a prescribed limit) is contrary to European Law (*Staatssectretaris van Financien v Verkooijen, Case C–35/98*) *[2000] SWTI 884*. Based on this case, there are technical arguments that the exemption from corporation tax for dividends from UK companies under *section 208* should be extended to cover dividends from EU subsidiaries.

4.78   In July 2001, the UK government published a consultation document entitled *Large Business Taxation: The Government's strategy and corporate tax reforms*. This concludes that the UK government would prefer to retain the current UK system of double tax relief as amended by *FA 2000* and *FA 2001* rather than consider the possible introduction of an exemption system for some types of foreign dividends. However, the government included in the document its initial thinking as to how such an exemption system for overseas dividends might operate if it were introduced and invited comments from business on this. The relevant extract from the consultation document is reproduced below. For the time being, however, it appears likely that the existing system will continue to apply for a number of years to come.

'**Annex B**:

Exemption of Foreign Dividends

Background

B.1   Internationally, there are two accepted ways of recognising that dividends from foreign companies may already have borne foreign tax (or have been paid out of profits on which foreign tax has been paid):

- charge tax on dividends received by companies, but reduce this by giving a credit for foreign tax already paid. This is what the UK does currently, along with Japan, the United States and many other countries; or

- exempt from tax some dividends received by companies, in recognition of the foreign tax already paid, while generally operating a credit regime for dividends in respect of which little or no foreign tax has been paid. This is what France does, for example.

B.2   The March 1999 Inland Revenue discussion paper "Double Taxation Relief for Companies" presented the economic and technical arguments on these alternative methods of relieving double taxation. This annex considers what a system of exempting some foreign dividends might look like if it were to be introduced in the UK.

A Minimum Level of Foreign Tax

B.3   A system for exempting certain foreign dividends in the UK would, of course, have to be consistent with fair tax competition. So it would have to avoid fostering harmful tax competition by encouraging, for example, the use of niche tax regimes outside the UK. And an exemption regime should not tilt the playing field unfairly against investment in the UK.

B.4   This suggests that exemption should apply only to dividends paid into the UK out of profits on which a minimum level of foreign tax has been paid. Dividends that did not meet this "minimum level of foreign tax" test would be taxed in the UK, with a credit for any foreign tax suffered, just as they are now.

B.5   The working assumption might be to mirror the controlled foreign companies (CFC) legislation so that an exemption system for the UK would apply to foreign dividends paid out of profits that had been subject to foreign tax of at least 75 per cent of the UK corporation tax rate (currently up to 30 per cent) – i.e. 22.5 per cent.

B.6   This could be calculated (like the CFC rules) as 22.5 per cent of what the foreign profits would be if they were calculated according to UK tax rules; or as 22.5 per cent of the foreign company's distributable profits calculated according to the other country's rules (which is how relief for underlying tax is calculated now under the credit method).

Other Approaches

B.7   If it was not possible to devise a satisfactory system based on the criterion of a minimum level of foreign tax, other proxies for a "minimum level of foreign tax" test might be easier to apply in practice.

B.8   One approach might be automatically to exempt dividends paid by foreign associates or subsidiaries in specified listed countries – such as those with which the UK has a tax treaty (which until recently was the German approach) or those with tax systems or rates broadly comparable to the UK's (which is the basis of the Australian approach).

B.9   On the one hand, the sheer size of the UK's tax treaty network, including some with countries with effective tax rates well below the main UK corporation tax rate might make the treaty approach inappropriate. On the other hand, a more sophisticated approach (like that used for the excluded countries test in the CFC rules) would inevitably be very complicated if it were to avoid running the risk of exempting dividends that have been taxed at a rate well below the UK corporation tax rate or been routed into the UK through listed countries.

B.10   Another approach might be to exempt dividends paid out of specified types of profit but to tax others (as France and Canada do) but this could also have high compliance costs for business.

Interaction with a Capital Gains Exemption for Substantial Shareholdings

B.11   A "minimum level of foreign tax" test, or one of the approaches explored in the preceding paragraphs, would restrict the range of companies from which dividends would be exempt. If the Government decided to introduce an exemption regime of this sort for dividends, consideration would need to be given as to whether such a restriction should be reflected in the exemption for gains on substantial shareholdings in foreign companies.

Dividends from CFCs

B.12   The CFC legislation prevents UK groups avoiding tax in this country by diverting income to subsidiaries in tax havens and in countries with preferential tax regimes. One of the main exclusions from the rules is where the CFC pays a dividend to its UK parent (the acceptable distribution policy or ADP exemption). The ADP works on the assumption that the dividend will be taxed in the UK. It would clearly be ineffective if dividends paid by CFCs were automatically exempted from tax. Dividends paid by a CFC in order to meet the ADP test for exclusion from the CFC regime would continue to be taxed in the UK. As now, a credit would be allowed for foreign tax attributable to such dividends.

Impact on Dividend Pooling

B.13 Dividends that were not exempted would continue to be subject to UK tax, with a credit for foreign tax. In the case of dividends that were exempted, neither they nor the foreign tax attributable to them would be able to be included in the onshore pooling regime introduced by Finance Act 2000. High levels of foreign tax on some dividends could not, therefore, be used to cover UK tax liability on other dividends with low levels of foreign tax if the latter were not exempted.

B.14 Again, it would be necessary to prevent such rules being circumvented by routing dividends into the UK through companies whose own dividends would qualify for exemption.

Control Threshold

B.15 If an exemption system were introduced, this would have to be consistent with the EU directive on parent companies and their subsidiaries. The control threshold for allowing relief for underlying tax is 10 per cent of the voting power in the foreign company. The threshold for the EU directive is 25 per cent of the capital of the subsidiary.

B.16 Short of negotiating new bilateral treaties with each Member State, an exemption system would have to be based on the capital of the overseas company. Even assuming that the specified percentage was 10 per cent (which would be more generous than the 25 per cent threshold mentioned in the EU directive), the change of criterion from voting rights to capital might mean in principle that, in some cases, companies whose foreign dividends qualify now for relief for underlying tax would not qualify for exemption.

Branches

B.17 It has already been suggested by some businesses that an exemption of some foreign dividends would have to be matched by an equivalent exemption for the profits of their overseas branches. Crafting an equivalent exemption for foreign branches of UK companies would add considerable complexity to the legislation required. It might also entail the need to create the equivalent of the CFC rules to cater for foreign branches on whose profits little or no overseas tax had been paid.

Tax Treaties

B.18 Tax treaties have been negotiated, or are currently under negotiation, on the basis that the UK taxes dividends received by UK companies from their foreign associates and subsidiaries, subject to a credit for foreign tax. It is not possible to forecast how other countries would react to the introduction of an exemption system into the UK, even if it had the features (such as a "minimum level of foreign tax" test) described in paragraphs B.3 to B.6 above.

B.19 It is already the case that, in around a dozen tax treaties, reductions in other countries' withholding taxes on dividends paid to the UK are given only if the dividends are subject to tax in the UK. Such reductions would not, therefore, be available in the case of dividends that were exempt from UK tax.

B.20 Article 16 of the current tax treaty between the UK and the US would allow the US to charge its full rate of withholding tax on dividends paid to a UK company if these were exempt from UK tax and 25 per cent or more of the capital of the UK company was owned, directly or indirectly, by one or more persons who were not individual residents of the UK and were not nationals of the US.

Summary

B.21 The introduction of an exemption system for some foreign dividends (and, potentially, for some profits of foreign branches) would involve considerable upheaval for businesses affected by the change. A key issue in deciding whether this is a price worth paying is whether the change would lead to considerable simplification. *Views are invited on whether changing to an exemption system on the above lines would be of advantage to business.*'

Chapter 5

Banks, Financial Traders and Insurance Companies

Introduction

5.1   The rules relating to double taxation relief are modified for banks, financial traders and insurance companies, reflecting the special commercial factors affecting these types of business. For accounting periods ending before 21 March 2000, one of the main differences was that tax credit relief was available to non-UK resident banks and life insurance companies by virtue of *TA 1988, s 794(2)(c)* and *Sch 19AC, para 13* respectively. For accounting periods ended after 20 March 2000, double taxation relief on a unilateral basis has now been extended to all non-residents, i.e. not just banks and insurance companies, in respect of income and chargeable gains of a UK branch or agency.

Credit relief for UK branches of banks and life insurance companies

5.2   Non-UK resident persons may claim double taxation relief in respect of interest on loans, subject to the following conditions:

(*a*)   the person in question is a company which, for the chargeable period in question, carries on a banking business in the UK through a branch or agency;

(*b*)   the loan was made by the company through the branch or agency in the UK;

(c)   the territory under whose law the tax was paid is not one in which the company is liable to tax by reason of domicile, residence or place of management; and

(d)   the amount of relief claimed does not exceed (or is by the claim expressly limited to) that which would have been available if the branch or agency had been a company resident in the UK and the loan had been made by it in the course of its banking business.

This relief was first introduced by way of a concession as a result of a Parliamentary answer in 1975 (Hansard, Vol 899, Col 194) and was made available for all accounting periods ending in the 1975 financial year (ended 31 March 1976) onwards. The concession was given statutory authority by *FA 1982, s 67*.

5.3   For chargeable periods beginning after 31 December 1992, non-UK resident life insurance companies have been able to claim credit for foreign tax paid in respect of their UK branch income or UK branch gains, if the following conditions are fulfilled:

(a)   the territory under whose law the tax was paid is not one in which the company is liable to tax by reason of domicile, residence or place of management; and

(b)   the amount of relief claimed does not exceed (or is by the claim expressly limited to) that which would have been available if the branch or agency had been a UK resident insurance company and the income or gains in question had been income or gains of that company.

The terms 'UK branch income' and 'UK branch gains' are defined in terms of income and gains from assets of the company's long-term business fund.

Interest on certain overseas loans

5.4   In 1982 special provisions were introduced restricting the amount of double taxation relief which could be claimed by banks engaged in overseas lending and other financial traders. Generally, when banks (and other financial traders) lend to non-residents they are subject to UK corporation tax only on the net profit from the transaction (i.e. interest receivable less interest expense). However, the interest received may be subject to a withholding tax at a fixed percentage of the gross amount in accordance with the laws of the country of the borrower (as modified by the provisions of a double taxation agreement, if applicable).

Prior to the 1982 provisions, UK resident banks (or UK branches of foreign banks) were entitled to set the full amount of the foreign tax against their UK corporation tax liabilities in respect of their profits as a whole. In this way they were able to lend at lower rates than they would otherwise have been able to, taking advantage of the availability of credit relief in the UK for the full amount of the foreign tax paid. In effect, they could use double taxation relief to reduce their UK corporation tax liabilities on UK source profits.

The 1982 provisions took effect where:

• any person (referred to as 'the lender') was subject to income tax or corporation tax in respect of interest on a loan to a person resident outside the UK;

• expenditure relating to the earning of the foreign loan interest was deductible in determining the liability of the lender to UK corporation tax or income tax; and

• the lender was entitled to double tax credit relief for foreign tax chargeable on or by reference to the foreign loan interest.

The 1982 provisions restricted the amount of double tax relief available on the foreign loan to 15% of the gross amount of the interest. In addition, where the foreign tax payable on the interest comprised, wholly or partly, spared tax (see 3.54), the amount of the spared tax by which the interest could be grossed up and which could be allowed as a credit under a double taxation agreement was limited to 15%. [*TA 1988, s 798(3)*].

5.5   However, the 1982 provisions were of limited effectiveness since credit for the foreign tax continued to be given against the full amount of the foreign loan interest before deduction of the cost of funds borrowed in order to make the loan. As the cost of borrowed funds is deductible for UK corporation tax purposes, in effect tax relief was being given twice. Accordingly, in 1987 further provisions (former *TA 1988, s 798(6)*) were introduced which applied to new loans from 1 April 1987 or from 1 April 1989 to loans already agreed. These now limit the credit for foreign tax to the lower of:

(*a*)   UK tax on net profit from the foreign loan; and

(*b*)   15% of the gross amount of the interest.

The excess tax which is not creditable under these provisions has been deductible as an expense in calculating the UK tax liability, as set out in Example 65 below.

5.6   As a result of the 1987 changes in computing the limit of credit relief, the foreign loan interest was reduced by the amount of the lender's financial expenditure in relation to the loan which was properly attributable to the period for which the interest was paid. The expression 'financial expenditure in relation to a loan' was the aggregate of:

(*a*)   interest and similar sums payable in connection with the provision of the loan, which are either charges on income for corporation tax purposes or are deductible in computing the profits of the lender which are brought within the charge to income or corporation tax;

(*b*)   where the loan is financed by the issue of securities at a discount, the amount of discount which is a charge on income for corporation tax or is deductible for UK tax purposes;

(*c*)   so much as is just and reasonable to attribute to the loan of any interest or other return foregone by a person connected or associated with the lender in connection with the provision of funds to the lender; and

(*d*)   any other sum (whether a refund of tax or interest, or a commission) which is paid by the lender (or a connected or associated person) to the borrower (or a connected or associated person), is deductible for UK tax purposes and is reasonable to regard as referable to the loan or the foreign loan interest. [former *s 798(7)*].

Items (*a*) and (*b*) represented the financial cost to the lender of providing the loan to the overseas borrower and which is deductible for UK tax purposes. Items (*c*) and (*d*) were included to prevent the manipulation of the net profit figure (and thereby also the amount of tax credit available) by certain non-arm's length transactions.

Where the lender's financial expenditure in relation to a loan is not readily ascertainable, the amount is determined by a basis which is just and reasonable having regard, in particular, to market rates of interest. The Board of Inland Revenue has made regulations by statutory instrument [*SI 1999/3330*] to determine such market rates of interest.

Example 65

Deo Bank Plc, which is resident in the UK, made a loan to a foreign client on which it received interest of £750,000 annually. Interest payments were subject to a 20% withholding tax which is deducted under the laws of the borrower's country of residence. There is no double taxation agreement in force with that country. To finance the loan the bank paid interest of £400,000 and received the benefit of an interest free loan from an associated company. It agreed with the Inland Revenue that it was just and reasonable to attribute £200,000 of interest foregone by the associated company to the overseas loan.

	£	£
Foreign loan interest		750,000
Foreign tax (20%)	150,000	
Foreign tax eligible for credit (restricted to 15% of £750,000)	(112,500)	
Excess foreign tax (available for relief by deduction)		(37,500)
Foreign loan interest treated as reduced to		712,500
Financial expenditure in relation to the loan		(600,000)
Amount of interest on which credit relief is available		£112,500
UK corporation tax at 30%		33,750
Tax credit of £112,500 available, but limited to UK tax actually chargeable		(33,750)
UK corporation tax payable		Nil

Example 66

The facts are the same as for Example 65, except the 20% withholding tax was 'spared' by the country of the borrower. Furthermore there is an agreement between the UK and the country of residence of the borrower which provides for tax credit relief in the UK on the tax spared by the foreign country.

	£	£
Foreign loan interest		750,000
Foreign tax spared (20%)	150,000	
Foreign tax spared available for relief (15% restriction)		112,500
Adjusted amount of foreign loan interest		862,500
Financial expenditure in relation to the foreign loan		(600,000)
Amount of interest on which credit relief is available		£262,500
UK corporation tax at 30%		78,750
Spared tax credit of £112,500 available, but restricted to		(78,750)
UK corporation tax payable		Nil

5.7 In April 1996 the Inland Revenue issued an Interpretation (No 149) setting out its views on the scope of *section 798*. This indicated that the section applies not only where the recipient actually made the loan, but to other cases where foreign loan interest is trading income, including cases where interest is received by:

(*a*) a securities dealer on overseas debt purchased on the secondary market; and

(*b*) a financial trader to whom loan interest has been assigned.

'Foreign loan interest' in the Inland Revenue's view includes manufactured interest on overseas debt securities ('manufactured overseas dividends') arising as a result of transfer of such securities where the manufactured overseas dividends are in respect of foreign loan interest to which *section 798* would have applied. This includes transfers by way of a 'repo' (sale and repurchase agreement), a stock loan or an outright sale. In such cases the lender's financial expenditure to be included by virtue of *section 798(7)* is that relating to the provision or purchase of the securities which have been transferred.

5.8 In his Budget statement on 17 March 1998, the Chancellor announced amended provisions to be contained in new *sections 798, 798A* and *798B*. While the existing rules prevented banks and other financial traders from obtaining excessive relief for foreign tax in respect of interest received from abroad, attempts had been made to avoid these rules by:

• arranging for the return from lending money to overseas borrowers to be in the form of dividends from redeemable preference shares, so that underlying relief was available; and

• arranging for the income to be received by (or the related cost to be borne by) a non-trading associate.

To counter this, the scope of these provisions has been extended to include dividends received in the course of a trade. They also apply to foreign interest and dividend income of associates of financial traders where arrangements have been made to avoid the restriction that would have applied had the income been received by the trader. The new rules apply to foreign interest and dividends paid from 17 March 1998, except when they are paid before 1 January 1999 in pursuance of arrangements entered into before (and not altered on or after) 17 March 1998. Amendments were also made to *TA 1988, s 803* from the same dates.

5.9   New *section 798* applies where:

- in any chargeable period the profits of a trade carried on by a qualifying taxpayer include an amount (computed in accordance with *section 795*) in respect of foreign interest or foreign dividends;

- the taxpayer is entitled to credit for foreign tax; and

- in the case of foreign dividends, foreign tax is (or includes) underlying tax.

For the purposes of *sections 798* and *798B*, 'qualifying taxpayer' means a person carrying on a trade which includes the receipt of interest or dividends and which is not an insurance business. However, where a company ('the company') connected or associated with a qualifying taxpayer is acting in accordance with a scheme or arrangement, the purpose (or one of the main purposes) of which is to prevent or restrict the application of *section 798* to the taxpayer, the company is treated as a qualifying taxpayer. In these circumstances the foreign interest or dividends received in pursuance of the scheme or arrangement are treated as profits of the trade carried on by the company. The *section 839* definition of 'connected' and the *section 783* definition of 'associated' apply.

For the purpose of the new sections:

- 'interest' in relation to a loan includes any introductory or other fee or charge which is payable in accordance with the terms on which the loan is made (or is otherwise payable in connection with the making of the loan);

- 'foreign dividends' means dividends payable out of or in respect of the stocks, funds, shares or securities of a body of persons not resident in the UK; and

- 'foreign interest' means interest payable by a person not resident in the UK or by a government or local authority in a country outside the UK. [*s 798(3)*].

5.10   Where *section 798* applies, for the purposes of income tax or corporation tax, the amount of foreign interest or foreign dividends is treated as increased by any spared tax up to a limit of 15%. In addition, if the amount of tax which is not spared tax exceeds 15% of the interest, then the foreign interest or dividends are reduced by the excess. For these purposes the provisions of *FA 1996, s 80(5)* are ignored.

Where *section 798* applies, the amount of the credit against income tax or corporation tax:

(*a*)   is limited by treating the amount of the foreign interest or foreign dividends (as increased or reduced under *section 798A*) as reduced by the taxpayer's 'financial expenditure' in relation to the interest or dividend; and

(*b*)   is not to exceed 15% of the interest or dividends (where the foreign tax on dividends is not underlying tax).

The meaning of 'financial expenditure' is:

• so much of the financial expenses (e.g. interest, discounts and similar sums or qualifying losses) incurred by the taxpayer (or by a person connected or associated with him) as is both:

(i)   property attributable to the earning of the interest or dividend; and

(ii)   taken into account when computing the taxpayer's (or the person's) liability to income tax or corporation tax; and

• any other sum as is reasonable to attribute to the earning of the interest or dividends paid by the taxpayer (or a person connected or associated with him) which falls within the previous paragraph and would not otherwise be taken into account. [*s 798B(1)*].

There is to be deducted from the financial expenditure so much of the 'qualifying gains and profits' accruing to the qualifying taxpayer (or a person connected or associated with him) as:

• is properly attributable to the earning of the interest or dividends, and

• is taken into account in computing the taxpayer's (or the person's) liability to income tax or corporation tax.

For these purposes 'qualifying gains and profits' means those arising in connection with the foreign exchange and financial instruments legislation. [*s 798B(2)* and *(5)*].

Where the qualifying taxpayer's financial expenditure is not readily ascertainable, a just and reasonable amount is attributed to the earning of the interest or dividends, regard being had to a market rate of interest. The Board of Inland Revenue may make regulations to determine what is 'just and reasonable' and to make provision for the determination of market rates of interest. [*s 798B(3)* and *(4)*].

Underlying tax reflecting interest on loans

5.11   Similar restrictions under *TA 1988, s 803*, were introduced in 1982 and amended in 1987 to limit underlying tax which UK banks can claim on dividends received from foreign related companies. These provisions prevent UK banks from claiming full double tax credit relief in the UK indirectly, through underlying tax relief on dividends received from, for example, their own subsidiaries. Prior to 17 March 1998 (or to 1 January 1999 where a dividend is paid before that date in pursuance of an arrangement made before 17 March 1998) the restrictions to underlying relief applied where:

(*a*)   a bank, or a company connected with a bank (which would include a UK company holding shares in overseas subsidiaries), made a claim for double tax relief for underlying tax on a dividend paid by an overseas company ('the second company');

(*b*)   the underlying tax was (or included) tax payable under the laws of a territory outside the UK on interest on a loan made in the course of its business (or by a third, fourth or subsequent company which paid dividends to the second company); and

(*c*)   expenditure relating to the earning of the interest on the loan would have been deductible in computing the company's taxable profits if it had been resident in the UK.

5.12   The restrictions introduced in 1982 had a similar scope to those relating to overseas lending introduced at the same time. Unless the underlying tax was spared tax, the dividend was treated as reduced by any excess of the underlying tax over 15% of the interest to which it was referable. In addition the credit for underlying tax was restricted to 15% of the loan interest included in the relevant profits. Where the underlying tax was spared tax, the dividend was treated as increased by the amount of the spared tax up to the limit of 15% of the loan interest.

In 1987 amendments to underlying tax relief for banks mirrored the amendments made at that time in relation to foreign loan interest. The amount of the underlying tax credit was further limited to the amount of the UK corporation tax which would have been payable on the interest after deduction of 'the lender's relevant expenditure' (i.e. which would be 'financial expenditure on the loan' if the company were resident in the UK (see 5.6 above)).

5.13   The scope of *section 803* was changed by *FA 1998* reflecting the changes to *section 798* and, as amended, applies where:

(*a*)   a bank (or a company connected with a bank) makes a claim for underlying tax relief on a dividend ('the overseas dividend') paid by an overseas company; and

(*b*)   that underlying tax is (or includes) foreign tax on interest or dividends earned or received in the course of its business by the overseas company (or by a third, fourth or successive company); and

(*c*)   if the company which received the interest or dividends ('the company') had been resident in the UK, *section 798* would apply.

The credit for underlying tax is not to exceed the UK corporation tax at the rate in force at the time when the foreign tax was chargeable, on the amount of interest or dividends less the company's relevant expenditure which is properly attributable to the earning of the interest or dividends.

For these purposes 'the company's relevant expenditure' means the amount which would be its financial expenditure (for the purposes of *section 798B*) in relation to the interest or dividends if it were a company resident in the UK. Where the underlying tax is (or includes) an amount of spared tax, for the purposes of corporation tax, the amount of the overseas dividends is treated as increased by the lower of the spared tax creditable under any double taxation agreement or 15% of the interest or dividends. Where the underlying tax is not spared tax and exceeds 15%, for the purposes of corporation tax the amount of the overseas dividend is reduced by the excess.

Where *section 803* applies, the amount of credit which is referable to the underlying tax payable is not to exceed 15% of the interest or dividends which are included in the relevant profits of the company paying the overseas dividend. For the purposes of this section:

(*a*) 'relevant profits' has the same meaning as for the purposes of the computation of underlying tax (see 4.11); and

(*b*) the amount of interest or dividends is determined without making any deduction for foreign tax. [*s 803(9)*].

Under the recent changes to the double taxation relief (DTR) legislation, however, *TA 1988* has a further impact on UK headquartered banks or financial institutions. *Section 806A(2)(d)*, which was inserted by *FA 2000, Sch 30, para 21*, excludes underlying tax on dividends falling within *section 803* from being treated as eligible unrelieved foreign tax. As mentioned previously, *section 803* is not limited to avoidance circumstances and this therefore means that where a non-UK subsidiary of a UK bank makes a loan to a third country resident and suffers withholding tax, the fact that the third country resident is a bona fide customer of the non-UK subsidiary and the lending has been approved by the non-UK subsidiary's management acting independently of the UK bank is not relevant. Any profits remitted to the UK by the non-UK subsidiary are likely to fall within *section 803* and therefore any surplus tax on the dividend cannot be treated as eligible unrelieved foreign tax.

The dividend paid up by the non-UK resident subsidiary is also excluded from being treated as a qualifying foreign dividend and hence is not eligible to have any eligible unrelieved foreign tax offset against it.

Finally, it should also be noted that *section 803* applies even if the overseas tax authorities operate similar restrictions to the UK's *section 798*.

UK insurance companies trading overseas

5.14   Special rules for UK insurance companies doing business abroad were contained in *TA 1988, s 802* which extended underlying tax credit relief to dividends from certain foreign companies in which the insurance company does not hold 10% of the voting power, which is the minimum shareholding normally required under an agreement or for unilateral relief. These rules were abolished for accounting periods beginning after 31 March 2000. They applied where a UK resident company was charged to tax under Schedule D Case I in respect of any insurance business and any part of that business is carried on abroad through a branch or agency. In respect of dividends referable to that business paid to the company by companies resident in that territory, any tax payable on their profits under the law of any overseas territory, or any UK income tax or corporation tax payable on those profits, is to be taken into account in the computation of underlying relief for the purposes of *TA 1988, s 799* (see Chapter 4). This is extended to unilateral relief by *section 790(5)(c)(iii)* which provides that the underlying relief applies to an insurance company within *section 802* if the dividend is of a kind described in that section.

5.15   However, the extension of the underlying tax credit provisions was limited by reference to the amount of insurance business carried out in the overseas branch as a proportion of the worldwide business of the UK insurance company. This limitation was set out in *section 802(2)* which provides that credit is not to be allowed to a company in respect of a greater amount of dividends paid by companies in the overseas country than is equal to the excess of:

- the 'relevant fraction' of the UK company's total income from investments (including franked investment income, foreign income dividends and group income) referable to the insurance business; over

- the amount of dividends paid to it in the year of assessment by companies in the overseas country and in respect of which credit may otherwise be allowed for underlying tax.

5.16   The 'relevant fraction' for this purpose is defined as the fraction where:

- the numerator is the UK company's foreign branch premium income referable to insurance business (A); and

- the denominator is the company's total premium income referable to insurance business (B).

Premium income is deemed to be foreign branch premium income if it consists of premiums under insurance contracts entered into at or through a branch or agency in the overseas country by persons not resident in the UK.

Example 67

Excelsior Insurance Plc, a UK resident company, had premium income of £1,000 million of which £100 million arose through a branch in Arcadia. It had worldwide investment income of £50 million which included £7 million of dividend income from companies resident in Arcadia. Of this amount, £4 million arose from companies in which Excelsior owned at least 10% of the voting power, so that underlying tax relief is available under *section 799*. The total qualifying for underlying relief was the smaller of:

the dividends arising in the territory $=$ £7,000,000

or $\frac{A}{B}$ × worldwide investment income

$=$ $\frac{100}{1000}$ × 50,000,000 $=$ £5,000,000

As the amount which qualified for relief apart from *section 802* was £4,000,000, the additional relief granted by *section 802* was £1,000,000.

5.17   ESC C1(b) extended the relief obtainable under *section 802* to tax paid by other companies which pay dividends to the overseas company on whose dividends underlying tax relief may be claimed, provided those other companies are resident in the same territory as the branch or agency. The concession indicates that where a UK insurance company is entitled to relief under *section 802*, the following items may, in practice, also be taken into account in respect of dividends paid by the overseas company:

- any UK or overseas tax paid on its income in a foreign country by a company paying dividends to, and resident in the same country as, the overseas company; and

- tax on dividends and income of companies further down the chain of shareholdings which are resident in the same country as the overseas company.

5.18   Under this concession, where a UK company controls directly or indirectly not less than 10% of the voting power of a company resident abroad ('the operating company') which carries on insurance business which would have been charged to tax under Schedule D Case I if that overseas operating company had been UK resident, the credit also takes into account in practice:

- any UK or overseas tax paid on its income in the same or another country by any company paying dividends to it and resident in the same country as the operating company, provided that such tax shall be reduced in the proportion that the overseas operating company's distributable surplus from insurance business bears to the total amount of its distributable surplus; and

- similarly, tax relating to dividends and income of companies further down a chain of shareholdings which are resident in the same country as the operating company.

Overseas life assurance business: restriction of credit

5.19   Under *TA 1988, s 441* the trading profit on overseas life assurance business (i.e. most properly certified business written for non-UK
residents by UK offices) is taxed under Schedule D Case VI. *Section 804A*
limits the credit relief as follows:

(*a*)   foreign tax charged by any territory by reference to trading profit
        arising in that territory is allowed as a credit against UK tax
        charged under Case VI; and

(*b*)   where foreign tax is charged wholly or partly on some other basis,
        for example by reference to investment income, the amount of such
        foreign tax is restricted by the fraction:

$$\frac{A}{B}$$

where: A = the Case VI profit, and
       B = the amount of receipts included in computing profits,
           apart from premiums and reinsurance claims, less expenses
           taken into account in computing those profits.

The resulting amount is available for credit if it is greater than foreign tax
charged by reference to trading profits.

Example 68

Regius Life Assurance Company Plc, a UK resident company, carries on overseas life
assurance business in Illyria and suffers tax of £1 million on its trading profit there. It also
suffers local tax of £14 million on its investment income in Illyria. Its profits on overseas life
assurance business assessed under Schedule D, Case VI are £10 million which includes an
investment return of £110 million. Expenses of £35 million were deducted in calculating
Case VI profit. The credit relief available is calculated as follows:

$\frac{A}{B}$ × foreign tax (14 + 1 = £15,000,000)

where A = profits of the company chargeable to Schedule D, Case VI under *section 441*;
and
      B = investment return less expenses and interest paid (110 − 35 = 75)

= $\frac{10}{75}$ × £15,000,000 = £2,000,000

As this is greater than the foreign tax on trading profits, credit will be given for £2 million.

5.20   There has been considerable uncertainty and dispute as to the
basis of calculating credit in respect of foreign investment income underlying UK life assurance business. Life assurance business is divided
into a number of categories including pensions business (taxed on trading
profit) and basic life business (taxed primarily on investment income plus
chargeable gains less expenses). It has been open to question whether
foreign taxes must be split according to these categories of business and
credit taken against corporation tax on each category separately.

In respect of pensions business taxable on trading profit, the Inland Revenue has been arguing that credit relief is available only to the extent of a fraction of foreign taxes suffered on investment income, being the ratio of trading profit to all positive items included in the calculation of the trading profit. The argument is that trading profit has to be divided rateably between its components, such as foreign income, other investment income and premiums, and that only the part of profit proportionate to foreign income is capable of being relieved by foreign tax credit. Generally, the life assurance companies have not accepted this view and have argued that all foreign taxes suffered in earning profit may be set against corporation tax on that profit. Some progress is being made on the passage of appeals through the legal system, which should (in the fullness of time) provide a solution to most of these issues.

Life assurance business — periods beginning after 31 March 2000

5.21   Some of the questions referred to above have largely been resolved by changes introduced as part of *FA 2000* for accounting periods beginning after 31 March 2000.

The reforms are two-fold:

- foreign tax is allocated between categories of business, and the limit for credit for each category is considered separately [*s 804B*]; and

- for Schedule D Case I computations — i.e. all categories except basic life assurance and general annuity business (BLAGAB), the limit on credit is based on only a proportion of the income allocated to the business. [*ss 804C–804E*].

In summary, *section 804B* establishes how foreign tax in relation to an item of relevant income is allocated between categories of business, and it provides that the amount of credit against corporation tax on the relevant income referable to a category cannot exceed the amount of foreign tax allocated to the same category. A simple example is set out below.

Example 69

A dividend of £90,000 is received net from a Belgian portfolio investment which has suffered £10,000 withholding tax; the total relevant income is therefore £100,000. Under *TA 1988, s 432A* apportionment of income and gains of an insurance company which carries on more than one category of business) say, £55,000 of the dividend is allocated to BLAGAB. For simplicity, it is assumed there is no pension profit. Before double tax relief in the UK, corporation tax of £11,000 is due on the BLAGAB element (at 20%) and nil on the pension element since there is no pension profit. Without *section 804B* the limit on credit would be £10,000. However, *section 804B* requires the tax to be allocated separately to BLAGAB and pensions. As a result £5,500 foreign tax is allocated to BLAGAB: the limit on credit is therefore £5,500.

In summary, the Belgian income of £100,000 has suffered £10,000 of Belgian (withholding) tax and £5,500 of UK tax. If this had been a UK dividend it would have suffered no tax while, if instead, it had been UK interest income, it would have suffered only £11,000 of tax.

5.22   *TA1988, ss 804C–804E* restrict relief where a company carries on any category of insurance business and the profits are computed under the principles of Case I of Schedule D. It applies to:

- general business;

- non-life long-term business taxed on a Schedule D Case I basis;

- pension business;

- life reinsurance business;

- overseas life assurance business; and

- individual savings account business.

The effect of these provisions is broadly to treat the relevant income as reduced by an allowance for 'relevant expenses', before calculating the limit for credit relief. Relevant expenses are defined by reference to insurance liabilities and claims.

Anti-avoidance provision

5.23   There is an anti-avoidance provision which applies where a 75% subsidiary is involved in a scheme aimed at avoiding the new rules. In overview, the anti-avoidance provision applies the calculations which would have applied in the parent company to determine the amounts of credit available in the subsidiary.

Articles in Agreements — Scope and Definitions

Introduction

6.1 The UK is constantly engaged in negotiating and renegotiating its network of double taxation agreements as it seeks both to extend the network to newly emerging international trading nations and to bring agreements with countries already in the network into line with current practice, legislation and commercial requirements. While most of the articles being negotiated in each new agreement have their basis in the OECD model, these new agreements do not follow the current model exactly. Instead, they tend to diverge from the model where there are matters of particular significance to one or both countries, which arise either from the particular tax systems or from special commercial factors. Nevertheless, because the UK is a member of the OECD it is considerably influenced by the model and no doubt bears in mind, when engaged in negotiations with other countries, the desirability of harmonising, so far as is possible, the international taxation arrangements of member countries. In the case of agreements between the UK and developing countries, the principles and wording of certain articles may be closer to the UN model agreement. However, in general, the UN model has been less influential than the OECD models in shaping the UK's agreements.

This chapter (and also Chapters 7 and 8) considers not only the wording of articles in the UK's agreements but also, where different, the corresponding articles in the OECD and UN models and the interpretation contained in the OECD commentary. References are made to several of the UK's agreements and the date appended to those agreements in the text represents the date the agreement was signed. A full list of the UK's current agreements appears in Appendix 2.

Status of the OECD commentaries

6.2   When considering a question where a double taxation agreement is relevant, it is essential to study the precise wording of that agreement and, where appropriate, to have regard to the provisions of, and commentaries on, the OECD models. The commentary notes observations by member countries on each article and reservations which indicate the extent to which they intend to adopt particular articles or wordings in their own agreements. Where the wording of an article follows the equivalent article in the OECD model the commentary may give an indication of the manner in which it is to be interpreted.

The status of the OECD commentaries in the interpretation of agreements has been given judicial consideration in the case of *Sun Life Assurance Society of Canada v Pearson [1984] STC 461*. In the Chancery Division Vinelott J quoted the OECD's Committee on Fiscal Affairs on the significance of the commentaries.

> 'As these Commentaries have been drafted and agreed upon by the experts appointed to the Committee on Fiscal Affairs by the Governments of Member countries, they are of special importance in the development of international fiscal law. Although the Commentaries are not designed to be annexed in any manner to the conventions to be signed by the member countries, which alone constitute legally binding international agreements, they can nevertheless be of great assistance in the application of the conventions and, in particular, in the settlement of any disputes.
>
> Observations on the Commentaries have sometimes been inserted at the request of some member countries who were unable to concur in the interpretation given in the Commentary on the article concerned. These observations thus do not express any disagreement with the text of the Convention, but furnish a useful indication of the way in which those countries will apply the provisions of the article in question.'

He concluded that 'the Commentaries can and indeed must be referred to as a guide to the interpretation of the [UK/Canada] Treaty'. When the case came to appeal at *[1986] STC 335*, the Court of Appeal did not consider itself bound to have regard to the commentaries, although it did in fact consider them. Accordingly, it would appear that the UK courts consider themselves entitled, but not necessarily bound, to take the commentaries into consideration when construing the terms of an agreement.

Personal scope

6.3   Most of the UK's agreements now contain a 'personal scope' article, although these have only been included in agreements concluded since about 1967. Most such articles are very brief, simply stating that 'this Convention shall apply to persons who are residents of one or both contracting states'. In the case of the older agreements there was generally no equivalent article. This may have been because it was considered that the application of the agreement to residents of one or both contracting states was implied by the various references to residents within the terminology of the agreement. However, the cases of *IRC v Commerzbank AG* and *IRC v Banco do Brasil SA [1990] STC 285* demonstrated that, without an express limitation of scope, it would be possible in some circumstances for a person resident in neither contracting state to claim the benefit of an agreement (see 3.3). However, in the case of agreements concluded by the UK since 1967, for example the 1976 agreement with Ireland and the 1975 agreement with Spain, there is a specific personal scope article which is often identical to that contained in the OECD model.

6.4   The 'personal scope' article in the 1975 US agreement is considerably more comprehensive than either OECD model, partly because of the US's system of taxing its citizens and lawful permanent residents (sometimes known as 'green card holders') on the basis of their worldwide income, and partly in order to prevent the use of the agreement by companies resident in both the US and the UK (usually referred to as 'dual resident' corporations). The same principles are reflected in the general scope and residence articles of the new draft US agreement.

As far as individuals are concerned, the agreement applies to persons who are residents of one or both of the contracting states. However, the contracting states reserve the right, with certain exceptions, to tax their residents and nationals as if the agreement had not come into effect. In practice this reservation affects mainly citizens and lawful permanent residents of the US who are resident in the UK.

The personal scope article of the 1975 US agreement also stipulates that dual resident corporations can obtain the benefit of the agreement only to a very limited extent as does the residence article of the new draft US agreement. However, this restriction does not apply where it is the recipient of the income rather than the dual resident corporation itself which claims relief under the agreement. For example, if a US corporation managed and controlled in the UK were to receive interest from a UK company it would not be entitled to receive it gross under the 'interest' article of the agreement. On the other hand, if the same dual resident company were itself to pay a dividend to its UK incorporated and resident parent company, the 30% rate of US dividend withholding tax under domestic law would be reduced to 5% under the 'dividends' article of the agreement. This relief is not available under the new draft US agreement.

The OECD and UN models

6.5   Both the OECD and UN models contain 'personal scope' articles identical to that in most of the UK's agreements as set out in 6.3 above.

The commentary on the OECD model describes in some detail the application of the convention to partnerships. No special provision relating to partnerships has been included in the OECD model because of the different tax treatment accorded to them under the laws of the various member countries. (However, the OECD published a report on the application of the OECD model to partnerships in 1999 which led to a number of changes in April 2000 to the commentary on the OECD model and an amendment to Article 23A.) For example, in some countries a partnership has a legal and tax status similar to that of a company, while in other countries it may have no separate tax or legal status apart from that of its partners. In certain countries there are several different forms of partnership, each with its own set of legal consequences. Accordingly, the Committee of Fiscal Affairs considered that the countries concerned should be able to consider the problems of partnerships in their bilateral negotiations and agree upon such special provisions which they consider to be necessary and appropriate.

The revised commentary highlights that difficulties can occur in applying agreements to partnerships because domestic laws can differ in their treatment of such entities. These difficulties are analysed in the OECD report mentioned above. While the revised commentary to the OECD model indicates that a partnership may qualify as a person it may not represent a resident of a contracting state. In particular, if it is fiscally transparent, the partnership may not be liable to tax in that state. As a result, the partnership may be unable to benefit from an agreement of that state. In this situation, the partners should broadly be allowed to benefit from the agreements entered into by the state in which they are resident in respect of their respective shares of the partnership income. The revised commentary also considers the effect that the application of the provisions of an agreement to a partnership can have on the taxation of the partners. For example, if a partnership is treated as a resident of a contracting state, the other contracting state may remain able to tax the individual partners. In addition, it is acknowledged that difficulties can arise in partnership cases involving three states.

6.6   In the UK the application of an agreement to a partnership was considered in the case of *Padmore v IRC [1989] STC 493.* This concerned the 1952 agreement with Jersey in which the term 'resident of Jersey' is defined as 'any person who is resident in Jersey for the purposes of Jersey tax . . . '. The term 'person' is also defined as including 'any body of persons, corporate or not corporate'. The Court of Appeal held that a partnership was, as a matter of the ordinary use of English, a body of persons and that it was improbable that, in the context, a partnership (which is a normal vehicle for carrying on a commercial activity) was intended to be excluded from the agreement.

It should be noted that in the *Padmore* case, a UK resident partner in a partnership controlled, managed and tax resident in Jersey was able to claim exemption from his share of the partnership profits under the

Jersey agreement. Following this case, legislation was inroduced in what is now *TA 1988, s 112*; this provides that a double tax treaty does not affect any liability to tax in respect of a UK resident partner's share of any income or gains of a non-UK resident partnership.

Early this year, in a case concerning a year of assessment after the introduction of the above legislation, the High Court dismissed the taxpayer's appeal that having regard to the literal words of *TA 1988, s 788(3)* and *s 112* could still be construed as being overridden by the Jersey agreement.

In other cases the application of the agreement to partnerships is expressed in the agreement. For example, the 1975 US agreement (but not the latest draft US agreement) includes 'partnership' in the definition of 'resident' but only to the extent that the income derived by such partnership is subject to tax as the income of a resident, either in its hands or in the hands of its partners.

6.7 The OECD commentary on the 'personal scope' article also notes that double taxation agreements should not be used to help tax avoidance or evasion, so that a country may preserve its own domestic anti-avoidance legislation in its agreements. In addition it comments that, through the use of 'artificial legal constructions', persons not normally able to benefit from tax treaties may be able to do so. For example, a person who is not a resident of a country with which the UK has an agreement may, by establishing a company in the jurisdiction of a country with such an agreement, take advantage of that agreement. The commentary suggests possible countermeasures, such as restricting the benefit of an agreement in cases where a company claiming the benefit of an agreement is not owned directly or indirectly by residents of the state in which the company itself is resident. However, the OECD model agreement does not itself contain an article restricting the benefits of the agreement in these (or other) circumstances. Several of the UK's agreements do contain provisions which deny the benefit of the agreement (or of specific articles) to certain companies which could otherwise be used for these purposes (see 8.3).

Taxes covered

6.8 The UK's agreements normally include a 'taxes covered' article which lists taxes to which the agreement applies and often states that taxes of an identical or substantially similar nature subsequently imposed in addition to, or in place of, existing taxes are included. The taxes listed are generally the national corporate and personal taxes of both countries on income and capital gains.

As far as the UK is concerned these taxes usually comprise income tax, corporation tax and capital gains tax, and may, depending on when the agreement was negotiated or amended, also include petroleum revenue tax and development land tax. There are, however, a number of agreements dating from before 1965 which have not been amended to reflect the introduction of corporation tax or capital gains tax. Examples of these are the 1953 agreement with Greece and the 1952 agreements with Jersey and Guernsey. Where the scope of such an agreement is to apply to 'taxes of a substantially similar character' which are imposed after the agreement has come into force (or been signed), the agreement is extended to corporation tax. However, agreements which refer specifically only to income tax and profits tax are not extended to cover capital gains tax or petroleum revenue tax.

There are many variations as far as the scope for foreign taxes is concerned. Several agreements do not include within the scope of the agreement taxes, such as state or provincial taxes, raised by political subdivisions. These include the 1975 US agreement (and the new draft US agreement) and the 1978 agreement with Canada. On the other hand, the 1964 agreement with Germany includes local trade tax (*Gewerbesteuer*). The fact that a foreign tax is included within the scope of the agreement does not necessarily mean that it is creditable against UK tax. For example, the agreement with Germany covers both local trade tax and capital tax (*Vermögensteuer*). However, later in the agreement the 'elimination of double taxation' article specifically excludes from double tax credit relief capital tax and also local trade tax if it is computed on a basis other than profits. This would not, of course, prevent other articles of the agreement, such as the 'business profits' or 'non-discrimination' articles, from applying to such taxes.

The OECD and UN models

6.9   The terms of the OECD and UN models are the same in so far as taxes covered are concerned. They are drafted to include taxes which are imposed on behalf of a political subdivision or local authority of the parties. They also refer to all taxes on income or capital or on both, as well as taxes on the total amount of wages and salaries paid by undertakings. The commentary indicates that 'taxes on the total amount of wages and salaries' refers to taxes such as the French *taxe sur les salaires* whose base is the wages and salaries bill of an undertaking and does not include social security or similar charges.

The models include provision for the extension of the agreement to identical or substantially similar taxes imposed after the date of signature of the agreement which are in addition to (or are in place of) the existing taxes. There is also a procedure laid down whereby the competent authorities notify each other of the changes which have been made in their respective taxation laws.

Paragraph 4 of the OECD model was amended in April 2000. As under the previous version, competent authorities of the contracting states are required to notify each other at the end of each year of any significant changes that have been made in their taxation laws. However, the phrase 'at the end of each year' has now been deleted. The commentary to the UN model indicates that the reason for this change was that the previous wording was very wide since in practice most contracting states do not communicate with each other on change in their own tax laws. In addition, the requirement to exchange information on changes in tax laws should extend only to significant changes in law which affect the application of the convention.

Paragraph 4 of the OECD commentary has now been amended to say that practice among countries varies with respect to whether interest and penalties are regarded as 'taxes covered' and that countries are free to claim this point in their bilateral negotiations.

General definitions

6.10　UK agreements generally define the geographical areas covered and also terms such as 'tax', 'person', 'company' and 'competent authority'. Other terms may be defined in their appropriate articles, e.g. 'permanent establishment', 'interest', 'royalties' and 'dividends'.

6.11　Following the commencement of development of the UK Continental Shelf and the extension in *FA 1973, s 38* (now *TA 1988, s 830*) of the UK's taxing rights to exploration or exploitation activities in designated areas, the definition of the 'United Kingdom' (and of the other party to the agreement) has been amended in the majority of the UK's agreements. Without such amendment the UK's right to tax a resident of another contracting state on its activities on the UK continental shelf outside territorial limits would be restricted since an enterprise of such a contracting state could operate in the UK sector of the North Sea without having a permanent establishment (PE) in the UK (i.e. within the boundary of the territorial sea). The United Kingdom is therefore now defined to include:

> 'any area outside the territorial sea of the UK which in accordance with international law has been or may hereafter be designated, under the laws of the UK concerning the Continental Shelf, as an area within which the rights of the UK with respect to the sea-bed and subsoil and their natural resources may be exercised'.

Similar wording is often used with regard to the continental shelf of the other territory. Examples of such wording are found, for example, in the agreements with Australia (1967), Belgium (1987) and The Netherlands (1980).

However, there are still some old agreements in force which do not refer to the continental shelf outside the UK's territorial waters. Prior to 6 April 1989 the Inland Revenue treated 19 such agreements as potentially exempting employment income received by residents of those contracting states for services performed on the UK continental shelf from UK income tax. However, after taking legal advice, the Inland Revenue issued a Press Release on 3 March 1989 indicating that, from 6 April 1989, residents of those countries would no longer be regarded as entitled to relief under the relevant agreement. Several of these agreements have since been renegotiated or amended.

6.12   The term 'person' is often defined to comprise 'an individual, a company and any other body of persons'. Certain older UK agreements, however, define the term as including 'any body of persons, corporate or not corporate'. Examples are the 1953 agreement with Greece and the 1952 agreements with Jersey and Guernsey. As discussed in 6.6 above, in the case of *Padmore v IRC [1989] STC 493* (which concerned the wording of the Jersey agreement) it was held that the term 'body of persons' included a partnership. The OECD commentary as recently amended now states that partnerships will also be considered to be 'persons' either because they fall within the definition of 'company' or, where this is not the case, because they constitute other bodies of persons.

The term 'company' is often defined as meaning 'any body corporate or any entity which is treated as a body corporate for tax purposes'. As far as the UK is concerned, under this definition the term would include an unincorporated association.

The latest version of the OECD model now includes a definition of the term 'enterprise' which applies to the carrying on of any business. There is now also a definition of business being the performance of professional services and other activities of an independent character. This addition ensures that the term 'business' includes the performance of activities previously covered in Article 14 (independent personal services) which has now been deleted from the OECD model. There are, of course, states where the domestic law does not consider that the performance of such services or activities can constitute a business. Contracting states for which this is not the case are free to agree bilaterally to omit the definition.

The term 'enterprise of a contracting state', which is of importance in several articles, is defined as 'an enterprise carried on by a resident of a contracting state'.

6.13   The term 'national' is sometimes defined in this article, although in some agreements the definition is contained in the 'non-discrimination' article, in which the concept of nationality frequently appears. In agreements concluded before the *British Nationality Act 1981* the term is often defined in relation to the UK as in this example from the 1977 agreement with Botswana:

> '... any citizen of the United Kingdom and Colonies, or any British subject not possessing that citizenship or the citizenship of any other

Commonwealth country or territory, provided that in either case he has the right of abode in the United Kingdom; and any legal person, association or other entity deriving its status as such from the law in force in the United Kingdom.'

The status of 'citizen of the United Kingdom and Colonies' was abolished by the *British Nationality Act 1981* and, from 1 January 1983, the term 'national' (or sometimes 'citizen') in relation to the UK now means a British citizen, a British dependent territories citizen or a British overseas citizen in accordance with that Act. Later agreements are worded differently to reflect these changes and several have been amended by protocol. For example, the 1980 agreement with Denmark was amended in 1991 to define the term 'national' as 'any British citizen or any British subject not possessing the citizenship of any other Commonwealth country or territory, provided he has the right of abode in the United Kingdom ... '.

Depending upon the terms of the particular agreement, the term 'national' may apply to legal persons, partnerships and associations deriving their status from the laws of the relevant territory. Accordingly, for example, a UK incorporated company will often be a national of the UK for the purposes of an agreement.

A partnership can also represent a national of a contracting state, although it is possible under the domestic laws of some countries for an entity to be a 'person' but not a 'legal person' for tax purposes. However, in certain agreements, including those with Denmark (1980) and Finland (1969), the definition specifically excludes partnerships.

6.14   The OECD commentary on the definition of 'international traffic' has been expanded considerably. In particular, the definition is clarified as applying where the journey of a ship or aircraft between places in the other contracting state forms part of a larger voyage of that ship or aircraft involving a place of departure or a place of arrival which is outside that other contracting state. However, the definition is not regarded as applying to any transport when the ship is operated between two places in the same contracting state, even if part of the transport takes place outside that state.

The 'general definitions' article normally defines the term 'competent authority'. As far as the UK is concerned, this is invariably the Commissioners of Inland Revenue or their authorised representative. In practice, the functions of the UK competent authority are carried out by senior Inland Revenue personnel, usually from International Division.

Many agreements contain a further paragraph indicating that any term not defined in the agreement shall, unless the context requires otherwise, have the meaning which it has under the law of the state concerning the taxes to which it applies.

The OECD and UN models

6.15   The 'general definitions' articles in the OECD and UN models are the same. The models' definitions of 'persons' are similar to those found in many of the UK's more recent agreements which is that the term 'includes an individual, a company and any other body of persons'. The term 'company' means 'any body corporate or any entity that is treated as a body corporate for tax purposes', which is similar to the definition usually adopted by the UK. There are also definitions of 'enterprise of a contracting state', and 'international traffic'. The OECD model defines the term 'national' to include legal persons, partnerships and associations.

The models also provide general rules of interpretation in relation to terms not defined in the agreement. Unless the context requires otherwise, the term is to have the meaning that it has under the law of the state for the purposes of the taxes to which the agreement applies. The OECD model added in the 1995 revision that this meaning is to prevail over the meaning given to the term under other laws of that state.

Residence/fiscal domicile

6.16   The majority of the UK's agreements define the term 'resident'. Many recent agreements follow closely the definition of 'resident' contained in the OECD model. The following example is taken from the 1967 agreement with France (as amended in 1987):

> 'For the purposes of this Convention, the term "resident of a Contracting State" means any person who, under the laws of that State, is liable to tax therein by reason of his domicile, residence, place of management, or any other criterion of a similar nature. But this term does not include any person who is liable to tax in that State in respect only of income from sources in that State.'

There are a number of variations on this definition, particularly in earlier agreements. For example, the 1973 agreement with Jamaica defines a 'resident of the United Kingdom' as 'any person resident in the United Kingdom for the purposes of United Kingdom tax'. There are a few older UK agreements which define a 'resident' as a person who is resident in one country and not resident in the other country under the domestic laws of those countries. Examples are the 1953 agreement with Greece, the 1952 agreements with Jersey and Guernsey and the 1955 agreement with the Isle of Man. These agreements also omit the tests (set out in 6.19 and 6.22 below) for determining residence for individuals and companies who are resident under the domestic laws of both countries. Such 'dual residents' are therefore generally unable to benefit from these agreements.

6.17   The 1975 US agreement refers to a partnership, estate or trust being a resident of a contracting state, but only to the extent that its income is subject to UK or US tax (as the case may be) as the income of a resident. The new draft US agreement does not refer to such entities per se. It includes as a resident of a contracting state a pension scheme along with certain other entities which are residents of a contracting state according to its laws, not withstanding that the income of such entities may be exempt from tax under the domestic law of that state.

The definition of 'UK resident' in the 1975 agreement as far as companies are concerned is 'a corporation whose business is managed and controlled in the UK', so that a UK registered company which is resident in the UK under *FA 1988, s 66* (see 3.6), but is managed and controlled outside the UK would not be UK resident for the purposes of this agreement. The basic definition of a resident of a contracting state under the new draft US agreement is any person who under the laws of that state is liable to tax therein by reason of his domicile, residence, citizenship, place of management, place of incorporation, or any other criteria of a similar nature. This term, however, does not include any person who is liable to tax in that state in respect only of income from sources in that state or of profits attributable to a permanent establishment in that state.

6.18   Most UK agreements then set out the tests to be applied if an individual or a person other than an individual is a resident of both countries by virtue of the domestic laws of each country. These are sometimes referred to as 'residence tie-breaker' clauses.

Residence of individuals

6.19   The 'residence' article of most UK agreements sets out the method of determining 'residence' for an individual *for the purposes of the agreement only* where, by virtue of the main definition, that individual is a resident of both countries which are parties to the agreement. There are normally four different tests which have to be considered in a strict order of priority, so that if one of the tests decides the issue the later tests are not considered. The tests are, in descending order of priority:

(*a*)   the individual has a permanent home in one (only) of the contracting states;

(*b*)   his 'centre of vital interests' is in one of the contracting states. (This test is considered only if the individual has a permanent home available in both contracting states. If he does not have a permanent home available in either country the tests move from (*a*) direct to (*c*));

(*c*)   he has an habitual abode in one (only) of the contracting states; and

(*d*)   he is a national of one (only) of the contracting states.

If these tests fail to break the tie, the individual's country of residence for the purpose of the agreement is to be settled by the mutual agreement of the competent authorities. Thus, under most agreements, an individual should not be resident for the purposes of the agreement in more than one country for the same period.

6.20   The UK's agreements follow closely the OECD model agreement and, therefore, it is appropriate to consider the OECD commentary as an aid to interpretation of the terms in this paragraph.

The concept of 'home' within (a) above includes any type of accommodation, whether it be a house or a flat and whether owned or rented. The essential test is its permanence, for example where arrangements are in force for the individual to have the 'home' available to him on a continuous basis and not merely when visiting the other country for a specific purpose which is to be for a short duration, such as travel for business, pleasure or education.

A person's 'centre of vital interests' is the country where his personal and economic relations are closest. Regard is to be had to family and social relations, and to the person's business, political and other activities. The commentary indicates that if a person who has a home in one state sets up a second in the other state while retaining the first, the fact that he retains the first and, *inter alia*, has his family and possessions there may demonstrate that he has retained his centre of vital interests in that country.

'Habitual abode' has a broader meaning than 'permanent home' and indicates any type of accommodation used by a person. Whilst 'permanent home' requires the home available in the country to be of a permanent nature, the 'habitual abode' test can apply to a person going from one hotel to another. The OECD commentary indicates that all stays in a state must be considered in determining whether there is an habitual abode in a contracting state. However, there is no specific period over which a comparison is to be made.

The term 'national' may be defined in the 'general definitions' article or elsewhere in the agreement.

6.21   A few agreements omit the test of nationality. Therefore, in these cases, after consideration of the test of 'habitual abode', the next step is to invoke the mutual agreement procedure.

The text of the 1969 agreement with Japan excludes all reference to the residence tie-breaker tests for individuals. However, on the day that the agreement was signed, the two countries exchanged notes under which it was agreed to follow these tests in practice.

Residence of persons other than individuals

6.22   The most common cases of 'persons other than individuals' are companies and therefore what follows, unless otherwise stated, refers to companies. The residence of a company for UK domestic law purposes is discussed in 3.6. A company may also be resident in another country which has an agreement with the UK and is therefore dually resident. Most recent agreements contain a 'tie-breaker' clause the effect of which is that, *for the purposes of the agreement only*, the company is resident in the country in which the company's place of 'effective management' is situated. This follows the OECD model agreement.

In its Statement of Practice (SP 1/90), the Inland Revenue recognised that there is a distinction between the meaning of 'central management and control' (referring to the highest level of decision making within the company, usually exercised by the board of directors) which is used to determine the place of company residence under UK domestic law and the meaning of 'effective management' as contained in the majority of the UK's agreements. The relevant part of SP 1/90 reads:

> 'It is now considered that effective management may, in some cases, be found at a place different from the place of central management and control. This could happen, for example, where a company is run by executives based abroad, but the final directing power rests with non-executive directors who meet in the UK. In such circumstances the company's place of effective management might well be abroad but, depending upon the precise powers of the non-executive directors, it might be centrally managed and controlled (and therefore resident) in the UK.'

The commentary has never been amended to clarify that the place of effective management is the place where key management and commercial decisions necessary for the conduct of the entity in business are in substance made. The place of effective management will ordinarily be the place where the most senior person or group of persons (e.g. a board of directors) makes its decisions, the place where the actions to be taken by the entity as a whole are determined. However, there is no definitive rule and all relevant facts and circumstances must be examined. An entity may have more than one place of management, but it can have only one place of effective management at any one time.

6.23 However, there are important variations. The 1975 US agreement does not contain a 'tie-breaker' clause for companies and furthermore severely restricts the benefits which dual resident companies can claim under the agreement. In addition, where an estate or trust is a resident of both the UK and the US, the residence position may be settled by agreement of the competent authorities. This method of settling the residence position applies to all entities other than individuals under the new draft US agreement. In certain earlier agreements, including the 1950 agreement with Myanmar (formerly Burma) a company is to be regarded as resident in the country in which its business is managed and controlled. The agreement with Japan (1969) makes the tie-breaker for companies the contracting state in which the head or main office is situated.

Pension funds, charities and other organisations are often exempted from taxation in many states but only if they meet all of the requirements for exemption specified in the tax laws. As a result such entities are often considered as residents for the purposes of an agreement. In some states, however, these entities are not considered liable to tax if they are exempt from tax under domestic laws. These states may not regard such entities as residents for the purposes of a convention unless these entities are expressly covered by the agreement.

The OECD commentary states that contracting states taking this view are free to address the issue in their bilateral negotiations. If a state disregards a partnership for tax purposes and treats it as fiscally transparent, taxing the partners on their share of the partnership income, the partnership itself is not liable to tax and may not therefore be considered as a resident of that state. As the partnership income flows through to the partners under the domestic law of that state, the partners are the persons liable to tax on that income and are thus the appropriate persons to claim the benefits or the agreements concluded by the states of which they are residents. This will be achieved even if, under the domestic law of the state of source, the income is attributed to a partnership which is treated as a separate taxable entity. For states unable to agree with this interpretation of the article, it would be possible to provide for this result in a special provision to avoid the resulting potential double taxation where the income of the partnership is differently allocated by the two states.

Notable reservations on the OECD model article have been expressed by France and Germany in the context of partnerships. Under French domestic law, a partnership is considered to be liable to tax, although technically that tax is collected from the partners. As a result, France reserves the right to amend the article in its tax conventions to specify that French partnerships must be considered as residents of France in view of their legal and tax characteristics. Germany reserves the right to include a provision under which a partnership that is not a resident of a contracting state under paragraph 1 is deemed to be a resident of the contracting state where its effective management is situated, but only to the extent that the income derived from the other contracting state or capital situated there is liable to tax in the first mentioned state.

The OECD and UN models

6.24   The texts of the two model agreements are the same. They both define a 'resident of a contracting state' in terms similar to those in many of the UK's recent agreements including the agreement with France (as set out in 6.16).

Both models contain the same residence 'tie-breaker' clauses as are in the majority of the UK's recent agreements in respect of individuals (as set out in 6.19). The test in both models for persons other than individuals is the contracting state in which the place of effective management is situated.

Permanent establishment

6.25   The main use of the concept of a permanent establishment (PE) is to determine the right of a contracting state to tax the profit of an enterprise of the other contracting state. Under the business profits article a contracting state cannot tax the profits of an enterprise of the other contracting state unless it carries on its business through a PE there. The PE article defines the activities which an enterprise of a contracting state may carry out in the other contracting state without becoming subject to tax in that other state. The existence of the OECD model agreements in particular has helped to standardise definitions of PE, not only in relationships between members of the OECD, but in double taxation agreements generally. The elimination of Article 14 (independent personal services) in 2000 reflected the fact that there were no intended differences between the concepts of PE used in Article 7 (business profits) and fixed base as used in Article 14.

6.26   The basic definition of PE, as contained in the OECD and UN models and in most of the UK's agreements, is 'a fixed place of business through which the business of an enterprise is wholly or partly carried on'. The OECD commentary indicates that this definition contains the three following conditions:

(*a*)   the existence of a 'place of business', i.e. a facility such as premises or, in certain circumstances, machinery or equipment;

(*b*)   the place of business must be 'fixed', i.e. must be established at a distinct place with a certain degree of permanence;

(*c*)   the carrying on of the business of the enterprise through this fixed place of business. This means usually that persons who, in one way or another, are dependent on the enterprise (personnel) conduct the business of the enterprise in the state in which the fixed place is situated.

6.27   The UK's more recent agreements usually continue (with some minor variations) by expanding on the basic definition by specifying that the term PE includes especially:

- a place of management;

- a branch;

- an office;

- a factory;

- a workshop;

- a mine, an oil or gas well, a quarry or other place of extraction of natural resources.

Some agreements, e.g. the 1980 agreement with the Gambia, do not refer to an oil or gas well. The 1986 agreement with Pakistan adds to the list 'a warehouse' and 'premises used for receiving or soliciting orders'. The 1993 agreement with India also refers to these, except that a warehouse is a PE only in relation to a person providing storage facilities for others. The 1967 agreement with Australia includes 'an agricultural, pastoral or forestry property'. The UK's older agreements, including many with Commonwealth countries, contain a much shorter and less specific definition referring to 'a branch, management or other fixed place of business'.

6.28   The OECD commentary indicates that the above list is not exhaustive. However, these examples are to be seen against the background of the general definition set out in 6.26 above and the commentary expects contracting states to interpret the terms 'a place of management', 'a branch' and 'an office' in such a way that they constitute PEs only if they also fall within the general definition.

6.29   Many of the UK's recent agreements have a separate paragraph (which follows the OECD model) to the effect that a building site or construction or installation project constitutes a PE only if it lasts more than twelve months. Agreements with some countries, including Australia (1967), India (1993) and Pakistan (1986), treat such sites and projects as PEs if they exist for six months. The agreement with India adds that a project or supervisory activity constitutes a PE if it is incidental to the sale of machinery or equipment, continues for a period not exceeding six months and the charges payable for the project or supervisory activity exceed 10% of the sale price of the machinery or equipment.

The OECD commentary indicates that where, for example, an office or workshop could be a PE under the terms outlined above but is part of a building site or construction project which lasts for less than twelve months, it would not, of itself, constitute a PE. It also indicates that it is not necessary for the construction or installation project to be carried out continuously at the same location. For example, if the activities at a particular location are part of a single project such as the construction of a pipeline, that project would be regarded as a PE if it lasts for more than twelve (or six) months even though the physical location of the project may move within that period.

6.30   Some recently negotiated treaties, including those with Argentina (1996) and Singapore (1997) provide that the furnishing of services by an enterprise through employees or other personnel in the host country for a total period of six months within any twelve-month period constitutes a PE in the host country. The agreement with Argentina also provides that the exploitation of mineral resources constitutes a PE, even though there is no fixed place of business, provided such activities continue for a period of more than six months within any twelve-month period.

In the case of fiscally transparent partnerships, the OECD commentary states that the twelve-month test is applied at the level of the partnership as concerns its own activities. If the period of time spent on the site by the partners and the employees of the partnership exceeds twelve months, the enterprise carried on by the partnership will therefore be considered to have a PE. Each partner will thus be considered to have a PE for the purposes of the taxation of his share of the business profit derived by the partnership regardless of the time he spends on the site.

6.31   The UK's agreements usually list a number of business activities which of themselves do not constitute permanent establishments, even if they are carried on through a fixed place of business. The exact wording in each agreement varies somewhat, but most follow broadly the following example taken from the 1987 agreement with Belgium:

'Notwithstanding the preceding provisions of the article, the term "permanent establishment" shall be deemed not to include:

(*a*)   the use of facilities solely for the purpose of storage, display or delivery of goods or merchandise belonging to the enterprise;

(*b*)   the maintenance of a stock of goods or merchandise belonging to the enterprise solely for the purpose of storage, display or delivery;

(*c*)   the maintenance of a stock of goods or merchandise belonging to the enterprise solely for the purpose of processing by another enterprise;

(*d*)   the maintenance of a fixed place of business solely for the purpose of purchasing goods or merchandise, or of collecting information, for the enterprise;

(*e*)   the maintenance of a fixed place of business solely for the purpose of carrying on, for the enterprise, any other activity of a preparatory or auxiliary character;

(*f*)   the maintenance of a fixed place of business solely for any combination of activities mentioned in ... [(*a*) to (*e*) above] ... , provided that the overall activity of the fixed place of business resulting from this combination is of a preparatory or auxiliary character.'

6.32   As mentioned above, there are many variations on this paragraph. For example, the 1975 US agreement (but not the new draft US agreement) omits (*e*) and (*f*) above but includes the maintenance of a fixed place of business for the purposes of advertising, the supply of information, scientific research and similar activities which have a preparatory or auxiliary character.

The OECD commentary indicates that the common feature of the exceptions listed in 6.31(*a*) to (*e*) is that the activities are, in general, preparatory or auxiliary. This is explicit in (*e*) which, according to the commentary, amounts to a general restriction in the scope of the main definition as set out in 6.26 above. On this basis the provisions of this paragraph prevent an enterprise of one state from being taxed in the other state if it carries on activities which are of a purely preparatory or auxiliary character.

6.33   The majority of the UK's agreements also deal with agents of an enterprise in a foreign country. The purpose of these paragraphs is to provide rules for dealing with persons who, under the domestic laws of the respective countries, may be treated as taxable branches of a foreign enterprise because of the nature of their activities, even though the foreign enterprise itself may have no fixed place of business in the country. Such persons are often referred to as 'dependent agents' and usually are deemed under the terms of an agreement to be a PE of their foreign principal.

6.34   The general rule under agreements is that a person acting in a contracting state on behalf of an enterprise of the other contracting state is deemed to be a PE of that enterprise if the person has, and habitually exercises in that state, an authority to conclude contracts in the name of the enterprise. However, if the activities are limited to those which are outlined in 6.31 above (i.e. generally those being of a preparatory or auxiliary character only), the person will not be deemed to be a PE. For example, a person who has authority only to conclude contracts for the purchase of goods for the enterprise and does, in fact, restrict his activities to this, will not be deemed to be a PE, since the maintenance of a place of business solely for the purchase of goods would not itself constitute a PE.

There is also generally an exception made for persons who are referred to as brokers, general commission agents and any other agents of an independent status. Such persons are not deemed to be PEs of their foreign principals provided they are acting in the ordinary course of their business.

6.35   The OECD commentary discusses the dependent agent paragraphs in some detail. A dependent agent can be an individual or company and, if an individual, need not be an employee of the enterprise. The important factors here, according to the commentary, are the scope of the authority and its repeated use. The phrase 'in the name of the enterprise' is not intended to be taken literally, but is to apply to an agent who concludes contracts which are binding on the enterprise even if those contracts are not 'in the name of the enterprise'.

A person is treated as an independent agent only if he is independent of the enterprise both legally and economically (which means, *inter alia*, that he is acting for a number of clients and is not economically dependent upon the foreign enterprise), and he acts in the ordinary course of his business when acting on behalf of that enterprise.

6.36   Articles in the UK's recent agreements generally include a paragraph (which is also in the OECD model) which applies where a company which is a resident of a contracting state controls or is controlled by a company which is a resident of the other contracting state or which carries on business in that other state (whether or not through a PE). In these circumstances the company is not, of itself, a permanent establishment of its foreign parent (or subsidiary). However, this does not, for example, prevent a subsidiary from being a PE of its parent where the subsidiary concludes sales contracts on behalf of the parent company.

6.37   Certain UK agreements also include a paragraph which is not in the OECD model which deems the collection of insurance premiums or the insurance of risks through an agent in the other country to be a permanent establishment in that other country, unless the agent is an independent agent as outlined in 6.35 above. Examples are the 1987 agreement with Belgium and the 1968 agreement with France.

The OECD and UN models

6.38   The text of the 'PE' article as contained in the OECD model agreement has been discussed above. The UN model is broadly similar to the OECD model, but is generally more favourable to the country in which the PE is situated. The main differences are as follows:

• A building site, construction assembly or installation project is a PE if it lasts for six months (rather than twelve months in the OECD model).

• The furnishing of services within a country by employees or other personnel engaged by an enterprise can constitute a PE if the activities continue in the country for a period of (or periods totalling) six months in any twelve-month period.

• A dependent agent will be a PE even if he has no authority to conclude contracts for the enterprise if he habitually maintains in a contracting state a stock of goods or merchandise from which he makes regular deliveries on behalf of the enterprise.

• There is a paragraph concerning the PEs of insurance companies collecting premiums or insuring risks in a contracting state similar to that discussed in 6.37 above.

Recent developments — electronic commerce

6.39   As part of its continuing work on the taxation aspects of electronic commerce, the OECD released on 12 February 2001 a comprehensive set of reports and technical papers. The content of these documents, which relate to treaty issues, is outlined below (see OECD & E-Commerce *Tax Journal*, 05/03/01):

Report titled: *Clarification on the Application of the Permanent Establishment Definition in E-Commerce: Changes to the Commentary on the Model Tax Convention on Article 5*

This report (dated 22 December 2000) was issued in January 2001 before the publication of the February 2001 press release. It sets out a revised commentary that indicates that a website alone cannot give rise to a PE. It indicates that where a server performs functions that are more than 'preparatory or auxiliary' it would constitute a PE even without human intervention (a position which does not accord with the UK Inland Revenue view on this issue — see below). Where in such circumstances the company utilises a server provided by a third party internet service provider, the server will not constitute a PE — except in the rare circumstance that an ISP could be shown to be acting as a dependent agent.

On 11 April 2000, the Inland Revenue published a press release which stated:

> 'In the UK we take the view that a website is not a permanent establishment. And we take the view that a server is insufficient of itself to constitute a permanent establishment of a business that is conducting e-commerce through a website on the server. We take the view regardless of whether the server is owned, rented or otherwise at the disposal of the business.'

Report titled: *Attribution of Profit to a Permanent Establishment Involved in Electronic Commerce Transactions*

This discussion paper considers the question of how profits should be allocated to e-commerce activities which qualify as a permanent establishment (PE). The conclusion is that the amount of profit to be attributed to a server PE is related to the nature of the functions that it performs and the ownership of the assets used — it will be necessary to examine each case and consider the functions of the enterprise as a whole and the nature of the permanent establishment in relation to that enterprise. Most PEs created by a web server will perform only routine functions, with little risk, and therefore under current guidelines are unlikely to warrant being attributed with a significant share of the profits generated by the activities carried on through the server. Where technology or website development or other functions making risk decisions are co-located with the server then the amount of profit attributable will increase substantially.

Report titled: *Treaty Characterisation Issues Arising from E-Commerce*

This report (dated 1 February 2001) was produced by the TAG on Treaty Characterisation of E-commerce Payments. The report recommends changes to be made to the commentary on Article 12 of the OECD model on royalties [see 7.35] such that products delivered digitally are broadly treated in the same way as their physical counterparts. As well as digitally supplied goods and services, the provision of 'know-how' is considered in some detail.

The report considers 28 different categories of e-business transaction. The vast majority are considered to give rise to business profits rather than royalties.

Report titled: *The Impact of the Communications Revolution on the Application of 'Place of Effective Management' as a Tie Breaker Rule*

The aim of residence tie-breaker clauses in agreements is to avoid double taxation where a person, as a result of domestic law, is liable to tax in both Contracting States. The OECD model [see 6.16 above] allocates the residence of a 'dual resident' non-individual person by virtue of its 'place of effective management'. For purposes of discussion, the TAG discussion paper suggests that the current test be replaced or enhanced by a tie-breaker rule that will produce a single territory result in all cases where dual residency arises.

Chapter 7

Articles in Agreements — Taxation of Income and Capital

Introduction

7.1   This chapter discusses the main substantive provisions contained in the UK's double taxation agreements and compares them with the articles in the OECD and UN model agreements. Reference is also made to the commentary to the OECD model where appropriate.

Income from immovable property

7.2   The 'immovable property' article in UK agreements invariably allows the contracting state in which immovable property is situated the right to tax income derived from it. For example, the first paragraph of this article in the 1980 agreement with Denmark reads:

'Income derived by a resident of a Contracting State from immovable property (including income from agriculture or forestry) situated in the other Contracting State may be taxed in that other State.'

The third and fourth paragraphs of the article indicate that this applies to income derived from the direct use, letting, or use in any other form of immovable property and that it extends to income from immovable property of an enterprise.

No comprehensive definition of 'immovable property' is set out in the article. The general approach is that the term is defined according to the laws of the country in which the property is situated. However, for the purposes of the agreement certain specified items, as set out in the article, are to be regarded as immovable property, for example livestock and equipment used in agriculture and forestry and rights to variable or fixed payments as consideration for the working of, or right to work, mineral deposits and other natural resources. On the other hand, ships, boats and aircraft are usually specifically excluded from the definition.

The article does not specify how income from immovable property is to be taxed, but simply preserves the right of the country in which the property is situated to tax income arising from the property in accordance with its domestic law.

Variations

7.3   There are many variations found in the UK's agreements, including the following:

- Several agreements do not include an article relating to income from immovable property, for example those with Australia (1967) and the Isle of Man (1955).

- Other agreements specifically provide that the article applies to income of agricultural and forestry enterprises, for example the 1964 agreement with Germany and the 1962 agreement with Israel.

- On the other hand, the agreements with Kenya (1973) and Zambia (1972) specify that income of agricultural, forestry or plantation enterprises are to be dealt with in accordance with the 'business profits' article.

- The agreements with Israel (1962) and Jamaica (1973) include profits from the alienation of immovable property within the scope of the article.

The OECD and UN models

7.4   The articles in the OECD and UN models are almost identical (except that in the OECD model, the reference has been removed to income from immovable property used for the performance of in-dependent personal services) and are also very similar to the wording of the article in the agreement with Denmark as set out in 7.2 above.

The commentary to the OECD model emphasises the priority of taxing rights of the country of source of the income and that the country of source has full taxing rights whether or not the person has a permanent establishment there.

Business (industrial or commercial) profits

7.5   It should be noted that the effect of the deletion of Article 14 is that income derived from professional services or other activities of an independent character is now dealt with under Article 7 as business profits. This was confirmed by the addition of a definition of the term 'business' which expressly provides that this term includes professional services or other activities of an independent character.

7.6   Recently negotiated agreements follow the OECD model in heading the article 'business profits', but many of the earlier UK agree-ments, for example the 1967 agreement with Australia, the 1964 agree-ment with Germany and the 1968 agreement with France, use the heading 'industrial or commercial profits'. This difference in terminology does not, in practice, have a material effect on the scope or interpretation of the article.

There are several different wordings in major UK agreements, but the first three paragraphs follow broadly the pattern of the article in, for example, the 1987 agreement with Belgium, which states that:

(*a*)   the profits of an enterprise of a contracting state may be taxed only in that state unless it carries on business through a permanent es-tablishment (PE) in the other contracting state. If it does so, the profits of the enterprise may be taxed in the other contracting state, but only so much of them as is attributable to the PE;

(*b*)   in each contracting state there are to be attributed to that PE the profits which it might be expected to make if it were a distinct and separate enterprise engaged in the same or similar activities under the same or similar conditions and acting wholly independently; and

(*c*)   in determining the profits of a PE there are to be allowed as de-ductions expenses (including executive and general administrative expenses) incurred for the purpose of the PE wherever they are incurred.

7.7   The article in the agreement with Belgium also contains a number of additional paragraphs which are contained in several agree-ments, as follows:

(a) that no profits are to be attributed to a PE by reason of the mere purchase by that PE of goods or merchandise for the enterprise;

(b) the profits to be attributed to the PE are to be determined by the same method from year to year unless there is good and sufficient reason to the contrary; and

(c) where the profits of a PE include items of income which are dealt with separately in other articles of the agreement, the provisions of the 'business profits' article do not affect the provisions of those articles.

Variations

7.8   While the majority of UK agreements have standard wording, some significant variations are used, including the following:

- Some agreements define 'business profits' or 'industrial or commercial profits'. These include, for example, the 1967 agreement with Australia, the 1975 agreement with the US and the 1968 agreement with Portugal. The definitions are different in each case, but, in general, income derived by an enterprise from a trade or business is included, as is income from the furnishing of services of employees or other personnel. Dividends, interest and royalties are excluded unless they are effectively connected with a trade or business carried on through a PE which the enterprise has in the other contracting state.

- A number of UK agreements contain a paragraph providing that, where it has been customary for a country to determine the profits of a PE on the basis of apportioning the total income of the enterprise, the country in which the PE is situated may determine the profits by that customary basis of apportionment, notwithstanding the arm's length principle referred to elsewhere in the article. The paragraph does, however, add that the method of apportionment adopted shall be such that the result is to be in accordance with the principles of the article. Agreements containing this paragraph include the 1968 agreement with France and the 1980 agreement with the Gambia.

- Some early UK agreements make no reference to the deduction of expenses in determining the profits of a PE, for example the 1953 agreement with Greece and the 1952 agreement with Jersey. Such paragraphs can be of significance in countries where local law or practice is to deny a deduction to a PE for expenses incurred by an enterprise outside the country in which the PE is situated.

The OECD and UN models

7.9   The OECD model has very similar wording for the 'business profits' article to that discussed in 7.6 and 7.7 above. It also contains a paragraph allowing a customary method of calculating profits as outlined in 7.8 above.

The commentary on the OECD model points out that this article is in many respects a continuation of, and a corollary to, the 'permanent establishment' article. When an enterprise of a contracting state is carrying on business in the other contracting state, two separate questions need to be addressed before tax can be levied on the profits of the enterprise by the other contracting state: does the enterprise have a PE in the contracting state? If so, what, if any, are the profits on which the enterprise should pay tax in that state? Some countries consider that, if a foreign enterprise has set up a PE in their territory, any income which the enterprise derives from within their territory may be taxed, whether or not it arises from the PE. This is usually referred to as the 'force of attraction' principle. However, the model and commentary support the contrary view that the right to tax the enterprise does not extend to other profits which it may have in that contracting state which are not attributable to the PE.

The commentary discusses the scope of the paragraph allowing a customary apportionment of the total profits of the enterprise to the PE. Such a method contemplates an attribution of profits otherwise than on the basis that the PE is a separate enterprise, for example by an apportionment of the total profits of the enterprise. The commentary indicates that such a method of allocation is generally not as appropriate as one which takes account only of the activities of the PE. Such a method should be used only where, exceptionally, it has been customary and is accepted in the country concerned as being satisfactory.

The UN model article contains some important differences from the OECD model:

(a) If an enterprise of a contracting state has a PE in the other contracting state, the profits of that enterprise that may be taxed in that contracting state are those attributable not only to the PE itself, but to sales in that contracting state of similar goods or merchandise to those sold through the PE and to other similar business activities carried on in that state. The model therefore allows the 'force of attraction' principle, but this is qualified to the extent that the non-PE profits must be attributable to sales and business activities similar to those of the PE itself.

(b) There is an extensive addition which restricts the deduction of charges made by the head office to the PE (and vice versa) except for reimbursement of actual expenses incurred.

(c) There is no provision preventing the attribution of profit to a PE by reason of the mere purchase by the PE of goods and merchandise for the enterprise. This is left open for negotiation between the contracting states.

Recent developments

7.10   Earlier in 2001, the OECD issued a consultative document considering how far the approach of treating a PE as a hypothetical distinct and separate enterprise can be taken. The OECD's intention is to formulate a preferred approach to attributing profits to a PE.

There is considerable variation in the domestic laws of OECD member countries regarding the taxation of PEs and there is no consensus as to the principles for attributing profits to PEs. However, as a first step to establishing a consensus opinion, the OECD has developed a working hypothesis which examines:

● how far the approach of treating the PE as a hypothetical distinct and separate enterprise can be taken; and

● how the OECD Transfer Pricing Guidelines (the Transfer Pricing Guidelines) could be applied, by analogy, to attribute profits (or losses) to a PE.

The OECD's efforts to establish a consensus opinion should help to provide taxpayers with greater certainty as to the taxation of branches in overseas territories. This is especially so as the historical practice and interpretation by tax authorities of the OECD model requires modification given modern-day operating practices of multinationals, including E-commerce (see below).

The OECD notes that the process of testing the working hypothesis is not yet complete, and that there is not yet a consensus on how the working hypothesis would be applied in practice in certain situations. The document considers the application of the working hypothesis to PEs in general and to PEs of banking enterprises. Testing of the working hypothesis is still under way for PEs of insurance companies and enterprises undertaking global trading of financial products. Testing is about to begin in the E-commerce sector for PEs created solely by the existence of a server.

The tax treatment or PEs of banking and other financial enterprises is complex, and requires consideration of issues that are not relevant to non-financial enterprises. A discussion of the working hypothesis for banking and other financial enterprises is not therefore included here.

The main thrust of the working hypothesis is to treat PEs as distinct and separate enterprises, and to apply (to the extent possible) the guidance set out in the OECD Transfer Pricing Guidelines in determining the profits (or losses) to be attributed to a PE.

The discussion document notes that there is still some way to go before a consensus can be reached. The working hypothesis represents a significant change from the existing interpretations and practices of many tax authorities (including the Inland Revenue).

The main issues raised in the discussion document as regards non-banking and financial enterprises are as follows.

Profits to be attributed to the PE are 'the profits that the PE would have earned at arm's length if it were a separate enterprise performing the same functions under the same or similar conditions, determined by applying the arm's length principle'. This approach is referred to as the 'functionally separate entity' approach and seeks to put PEs on the same footing as subsidiaries as regards determining appropriate level of profits to attribute to the PE.

This may result in the taxing authorities attributing higher profits to PEs in their territories as the working hypothesis rejects the 'relevant business activity' approach which is adopted by certain OECD member countries.

This 'relevant business activity' approach limits the profits that can be attributed to a PE to the profits that the *whole enterprise* earns from the relevant business activity in which the PE has some participation. Under this approach, where the relevant activity is carried on by the PE and other parts of the enterprise, there is a greater likelihood that the performance of other parts of the enterprise will limit the attribution of profit to the PE. For example, if those other parts of the enterprise made a 'loss' in respect of the relevant activity, this would effectively reduce the profits that can be attributed to the PE as the 'loss' would reduce the overall profits of the enterprise from the relevant business activity.

Although the Transfer Pricing Guidelines were drafted to provide guidance on the application of the arm's length principal to legally distinct and separate entities, the working hypothesis is that the guidelines should be applied, by analogy, to the attribution of profits to a PE.

Under the working hypothesis, taxpayers will be able to apply a broadly similar approach to dealing with the transfer pricing issues of their PEs as they do for group companies. This should assist groups in managing their transfer pricing risk.

The document notes that any functional analysis of the PE should consider what assumption of risks should be attributed to the PE.

The main issue for PEs is how to determine the risks attributable to the PE in the absence of contracts which would set out the terms of the transaction (i.e. as would be available if the PE was a distinct and separate enterprise). Any determination of what risks should be attributed to the PE will be highly specific, i.e. it will have to be deduced by examining internal practices of the enterprise, by making a comparison with what similar independent enterprises would do and by examining any internal data or documentation purporting to show how the attribution or risk has been made.

This is a significant proposal. In the past, the Inland Revenue has argued that risks should be attributed to the activities of PEs, but have lacked any guidance from the OECD to support such a stance.

The document raises the possibility of notional royalty charges to the PE where it uses intangible property developed by other parts of the enterprise in carrying out its activities. This represents a rejection of the general presumption as set out in the commentary to the OECD model and a marked departure from the approach adopted by the Inland Revenue, although the document recognises that this is a complex area and specifically requests comment on this issue as part of the consultative process.

In relation to internal services, the working hypothesis is to attribute profit to the PE in respect of services performed by the PE for other parts of the enterprise (and vice versa) by following the guidance given in the Transfer Pricing Guidelines. This represents a departure from previous interpretations and leaves open the possibility of costs being recharged at a mark-up rather than simply at cost.

The discussion document also considers:

- how to determine the capital structure and debt/equity ratio of the PE (especially how to allocate 'free' capital to the PE);

- whether the movement of funds between the PE and other parts of the enterprise could give rise to interest charges;

- how to determine the amount of interest that should be attributable to the PE;

- how to determine what credit rating should be attributed to the PE.

These issues are important, as they affect on the amount of interest expense that can be claimed as a deduction by the PE.

Associated enterprises

7.11   The 'associated enterprises' article deals with the position where an enterprise of a contracting state participates, directly or indirectly, in the management, control or capital of an enterprise of the other contracting state, or the same persons so participate in both enterprises. If conditions are made or imposed between the two enterprises in their commercial or financial relations which differ from those which would be made between independent enterprises, any profits which would, but for those conditions, have accrued to one of the enterprises may be included in the profits of that enterprise and be taxed accordingly.

There are two methods of dealing with the profit which would be taxed in both jurisdictions following an adjustment under this article. The first is to make a corresponding adjustment reducing the profits of the enterprise in the jurisdiction in which the profits are overstated. This approach is taken, for example, in the 1975 and the new draft agreement with the US. The other method is to treat the adjustment as foreign source income of the enterprise whose profits were overstated and to allow a credit for the foreign tax paid by the associated enterprise on the adjustment. Where the second approach is adopted, as in the 1979 agreement with Sri Lanka, it is often contained in the 'elimination of double taxation' article.

Other variations

7.12   The UK's agreements contain a number of variations to this article, including the following:

(*a*)   The 1967 agreement with Australia provides that, if there is inadequate information to determine the profits of an associated enterprise in accordance with the article, the law of either country may be applied to make the enterprise liable to pay tax on an amount determined by the exercise of a discretion or the making of an estimate, provided that the discretion is exercised or the estimate is made in accordance with the principles stated in the article.

(*b*)   The 1975 US agreement also contains some additional paragraphs, as follows:

    (i)   the mutual agreement procedure is to apply if the contracting states disagree on the amount of any expense or income to be taken into account in their respective jurisdictions;

    (ii)   as published in 1975, Article 9(4) expressly prevented US states from applying the unitary basis of taxation (i.e. one based on an apportionment of the worldwide income of a 'unitary business' rather than on the arm's length principle) in relation to UK enterprises. As ratification by the US Senate could not be obtained on that basis, the article was amended so that, as ratified, it applies only to federal tax. This allowed individual states to tax UK enterprises on the unitary basis and other solutions have had to be sought to the problem of the application of unitary taxation to UK enterprises.

The new draft US agreement broadly follows the OECD model.

The OECD and UN models

7.13   The OECD and UN model articles are broadly similar to each other and adopt the 'corresponding adjustment' method for eliminating double taxation. The commentary to the OECD model indicates that the article deals only with 'primary adjustments', i.e. adjustments to the taxable profits of the companies themselves. It does not seek to restore fully the position of the enterprises to the position the parties would have been in if the original transactions had been on arm's length terms. This might entail, for example, withholding tax on a notional dividend from a subsidiary company to its parent. However, nothing in these model articles prevents either country from making a secondary adjustment if it may do so under its domestic law.

Shipping and air transport

7.14   This article usually provides that profits from the operation of ships or aircraft in international traffic are taxable only in the territory in which either the enterprise is resident or its place of effective management is situated. The term 'international traffic' is variously defined in the UK's agreements. For example, the 1980 agreement with Denmark (as amended by protocol in 1996) defines the term as:

> 'any transport by a ship or aircraft operated by an enterprise of a contracting state, except when the ship or aircraft is operated solely between places in the other contracting state'.

It should be noted that a transport enterprise may be required to have assets or personnel in a foreign country for the purposes of operating its ships or aircraft in international traffic. Such an enterprise may derive income from providing goods or services in that country to other transport enterprises. The commentary in the OECD model takes the view that such income would not be related to the operation of ships or aircraft by the operation itself and so it would not normally fall within the scope of the shipping and air transport article, unless the provision of goods and performance of services for other transport enterprises in that country are incidental or supplementary to the enterprise's operation of ships or aircraft in international traffic. Similar considerations apply to operations carried on by a pool.

In addition, the commentary has been amended to say that certain investment income may now fall within this article where it is made as an integral part of the carrying on of the business of operating the ships or aircraft in international traffic in the contracting state.

A further amendment to the commentary has been made such that where ships or aircraft are operated in international traffic, the application of the article to the profits from such operation will not be affected by the fact that the ships or aircraft are operated by a PE which is not the place of effective management of the whole enterprise.

Some variations

7.15   There are several variations to this article in the UK's agreements, including the following:

(*a*)   The 1976 agreement with the Philippines does not contain an article concerning the operation of ships and aircraft.

(*b*)   There is no reference to 'international traffic' in the 'shipping and air transport' article in the 1953 agreement with Greece. Therefore it would appear possible for the UK operator of a ship or aircraft to pay no local tax on profits earned from the use of the ship or aircraft solely between ports or airports in Greece and vice versa. Similarly, the shipping and air transport articles in the agreements with Jersey (1952), Guernsey (1952) and the Isle of Man (1955) are not limited in scope to 'international traffic'.

(*c*)   Several agreements, including those with The Netherlands (1980), Belgium (1987), Luxembourg (1967) and Poland (1976) refer specifically to the situation where the effective management of a shipping enterprise in international traffic is on board a ship. In these cases the effective management of the enterprise is deemed to be situated in the country in which the ship's home harbour is situated or, if there is no such home harbour, in the country where the ship's operator is resident. This paragraph is included in the OECD model.

(*d*)   A few agreements, including that with Switzerland (1977), refer to profits from the operation of boats engaged in inland waterways transport. These are normally taxable only in the contracting state in which the effective management of the enterprise is situated.

(*e*)   Some agreements provide that, where profits within the first paragraph of the article (i.e. those referred to in 7.14 above) are derived by an enterprise from participation in a pool, a joint business or an international operating agency, the profits attributable to that enterprise are to be taxed only in the state in which the effective management of that enterprise is situated.

(*f*)   Several agreements include paragraphs concerning the use, maintenance or rental of containers (including trailers and related equipment) used for the transport of goods in international traffic. In such circumstances the profits earned from this activity are taxable only in the country of residence of the operator. Examples include the agreements with the US (1975) and Poland (1976).

Consideration should also be given to the limited agreements covering the taxation of shipping and air transport profits which are referred to in 2.20.

The OECD and UN models

7.16   The OECD model article contains four paragraphs. The first two deal with the operation of ships in international traffic and to the operation of boats in inland waterways transport, the profits from which are to be taxable only in the country of effective management of the enterprise. The model also has paragraphs dealing with the situation where the place of effective management is aboard a ship or boat, and with the profits of a pool, joint business or international operating agency similar to those discussed in 7.15 (*c*) and (*e*) above.

The UN model has two alternative articles. The first is almost identical to the OECD model. The second contains a different method of dealing with profits from the operation of ships in international traffic. The profits from these activities are to be taxable only in the state of effective management unless the shipping activities arising from the operation in the other contracting state are 'more than casual'. If so, the profits may be taxed in the other state. The amount of taxable profits is to be determined on the basis of an appropriate allocation of the overall net profits derived by the enterprise from its shipping operations. The tax computed in accordance with the allocation is to be reduced by a percentage figure to be agreed by negotiation between the parties to the agreement.

Neither the OECD nor the UN model refers to the operation of container traffic, although the OECD commentary indicates that profits derived by an enterprise engaged in international transport from the lease of containers which is supplementary or incidental to its international operation of ships or aircraft fall within the scope of the article.

Dividends

7.17   The 'dividends' article in UK agreements is often lengthy and complex due largely to the UK's imputation system introduced in *FA 1972* and the payment to non-resident shareholders of part of the tax credit to which UK resident individual shareholders are entitled. Many agreements contain anti-avoidance provisions relating to the payment of the tax credit.

As far as UK groups of companies with subsidiaries in the EC are concerned, the importance of dividend articles in agreements may be significantly reduced by the EC Parent/Subsidiary Directive which came into force on 1 January 1992. Where the EC Directive applies and gives more favourable treatment than the dividends article in the relevant agreement (usually a complete exemption from foreign dividend withholding tax), the terms of the dividends article in the agreement may be of academic interest only. However, the dividends article in the relevant agreement often applies in cases which are outside the Directive, for example where the shareholding in the foreign company is less than 25% or where the shares are not held for the requisite period (up to two years) under the law of the foreign country.

Dividends articles in the UK's agreements are subject to many variations. The following sets out the contents of article 10 of the agreement with Spain (1975). Important variations in other agreements are discussed later.

7.18   The Spain agreement contains the following paragraphs. *Paragraph 10(1)*. A statement that dividends derived from a Spanish resident company by a resident of the UK may be taxed in the UK. However, such dividends may also be taxed in Spain according to the laws of Spain, although the tax charged is not to exceed:

(*a*) 10% of the gross dividend if the beneficial owner is a company which controls directly or indirectly at least 10% of the voting power in the paying company; or

(*b*) in all other cases 15% of the gross dividend.

7.19 *Paragraph 10(2).* A similar statement to the effect that dividends derived from a UK resident company by a resident of Spain may be taxed in Spain. However, the dividends may also be taxed in the UK in accordance with the laws of the UK, although the tax charged is not to exceed:

(*a*) 10% of the gross dividend if the beneficial owner is a company which controls directly or indirectly at least 10% of the voting power in the paying company; or

(*b*) in all other cases 15% of the gross dividend.

Since the introduction of the system of advance corporation tax in 1973 the UK has not levied a dividend withholding tax (although advance corporation tax has now been abolished). Accordingly, article 10(2) has no effect at present.

7.20 *Paragraph 10(3).* This provides that so long as an individual resident in the UK is entitled to a tax credit in respect of dividends paid by a company resident in the UK (i.e. under the present imputation system) the following rules apply:

(*a*) Dividends derived from a UK resident company by a resident of Spain may be taxed in Spain.

(*b*) Unless the beneficial owner of the dividend is a Spanish company which owns (together with associated companies) directly or indirectly at least 10% of the voting power of the UK company, the Spanish shareholder is entitled to a tax credit equal to the tax credit to which a UK resident individual would be entitled. UK tax may be charged on the dividend, but the UK tax charge is limited to 15% of the sum of the dividend and the tax credit.

(*c*) No tax credit is available if the shareholder is a Spanish company controlling 10% or more of the voting power in the UK resident company, but the dividend is exempt from any UK tax which is chargeable on dividends.

Example 70

Isabella, a Spanish resident individual, owns shares in a UK company on which she received a dividend (before tax credit) of £50,000 on 31 December 1997. Her UK tax position is as follows:

	£
Dividend received (net)	50,000
Tax credit (20/80)	12,500
Dividend plus tax credit	62,500
Tax deducted (15%)	(9,375)
Dividend after withholding tax	£53,125

Therefore, a payment of tax credit of £3,125 (i.e. £12,500 − £9,375) is due to Isabella. This may be claimed by an application on the relevant forms to FICO (International), Nottingham.

From 6 April 1999, the rate of tax credit on dividends for a UK resident individual is reduced to 10/90 of the net dividend. From that date, the amount of tax which may be deducted from the amount of the dividend plus tax credit (15%) exceeds the amount of the tax credit. On dividends paid from 6 April 1999, therefore, no payment of tax credit will be due to Isabella.

7.21   *Paragraph 10(4).* This gives a definition of 'dividends' as follows:

'The term "dividends" as used in this article means income from shares, or other rights, not being debt claims, participating in profits as well as income from corporate rights assimilated to income from shares by the taxation law of the State of which the company making the distribution is a resident and also includes any other item (other than interest relieved from tax under the provisions of Article 11 of this Convention) which, under the laws of the Contracting State of which the company paying the dividend is a resident, is treated as a distribution or dividend of a company.'

Therefore the definition for the purposes of the agreement is significantly wider than that of 'dividend' in the *Taxes Acts*, encompassing items (listed in *TA 1988, s 209* and following) which are treated as distributions under UK tax law. However, it excludes items which are defined as 'interest' later in the agreement to the extent that those items are relieved from tax under the 'interest' article.

7.22   *Paragraph 10(5).* The normal provisions are excluded where the shareholder has a PE in the other country and the holding of shares is effectively connected with the business carried on through the PE. In that case, the dividend is treated as income of the PE under the 'business profits' article of the agreement and may be taxed accordingly.

7.23   *Paragraph 10(6).* This is a 'dividend stripping' provision which applies where a shareholder owns 10% or more of the class of a company's shares on which a dividend is paid. The withholding tax reliefs and imputation credits do not apply to the extent that the dividends can only have been paid out of profits which the paying company earned in a period ending twelve months or more before the date on which the recipient of the dividend became the owner of 10% or more of the shares. This provision does not, however, apply if the shares were acquired for bona fide commercial reasons and not primarily for the purpose of securing the benefit of the 'dividends' article.

7.24 *Paragraph 10(7).* Where a company resident in one of the contracting states derives profits or income from the other (the source country), the source country may not impose any tax on the dividends paid by that company (unless those dividends are beneficially owned by residents of the source country). It also provides that no tax may be imposed by the source country on the undistributed profits of the company. However, where a company of one of the contracting states has a PE in the other state, the contracting state in which the PE is situated is allowed to impose a withholding tax not exceeding 15% of the distributed profits of the company attributable to the post-tax profits of the PE.

Paragraphs of this type have no practical effect on foreign companies which have PEs in the UK since UK domestic law does not impose a withholding tax on dividends or undistributed profits of non-resident companies. However, UK companies with PEs in countries which do impose such taxes would benefit from these provisions.

Tax credits for foreign corporate shareholders

7.25 Since the introduction of the UK's imputation system of corporation tax in 1973 most of the UK's agreements have been renegotiated or amended by protocol to allow a foreign non-corporate shareholder, or a corporate shareholder owning less than 10% of the voting power in a UK company, to obtain the same tax credit as a UK resident individual shareholder would have obtained less a deduction at a rate of (usually) 15% of the amount of the dividend plus the tax credit. This is discussed in 7.18 above with respect to the agreement with Spain.

However, a number of agreements make provision for the payment of a tax credit to foreign corporate shareholders owning at least 10% (or, in some cases, 25%) of the voting power of a UK company. Seven such agreements, namely those with Belgium (1987), Italy (1988), Luxembourg (1984 protocol), The Netherlands (1980), Sweden (1983), Switzerland (1982 protocol) and the US (1975, but not the new US agreement) currently allow such a foreign corporate shareholder to obtain payment of one-half of the tax credit to which a UK resident would have been entitled, less a deduction of 5% of the aggregate of the amount of the dividend plus the tax credit (see also 2.7 for a discussion of the European law issues of this deduction).

Until 5 April 1999, these provisions reduce the effective rate of UK corporation tax on distributed profits from 31% to approximately 26.3%. Where the UK subsidiary is paying tax at the small companies' rate of 21% the effective rate of corporation tax is reduced to approximately 15.6% — see Example 71 below. In an agreement with Canada (1985 protocol), a similar tax credit is paid, subject to a deduction of 10% of the dividend plus tax credit. Payments of tax credits which were previously available under the agreements with Denmark and Finland were withdrawn with effect from 1 April 1998. From 6 April 1999, the benefit of these articles is considerably reduced, so that it becomes marginal. See Example 71 below.

In *Union Texas International Corpn v Critchley [1990] STC 305*, the company contended that the 5% deducted from the tax credit under the 1975 agreement with the US was invalid since there was no provision in UK domestic law authorising the deduction. The Court of Appeal held that the 5% deduction was properly made, although it agreed with the taxpayer's calculation of the amount of the deduction under the specific wording of the agreement. *FA 1989, s 115* has since changed the construction of the relevant paragraph, so that the 5% deduction under this paragraph in the 1975 US agreement is calculated on the total of the dividend and the half tax credit given by the agreement.

Example 71

Tenedos BV is a Netherlands resident company controlled by Netherlands resident individuals. It owns 100% of the shares of Tenedos Ltd, a UK company which distributes all its post-tax profits. Until 5 April 1999 the effective rate of UK tax on the basis that Tenedos Ltd pays UK corporation tax at the full rate of corporation tax (31%) and the small companies' rate (21%) is as follows:

		31% CT rate		21% CT rate
Profit before UK corporation tax		100,000		100,000
UK corporation tax at 31%/21%		(31,000)		(21,000)
Profit after UK corporation tax		69,000		79,000
Dividend paid		69,000		79,000
Tax credit (20/80)	17,250		19,750	
50% thereof		8,625		9,875
Dividend plus half tax credit		77,625		88,875
Less: 5% tax deducted		(3,881)		(4,444)
Cash received by Tenedos BV		£73,744		£84,431
Effective rate of UK tax		26.26%		15.57%

From 6 April 1999 the position is to be as follows:

		30% CT Rate		20% CT Rate
Profit before UK corporation tax		100,000		100,000
UK corporation tax at 30%/20%		(30,000)		(20,000)
Profit after UK corporation tax		70,000		80,000
Dividend paid		70,000		80,000
Tax credit (10/90)	7,778		8,889	
50% thereof		3,889		4,445
		73,889		84,445
Less: 5% tax deducted		(3,694)		(4,222)
		70,195		80,223
Effective rate of UK Tax		29.80%		19.78%

7.26   For the purpose of ascertaining whether there is 10% voting control, agreements usually provide for the aggregation of the holdings of associated companies, which prevents the fragmentation of shareholdings in order to obtain larger benefits under the agreement. For example, Article 10(3)(c) of the agreement with Sweden gives a half tax credit (less 5%) rather than a full tax credit (less 15%) where the 'beneficial owner of the dividend is, or is associated with, a company which either alone or together with one or more associated companies controls directly or indirectly at least 10% of the voting power of the company paying the dividend'. This paragraph defines two companies as 'associated' for these purposes where 'one is controlled directly or indirectly by the other, or both are controlled directly or indirectly by a third company; and a company shall be deemed to be controlled by another company if the latter controls more than 50% of the voting power in the first-mentioned company'. The definition refers only to control by companies and therefore does not aggregate the shareholdings of, for example, two companies controlled by the same individual or trust.

Other variations

7.27   There are many significant variations articles in UK agreements, including the following:

- Some agreements such as the 1953 agreement with Greece and the agreements with Jersey (1952), Guernsey (1952) and the Isle of Man (1955) do not contain 'dividends' articles.

- Many agreements offer no tax credits to residents of the treaty partner. Examples include those with Hungary (1977), China (1984) and Pakistan (1986).

- Some agreements (including those with Australia (1967 as amended), India (1993) and New Zealand (1983)) restrict the tax credit to *individuals* resident in the country of the treaty partner. Corporate 'portfolio' shareholders (i.e. those holding less than 10% of the voting power in a UK company) may not therefore benefit from a payment of tax credit.

- The agreement with Finland (as amended by a 1996 protocol) provides that dividends paid by a company resident in one of the contracting states to a resident (whether an individual or company) of the other contracting state who is the beneficial owner is taxable only in the country of residence of the recipient. Accordingly, no withholding tax can be applied by either country on dividends paid to a resident of the other.

- A number of agreements contain no 'dividend-stripping' paragraph, including the 1969 agreement with Japan (as amended).

- The 1964 agreement with Germany contains a special provision which relates the rates of withholding tax on dividends paid to a UK corporate shareholder owning at least 25% of the voting shares in a German company to the rates of corporate tax levied in Germany on distributed and undistributed profits. This would currently restrict the German withholding tax to 15%. However, UK companies holding 25% or more of the voting shares of a German company are normally entitled to the benefit of the EC Parent/Subsidiary Directive which reduced the rate of German withholding tax on dividends to 0% from 1 July 1996 (and to 5% before that date).

• There are many different definitions of 'dividends', reflecting the diverse systems of company law of the countries with which the UK has negotiated agreements. The term 'dividends' usually encompasses any item which is a distribution of a company under the laws of the UK.

• In cases where a payment of a tax credit is available to substantial corporate shareholders, there are usually anti-avoidance provisions denying the benefit of the provision in specified circumstances. In the agreement with the Netherlands, unless the Netherlands company receiving the dividend is officially quoted on a Netherlands stock exchange, it must show that it is not controlled by a person (or persons) who would not have been entitled to a tax credit if he (or they) had been the beneficial owner of the dividend. Other agreements, including those with Belgium and Switzerland, provide that the recipient of the dividend must show that the shareholding in respect of which the dividend was paid was acquired by it for bona fide commercial reasons or in the ordinary course of making or managing investments and that it was not the main object (or one of the main objects) of that acquisition to obtain entitlement to the tax credit.

• A number of agreements with countries, including France and Italy, which have imputation systems of corporation tax give tax credits to UK resident shareholders. For example, the agreement with Italy (1988) gives UK resident shareholders of an Italian company (other than companies owning 10% or more of the voting power) the tax credit to which an individual resident in Italy would be entitled, subject to a 15% withholding tax. A UK resident company owning 10% or more of the voting power of the Italian company is entitled to half of the Italian tax credit, subject to a 5% withholding tax. At present there is a tax credit available to Italian shareholders in an Italian company of 56.25% of the amount of the dividend. The position of UK shareholders may be illustrated as follows:

Example 72

The dividends from an Italian company to a UK shareholder are as follows:

	Individual	Corporate < 10%	Corporate > 10%*
	£	£	£
Net dividend	100,000	100,000	100,000
Italian tax credit	56,250	56,250	28,125
UK taxable income	156,250	156,250	128,125
Withholding tax (15%/5%)	(23,438)	(23,438)	(6,406)
Net cash received in UK	132,812	132,812	121,719

UK taxable income	156,250	156,250	128,125
Income tax (40%)	(62,500)		
Corporation tax (30%)		(46,875)	(39,718)
Double taxation relief	23,438	23,438	6,406
UK tax after double taxation relief	(39,062)	(23,437)	(33,312)
Net income after tax	£93,750	£109,375	£88,407

*NB ignores relief for underlying tax.

The OECD and UN models

7.28   The wording of 'dividends' articles contained in these models is broadly similar. The first paragraph gives the general rule that a dividend paid by a company which is a resident of a contracting state to a resident of the other contracting state may be taxed in that other state. The second provides that such dividends may also be taxed in the country of residence of the company paying the dividends. However, if the recipient of the dividends is the beneficial owner of the dividends, the tax charged shall not exceed certain percentages. In the OECD model, the percentages are 5% of the gross amount of the dividends if the beneficial owner is a company (other than a partnership) which holds directly at least 25% of the capital of the company paying the dividends and 15% in all other cases. The UN model leaves the percentage of withholding tax open for negotiation between the contracting states, but sets the percentage shareholding at which the withholding tax rate changes at 10% rather than 25%.

The next two paragraphs of both model articles provide a definition of 'dividends' and deal with dividends connected with a PE in the contracting state of the company paying the dividend (which are treated as business income in the state in which the PE is situated).

The final paragraph of both models provides that, where a company of one of the contracting states derives profits or income from the other (the source country), the source country may not impose any tax on the dividends paid by that company (unless those dividends are paid to a resident of the source country or the holding in respect of which the dividends are paid is effectively connected with a PE there). It also provides that no tax may be imposed by the source country on the undistributed profits of the company. This is to apply even if the dividends paid or the undistributed profits consist wholly or partly of profits or income arising there.

The OECD commentary on this article contains a discussion of the effects of special features in the domestic tax laws of certain countries, in particular the system of corporation tax prevailing (classical, imputation and split-rate) and the consequential effect on shareholders. It also draws a distinction between dividends being the distribution of profits to the shareholders by companies limited by shares, limited partnerships with share capital, limited liability companies or other joint stock companies and the profits of a business carried on by a partnership as the partners' profits derived from their own exertions, being business profits.

Interest

7.29   The structure of the 'interest' article in UK agreements varies according to whether the agreement grants an exemption from tax in the country in which the interest arises (the 'source country') or merely grants a reduction in the rate of tax which may apply. Where there is a complete exemption, for example as in agreements with many western European countries, the opening paragraph may provide, as in the 1969 agreement with Finland, that interest arising in a contracting state which is derived and beneficially owned by a resident of the other contracting state is taxable only in the state of residence.

7.30   Where the agreement does not give a full exemption in the source country, as in the agreements with Canada (1978) and New Zealand (1983), the first paragraph may contain a statement confirming the rights of each contracting state to tax its own residents on interest arising in the other contracting state. In these cases, the source country retains the right to levy tax at a specified maximum rate which is usually lower than the withholding tax rate applying under its domestic law. The maximum rate of tax on interest is 10% in the agreements with Canada, Australia, Portugal and Italy, 12.5% in those with Ghana, Jamaica and Nigeria and 15% in those with, for example, Belgium and the Ivory Coast.

7.31   There is usually a definition of 'interest', which may refer to income treated as interest by the taxation laws of the country in which the income arises. For example, the agreement with Italy (1988) defines 'interest' for the purposes of the article as:

' ... income from Government securities, bonds or debentures, whether or not secured by mortgage and whether or not carrying a right to participate in profits, and debt claims of every kind as well as other income assimilated to income from money lent by the taxation law of the state in which the income arises, but does not include income dealt with in Article 10 of this convention [dividends].'

In most agreements there is a paragraph excluding relief where the beneficial owner of the interest, who is a resident of one of the contracting states, has a PE in the other contracting state. Where the debt claim producing the interest is effectively connected with the PE the interest may be taxed as part of the profits of the PE.

7.32   Other provisions contained in many of the UK's agreements include the following:

(*a*)   A paragraph which deems the source of the interest to be the country of residence of the payer (or the country of a PE of the payer if the interest was incurred in connection with the PE).

(*b*)   A paragraph which provides that 'any provision in the law of a contracting state relating only to interest paid to a non-resident company shall not operate so as to require such interest paid to a company which is a resident of the other contracting state to be treated as a distribution of the company paying such interest'. As far as the UK is concerned, this referred to *TA 1988, s 209(2)(e)(iv)* and *(v)* which were repealed with effect from 29 November 1994. Under *s 209(2)(e)(iv)* all interest paid by a UK resident company to a foreign parent or fellow subsidiary where there was a 75% shareholding relationship was treated as a distribution in the absence of the application of such a paragraph in a double taxation agreement. *FA 1995* introduced new provisions, contained in *TA 1988, s 209(2)(da)*, which apply, subject to exceptions, to interest paid to a 75% parent or fellow group company (whether UK resident or not). These provisions treat as a distribution only that part of the interest which exceeds the amount which would have been paid in the absence of the relationship.

(*c*)   A paragraph which states that, where interest paid exceeds an arm's length amount (or, in some cases, exceeds an arm's length rate) because there is a 'special relationship' between the payer and the recipient or between both of them and some other person, the benefit of the 'interest' article extends only to the amount (or rate) of interest which would have been agreed on in the absence of such special relationship. In that case the excess part of the payments remains taxable according to the domestic laws of each contracting state. *TA 1988, s 808A* sets out in which circumstances the Inland Revenue apply this 'special relationship' provision.

(*d*)   Some agreements contain a paragraph which denies any benefit under the article if the debt claim in respect of which the interest was paid was created or assigned mainly for the purpose of taking advantage of this article and not for bona fide commercial reasons. This is to be found in many agreements including those with the Netherlands (1980) and France (1968, as amended by protocol).

Variations

7.33   A significant number of variations arise in UK agreements. These include the following:

(*a*)   The 1952 agreements with Jersey and Guernsey and the 1955 agreement with the Isle of Man contain no 'interest' article.

(*b*)   The 1964 agreement with Germany and the 1953 agreement with Greece treat interest and royalties in a similar manner in the same article.

(*c*)   The 'distribution' clause is absent in agreements with a number of countries, for example the 1953 agreement with Greece, the 1976 agreement with the Irish Republic and the 1973 agreement with

Malaysia. However, the absence of this paragraph is less important as far as interest paid by UK resident companies to overseas affiliates are concerned following the changes to *TA 1988, s 209* introduced from 29 November 1994 noted in 7.32(*b*) above.

(*d*)   There is no 'deemed source of interest' paragraph in many agreements, for example the 1964 agreement with Germany, the 1976 agreement with the Irish Republic and the 1980 agreement with the Netherlands. In addition the 1975 US agreement omits this paragraph.

(*e*)   Several UK agreements contain a clause which denies relief where:

   (i)   the interest relates to a debt dealt in on a stock exchange;

   (ii)   the beneficial owner of the interest does not bear tax in respect of it in his country of residence; and

   (iii)   the beneficial owner sells the debt within three months of the date on which it was acquired.

An example of this type of paragraph is found in the 1973 agreement with Jamaica and a broadly similar paragraph is contained in the 1975 US agreement (although not in the new draft US agreement).

(*f*)   A number of agreements do not contain a paragraph which denies relief if the debt claim was created or assigned in order to take advantage of the article and not for bona fide commercial reasons. Examples are the 1987 agreement with Belgium and the 1962 agreement with Israel.

(*g*)   The agreement with Iceland (1991) contains an anti-avoidance provision. Briefly, the benefit of the 'interest' article is denied where the beneficial owner of the interest is a company (other than a quoted company) unless the company shows that it is not controlled by a person (or associated persons) who would not be entitled to relief under the article if he had been the beneficial owner of the interest. A similar paragraph in the agreement with Denmark has been removed by a 1996 protocol.

(*h*)   In the majority of the UK's agreements the scope of the article is limited to interest arising in one of the contracting states. In many of these agreements interest arising outside the contracting states would fall within the 'other income' article (see 7.65 below). However, the 'interest' article in other agreements (including that with the US (1975)) applies to interest wherever it arises.

The OECD and UN models

7.34   The OECD and UN model articles are very similar to each other. The OECD model allows the country of source of the interest to levy tax at a maximum of 10%, although the UN model leaves the percentage to be established through bilateral regulations. Both model articles provide for the competent authorities of the contracting states to settle the method of application of this limitation by mutual agreement. The models also contain paragraphs (similar to many contained in the UK's agreements) which define 'interest', deal with the case where the recipient has a PE in the source country, provide 'deemed source' rules and restrict the application of the article (and fixed base in the case of the UN model) where there is a 'special relationship' between the parties.

Royalties

7.35 The UK's agreements follow two main patterns in determining where relief falls under this article, depending upon whether the country in which the royalty arises (the 'country of source') retains the right to tax them. Several of the UK's agreements with OECD countries specify that no tax is to be levied on royalties by the country of source. However, several OECD countries which have historically been net importers of capital, such as Australia and New Zealand, and many developing countries, have negotiated agreements allowing the country of source to tax the royalty at a maximum rate, often 10%. The 1969 agreement with Japan also provides for a 10% rate of tax in the country of source. The agreement with India (1993) is unusual in that it provides for various rates from 10% to 20% depending on the type of royalty and the period during which it arises.

The detailed wording of royalties articles varies. Several provide that the article applies to royalties 'derived and beneficially owned' by a resident of a contracting state (as in the 1967 agreement with Australia, the 1976 agreement with the Irish Republic and the 1975 US agreement). However, there are variants to this, including that in the 1968 agreement with South Africa which refers to royalties 'paid to a resident of the other contracting state who is subject to tax there in respect thereof'. For the Inland Revenue's view of circumstances in which income is 'subject to tax' in the UK see 2.17.

7.36 The UK's agreements provide a number of definitions of the term 'royalties'. This example is contained in the agreement with Belgium (1987), which defines them as:

> 'payments of any kind received as a consideration for the use of, or right to use, any copyright of literary, artistic or scientific work (including cinematographic films and films or tapes for radio or television broadcasting), any patent, trademark, design or model, plan, secret formula or process, or for information concerning industrial, commercial or scientific experience.'

Earlier agreements often give a less comprehensive definition and may not specifically include films and tapes for radio and television broadcasting. They may also specifically *exclude* amounts paid in respect of the operation of mines or quarries or in respect of the extraction or removal of natural resources.

Some agreements, for example those with Australia (1967) and New Zealand (1983) specifically include payments for the right to use industrial, commercial or scientific equipment (leasing charges). Fees for technical services and assistance are also included within the definition in several agreements, perhaps most notably in the agreement with India (1993).

7.37   Royalties articles in most UK agreements contain a paragraph to the effect that the exemption or withholding tax reduction as specified in the earlier paragraphs will not apply if the person claiming relief has a PE in the country in which the royalties arise. This allows a country to levy tax at full rates on a royalty arising in that country which is paid in respect of a right or property which is effectively connected with the PE. In such a case the royalty may be taxed as part of the business profits of the PE. Many agreements extend this paragraph to cover royalties which are effectively connected with a fixed base from which a resident of the other country performs professional services.

7.38   Other matters normally covered in the 'royalties' article are as follows:

• Most of the UK's more recent tax treaties contain a provision in the royalty article denying the relief available under that article where:

   (i)   a 'special relationship' exists between the payer and the beneficial owner of the royalty or between them and some other person; and

   (ii)   the amount of the royalty is greater 'for whatever reason' than it would otherwise have been if agreed between two independent parties.

In some treaties, the words 'for whatever reason' are omitted. In either event, the intention is that the provision should apply not only where the rate of royalty is greater than the arm's length rate but also where no such agreement would have been concluded at all in the absence of the special relationship.

However, the wording is sufficiently ambiguous to leave some area of doubt. Therefore, *TA 1988, s 808B* (introduced by *FA 2000, Sch 25 para 30*, in relation to royalties payable on or after 28 July 2000) requires the special relationship provision in a royalties article to be construed as requiring account to be taken of all factors. Thus, where the royalties paid are, all things considered, excessive, the Inland Revenue can apply this provision to exclude the excess royalties from the benefit of the treaty and apply the normal rate of withholding tax to the excess — no matter what the exact wording of the 'special relationship' provision may be.

This refinement was introduced as part of the *FA 2000* reform of double tax relief. *Section 808B* sets out factors to be taken into account when construing the special relationship. Its wording follows, with necessary adjustments, the existing *s 808A* for interest payments, but is more comprehensive.

• In some agreements royalties are deemed to arise in the country where the payer is resident, unless the obligation is incurred by, and the expense borne by, a PE or a fixed base, in which case they arise where the PE or fixed base is situated.

• A number of agreements contain a paragraph preventing royalties from being treated as distributions (for example the 1969 agreements with Austria and Japan). Others (for example the 1969 agreement with Finland), qualify this principle by permitting the treatment of royalties as distributions where the paying and receiving companies are under common control and 50% or more of the recipient company's shares are owned by residents of the country in which the payer is resident.

• The new draft US agreement includes a paragraph containing anti-conduct rules.

Other variations

7.39   Royalties articles in the UK's agreements contain many other variations, including the following:

(*a*)   Certain agreements provide that capital gains realised on the sale of patents or other rights or property are treated as royalties to be taxed in accordance with this article. This is achieved either by means of a separate paragraph in the article (for example the 1964 agreement with Germany) or by extending the definition of 'royalties' to include such gains (for example the 1968 agreement with France and, to a more limited extent, the 1975 and new draft agreement with the US).

(*b*)   The 1978 agreement with Canada provides for exemption from tax on royalties in respect of the production or reproduction of any literary, dramatic, musical or artistic work (but not including rents or royalties in respect of motion picture films and films or video tapes for use in connection with television). There is a 10% tax on all other royalties.

(*c*)   The agreement with Iceland (1991) contains an anti-avoidance provision similar to that contained in the 'interest' article of that agreement. Briefly, the benefit of the 'royalties' article is denied where the beneficial owner of the royalties is a company (other than a quoted company) unless the company shows that it is not controlled by a person (or associated persons) who would not be entitled to relief under the article if he had been the beneficial owner of the royalty. A similar article in the agreement with Denmark was removed by a 1996 protocol.

The OECD and UN models

7.40   The OECD model article exempts royalties arising in a contracting state and beneficially owned by a resident of the other contracting state from tax in the country of source. It has a similar definition of 'royalties' to that contained in the agreement with Belgium as set out in 7.36 above, except that the OECD model does not refer to films or tapes for radio and television broadcasting. It also contains paragraphs dealing with royalties arising in connection with a PE and with non-arm's length terms where a 'special relationship' exists.

The latest version of the OECD model commentary has been revised to reflect the changes to Article 7 following the deletion of Article 14. Some detailed comments on the taxation of computer software have also been added to refine the analysis by which business profits are distinguished from royalties in computer software transactions.

The UN model article allows the country of source to tax royalties at a maximum rate to be agreed between the contracting parties. The definition contained in this model includes payments for films or tapes used for radio or television broadcasting and also payments for the use of, or right to use, industrial, commercial or scientific equipment.

The paragraph dealing with PEs and fixed bases allows the 'force of attraction' principle to a limited extent as royalties may be taxed as business profits or as income from independent personal services if the right or property concerned is effectively connected not only with a PE or fixed base, but also with other business activities carried on in the country of source which are of the same or similar kind as those effected through the PE.

The UN model also contains a 'special relationship' paragraph similar to that in the OECD model and a 'deemed source' paragraph similar to several in the UK's agreements.

Management fees

7.41   A few UK agreements contain a separate 'management fee' article, including the 1973 agreements with Jamaica and Kenya and the 1985 agreement with the Ivory Coast. Neither the OECD model nor the UN model contains a 'management fee' article although it is relatively common for developing countries to impose a withholding tax on such fees. However, management fees may fall within the definition of 'royalties' in certain agreements.

The UK agreements with Jamaica, Kenya and the Ivory Coast deal with management fees in a similar way to interest and royalties:

- The country of residence of the recipient retains the right to tax the fees.

- The country of source may tax management fees at the rate of 10% or 12.5%.

- The term 'management fees' is defined variously to include payments in consideration for services of a managerial, technical, and consultancy nature and, in the case of Jamaica, fees for industrial or commercial advice.

- No relief is given under the article if the fees are connected with a PE. The later agreement with the Ivory Coast also refers to a fixed base in which independent personal services are performed.

- A 'deemed source' paragraph is included, making the source of the fees the country of residence of the payer (or, if the management fees are incurred in connection with a PE, the country of the PE).

The agreements with Jamaica and the Ivory Coast (but not the agreement with Kenya) include a 'special relationship' paragraph similar to those commonly contained in 'interest' and 'royalties' articles. Accordingly, if there is a special relationship and the management fee exceeds the amount which would have been paid in the absence of that relationship, the excess may be taxed in accordance with the domestic laws of each country.

Capital gains

7.42   In several of the UK's agreements this article provides as follows:

(*a*) Gains derived by a resident of a contracting state from the alienation of immovable property may be taxed in the contracting state in which the property is situated.

(*b*) Gains from the alienation of movable property forming part of the business property of a PE which an enterprise has in a contracting state or pertaining to a fixed base there may be taxed in the state where the PE or fixed base is situated. These are to include gains from the disposal of the PE or fixed base itself.

(*c*) Gains from the sale of ships and aircraft operated in international traffic, and movable assets relating to the operation of the ships and aircraft, may be taxed only in the person's country of residence (or, in some cases, the place of effective management of the enterprise).

(*d*) Gains from the disposal of any other property may be taxed only in the alienator's country of residence.

Variations

7.43   There are a number of variations from these standard paragraphs in UK agreements, the following being significant examples.

(*a*)   There is no 'capital gains' article in many agreements, including the 1967 agreement with Australia and several agreements pre-dating the introduction of capital gains tax in 1965.

(*b*)   The article in the 1975 agreement with the US allows each country to tax capital gains according to its own domestic law. However, the new draft US agreement broadly attributes taxing rights to the source country in respect of gains relating directly or indirectly to the alienation of real property. Gains from the alienation of most other types of property with the exception of property forming part of the business assets of a PE are taxable only in the alienator's country of residence.

(*c*)   Some agreements, including the 1968 agreement with South Africa, allow immovable property to be taxable in the country of its location only if it forms part of the business property of a PE or pertains to a fixed base there.

(*d*)   The 1953 agreement with Greece provides that a resident of a contracting state is exempt from any tax on gains in the other contracting state unless it has a PE there. The 1966 agreement with Singapore (now superseded) contained a similar provision.

(*e*)   A number of agreements, including that with Switzerland (1977), allow a contracting state to tax gains on the alienation of shares in a company whose assets comprise principally immovable property situated in the contracting state.

(*f*)   Some agreements, for example that with Kenya (1973), contain a paragraph preserving the right of a country to levy a tax on capital gains under its own law if the seller is a resident of the other country and has been a resident of the first country at any time during the period of (usually) five or ten years immediately preceding the sale. Another, more limited, example of this kind of provision is included in the agreement with France (1968).

(*g*)   Several agreements, including those with Denmark (1980) and Finland (1969, as amended), contain paragraphs concerning the alienation of exploration and exploitation rights in connection with the sea-bed and subsoil. These allow the country in which the rights and property are situated to tax gains arising from them. The scope of these paragraphs varies, but in the Danish agreement property situated in the other contracting state (which includes designated areas of the Continental Shelf) used in connection with offshore activities is included, and also shares deriving the greater part of their value from such rights and property.

The OECD and UN models

7.44   The 'capital gains' article in the OECD model is similar to the article in some of the UK's agreements as set out in 7.42 above. There are, however, differences of detail; for example, the paragraph in the OECD model concerning the alienation of ships and aircraft includes a reference to 'boats engaged in inland waterways transport', which the UK's agreements do not usually cover. The latest version of the capital gains article in the OECD model together with the commentary has been revised to reflect the deletion of Article 14.

The UN model is broadly similar to the OECD model, except that it makes provision to allow a contracting state to tax gains on shares whose property consists principally of immovable property situated in the contracting state. In addition, it allows a contracting state to tax gains made by a non-resident on substantial shareholdings in other companies resident in its jurisdiction. In this case the required percentage holding is to be established by negotiation between the contracting states.

There is no definition of 'capital gains' in the models. Agreements use the word 'alienation' to cover all disposals such as the sale, gift or exchange of assets and the transfer of rights affecting assets. There are certain countries where capital appreciation, or gains on revaluation of assets, are taxed even if no alienation takes place. The OECD commentary indicates that the same principles should apply to taxes levied in these circumstances as apply on the disposal of such assets.

Independent personal services

7.45   While the heading of this article in many agreements is 'independent personal services', the text of the articles themselves tend to refer to 'professional services'. UK agreements usually contain two paragraphs dealing with the basis of taxation and the definition of 'professional services'. A person carrying on professional services or other activities of an independent character is taxable only in his country of residence unless he has a fixed base regularly available to him in the other country for the purpose of performing his activities. In that event the income attributable to that fixed base may be taxed in the other country. The agreement with Switzerland (1977), for example, defines the term 'professional services' as including especially 'independent scientific, literary, artistic, educational or teaching activities as well as the independent activities of physicians, lawyers, engineers, architects, dentists and accountants'. The expression therefore includes many of the occupations traditionally considered to be professions, but others, such as surveying, are not referred to specifically. However, since it is an inclusive definition, such professional people are likely to be taxed in accordance with this article if their services are clearly of an independent and professional character.

Variations

7.46   There are several variations, especially in the earlier UK agreements:

(*a*)   Among others, the 1967 agreement with Australia and the 1968 agreement with South Africa contain no definition of 'independent personal services' or of 'professional services'.

(*b*)   The article in the 1953 agreement with Greece refers to all personal services, whether they are professional, independent or dependent, in one article. In this case the treatment of independent personal service income is similar to that for wages and salaries (see 7.46 below).

(*c*)   The 1968 agreement with France refers to 'independent professional activities' and these are defined as 'all the activities, other than commercial, industrial or agricultural activities, carried on by a person who receives the proceeds or bears the losses arising from those activities'.

(*d*)   The 1976 agreement with the Irish Republic does not contain any reference to independent personal services. Accordingly, these may fall under Article 20 (income not expressly mentioned), in which case they are taxable only in the country of residence.

(*e*)   Several agreements allow a contracting state to tax a non-resident performing independent personal services in its jurisdiction, not only if he has a fixed base there, but also if his stay in the contracting state exceeds a certain period. An example of such a provision is contained in the 1975 US agreement, the relevant period being 183 days in the tax year. There is no independent personal services article in the new draft US agreement.

The OECD and UN models

7.47   The independent personal services article was deleted from the OECD model on 29 April 2000 on the basis of the report entitled *Issues Related to Article 14 of the OECD Model Tax Convention*. This reflects the fact that there are no intended differences between the concepts of permanent establishment as used in Article 7, and fixed base, as used in Article 14, or between how profits were computed and tax was calculated according to which of Article 7 or Article 14 applied. In addition, it was not always clear which activities fell within Article 14 as opposed to Article 7. The effect of the deletion of Article 14 is that income derived from professional services or other activities of an independent character is now dealt with under Article 7 as business profits.

There was no definition of the term 'fixed base' in the previous OECD model or in the UK's agreements. However, the previous OECD commentary indicated that the term would include, for instance, a physician's consulting room or the office of an architect or a lawyer, provided that such a centre of activity is of a fixed or permanent character.

The UN model allows a contracting state to tax income from professional services of a resident of the other contracting state in two circumstances:

(*a*)   where the person has a fixed base in the contracting state; and

(*b*)   if the person performing the services stays in the contracting state for more than 183 days in a fiscal year.

Dependent personal services

7.48   The 'dependent personal services' article covers the taxation of wages, salaries and other similar remuneration arising from an employment. UK agreements normally contain the following provisions:

(*a*)   Salaries, wages and other similar remuneration derived by a resident of one contracting state in respect of an employment is taxable only in that state, unless the employment is exercised in the other contracting state. If the employment is exercised in the other contracting state, such remuneration as is derived *therefrom* (generally taken to refer to the contracting state, rather than the employment) may be taxed there.

(*b*)   The income mentioned in (*a*) above does not include income dealt with in other articles, for example directors' fees, income of artistes and athletes, remuneration from government service and pensions.

(*c*)   Notwithstanding the principle in (*a*) above, the remuneration derived by a resident of one of the countries is taxable only in the country of residence if the following three conditions are met:

   (i)   the recipient is present in the other country (in which he performs duties) for not more than 183 days in any period of twelve months; and

   (ii)   the remuneration is paid by, or on behalf of, an employer who is not a resident of the other country; and

   (iii)   the remuneration is not borne by a PE or fixed base which the employer has in the other country.

(*d*)   The income of crews of ships or aircraft are usually taxable only in the country in which the ship or aircraft operator is effectively managed.

The Inland Revenue considers that 'salaries, wages and other similar remuneration' includes share option gains chargeable under *TA 1988, s 135* and bonus payments, such as those arising under phantom share option schemes. In its view share option gains should usually be regarded as accruing evenly between the grant and exercise dates. If, subsequent to the date when the option was granted, the employee ceases to be a resident of the UK and becomes a resident of a state with which the UK has a double taxation agreement, the individual may claim that part of the gain as exempt under the agreement (see the Inland Revenue Double Taxation Relief Manual paragraph 1925).

Variations

7.49   There are a number of significant variations in the UK's agreements, including the following:

- In (c)(i) above, older agreements, for example those with Germany (1964) and Canada (1978), may specify that the 183-day period is in a *fiscal* or *calendar* year. This may give the opportunity for an individual arriving in a country midway through a tax or calendar year to work for almost a complete year in the country without paying tax there.

- In many agreements condition (c)(ii) above is satisfied if the remuneration is *not* paid by, or on behalf of, a resident of the country of employment. Some agreements, for example the 1953 agreement with Greece and the 1980 agreement with Denmark, require that the duties must be performed for an employer who is a resident of the country of which the employee is a resident.

- Agreements such as the 1967 agreement with Australia and the 1976 agreement with the Irish Republic specifically extend the application of the 'dependent personal services' article to directors' remuneration as if it were employees' remuneration and therefore make no practical distinction between directors' fees and employment income.

- The 1953 agreement with Greece requires that for exemption to be given in the country of source the remuneration has to be subject to tax in the country of residence.

- Many agreements now have paragraphs (usually found in the 'miscellaneous provisions' article) restricting relief where an individual is subject to tax in the UK on a remittance basis. The relief in the country where the duties are performed is restricted to the proportion of the income remitted to the UK.

- Some of the earlier UK agreements, for example the 1953 agreement with Greece, make no reference to the crews of ships or aircraft.

- The agreement with Canada (1978) contains an unusual provision which prevents tax being deducted from remuneration in more than one jurisdiction. Where the country of source is entitled to (and does) deduct tax from remuneration, the country of residence is prevented from doing so.

- The 1980 agreement with Denmark contains a provision which denies any exemption in the country where the employment is exercised if the employer is, for example, merely loaning out the services of the employee and is not itself responsible for carrying out the purposes for which the services are performed.

The OECD and UN models

7.50   The OECD model article has now been renamed 'income from employment'. It is similar to the provisions found in many UK agreements as discussed in 7.48 above. The exemption in 7.48(*a*) is available unless the recipient is present in the contracting state for a period exceeding '183 days in any twelve month period commencing or ending in the fiscal year concerned' although the reference to remuneration being borne by a fixed base (as opposed to a permanent establishment) has been removed. It also contains a reference to remuneration from employment on a boat engaged in inland waterways transport, which may be taxed in the place of effective management of the enterprise.

The OECD commentary states that, in computing the 183-day period within a contracting state, any day during part of which the individual is present should be counted as a day of presence in that state. The only exception to this is that a day when the individual is in transit in the course of a trip between two points outside the state of activity should be excluded from the computation. The Inland Revenue counts days of arrival, departure and transit through the UK as part-days of presence in the UK. In marginal cases it is their practice to take into account the actual time (counting the hours and minutes) spent in the UK (see the Inland Revenue Double Taxation Relief Manual paragraph 1921).

The commentary also discusses the abuse of this article by the practice of what it refers to as the 'international hiring of labour', whereby foreign labour is supplied for periods of less than 183 days to a local employer through an intermediary established abroad which purports to be the employer. The view expressed in the commentary is that substance should prevail over form and that each case should be examined to see whether the functions of an employer are exercised by the intermediary or by the user. However, there is nothing in the model itself similar to the paragraph in the UK's agreement with Denmark noted in the last paragraph of 7.49 above.

It should be noted that the OECD model commentary states that it may be inappropriate to extend the exception to cases where the employer is not a resident of the state of residence of the employee as there might then be administrative difficulties in establishing the employment income of the employee or in enforcing withholding obligations on the employer. The OECD model commentary therefore offers an alternative wording for countries that take this view. In the case of fiscally transparent entities such as partnerships, the commentary broadly takes the view that the concepts of employer and resident should be applied at the level of the partners themselves. The commentary now also defines the meaning of 'borne' in subparagraph (c) of paragraph 2 of the article, i.e. deductible in computing the profits of a PE in the state in which the employment is exercised.

The Inland Revenue adopts a similar approach to that set out in the OECD commentary with effect to claims from employees who commence a work assignment in the UK from 1 July 1995 and to all claims for 1996/97 and future years — see Inland Revenue Tax Bulletin, June 1995 (and the Double Taxation Relief Manual paragraphs DT 1922–1924). A claim for relief from UK income tax on an employee's salary under an agreement is not to be admitted where:

(a)   the employee remains formally employed by a company which is not resident in the UK;

(b)   he is seconded to work for a UK company;

(c)   the UK company functions as his employer for practical purposes; and

(d)   the UK company bears the cost of the employee's remuneration either by a direct recharge or as part of a management charge made by the non-resident employer.

The UN model on dependent personal services has very similar wording to the OECD model.

Directors' fees

7.51   This article is often worded in the same way as the OECD model article, an example being from the agreement with China (1984):

'Directors' fees and other similar payments derived by a resident of a Contracting State in his capacity as a member of the board of directors of a company which is a resident of the other Contracting State may be taxed in that other State'.

The article on directors' fees relates solely to fees and similar payments derived by a resident of one of the countries *in his capacity as a member of the board of directors of a company resident in the other country*. Therefore, if a director is paid fees for board attendances and a salary in his capacity as, for example, an executive in charge of marketing, the taxation of the salary would be in accordance with the article covering dependent personal services.

Variations

7.52   Several variations from the normal wording exist, including the following:

(a)   Some UK agreements deal with directors' fees in the 'dependent personal services' article. Similarly, a few UK agreements include all personal services, whether employed or self-employed, in a 'personal services' article.

(*b*)   In other agreements, even where there is no single 'personal services' article, there may be no reference to directors' fees, for example the 1968 agreement with Portugal.

(*c*)   The 1987 agreement with Belgium specifically states that remuneration of a director of a company in respect of the discharge of day-to-day functions of managerial or technical nature are to be considered under the 'dependent personal services' article of the agreement.

(*d*)   The 1976 agreement with the Philippines, on the other hand, allows the country in which the company is resident to tax both fees and remuneration earned in respect of the discharge of day-to-day functions of a managerial and technical nature.

The OECD and UN models

7.53   The 'directors' fees' articles of both models have identical wording to that quoted in 7.51 above from the China agreement. However, the UN model adds a second paragraph allowing the contracting state in which the company is resident to tax salaries, wages and other similar remuneration derived by the director in his capacity as an official in a top-level managerial position of the company.

Artistes and athletes

7.54   Most UK agreements have an article dealing specifically with artistes and athletes. This paragraph, covering individuals such as actors, musicians, radio and television artistes and athletes, generally allows income to be taxed in the country in which the activities are exercised. This example of a provision in a UK agreement is from the agreement with The Netherlands (1980):

'(1) Notwithstanding the provisions of Articles 14 and 15 [dealing with independent and dependent personal services], income derived by a resident of one of the States as an entertainer, such as a theatre, motion picture, radio or television artiste, or a musician, or as an athlete, from his personal activities as such exercised in the other state, may be taxed in that other state.

(2) Where income in respect of personal services exercised by an entertainer or an athlete in his capacity as such accrues not to the entertainer or athlete himself but to another person, that income may notwithstanding the provisions of Articles 7 [business profits], 14 and 15 be taxed in the State in which the activities of the entertainer or athlete are exercised.'

The second paragraph is usually found in more recent agreements and is designed to ensure that income from performances and appearances by an artist or athlete is taxable in the country in which it takes place even if it is paid not to the performer directly, but, for example, to a company which hires out his services.

Variations

7.55   Certain earlier agreements have no separate article dealing with artistes and athletes. The only reference to those activities in these particular agreements may be that the article dealing with personal services may indicate that it does not cover artistes and athletes. An example is the 1964 agreement with Germany, which allows such income to be taxed in the country in which the activities are exercised. In such cases the profits or remuneration from such activities could fall under one of a number of different headings, including business profits and independent personal services, depending on how the contractual arrangements are structured and the provisions of the particular agreement.

The 1975 US agreement permits the taxation of the activities of an artist or athlete in the country in which they are performed except where the gross amount of the receipts derived from the activities does not exceed US$15,000 or its sterling equivalent in the tax year concerned. The new draft US agreement increases this threshold to US$20,000.

The OECD and UN models

7.56   The OECD model has very similar wording to the article in The Netherlands agreement set out in 7.54 above, except that an amendment was made in 1992 so that it now refers to 'sportsmen' rather than 'athletes'. This is considered a better description of the persons intended to be covered by this article as they include, for example, golfers, jockeys, footballers, cricketers, and tennis, snooker, chess and bridge players. In addition, references to what used to be Article 14 (independent personal services) in the OECD model have now been removed.

Pensions and annuities

7.57   Pensions and annuities are dealt with in several different ways in UK agreements and the treatment depends upon the type of pension concerned. For example, pensions paid by a private occupational or personal pension scheme need to be distinguished from social security pensions and pensions in respect of services to governmental bodies and local authorities. The agreement with Denmark (1980, as amended by protocol), deal with pensions as follows:

●   Pensions and other similar remuneration paid in consideration of past employment and any annuity paid to a resident of a contracting state is taxable only in the state of residence, provided that it is subject to tax there. However, where an individual who was a resident of one of the contracting states has become a resident of the other and the pension arises in the state where he was formerly resident, the pension may be taxed in the contracting state in which it arises.

- Pensions paid under the social security legislation of a contracting state may be taxed only in the state in which it arises.

- The rules for government pensions are often set out in the 'government service' article — see 7.60 below. Normally, pensions paid by or out of funds created by a contracting state (including a political subdivision or local authority) in respect of services rendered to that state by a pensioner resident in the other state are taxable in the state from which the pension is paid. However, if the pensioner is both a resident and a national of the other contracting state, the pension is taxable only in the state of residence.

- Annuities are usually treated in the same way as private occupational pensions and appear in the same article. There is no definition of the word 'pension' but 'annuity' is defined as 'a stated sum payable periodically at stated times during his life or during a specified or ascertainable period of time, under an obligation to make the payments in return for adequate and full consideration in money or money's worth'.

Variations

7.58   There are a number of variations in the UK's agreements:

(*a*)   Many agreements do not refer specifically to social security pensions. Others allow such pensions to be taxed in both states, subject to the provisions of the 'elimination of double taxation' article.

(*b*)   Some UK agreements, in relation to the taxation of governmental pensions, refer to 'ordinary residence' rather than nationality. For example, the 1962 agreement with Israel and the 1952 agreement with Jersey provide that governmental pensions are taxable only in the country of the paying government unless the pensioner is ordinarily resident in the other country. If the pensioner is ordinarily resident in the other country both states may tax the pension, subject to the provisions of the 'elimination of double taxation' article in the agreement.

(*c*)   The 1967 agreement with Australia effectively treats government pensions in the same way as ordinary pensions. All pensions and annuities derived from sources within one of the territories by an individual who is resident of the other territory are exempt from tax in the country of source.

(*d*)   The 1952 agreement with Jersey makes no reference to pensions other than government pensions. Thus the taxation of, for example, private occupational and personal pensions earned in the UK by a

Jersey resident is in accordance with UK domestic law (and vice versa). This also applies to the agreements with Guernsey (1952) and the Isle of Man (1955).

(*e*) The 1978 agreement with Canada (as amended) exempts all pensions (including government and social security pensions) from tax in the country of source. Annuities may be taxed in the source country at a rate not exceeding 10% on the portion of the annuity that is subject to tax in that state.

(*f*) The 1976 agreement with the Philippines provides that government and local authority pensions paid to any individual in the discharge of functions of a governmental nature are exempt from tax in the other country.

(*g*) The 1975 and new draft agreements with the US (1975) refer also to the taxation of alimony payments.

The OECD and UN models

7.59   The OECD model allows only the state of residence of the recipient to tax private employment pensions. Government pensions may be taxed only by the country for which the services were rendered, except in the case of an individual who is both a resident and a national of the other country, in which case the pension is to be taxable only in the country of residence. There is no specific provision concerning social security pensions, although these are discussed in the commentary.

The article also covers contributions to foreign pension schemes and seeks to ensure as far as possible that an employee is not discouraged from taking up an overseas assignment by the tax treatment of contributions made to a home country pension scheme by an employee working abroad.

The UN model treats government pensions in the same way as the OECD model. With regard to other pensions, two alternative models are provided. The first (alternative A) allows exclusive taxing rights to the country of residence of the recipient, except for social security pensions which are to be taxed exclusively by the country making the payment. The second (alternative B) allows both the country of residence and the country of payment to tax the pension (subject to the provisions of the 'elimination of double taxation' article), except for social security pensions which are to be taxable only in the country of the payer.

Government service

7.60   Reference has been made in 7.57–7.59 above to the taxation of government pensions. The references in this section are solely to remuneration for such services *other* than pensions. There are several different types of wording, often producing a similar result in practice, to be found in UK agreements. Some of the alternatives are set out below:

(*a*)   The 1967 agreement with Australia provides that remuneration paid by a government to an individual for services to that government in the discharge of governmental functions will be exempt from tax in the country where the duties are performed if the individual is not ordinarily resident there (or 'resident' in Australia), or is ordinarily resident there (or 'resident' in Australia) solely for the purpose of rendering those services.

(*b*)   The 1968 agreement with Finland (as amended) provides that remuneration paid by the government of one country to an individual for services rendered to that country (or political subdivision, public community or local authority) in respect of services rendered to that country is to be taxable only in that country. However, if the services are performed in the other country, the remuneration is taxable only in that country (i.e. in which the services are performed) if:

   (i)   the individual is a national of that country; and

   (ii)   he did not become a resident of that country solely for the purpose of rendering the services.

(*c*)   The 1976 agreement with the Irish Republic provides that remuneration paid by the government of one contracting state (or local authority) in respect of services rendered to it in discharge of functions of a governmental nature is to be taxable only in that state unless the individual is a national of the other contracting state without also being a national of the employing state.

(*d*)   The 1975 and new draft US agreements provide that remuneration paid by a contracting state to any individual is taxable only in the state paying the remuneration. However, if the services are performed in the other contracting state and the individual is both a national and a resident of that state, the remuneration is taxable only in the state of residence.

Many agreements contain a paragraph providing that the 'government service' article does not apply to remuneration and pensions in respect of services rendered in connection with a business carried on by a contracting state, political subdivision, local authority or wholly owned state agency. The scope of these paragraphs varies considerably, but examples are contained in the agreements with France (1968), the US (1975 and new draft agreements) and Estonia (1994).

The OECD and UN models

7.61   The 'government service' articles in the OECD and UN models are the same. They provide that remuneration in respect of services rendered to a contracting state or subdivision or authority is taxable only in the country to which the services are rendered. However, such remuneration is taxable only in the other country if the individual is a resident of that country and is either a national of that country, or did not become a resident of that country solely for the purpose of rendering the services. The models also contain a paragraph providing that remuneration and pensions paid in respect of services rendered in connection with a business carried on by a contracting state, political subdivision or local authority are taxable according to the articles concerning 'dependent personal services', 'directors' fees', 'artistes and sportsmen' or 'pensions', whichever is appropriate.

Students and apprentices

7.62   There are several different wordings for articles relating to students and apprentices. Some examples are listed below:

• The 1987 agreement with Belgium contains a single paragraph which follows exactly the wording of the OECD model. This applies to payments which a student or business apprentice who was immediately before visiting one of the states ('the country of study') a resident of the other country and who is present in the country of study for the purpose of full-time education or training. Such payments are exempt from tax in the country of study if received for the purpose of maintenance, education or training, provided that the payments are received from sources outside the country of study. This form of wording is found in many of the UK's agreements, subject to some minor variants.

• The 1967 agreement with Australia is similar, but refers only to students and not to business apprentices.

• The 1969 agreement with Austria also contains the paragraph which is in the 1987 Belgian agreement (above), but adds a further provision which exempts from tax in the country of study remuneration from employment directly related to the studies or apprenticeship if the employment is exercised in the country of study for no more than 183 days in the fiscal year concerned.

• The 1993 agreement with India contains an extensive article which, in addition to exempting grants, allowances and gifts from abroad from tax in the country of study, enables a student to earn up to £750 per year (or its equivalent in Indian currency) from certain personal services in the contracting state of study. These provisions apply for a period of five years. Other exemptions are available for those undergoing short-term study or training and who are present in the country of study for up to twelve months.

The OECD and UN models

7.63   The wording of the OECD model is as discussed in the first example of 7.62 above. The UN model is very similar to the OECD model concerning this article.

Professors and teachers

7.64   Some of the UK's agreements contain an article dealing with professors and teachers, although there is no equivalent in either the OECD or the UN models. Several recently negotiated agreements do not contain an article of this kind.

The article in the agreement with Australia (1967) applies to a professor or teacher who visits one of the territories for a period not exceeding two years for the purpose of teaching at a university, college, school or other educational institution in that territory. If he is, or was immediately before that visit, a resident of the other territory he is exempt from tax in the territory which he is visiting on any remuneration for such teaching in respect of which he is subject to tax in the other territory. The agreements with several other countries, including France (1968), Poland (1976) and Greece (1953), contain an important difference in that the exemption does not depend upon the remuneration being subject to tax in the other territory.

The case of *IRC v Vas [1990] STC 137* illustrates the workings of this article and the two-year time limit. Mr Vas, a Hungarian national previously resident in Hungary, visited the UK as a university research associate from 21 January 1979 to 22 January 1981 (thereby slightly exceeding the two years on his first appointment) and then again from 19 February 1981 to 28 January 1982. The Special Commissioners rejected his claim under Article 21 of the Hungary agreement (1977) for exemption from UK tax in 1979/80 and 1980/81 in respect of his first visit. Later he claimed exemption from UK tax for 1981/82 under the same article on the basis that each of his two appointments should be regarded in isolation. In the High Court, Vinelott J held that, on the facts of the case, any entitlement to exemption ceased immediately before the expiry of two years from the day of his first arrival in the UK and therefore rejected Mr Vas' claim to exemption with respect to his second appointment. Having decided that, it was unnecessary for him to give a judgment on the precise method of applying this paragraph and he declined to do so.

Strictly speaking, a visiting professor or teacher is not in a position to claim an exemption until his visit to the UK has ended. However, where the individual states at the outset that his visit will not exceed the requisite period, a nil tax (NT) coding may be issued. The Inland Revenue's practice is to inform the individual in writing that, if his visit exceeds the requisite period, tax will be payable for the whole period of the visit.

However, teachers from Jamaica, Korea, Mauritius, Poland and Romania are exempt from UK tax for the first two years, even if their visit exceeds this period.

Income not expressly mentioned/other income

7.65   Many UK agreements contain an article relating to 'income not expressly mentioned' in the agreement, sometimes headed 'other income'. This can be an important article in practice, since it deals with any income of a type or from sources not included elsewhere in the agreement and often allows the income to be taxed only in the country of residence of the taxpayer. As with many articles, there are several variations to the wording and scope. Among these are the following:

(a)   An example of the simplest form of this article is contained in the agreement with Hungary (1977). It provides that 'items of income of a resident of a Contracting State, wherever arising, being income of a class or from sources not expressly mentioned in this Convention shall be taxable only in that State'.

(b)   The agreement with Germany (1964) provides a similar exemption, but only if the income is subject to tax in the country of residence.

(c)   The 1968 agreement with France requires that the income be 'beneficially owned' by a resident of a contracting state for the exemption to apply. It also denies the exemption if the income is effectively connected with a PE or fixed base in the other contracting state.

(d)   The 1975 and new draft US agreements specifically deny the exemption in respect of income paid out of trusts.

Certain of the UK's earlier agreements and those with many Commonwealth countries do not contain an article dealing with 'other income' and therefore in these cases income which does not fall within the terms of any article in the agreement will be taxed in the country of source in accordance with that country's domestic law. Examples are the agreements with Australia (1967) and New Zealand (1983).

The OECD and UN models

7.66   The OECD model article has two paragraphs, the first of which provides that other income, wherever arising, is taxable only in the country of residence. The second denies exemption if the income is effectively connected with a PE in the other contracting state. In these circumstances either the 'business profits' or 'independent personal services' article applies.

The UN model has three paragraphs, the first two of which are similar to the OECD model. However, the third paragraph changes the effect considerably as it provides that, notwithstanding the provisions of the first two paragraphs, items of income of a resident of a contracting state arising in the other state may also be taxed in the state in which they arise.

Capital

7.67   A few UK agreements contain an article dealing with the taxation of 'capital' (i.e. net worth). These include the agreement with Finland (1969, as amended) and Kenya (1973). The article in the Finland agreement provides that:

(*a*)   capital represented by 'immovable property' (as defined in the 'immovable property' article) owned by a resident of a contracting state and situated in the other state may be taxed in the other state (i.e. the state in which the property is located);

(*b*)   capital represented by shares or other corporate rights (other than shares quoted on an approved stock exchange) deriving more than half of their value directly or indirectly from immovable property situated in a contracting state may be taxed there. This applies also to an interest in a partnership or trust, the assets of which derive more than half of their value from immovable property situated there;

(*c*)   capital represented by movable property forming part of the business property of a PE may be taxed in the state in which the PE is located;

(*d*)   all other elements of capital of a resident of a contracting state are taxable only in the state of residence.

The OECD and UN models

7.68   The OECD and UN models both contain clauses similar to 7.67(*a*), (*c*) and (*d*) above. However they have no provision similar to (*b*), although they do include a paragraph which provides that ships and aircraft in international traffic, boats engaged in inland waterways transport and related movable property are to be taxed in the contracting state where the place of effective management of the enterprise is situated.

Chapter 8

Articles in Agreements — Relieving, Special and Other Provisions

Personal allowances

8.1   Several UK agreements, including that with France (1968) contain a separate article dealing with 'personal reliefs'. Such articles generally provide that individuals who are resident in one of the countries are entitled to the same personal allowances, reliefs and reductions in computing the other country's tax to which non-resident nationals of that country are entitled. For example, under this article a resident of France would be entitled to the same allowances for UK tax purposes as a British subject not resident in the UK. Since the tax year 1990/91, British subjects not resident in the UK have been entitled to full UK personal allowances under *TA 1988, s 278*. Before this, the entitlement was restricted to a proportion of the allowances based on the ratio of UK source income to worldwide income. From 1996/97, the scope of *section 278* has been widened considerably so that non-UK resident nationals of the European Economic Area are now entitled to personal allowances under UK domestic law.

In some agreements there is a second paragraph which denies the reliefs, allowances and reductions in the country of source to a resident of the other country where the relevant income consists solely of dividends, interest or royalties. This second paragraph is not included in all agreements; for example, it is not present in that with Greece (1953). The trend in more recent agreements is not to include a 'personal allowances' article, and this article was removed from the agreement with Finland by a 1996 protocol. However, there are sometimes paragraphs in other articles (often headed 'miscellaneous rules' — see 8.25 below) which contain equivalent provisions. Examples of these are contained in the agreements with The Netherlands (1980) and Sweden (1983).

The OECD and UN models

8.2   There is no comparable article in either the OECD or the UN model.

Holding companies and other excluded persons

8.3   Several UK agreements contain articles dealing with certain holding companies and other persons who are excluded from benefiting either from the agreement as a whole or from certain articles in the agreement. Examples of such companies and other persons are given below:

- Article 23 of the 1970 agreement with Barbados states that no part of the agreement is to apply to companies entitled to any special tax benefit under the *Barbados International Business Companies (Exemption from Income Tax) Law 1965–50*, as in effect on 26 July 1965, or any substantially similar law enacted by Barbados after that date.

  A Barbados international business company may be formed by foreign investors for the purpose of engaging in trade or business outside Barbados and is liable to Barbados income tax on the profits at a special low rate of tax. However, such a company cannot claim reliefs under Barbados' agreement with the UK, for example by the reduction of the UK's withholding tax on interest or exemption from UK tax on UK source trading profits under the 'business profits' article.

- Article 30 of the 1967 agreement with Luxembourg states that the agreement is not to apply to holding companies entitled to any special tax benefit under the Luxembourg laws of 31 July 1929 or 27 December 1937, or any similar law enacted by Luxembourg thereafter.

  This type of Luxembourg holding company is often used by international organisations for international finance or to hold shares in group operating companies. Article 30 does not apply to companies set up in Luxembourg under more recent legislation (1991) which created a new type of holding company commonly referred to as a 'SOPARFI'. Such companies are entitled to an exemption in Luxembourg on dividend income and on profits from the disposal of shares in qualifying subsidiaries. However, they are subject to a dividend withholding tax in Luxembourg unless this is reduced either by an agreement or by the EC Parent/Subsidiary Directive.

- Changes were made in 1994 to the agreements with Jersey, Guernsey and the Isle of Man which prevent certain companies resident in those territories from claiming the benefit of an agreement with the UK. For example, in Guernsey any person who is assessed in accordance with, or is exempt from assessment by virtue of the *Income Tax (Exempt Bodies) (Guernsey) Ordinances 1989 and 1992*, or the *Income Tax (International Bodies) (Guernsey) Law 1993* is not entitled to any relief or exemption from UK tax under the agreement with Guernsey unless that person is assessed on the whole of those profits at a rate which is not less than the standard rate of Guernsey income tax (currently 20%). Therefore companies and other persons who are exempt from Guernsey income tax or who pay tax at less than the standard rate in Guernsey cannot take advantage of the agreement.

- Article 16 of the 1975 agreement with the US contains a number of provisions affecting investment or holding companies. The basic rule is that the 'dividends', 'interest' and 'royalties' articles are not to apply to a corporation resident in one of the countries if 25% or more of the capital of the corporation is owned by individuals who are not residents of the same country as the corporation and who are not US nationals if either:

    (*a*) the tax imposed by the country of residence on dividends, interest and royalties is substantially less than the tax generally imposed by that country on profits, or

    (*b*) the company is a resident of the US and receives more than 80% of its gross income from non-US sources.

    There is an exception to these provisions in the second paragraph of the article. Relief can be claimed under the relevant articles where more than 75% of the company's capital is directly or indirectly owned by:

    (i) a US corporation receiving 20% or more of its gross income from US sources;

    (ii) a corporation (other than a US corporation) which would not fall to be treated in the UK as a close company; or

    (iii) a UK resident corporation in which more than 50% of the voting power is controlled directly or indirectly by UK resident individuals.

These provisions will be replaced by Article 23 (limitation of benefits) in the new draft US agreement).

- An exchange of notes relating to the 1994 agreement with Malta identifies various persons who are not entitled to the benefits of the agreement because of special tax exemptions or benefits in Malta. They are persons who:

(i)   are entitled to a special tax benefit under the *Malta International Business Activities Act 1988* (unless they opt to be taxed at full rates in Malta);

(ii)   have a tax exemption under the *Merchant Shipping Act 1973* and are not subject to tax on the profits derived from the operation of ships in international traffic;

(iii)   are entitled to any special tax benefit in respect of distributions by a trust subject to the *Offshore Trusts Act 1988*; and

(iv)   are entitled to any special tax benefit under any substantially similar law subsequently enacted, as agreed by the competent authorities.

- Article 24A of the 1974 Cyprus agreement (as amended) prevents various residents of Cyprus from benefiting from the 'interest', 'royalties' and 'dividends' articles of the agreement. Excluded persons include Cyprus offshore companies which pay Cyprus tax at the rate of 4.25%. However, these companies can benefit from other articles in the agreement, including the 'business profits' article which exempts the business profits of a Cyprus resident company from UK tax unless it has a permanent establishment (PE) in the UK.

The OECD and UN models

8.4   No reference to these types of special company or other excluded persons appears in either the OECD or the UN model, although the commentary to the 'personal scope' article discusses these issues (see 6.7).

Elimination of double taxation

8.5   All UK agreements contain an article setting out the method of eliminating double taxation in respect of the various taxes on income and capital gains which are covered in the agreement. There are two main methods of granting double taxation relief. The UK and other (mainly common law) countries, including the US and Ireland, use the credit method under which foreign income is subject to tax in the country of residence but credit is given for foreign taxes paid. The UK system of granting double tax credit relief is discussed in detail in Chapters 3 and 4. Other countries, particularly civil law jurisdictions in continental Europe, use the exemption (or partial exemption) method under which foreign source income, especially dividend income, which has suffered tax in the country of source is exempt from tax in the country of residence.

These two methods are reflected in the OECD and UN models which provide alternative model articles depending on whether the contracting states use the credit or the exemption method. Many UK agreements with countries which use the exemption method incorporate both forms into the 'elimination of double taxation' article.

8.6   The 1976 agreement with Ireland is an example of an agreement which applies the credit method in both countries. The effect of the article is as follows:

(*a*)   UK tax payable under the laws of the UK and in accordance with the agreement on profits, income or chargeable gains from sources within the UK is allowed as a credit against any Irish tax computed by reference to the same profits, income or chargeable gains by reference to which the UK tax is computed.

(*b*)   In the case of a dividend paid by a company which is a resident of the UK to a company which is a resident of Ireland and which controls directly or indirectly 10% or more of the voting power in the company paying the dividend, the credit also takes into account the UK tax payable by the company in respect of the profits out of which such dividend is paid (underlying tax).

Mutatis mutandis, the same provisions for relief are to apply in the UK, as follows:

(*c*)   Irish tax payable under the laws of Ireland and in accordance with the agreement on profits, income or chargeable gains from sources within Ireland is allowed as a credit against any UK tax computed by reference to the same profits, income or chargeable gains by reference to which the Irish tax is computed.

(*d*)   In the case of a dividend paid by a company which is a resident of Ireland to a company which is a resident of the UK and which controls directly or indirectly 10% or more of the voting power in the company paying the dividend, the credit shall also take into account the Irish tax payable by the company in respect of the profits out of which such dividend is paid.

(*e*)   There follows a statement that profits, income or gains owned by a resident of a contracting state which may be taxed in the other state in accordance with the agreement is deemed to arise from sources in that other state. This paragraph can be of considerable practical importance as is illustrated by the case of *Yates v GCA International Ltd [1991] STC 157* (see 3.9).

(*f*)   The final paragraph deals with the situation where profits of an enterprise of a contracting state ('the first enterprise') have been charged to tax in the country of residence and those same profits are also included in the profits of an enterprise of the other state following a transfer pricing adjustment. In these circumstances, the amount included in the profits of both enterprises is to be treated for the purposes of this article as the first enterprise's income from a source in the other state and double taxation relief is to be given accordingly.

Therefore, if a UK manufacturing company were to sell goods to an Irish subsidiary which distributed them and the Irish tax authorities made a transfer pricing adjustment so that increased profit was attributed to the Irish company, that increased profit would be treated as Irish source income of the UK company. Double tax credit relief would be available in the UK for the Irish tax payable on the profit adjustment.

Variations

8.7 An example of an agreement where one of the countries applies the exemption method is that with The Netherlands (1980). As far as the UK is concerned, the main provisions for credit for Netherlands tax are similar to those contained in the agreement with Ireland as set out in 8.6(*c*), (*d*) and (*e*) above. However, as far as The Netherlands is concerned, the paragraph provides as follows:

(*a*) The Netherlands, when imposing tax on its resident, may include in the basis upon which such taxes are imposed the items of income which, according to the agreement, may be taxed in the UK.

(*b*) However, where a resident of The Netherlands has income or capital gains from the UK which may be taxed in the UK under the agreement, such income is to be exempt from Netherlands tax. This income is as follows:

(i) income from UK immovable property;

(ii) business profits (including dividends, interest and royalties) connected with a UK PE;

(iii) capital gains from UK immovable property or the movable property of a UK PE;

(iv) income from independent personal services attributable to a UK fixed base;

(v) income from employment, from performances as a performer or athlete and from government service.

The exemption is computed in accordance with the provisions of Netherlands law which currently applies the 'exemption with progression' method. The taxpayer's total income (including exempt income) is aggregated and Netherlands tax is computed on this total. The tax liability is then reduced by applying the formula:

$$\frac{\text{Income qualifying for exemption} \times \text{Netherlands tax on total income}}{\text{Total income}}$$

(*c*) Other types of UK source income which are taxed in the UK may also be taxed in The Netherlands, subject to a deduction from Netherlands tax of the related UK tax. However, the deduction for the UK tax is not to exceed the reduction in Netherlands tax which would occur if these items were exempt from tax under Netherlands law.

Variations can be found in other agreements, e.g. the new draft US agreement contains a provision which denies relief for US underlying tax to a UK company with more than 10% of the voting power in the US company where the dividend is treated as tax deductible for US purposes.

Tax sparing relief

8.8   UK agreements with several countries, including Indonesia, Malaysia, Singapore and Sri Lanka, provide that a UK resident is entitled to credit for foreign tax which would have been payable but for a reduction under specific legislation designed to attract foreign investment. Tax sparing relief enables a UK company or group of companies to retain the benefit of tax laws which grant a tax holiday or partial exemption from, for example, tax on profits earned in certain industries with pioneer status. In the paragraph concerning the granting of double taxation relief in the UK, the term 'Malaysian tax payable' is deemed to include:

'... any Malaysian tax which would have been payable but for an exemption or reduction of tax granted for that year under, inter alia, the *Malaysian Promotion of Investment Act 1986* (or any other subsequent provisions of substantially similar character as agreed by the competent authorities.'

In recently negotiated agreements with Singapore, Korea and Malaysia, tax sparing relief is granted for limited periods only. For a fuller discussion of tax sparing relief in the UK see 3.47 and 4.27.

The latest version of the OECD model commentary refers to a 1998 report published by the OECD Committee of Fiscal Affairs entitled *Tax Sparing: a reconsideration*. The report identified a number of concerns relating to the potential abuse offered by tax sparing, the effectiveness of tax sparing as an instrument of foreign aid to promote the economic development of the source company and general concerns with the way in which tax sparing may encourage countries to use tax incentives. The committee concluded that countries should not necessarily refrain from adopting tax sparing provisions. However, tax sparing should be considered only with regard to countries the economic level of which is considerably below that of OECD countries, and the 'best practices' set out in the report should be followed.

The OECD and UN models

8.9   Both the OECD and the UN model agreements give alternative wordings for this article depending on whether the contracting states apply the exemption or the credit method in their domestic laws.

Article 23A of the OECD model is generally suitable for use by countries using the exemption method, and provides as follows:

(a)   Where a resident of a contracting state derives income or owns capital which, in accordance with the provisions of the agreement, may be taxed in the other contracting state, the country of residence shall, subject to certain exceptions, exempt such income or capital from tax.

(b)   The exceptions, as mentioned in (a) above are dividends and interest, which may be taxed in accordance with the agreement in both contracting states. In that case the country of residence is to allow the tax paid in the other state as a credit against its own tax, but only up to the amount of its own tax attributable to that income.

(c)   The country of residence is allowed to operate an 'exemption with progression' method (as set out in 8.7 above).

The latest version of the OECD model adds a new paragraph to the broad effect that the recipient state shall not exempt foreign income where it is exempted from tax in the source state. The purpose of this paragraph is to avoid double non-taxation.

8.10   Article 23B of the OECD model is generally suitable for use by countries using the credit method, and provides as follows:

(a)   Where a resident of a contracting state derives income which in accordance with the agreement may be taxed in the country of source, the country of residence shall allow a credit for the tax paid in the country of source. However, the credit is not to exceed the tax attributable to the income which is taxed in the country of source.

(b)   Where in accordance with the agreement income is exempt from tax in the country of residence, the agreement allows the country of residence to apply an 'exemption with progression' method for computing the tax payable.

The commentary to the OECD model accepts that conflicts of qualification of income can arise between the state of residence and the state of source, but this should not prevent the state of residence from giving relief from double taxation. Where a particular conflict cannot be resolved it is recommended that the provisions of Article 25 (mutual agreement procedure) are followed.

The latest version of the OECD model commentary also acknowledges that problems may arise where contracting states treat entities such as partnerships in a different way, e.g. where the state of source treats the partnership as a company and the state of residence of a partner treats it as fiscally transparent, and makes a number of recommendations for resolving this type of situation.

The UN model is very similar to the OECD model, but the second paragraph of Article 23A treats royalties in the same way as dividends and interest. This reflects the fact that the UN model allows the country of source to tax royalties paid to a resident of the other contracting state.

Non-discrimination

8.11   The 'non-discrimination' article of many UK agreements follows a fairly uniform pattern, but there are a number of variations. The following is from the 1980 agreement with Denmark.

(*a*)   Nationals of one of the contracting states shall not be subject in the other contracting state to any taxation (or taxation requirements) which are other or more burdensome than those to which nationals of the other contracting state are subject in the same circumstances.

(*b*)   The second paragraph deals with the taxation of a PE which one enterprise has in the other country. It provides that such taxation shall not be less favourably levied than the taxation levied on enterprises of that other country carrying on the same activities. This paragraph may be used to obtain the small companies' rate of corporation tax for a non-resident company. However, in applying this rate the Inland Revenue takes into account the total profits of the non-resident company and not just the profits of the UK PE.

(*c*)   Nothing in the article is to be construed as obliging either contracting state to grant to individuals not resident in that state any of the personal allowances, reliefs and reductions for tax purposes which are granted to resident individuals. However, in many agreements personal allowances are granted to residents of the other contracting state in other articles, either dealing with 'personal allowances' or 'miscellaneous provisions' — see 8.1 above.

(*d*)   Except where the 'special relationship' provisions apply to non-arm's length transactions, interest, royalties and other disbursements paid by an enterprise of a contracting state to a resident of the other contracting state are to be deductible under the same conditions as if they had been paid to a resident of the country of the enterprise making the payment. This is to prevent indirect discrimination where, for example, interest, royalties or management fees paid to a non-resident are disallowed for tax purposes in circumstances where they would be allowed if paid to a resident of that country.

(*e*)   Enterprises of a contracting state, the capital of which is wholly or partly owned by residents of the other, may not be subjected to any taxation in its country of residence that is more burdensome than the taxation to which other similar enterprises of that state are subjected.

(*f*)   The provisions of the article apply to taxes of every kind and description.

Variations

8.12   There are several variations in the UK's agreements. These include:

(a)   a number of agreements, including those with Australia (1967), Jersey (1952), Guernsey (1952), the Isle of Man (1955) and the early Commonwealth agreements do not contain a 'non-discrimination' article;

(b)   some agreements limit the application of the article to taxes which are the subject of the agreement.

As far as EU nationals and residents are concerned (or UK residents and nationals claiming benefit of non-discrimination articles in agreements with other EU member states), consideration should also be given to whether the particular tax treatment which is considered discriminatory may be contrary to the Treaty of Rome following a number of cases on discrimination that have been heard by the European Court of Justice in recent years, e.g. the *Commerzbank* and *Halliburton* cases (see 3.8).

The OECD and UN models

8.13   The OECD model 'non-discrimination' article has many points of similarity with articles in UK agreements, but there are some important differences:

- While the first paragraph is similar to that set out in 8.11(*a*) above, it contains a further sentence indicating that the article applies to persons who are not residents of one or both contracting states notwithstanding the 'personal scope' article.

- A paragraph was introduced into the 1977 OECD model dealing with 'stateless persons'. This provides that stateless persons who are residents of a country are not to be subjected in either contracting state to any taxation or any requirement connected with tax which is different or more burdensome than those to which nationals of the state of residence may be subjected in the same circumstances. This paragraph has been adopted by the UK in some agreements, an example being that with Estonia (1994).

- There is a paragraph dealing with the taxation of PEs of enterprises of a contracting state. The second sentence of this paragraph indicates that it shall not be construed as obliging a state to grant to residents of the other contracting state personal allowances, reliefs and reductions for tax purposes on account of civil status or family responsibilities.

- The model also provides that (with the usual exceptions for non-arm's length transactions) interest, royalties and other disbursements paid by an enterprise of one country to a resident of the other country will be a deductible expense in computing the taxable profits of the payer under the same conditions as would have been applicable had the payments been made to a resident of the country in which the enterprise is carried on. It adds that any debts of an enterprise of a contracting state to a resident of the other contracting state shall, for the purpose of determining the taxable capital of such enterprise, be deductible under the same conditions as if they had been contracted to a resident of the contracting state where the debtor is resident.

- Enterprises of a contracting state, the capital of which is wholly or partly owned by residents of the other may not be subjected to any taxation or taxation requirement in its country of residence that is more burdensome than the taxation or connected requirements to which other similar enterprises of that state are subjected. This is found in many UK agreements.

- The OECD model indicates that the non-discrimination article applies, notwithstanding the 'taxes covered' article, to taxes of every description. The UK has reserved the right to restrict the scope of this provision to taxes covered by the agreement. There are several examples of both positions in the UK's agreements.

The UN model article is the same as that in the OECD model.

Mutual agreement procedure

8.14   Many UK agreements contain a four-paragraph article on mutual agreement, as follows:

- Where a person (or 'resident of a contracting state') considers that the actions of one or both of the contracting states result or will result in taxation not in accordance with the provisions of the agreement, he may, irrespective of the remedies provided by the domestic law of those states, present his case to the competent authorities of the contracting state of which he is a resident.

- The competent authority shall endeavour, if the objection appears to be justified and if it is not itself able to arrive at a satisfactory solution, to resolve the case by mutual agreement with the competent authority of the other contracting state, with a view to the avoidance of taxation which is not in accordance with the agreement.

- The competent authorities shall endeavour to resolve by mutual agreement any difficulties or doubts arising as to the interpretation or application of the agreement.

- The final paragraph allows the competent authorities of the contracting states to communicate directly with each other for the purpose of reaching a solution and to give effect to the provisions of the agreement.

In most agreements the term 'competent authority' is defined. In the UK this invariably refers to the Commissioners of the Inland Revenue or their authorised representative. In practice the functions of the competent authority are usually carried out by senior members of the Inland Revenue's International Division.

Variations

8.15   There are several variations to this article, including those listed below:

(*a*)   The 1952 agreements with Jersey and Guernsey, the 1955 agreement with the Isle of Man and several early Commonwealth agreements contain no 'mutual agreement' article.

(*b*)   The 1967 agreement with Australia allows a taxpayer to present his case to either tax authority, and not just to the tax authority of his country of residence.

(*c*)   A few agreements state a time limit within which the case must be presented. For example the agreement with Belgium (1987) indicates that the case must be presented within three years from the first notification of the action resulting in taxation not in accordance with the agreement. This follows the OECD model — see 8.16(*b*) below.

(*d*)   Some agreements, including that with Belgium, indicate that the competent authorities may also consult with each other to consider measures to counteract improper use of the provisions of the agreement.

(*e*)   The article in the agreement with Germany contains a paragraph allowing the contracting states to apply full rates of withholding tax under domestic law and specifying that claims for refunds for the excess tax deducted must be made within three years of the receipt of the income.

The OECD and UN models

8.16   The OECD model is quite close to the wording contained in most of the UK's agreements. However, there are some significant differences:

(*a*)   Where the case for mutual agreement concerns 'nationals' of a country, the model provides that the person should present his case to the authorities of the country of which he is a national.

(*b*)   A time limit is included for claims under the mutual agreement procedure. The claim must be made within three years from the first notification of the action resulting in taxation not in accordance with the agreement. The UK has reserved its position on this time limit on the grounds that it conflicts with the six-year time limit under its domestic legislation.

(c) In relation to a case being resolved by mutual agreement, the model states that an agreement is to be implemented notwithstanding any time limits in the particular country's domestic law. The UK has reserved its position on this as it considers that the implementation of reliefs and refunds following mutual agreement ought to remain linked to time limits prescribed by its domestic law.

(d) The third paragraph of the model allows the competent authorities to consult together for the elimination of double taxation in cases not provided for in the agreement.

(e) The model also provides that, where it seems advisable in order to reach agreement to have an oral exchange of opinions, such exchange may take place through a commission consisting of representatives of the competent authorities of the contracting states.

The UN and OECD model articles are quite similar. However, the UN model provides that the competent authorities are to develop appropriate bilateral procedures, conditions, methods and techniques for the implementation of the mutual agreement procedures. In addition, a competent authority may devise similar unilateral procedures to facilitate the implementation of the mutual agreement procedure.

8.17   The mutual agreement procedure is commonly used to:

• allocate the proportion of executive and general administrative expenses attributable to a PE;

• establish the amount of excess interest and royalties where a special relationship exists between the payer and payee;

• resolve generally transfer pricing disputes under the 'associated enterprises' article of the agreement.

8.18   In practice there are a number of difficulties with the mutual agreement procedure as set out in bilateral double taxation agreements:

• there are no time limits laid down within which the competent authorities must reach agreement and the negotiations may be protracted;

• once the taxpayer has made representations to the competent authority (usually of his country of residence) he has no further right of representation — accordingly, the negotiations between the competent authorities may be conducted without his being represented;

• there is no obligation on the part of the competent authorities to reach agreement.

Where the dispute in question is also covered by the EC Arbitration Convention, it may be beneficial to the taxpayer to use the provisions of that Convention rather than the procedure laid down in the agreement since it contains provisions to ensure that a resolution to the dispute avoiding double taxation is reached within a specified time limit. It also gives the taxpayer the right to appear or be represented before the advisory commission appointed to resolve a dispute where the competent authorities have failed to reach agreement. (See 2.8).

Exchange of information

8.19 There are a number of variations found in 'exchange of information' articles in the UK's agreements, including the following:

(*a*) The agreements with Australia (1967) and Canada (1978) contain a single paragraph article with almost identical wording to the effect that the tax (or 'competent') authorities of the contracting states are to exchange such information (being information which is at their disposal under the respective taxation laws in the normal course of administration) as is necessary for the carrying out of the provisions of the agreement or for the prevention of fraud or for the administration of statutory provisions against legal tax avoidance in relation to the taxes which are the subject of the agreement.

Any information so exchanged is to be treated as secret and is not to be disclosed to persons other than persons (including a court or administrative tribunal) concerned with the assessment, collection or enforcement of the taxes which are the subject of the agreement. No information is to be exchanged which would disclose any trade, business, industrial or professional secret or trade process.

(*b*) The 1975 and new draft agreements with the US contain a very similar first paragraph, but includes three additional paragraphs. The first provides that the contracting states will endeavour to collect on behalf of the other contracting state such amounts as may be necessary to ensure that that relief granted by the agreement from taxation imposed by the other contracting state does not enure to the benefit of persons not entitled to the relief. However, this obligation is not to impose upon either contracting state the obligation to carry out administrative measures which are of a different nature from those used in the collection of its own tax, or which would be contrary to its sovereignty, security or public policy. In view of the general position under UK domestic law that no action is taken to enforce tax laws of other countries, the practical scope of this provision is unclear. The article also provides that the competent authorities of the contracting states are to consult each other for the purpose of co-operating and advising in respect of any action to be taken in implementing this article.

(c) In a number of UK agreements, for example those with France and Germany, there is a second paragraph which states that the relevant tax authorities shall have no obligation to:

(i) carry out any administrative measure at variance with the laws or practice prevailing in either territory;

(ii) supply details not obtainable under the laws of, or in the normal course of the administration in, either territory; or

(iii) supply information which would disclose any trade, business, industrial, commercial or professional secrets or supply information the disclosure of which would be contrary to public policy.

(d) Many recent UK agreements do not refer to the exchange of information for the 'administration of statutory provisions against legal avoidance', for example the 1976 agreement with Poland and the 1980 agreement with Denmark. These agreements follow more closely the OECD model.

The OECD and UN models

8.20 The OECD model article contains a paragraph similar to that contained in the agreements with France and Germany as set out in 8.19(c) above. It also indicates that disclosure is not limited by reference to the residence of the taxpayer concerned.

Recently, the OECD model has been amended to allow the exchange of information regarding taxes not specifically covered in an agreement, for example indirect taxes, except broadly where such taxes are covered by other international agreements.

The UN model is similarly worded to the OECD model, but there are some differences:

(a) the UN model specifically mentions the prevention of fraud and evasion of taxes;

(b) disclosure in the receiving country is only restricted if it is regarded as secret in the transmitting state; and

(c) the competent authorities, through consultation, are to develop appropriate conditions, methods and techniques concerning the matters in respect of which exchanges of information are to be made, including those relating to tax avoidance.

Diplomatic agents and consular officers

8.21 This is a brief article which appears in some UK agreements, including the 1976 agreements with Ireland and the Philippines, the 1968 agreement with Portugal and the 1975 agreements with Spain and the US.

It can also be found in the new draft agreement with the US. Diplomatic and consular officials are often exempt from tax in the country in which they are posted and the article is included to ensure that those privileges are preserved. The article normally states that nothing in the agreement is to affect the fiscal privileges of 'diplomatic or consular officials' under the general rules of international law or under the provisions of special agreements. However, some agreements refer to 'members of diplomatic or permanent missions or consular posts' both in the heading and the text of the article.

Some agreements contain a second paragraph which provides that the agreement does not apply to international organisations, to organs or officials of international organisations, or to members of diplomatic or permanent missions or consular posts of a third state who are present in a contracting state but who are not subject to the same tax obligations as residents of that state.

The OECD and UN model

8.22 The OECD and UN model agreements both contain a single paragraph similar to that set out in 8.21 above. The commentary to the OECD model states that the aim of the provision is to ensure that members of diplomatic and consular posts receive under double taxation agreements no less favourable treatment than that to which they are entitled under international law or special international agreements.

Territorial extension

8.23 Many UK agreements contain a 'territorial extension' article under which the agreement, either in its entirety or with modifications, may be extended to any territory for whose international relations either contracting state is responsible and which impose taxes substantially similar in character to those covered in the agreement. Such extensions are to take effect from such date and subject to such conditions as may be specified and agreed in an exchange of notes through diplomatic channels. Unless otherwise agreed, the termination of the agreement also terminates its application to any territory to which it has been extended under the provisions of the article.

The 1968 agreement with France specifies that the territories to which this article applies are:

- in relation to the UK, any territory other than the UK for whose international relations the UK is responsible; and

- in relation to France, the French overseas territories.

By virtue of the definition of 'France' contained in Article 2(1)(*b*) of the agreement, the agreement applies to the Overseas Departments (Guadeloupe, Guyana, Martinique and Réunion). However, there have not been any extensions to the agreement under this article and, in general, the provisions of such 'territorial extension' articles have not been commonly used in recent years; nevertheless the agreements with Namibia and the Faroe Islands (now terminated) are the result of extensions of the agreements with South Africa and Denmark respectively. Many agreements, including those with the US (1975), India (1993) and Estonia (1994) do not contain such an article.

The OECD and UN models

8.24   The OECD model contains similar wording to that contained in most UK agreements. There is no equivalent article in the UN model.

Miscellaneous rules

8.25   Many of the UK's agreements now contain an article dealing with 'miscellaneous rules'. No equivalent article is found in either the OECD or UN model agreements. By its nature, this article does not have a standard format or content, although some paragraphs are found in more than one agreement. The 1980 agreement with Denmark (as amended by protocol) provides an example of this article:

(*a*)   The first paragraph provides for the situation where under the agreement an individual's income is relieved from Danish tax, but is taxed in the UK only on the remittance basis. In these circumstances the relief allowed in Denmark is to apply only to the amount remitted to the UK. Similar provisions are found in many of the UK's agreements, often inserted by an amending protocol.

(*b*)   The second paragraph defines 'political subdivision' in relation to the UK as including Northern Ireland.

(*c*)   There follow provisions which apply where an individual who is a resident of a contracting state is a member of a pension scheme which is established in (and is recognised for tax purposes by) the other contracting state. If the individual is employed in the state in which he is resident, contributions paid by the individual to that pension scheme are to be relieved from tax in the state of residence as if the pension scheme were recognised by it. In addition, payments made to the pension scheme by (or on behalf of) the individual's employer are not to be taxed as income of the individual and are to be a deduction in computing the profits of the employer as if the pension scheme were recognised for tax purposes in the state of residence.

This is subject to various conditions, namely that:

● the individual exercises his employment in the state of residence for an employer who was his employer immediately before he began to be employed there (or for an associated employer);

- the individual was a member of the pension scheme immediately before he became a resident there; and

- the pension scheme is accepted by the competent authority of the state of residence as corresponding to a pension scheme which is recognised for tax purposes there.

Variations

8.26   The agreement with Sweden (1983) has a provision similar to that in the Denmark agreement outlined in 8.25(*a*) above, except that it refers to chargeable gains (as well as income) taxed in the UK on the remittance basis. It also contains a provision concerning the undivided estates of deceased persons. Where, under the agreement, a UK resident is entitled to exemption or relief from Swedish tax, similar exemption or relief is to be applied to the undivided estate of a deceased person insofar as one or more of the beneficiaries is UK resident. If Swedish tax is chargeable on the undivided estate, a UK resident beneficiary is entitled to a credit for the Swedish tax.

The next three paragraphs of the Sweden agreement contain provisions which are often found in separate 'personal allowances' articles — see 8.1 above. These entitle residents of Sweden to the same personal allowances, reliefs and reductions for the purposes of UK tax as are available to British subjects not resident in the UK and vice versa. These are not available to an individual resident in a contracting state whose income from the other contracting state consists solely of dividends, interest or royalties.

Taxation of offshore activities

8.27   Many of the UK's agreements contain 'taxation of offshore activities' articles which deal with oil related activities on the continental shelves of the contracting states. There is no equivalent article in either the OECD or UN model agreements. This example is from the 1980 agreement with Denmark which was inserted by protocol in 1991:

(*a*)   The provisions of this article are to apply (notwithstanding any other provision in the agreement) where activities are carried on offshore in connection with the exploration for or exploitation of oil or gas in the sea-bed and subsoil situated in a contracting state. (Such activities are defined as 'offshore activities'.)

(*b*)   An enterprise of a contracting state which carries on offshore activities in the other contracting state is deemed to be carrying on a business in that other contracting state through a PE situated there.

(*c*)   Similarly, a resident of a contracting state who carries on offshore activities consisting of professional services or other services of an independent character is deemed to be performing those activities from a fixed base in that contracting state.

(*d*)   Notwithstanding (*b*) above, profits derived by an enterprise of a contracting state from the operation in connection with offshore activities of ships and aircraft designed primarily for the purpose of transporting supplies or personnel, or of tugboats or anchor handling vessels, are to be taxable only in the state where the effective management of the enterprise is situated. However, this provision does not apply to profits derived during any period in which such a ship or aircraft is contracted to be used mainly for purposes other than to transport supplies or personnel to or between places where offshore activities are being carried on.

(*e*)   Salaries, wages and similar remuneration derived by a resident of a contracting state in respect of an employment connected with offshore activities in the other contracting state are to be taxable only in that state, to the extent that the duties are performed offshore in that contracting state. However, this does not apply to remuneration from an employment to which (*d*) applies, which is to be taxable only in the contracting state in which the effective management of the enterprise is situated.

(*f*)   In order for the exemptions from tax on remuneration to apply, documentary evidence must be produced to the tax authorities of the country in which the income is exempt that arrangements have been made for the payment of tax to the contracting state which has sole taxing rights.

Entry into force

8.28   The 'entry into force' article of the UK's agreements is usually contained in three or four paragraphs, its wording depending on whether the agreement is the first between the countries or replaces an existing agreement. An example of the latter is the 1967 agreement with Australia which replaced an agreement dating from 1946. It provides as follows:

•   The agreement is to enter into force when 'the last of all such things shall have been done both in the UK and Australia as are necessary to give the agreement the force of law in the UK and Australia respectively'. The agreement is then to have effect from the dates specified in the paragraph.

•   The second paragraph terminates the previous agreement.

•   Where the provisions of the 1946 agreement would have afforded greater relief from tax than is afforded by the new provisions, those provisions are to continue to have effect for any tax year beginning before the entry into force of the new agreement.

The agreement was given the force of law in the UK on 4 March 1968 and in Australia on 8 May 1968 and consequently entered into force on the latter date.

8.29   Owing to the time taken to negotiate and ratify agreements, it often happens that an agreement takes effect from a date earlier than it enters into force. For example, the 1967 agreement with Australia took effect in the UK with respect to corporation tax from 1 April 1964 and with respect to capital gains tax from 6 April 1965. The most notable example of such an occurrence was the current agreement with the US which was signed on 31 December 1975. However, it was not ratified until 1980 owing to difficulties over the issue of unitary taxation levied by certain US states. The agreement took effect for some purposes from 6 April 1973. However, the provisions of the agreement, including those concerning the payment of tax credits on dividends, could not be implemented until the agreement had been ratified in 1980. Accordingly, a special paragraph (Article 28(7)) was introduced by protocol extending the time limit for applications for relief under the agreement to three years from the end of the year in which the agreement entered into force (which occurred on 25 April 1980).

Variations

8.30   An example of an agreement with a contrasting 'entry into force' article is the 1987 agreement with Belgium. This contains a shorter article which provides that the agreement enters into force 15 days after both parties have notified each other that the procedures for bringing the agreement into force have been completed. The agreement then enters into force from specified dates in the following calendar year. There is no provision for the previous agreement to continue to apply for a period if this is more advantageous to the taxpayer.

The OECD and UN models

8.31   The OECD and UN model articles are identical and very brief. They refer to the instruments of ratification being exchanged at a place to be specified as soon as possible. The agreement is to enter into force upon the exchange of instruments and to have effect in each contracting state on specified dates. These dates depend on the period of assessment in each contracting state.

Termination

8.32   This final article in UK agreements provides for termination of the agreement. Several agreements, including that with Canada (1978), provide for the agreement to remain in force indefinitely, but the government of either country can give notice of termination on or before 30 June in any year, subject to a minimum duration of two or three years. It then ceases to be effective in each country for any year of assessment or financial year beginning on or after dates specified for the various taxes in the following calendar year. For UK income tax and capital gains tax the agreement invariably ceases to have effect for any year of assessment beginning on or after the following 6 April and for corporation tax for any financial year beginning on or after the following 1 April. The effective date of termination varies in the other country, but is usually the following 1 January where it uses the calendar year as the tax year.

There are several variations from this wording, including the following:

- a few agreements, including that with Denmark, use the word 'denounce' instead of 'terminate' — this would appear to have no practical significance, although the more common wording is considered more appropriate;

- many agreements specify that termination is to be effected through diplomatic channels;

- the 1993 agreement with India specifies a minimum duration of the agreement of ten years;

- in several agreements, including the 1980 agreements with Denmark and The Netherlands and the 1975 US agreement (but not the new draft US agreement), it is specifically provided that the termination of the agreement does not have the effect of reviving any earlier agreement which has been abrogated, either by the agreement which is being terminated or by previous agreements between the contracting states.

The OECD and UN models

8.33   The OECD and UN model articles are identical to each other and comprise a single paragraph similar to the first paragraph in many of the UK's agreements. They specify that the termination is to be effected through diplomatic channels.

Chapter 9

Relief against Inheritance Tax

Introduction

9.1   UK inheritance tax (IHT) is chargeable on transfers of value by persons domiciled (or deemed to be domiciled) in the UK wherever the assets concerned are situated. IHT is also chargeable on transfers of value of most UK assets by non-UK domiciled persons.

Many other countries impose gift and estate taxes which apply to lifetime gifts, devolutions on death or both. According to the laws of each country, liability to these taxes may depend upon the domicile, residence or nationality of the person concerned and on the location of the assets. A transfer of value may therefore be subject to gift or inheritance taxes in more than one country. Accordingly, measures are necessary (either by agreement or unilaterally) to avoid or relieve such potential double taxation.

9.2   Since the introduction of IHT in 1986, the *Capital Transfer Tax Act 1984* has been cited as the *Inheritance Tax Act 1984* (*IHTA*) and references in that Act to capital transfer tax (CTT) have effect as if they are references to IHT. [*FA 1986, s 100(1)*].

IHTA 1984, s 158 provides that Orders in Council may be made giving effect to agreements affording relief from IHT, or for determining the location of property for the purposes of IHT. On the abolition of estate duty and the introduction of CTT in 1974 there were in existence a number of agreements covering estate duty. Some of these agreements, together with a number of CTT agreements which were concluded between 1975 and 1986, continue in force and now apply to IHT. For convenience, the CTT agreements and the agreement with Switzerland concluded since the introduction of IHT are referred to as 'IHT agreements'. A list of estate duty and IHT agreements currently in force is included as Appendix 3.

Unilateral relief

9.3   *IHTA 1984, s 159(1)* provides that credit is to be allowed for overseas tax where the Board of Inland Revenue is satisfied that foreign tax, which is of a character similar to that of IHT or is chargeable on or by reference to death or gifts *inter vivos*, is imposed by reason of any disposition or other event, and IHT is chargeable on the value of the same property. There is no requirement that the overseas tax is payable in the foreign country by the same person who is liable to IHT. Accordingly, taxes paid by the recipient of a gift or devolution on death are available for credit against IHT chargeable on the donor or on the deceased's estate.

9.4   The amount of unilateral credit for foreign tax depends on where the asset is situated. If the asset is situated in the foreign country imposing the tax, and not situated in the UK, the credit is the whole amount of the foreign tax, subject to a limit of the IHT payable. The foreign tax paid for which credit is claimed is converted to sterling on the date of payment.

Example 73

Philip was domiciled in England at the date of his death leaving a house in Denmark valued at £100,000 to his children on which Danish inheritance tax of £20,000 was payable. His worldwide chargeable estate exceeded £500,000 and IHT was payable at 40%. The Danish inheritance tax liability of £20,000 is available as a credit against IHT payable in the UK.

9.5   Where, however, the asset is situated:

(*a*)   in neither the UK nor the overseas territory imposing the tax; or

(*b*)   in both the UK and the overseas territory (which includes cases where UK law regards the asset as situated in the UK and the law of the foreign country regards it as situated in its own jurisdiction),

the credit is calculated by what is known as the 'split credit' method, according to the following formula:

$$\frac{A}{A+B} \times C$$

where: A = the IHT payable;
      B = the overseas tax; and
      C = whichever of A and B is the smaller.

Example 74

Peter died domiciled for UK purposes in England, but was also resident in Narnia for the purposes of Narnian inheritance tax. At the date of death he owned a property in the Bahamas valued at £500,000 which he left to a distant relative. No tax is payable in the Bahamas, but Narnian inheritance tax of £225,000 is payable. The IHT liability before double taxation relief is £200,000. Applying the formula:

9.6   Relief against Inheritance Tax

$$\frac{A}{A+B} \times C$$

gives double tax credit relief in the UK of:

$$\frac{£200,000}{£200,000 + £225,000} \times £200,000 = £94,117$$

9.6 Where tax is imposed in two or more overseas territories in respect of an asset which:

(*a*)   is situated neither in the UK nor in any of those territories, or

(*b*)   is situated both in the UK and in each of those territories,

then the formula:

$$\frac{A}{A+B} \times C$$

is applied where:

A = the IHT payable;

B = the aggregate of the overseas taxes imposed in each of those territories; and

C = the aggregate of all, except the largest of IHT and the overseas tax imposed in each territory.

Example 75

The facts are the same as in Example 74 above, except that Peter was also at the time of his death a resident of Ruritania, and is liable to Ruritanian gift tax of £150,000 on the Bahamas property. The double taxation relief available in the UK becomes:

$$\frac{£200,000}{£200,000 + £375,000} \times £350,000 = £121,739$$

9.7 Where a full credit for foreign tax has been allowed either unilaterally (i.e. where the asset is situated in an overseas territory and not in the UK) or under a double taxation agreement, and tax is also payable in a third country, *section 159(5)* applies. In that case, the formula:

$$\frac{A}{A+B} \times C$$

is applied treating the IHT as reduced by the amount of the first credit.

Example 76

The facts are as in Example 47 above, except that, in addition to his house in the Bahamas, Peter also owned a property in Norway valued at £600,000 on which the following taxes were payable:

Norwegian inheritance tax — £180,000
Narnian inheritance tax — £260,000
IHT (before double taxation relief) — £240,000

The Norwegian tax is fully creditable against IHT. Therefore the IHT in the formula becomes £60,000 (i.e. £240,000 − £180,000). A further credit is then given for Narnian tax in accordance with the formula:

$$\frac{£60,000}{£60,000 + £260,000} \times £60,000 = £11,250$$

The total IHT payable is therefore £48,750 (i.e. £240,000−£180,000−£11,250).

9.8   Where tax is imposed in two or more overseas territories and a credit is allowed for tax in one territory against tax paid in the territory where the asset is situated, then, in calculating the credit against IHT under the formula, the overseas tax is reduced by the credit.

Example 77

The facts are as in Example 76 above except that Narnia gives a partial credit for Norwegian inheritance tax when computing the Narnian tax liability. As a result the Narnian tax is reduced to £100,000. The formula for calculating double tax relief for IHT purposes becomes:

$$\frac{£60,000}{£60,000 + £100,000} \times £60,000 = £22,500$$

The total IHT payable is therefore £37,500 (i.e. £240,000 − £180,000 − £22,500).

It will be noted that the result of the split credit method would appear illogical when compared to the result in Example 76, since greater relief is given for a smaller amount of foreign tax paid. The formula gives the optimum result when the IHT and the foreign tax are equal, at which point a credit is given for half the foreign tax paid.

9.9   Credit relief is given only for tax imposed in an overseas territory if tax is chargeable under the law of that territory and is paid by the person liable to pay it. [*IHTA 1984, s 159(6)*]. This prevents, for example, credit being obtained for tax imposed by a foreign country which it has been unable to enforce. However, it may be possible to negotiate a provisional credit for foreign tax which has yet to be paid.

Where relief can be given both unilaterally and under an agreement, it is given under whichever provides the greater relief. [*IHTA 1984, s 159(7)*].

Relief under double taxation agreements

9.10   *IHTA 1984, s 158* provides that an Order in Council may be made with a view to giving relief from double taxation in relation to IHT and any tax imposed under the laws of any territory which is of a similar character to IHT, or is chargeable on or by reference to death or gifts *inter vivos*. Provision is also made for making arrangements for exchange of information necessary for carrying out UK and foreign domestic law and including, in particular, the prevention of evasion of taxes. [*s 158(1A)*].

Existing double taxation agreements relating to estate duty continue to apply as if any provision in the agreement relating to estate duty extended to IHT on transfers on death. [*s 158(6)*].

There are currently ten agreements which apply to IHT. Four of these, namely those with France (1963), India (1956), Italy (1966) and Pakistan (1957) are estate duty agreements which apply only to transfers on death. The agreements with India and Pakistan are now of limited effect since death duties have been abolished in those countries. However, they do operate to override the application of the UK's 'deemed domicile' rules under *IHTA 1984, s 267*. On the death of a person domiciled for the purposes of one of the agreements in India or Pakistan, who is deemed to be domiciled in the UK under *section 267*, the charge to UK IHT is restricted to property situated in the UK.

The five agreements negotiated when CTT was in force cover IHT on lifetime transfers as well as transfers on death. These are the agreements with Ireland (1977), The Netherlands (1979), South Africa (1978), Sweden (1980) and the US (1978). The 1993 agreement with Switzerland is the only agreement concluded since the introduction of IHT, although a protocol amending The Netherlands agreement entered into force in June 1996.

9.11   The general scheme of relief from double taxation in the IHT and estate duty agreements is outlined briefly below. The agreements are discussed in more detail in Chapter 10:

- Agreements specify which taxes they cover and normally include 'any identical or substantially similar taxes' imposed by either country after the date of the agreement.

- For the purposes of IHT and estate duty agreements, the term 'domicile' of an individual is used in the agreement to determine which country has worldwide taxing rights. However, the term 'domicile' is primarily a UK term and a further definition is therefore necessary to determine whether an individual is 'domiciled' in the country of the other party to the agreement. The agreement will normally provide for the determination of the country of domicile if the individual is 'domiciled' in both countries under their respective domestic laws. Where a person is domiciled in both countries, there is usually a 'tie-breaker' clause for determining the place of domicile for the purposes of the agreement.

- Deductions and exemptions are to be allowed according to the laws of the country imposing the tax in determining the amount of tax payable.

- Estate duty agreements (and also the IHT agreement with Ireland) lay down rules for determining the situs of assets. The country of situs has the primary taxing rights and the country of domicile gives relief for that tax in accordance with the agreement. The approach of the other IHT agreements is to allow immovable property and the business property of a PE or fixed base situated in the other contracting state (and sometimes certain other assets) to be taxed in the country in which they are situated. The country of domicile has secondary rights to tax these assets, and exclusive rights to tax all other assets.

- If property may be taxed in both contracting states, credit is given by the country of domicile for tax imposed by the country in which the asset is situated.

- There is usually a provision for the exchange of information necessary for carrying out the provisions of the agreement.

Chapter 10

Articles in Agreements — Inheritance Tax and Estate Duty

Introduction

10.1   Following the end of the Second World War the UK negotiated a number of agreements for the avoidance of double taxation with regard to estate duty. Those with France, India, Italy and Pakistan are still in force, although India and Pakistan have since abolished death duties, so that these two agreements are of very limited effect (see 9.10). Since the introduction of CTT in *FA 1975* the UK has signed six agreements (referred to as 'the IHT agreements') with the Republic of Ireland, The Netherlands, South Africa, Sweden, Switzerland and the US.

In 1966 the OECD published a draft Double Taxation Convention on Estates and Inheritances (with commentary) which was limited in scope to the estates of deceased persons. A further model and commentary was published in 1982 which covered taxes on lifetime gifts in addition.

This chapter compares the provisions of the UK's six current IHT agreements with the 1982 OECD model agreement. It also considers the estate duty agreements with France and Italy.

Scope

10.2   Of the IHT agreements concluded, those with South Africa (1978), Sweden (1980) and the US (1978) have identical wording as to their scope. The article provides simply that the agreement is to apply to any person who is within the scope of a tax which is the subject of the agreement. The article in the agreement with Ireland (1977) adds that it also applies to any asset which is the subject of a charge to a tax covered in the agreement.

The scope of the agreement with The Netherlands (1979) is to:

• estates of and gifts made by persons domiciled in one or both states at the time of their death or the time of the gift, as the case may be; and

• property comprised in settlements made by persons domiciled in either state at the time the settlement was made.

The scope of the 1993 agreement with Switzerland is more restrictive, applying to:

• estates and inheritances where the deceased was domiciled, at the time of his death, in one or both of the contracting states; and

• property comprised in a settlement made by a person who was domiciled, at the time the settlement was made, in one or both of the contracting states.

10.3   The 1982 OECD model has an article entitled 'estates, inheritances and gifts covered' which has a similar purpose in defining the scope of the agreement. It indicates that the agreement applies to:

(*a*)   estates and inheritances where the deceased was domiciled, at the time of his death, in one or both of the contracting states; and

(*b*)   gifts where the donor was domiciled, at the time of the gift, in one or both of the contracting states.

Taxes covered

10.4   All six IHT agreements list the taxes covered in the agreements (both in the UK and in the other country) and then extend the application of the agreement to any identical or substantially similar tax imposed subsequently in addition to, or in place of, the existing taxes. The taxes involved are, for example, in Ireland, the gift and inheritance taxes, in South Africa, the estate duty and donations tax and in the US, the federal gift and estate taxes (including the tax on generation-skipping transfers). In Switzerland the taxes covered are cantonal and communal taxes imposed upon estates and inheritances, as there are no such taxes at the federal level.

In relation to taxes imposed subsequently, the agreements with the US, The Netherlands and Switzerland state that the competent authorities of the respective states are to notify each other of changes made in their taxation laws which are relevant to the agreement. The competent authority for the UK is invariably the Commissioners of Inland Revenue. Similarly, the estate duty agreements with France and Italy refer to UK estate duty and to specific taxes in the other country and apply to 'any other duties of a similar character' imposed after the date of signature of the agreement.

General definitions

10.5   Each of the IHT agreements contains a number of definitions which are necessary for the purposes of the agreement. For example, the 1978 agreement with the US defines 'United States', 'United Kingdom', 'enterprise', 'competent authority', 'nationals', 'tax' and 'contracting state'. In addition, it is normally provided that, as regards the application of the agreement by a contracting state, any term not defined is, unless the context requires otherwise, to have the meaning normally attributed to it under that country's domestic legislation.

10.6   The 1982 OECD model agreement has a short 'general definitions' article which defines 'property which forms part of the estate of, or a gift made by, a person domiciled in a contracting state' as including any property the devolution or transfer of which, under the law of a contracting state, is liable to a tax covered by the agreement. Other terms, such as 'immovable property', 'domicile', 'permanent establishment' and 'nationals' are defined elsewhere in the agreement.

There is also a general paragraph indicating that, as regards the application of the convention by a contracting state, any term not defined in the agreement shall, unless the context otherwise requires, have the meaning which it has under the law of that state concerning the taxes to which the convention applies.

Fiscal domicile

10.7   The UK's concept of domicile is an important element in determining the IHT liability arising on assets devolving on death or by certain lifetime gifts. The definition of 'domicile' is extended, for the purpose of IHT only, by *IHTA 1984, s 267*. A person is treated for IHT purposes as domiciled in the UK if:

(*a*)   he has been domiciled in the UK within the last three years; or

(*b*)   he has been resident in the UK for at least 17 of the last 20 years of assessment ending with the year of assessment in which the relevant time falls.

Accordingly, a person who has been domiciled in the UK or a non-UK domiciled person who has been a continual long-term resident of the UK may be deemed to be domiciled in the UK for at least three years following his departure from the UK for permanent residence abroad. Such a person continues to be liable to IHT on his worldwide estate during that period.

The term 'domicile' has been widely adopted in agreements (whether or not the UK is a party) as a factor in determining the taxation rights of each contracting state. However, the meaning of the term 'domicile' as used for the purposes of agreements and the OECD model is clearly different from its technical meaning under UK domestic law. Many countries retain under their domestic laws the right to levy inheritance or gift taxes on the worldwide property of individuals who are their residents (or, in some cases, long-term residents), citizens or nationals. Such individuals are normally considered to be 'domiciled' in that country for the purposes of any agreement.

10.8   A person's 'domicile' for the purposes of the IHT agreements is therefore first ascertained by reference to the laws of the UK and the other country which is a party to the agreement. If a person is (or, in the case of a deceased person, was) domiciled in both countries, the matter is to be determined by means of further tests contained in the 'fiscal domicile' article. The tests (which apply in descending order of priority) in the agreements with Ireland and Sweden provide that the person was domiciled in:

(*a*)   the country in which he had a permanent home available to him;

(*b*)   the country where his centre of vital interests lay (where his personal and economic relations were closer);

(*c*)   the country in which he had a habitual abode; or

(*d*)   the country of which he was a national.

If these tests fail to determine an individual's domicile, this is to be determined by mutual agreement between the contracting states. The US and South African agreements are somewhat different in that there is an additional test to be applied before the tests (*a*) to (*d*) above. These agreements provide that a person who was domiciled in both contracting states and:

(i)   was a national of the UK and not the US/South Africa,

(ii)   has not been resident for tax purposes in the US/South Africa for seven or more of the last ten tax years, is deemed to be domiciled in the UK at that time. The converse also applies. The 1979 agreement with The Netherlands contains a similar provision.

10.9   A protocol to the 1993 agreement with Switzerland also makes provision for individuals living in the other country on a temporary basis. It provides that an individual who was a national of one of the countries and who was domiciled in that country immediately before coming to the other country (the country of residence) shall not be domiciled in the country of residence if:

- he was temporarily present in the country of residence by reason only of his employment (or was a spouse or other dependant of a person temporarily employed in the country of residence);

- the individual had retained the domicile of the country of which he was a national; and

- the individual had no intention of becoming a permanent resident of the country of residence.

The 1982 OECD model agreement

10.10   The 1982 OECD model agreement defines 'person domiciled in a contracting state' as 'any person whose estate or whose gift, under the law of that state, is liable to tax therein by reason of the domicile, residence or place of management of that person or any other criterion of a similar nature'. It clearly therefore covers persons other than individuals. However, this term does not include a person whose estate or gift is liable to tax in that state only in respect of property situated there.

Where an individual is domiciled in both contracting states, the tests to be applied to determine domicile for the purposes of the agreement are the same as those set out in 10.8(*a*) to (*d*) above, failing which the matter is to be decided by mutual agreement.

Where a person other than an individual is domiciled in both contracting states, it is deemed to be domiciled in the place of its effective management.

Taxing rights

10.11   With the exception of the agreement with Switzerland, all of the UK's IHT agreements have 'taxing rights' articles which (when read in conjunction with other relevant articles) determine where assets passing on death or by gift may be taxed. There is little uniformity in these articles, which reflects the number of different positions taken by the various countries, particularly with regard to persons who change their country of domicile within a few years before death or making a gift.

Each of the six IHT agreements must therefore be considered separately in this regard.

10.12   The agreement with Ireland provides that each country retains its normal rights to tax, subject to the provisions of the agreement. Where both countries impose tax on an asset situated in the UK or Ireland, the country with primary taxing rights is the country where the asset is situated. In cases where assets are situated in a third country, the country in which the person is (or was) not domiciled has subsidiary taxing rights (i.e. gives credit for tax payable in the other), unless the property is settled property. As far as property situated in a third country and comprised in a settlement is concerned, the position is determined by the proper law of the settlement when it was made, the settlor's domicile at that time and (in some cases) the proper law of the settlement at a later date.

10.13   The agreement with Sweden provides the basic rule that (with the exceptions of immovable property, business property of a permanent establishment (PE) or fixed base, and ships and aircraft in international traffic) if the deceased or transferor was domiciled in one of the contracting states at the relevant time his property is not to be taxed in the other contracting state unless he was a national of the other state and had been domiciled in that other state within the previous ten years. There are, however, reciprocal rules which apply where a person has only recently become domiciled in the other country. For example, if an individual is:

- a UK national and is not a national of Sweden;

- has been domiciled in Sweden for less than seven of the previous ten years; and

- is domiciled (or deemed domiciled) in the UK under UK domestic law,

he is taxable (subject to the usual exceptions noted above) only in the UK. This rule also applies *mutatis mutandis* to Swedish nationals who have recently become domiciled in the UK.

10.14   In the agreement with South Africa, property (apart from that dealt with in four specific articles, including an unusual one relating to securities) is taxable only in the country of domicile, unless the individual has been domiciled in the other country within the preceding ten years. This does not apply in the UK to settled property, which (apart from the same exceptions) is not taxable in the UK if the settlor was domiciled in South Africa when the settlement was made and had not been domiciled in the UK within the preceding ten years.

If tax, though chargeable under the terms of the agreement only in one country, is not in fact paid (otherwise than because of a specific exemption or other relief), it may be imposed by the other country. A similar provision is found in several of the IHT agreements.

10.15 In the agreement with the US the basic rule is that, if the deceased or transferor was domiciled at the relevant date in one of the contracting states and at the relevant time was not a national of the other state, assets are not to be taxable in the other state. This rule does not, however, apply to immovable property or to property forming part of a PE, which are dealt with in separate articles.

If, on the relevant date, the deceased or transferor was domiciled in neither country, but was a national of one of the countries (but not both), assets taxable in the country of nationality are not to be taxable in the other country. Further paragraphs apply in the US to generation-skipping trusts and in the UK to settled property.

10.16 The agreement with The Netherlands (1979) contains an article headed 'subsidiary taxing rights'. If the deceased or donor was domiciled in one of the contracting states at the relevant time, but was at that time a national of the other state and had been domiciled there within the last ten years, that state may impose tax according to its domestic law. However, the taxing right given by this article is a subsidiary taxing right, so that credit must be given for tax paid in the other state. In addition, the UK is allowed subsidiary taxing rights with regard to property comprised in a settlement unless at the time the settlement was made the settlor was:

- domiciled in The Netherlands; and

- not a national of the UK who had been domiciled in the UK at any time within the last ten years.

10.17 The 1993 agreement with Switzerland does not contain a 'taxing rights' article, but in substance the issue is dealt with in an 'other property' article. Apart from the usual exceptions of immovable property, movable property of a PE or fixed base and ships and aircraft in international traffic, property situated in one of the contracting states may be taxed as follows:

- where the deceased person was domiciled for domestic law purposes in only one of the contracting states, it is taxable only in that state;

- where the deceased was domiciled for domestic law purposes in both contracting states, it is taxable only in the contracting state in which it is situated.

If the property is situated in neither contracting state the taxing rights are as follows:

- if the deceased was domiciled for domestic law purposes in only one of the contracting states, the property is taxable only in the state of his domicile;

- if the deceased was domiciled in both contracting states, it is only then that the domicile tie-breaker paragraph comes into operation

— these tests decide where the deceased was domiciled for the purpose of this paragraph and the property is taxable only in that contracting state (see 10.8 above).

The UK is also given subsidiary taxing rights with regard to shares in UK companies owned by Swiss domiciled persons and to property located in Switzerland or a third country of a Swiss domiciled person who was at the time of his death a UK (and not a Swiss) national and had been domiciled in the UK within the five years preceding his death.

10.18   The estate duty agreements differ from each other in their approach to taxing rights, although the intention is generally that an asset passing on the death of a person domiciled in one country is not to be subjected to the other country's tax unless the asset is situated in, or (in some cases) devolves under the laws of, the other country. Each agreement needs to be considered individually.

10.19   The 1982 OECD model does not contain a taxing rights article. It does, however, contain a short 'other property' article which provides that property, wherever situated, which forms part of the estate of, or a gift made by, a person domiciled in a contracting state, which is not dealt with in the 'immovable property' or 'permanent establishment/fixed base' articles is to be taxed only in the country of domicile.

Situs

10.20   The UK's IHT agreement with Ireland is the only one which contains an article dealing with the situs of property since in the other IHT agreements the situs of the property is not normally a central issue. In the agreement with Ireland the situs of an asset is usually determined under each country's domestic law. However, where the situs of assets is not the same under both countries' domestic laws and the credit provisions will be affected, the situs of the assets is to be determined under the law of the country which has subsidiary taxing rights. If neither country has such rights, the situs is to be determined by mutual agreement.

In other IHT agreements, including those with South Africa, Sweden and the US, any dispute about the situs of assets which would result in tax being imposed in both states is to be resolved by mutual agreement of the competent authorities. A protocol to the agreement with Switzerland provides that for the purposes of the 'other property' article in the agreement, the situs of assets is to be determined in accordance with UK law in force at the date of the agreement.

10.21   The estate duty agreements with France and Italy do have detailed 'situs' articles covering most types of asset, since the situs of the asset is a major factor in determining taxing rights under those agreements. The situs of some of the more important types of asset is as follows:

- immovables — where they are situated;

- tangible movables — where they are situated;

- contract debts — in France, the place of the deceased's domicile, but in Italy the relevant place is the debtor's residence;

- shares — the place of incorporation of the company;

- goodwill — where the trade is carried on;

- ships and aircraft — where they are registered;

- patents, trade marks and designs — in the agreement with Italy it is the country of registration, whereas in the agreement with France the deceased's domicile is relevant.

Immovable property

10.22   The IHT agreements, with the exception of that with Ireland, contain 'immovable property' articles. These define 'immovable property' and give primary taxing rights to the contracting state in which the immovable property is situated. It is then necessary to consider the terms of the relevant 'elimination of double taxation' article to determine the treatment in the other contracting state.

The agreement with Switzerland allows the UK to tax the Swiss immovable property of a person domiciled in the UK, subject to a credit for Swiss tax payable in connection with the same event as is taxed in the UK. The UK immovable property of a Swiss domiciled person on which tax may be imposed in the UK in relation to the same event is exempt from Swiss tax.

The agreements with The Netherlands, the US, Sweden and South Africa all give subsidiary taxing rights to the country of domicile.

There is also a paragraph which indicates that immovable property of an enterprise and immovable property used for the performance of professional services or other services of an independent character falls within this article.

In the 'situs' articles of the estate duty agreements immovable property is situated in the contracting state where the property is situated and primary taxing rights are given to that contracting state.

The 1982 OECD model agreement contains an 'immovable property' article which gives primary taxing rights to the contracting state in which the property is situated. It also contains a definition of 'immovable property' identical to that in the 1992 OECD model agreement on income and capital. This article also covers immovable property of an enterprise and immovable property used for the performance of professional services or other services of an independent character.

Movable property of a permanent establishment or fixed base

10.23   Five IHT agreements (i.e. those with The Netherlands, South Africa, Sweden, Switzerland and the US) contain articles dealing with the movable property of a PE or a fixed base. The treatment is very similar to that of immovable property in that primary taxing rights are given to the contracting state in which the PE or fixed base is situated. The definitions of PE are very similar to those contained in the UK's agreements on income (see 6.25), except that the UK's agreements with Sweden (1980) and Switzerland (1993) contain no references to dependent agents. As with the UK's agreements on income, the term 'fixed base' is not defined. The agreements with Switzerland and South Africa specifically exclude from the scope of this article shares and other securities which are covered by other articles.

For its definition of PE the 1982 OECD model agreement follows the wording of the OECD model agreement on income and capital. However, like the UK's agreements with Sweden and Switzerland, it does not include references to dependent agents.

Ships and aircraft in international traffic

10.24   Four of the UK's IHT agreements, namely those with The Netherlands, South Africa, Sweden and Switzerland, contain an article concerning ships and aircraft in international traffic and movable property pertaining to the operation of such ships. The articles in the agreements with The Netherlands and Sweden also refer to boats engaged in inland waterways transport. Primary taxing rights over these assets are given to the contracting state in which the effective management of the enterprise is situated.

The 1982 OECD model agreement does not contain an equivalent article.

Deductions

10.25   Five of the IHT agreements, the exception being that with Switzerland, contain an article dealing with deductions in determining the amount on which tax is payable. The agreements with Ireland, The Netherlands and Sweden contain a very short article which indicates that, in determining the amount on which tax is to be computed, deductions are to be allowed under the law in force of the country imposing the tax. The matter is therefore left to the domestic laws of each country. Although the articles themselves are worded in general terms, the article in the agreement with Ireland is headed specifically 'deduction of debts'.

The South African agreement is similarly worded, but contains an additional paragraph stating that the agreement does not oblige either country to grant to non-domiciled individuals or their estates any personal allowances, reliefs and reductions which are granted to domiciled individuals or to their estates.

The US agreement also contains a paragraph similar to that contained in the agreements with Ireland, The Netherlands, Sweden and South Africa, but deals with a number of other exemptions and reliefs. These relate to assets passing to the spouse of a person domiciled in (or a national of) the UK or the US and to assets comprised in a settlement on the death of a person domiciled in the UK. Finally, the US agreement provides that, where assets are taxed in the US on the death of a UK national who was neither domiciled in, nor a national of, the US, the US tax to be imposed is limited to the tax which would have been imposed if the deceased had become domiciled in the US immediately before his death, on the property which would in that event have been taxable.

The estate duty agreement with Italy contains an article similar to those in the five IHT agreements. It adds that, where duty is imposed by one contracting party on the death of a person domiciled in the other, no account is to be taken in determining the rate of duty of property situated outside its territory, except where the property passes under a settlement governed by its law.

The 1982 OECD model

10.26   The OECD model provides that debts especially secured on the value of immovable property are to be deducted from the value of that property. Other debts associated with the acquisition, conversion, repair or upkeep of immovable property are also to be deductible. Debts relating to a PE or fixed base are to be deductible from the value of the PE or fixed base.

Other debts are to be deducted from the value of property taxable only in the state of domicile, although if the debt exceeds the value of the property from which it is deductible in a contracting state, the excess is to be deducted from any other property taxable in that state. However, where these rules would oblige one contracting state to deduct debts to a greater extent than it would under its domestic law, they are to apply only to the extent that the other contracting state does not deduct the same debts under its own law.

Elimination of double taxation/credit provisions

10.27   All six IHT agreements have detailed articles headed 'elimination of double taxation', 'credit provisions' or 'credits' which set down the rules for allowing double taxation relief. The articles vary considerably in length and complexity, but, broadly, each agreement provides:

(*a*)   for the granting of a credit for tax paid in the country with primary taxing rights against tax levied in the other country in connection with the same event (the tax credit is limited to the amount of tax payable in the country granting the credit);

(*b*)   that the tax attributable to assets is the amount chargeable, as reduced, for example, by credit given for tax paid in a third country in which the property is situated; and

(*c*)   that the tax must have been paid for credit to be given.

The exception to (*a*) is in the agreement with Switzerland which provides that, where the UK has primary taxing rights, the property is to be exempt from Swiss tax, although it may be taken into account in computing Swiss tax on other property. This is an 'exemption with progression' method similar to that found in agreements relating to income and capital gains.

10.28   In many cases there are special provisions for granting credits in the case of settled property. For example the agreement with the US contains the following provisions which apply where trust property is chargeable to both US and UK tax:

(*a*)   if the property is referred to in specific articles giving one country the primary taxing rights (i.e. it is either immovable property or a PE/fixed base in the US or the UK), the other country will give the credit against its own tax;

(*b*)   if the US imposes tax on the property and it is not referred to in specific articles, the UK will give credit for US tax paid against its tax where the event giving rise to the liability was:

(i)   a generation-skipping transfer where the deemed transferor is domiciled in the US, or

(ii)   the event giving rise to the liability was the exercise or lapse of a power of appointment by a person domiciled in the US at the time of that event.

If (i) and (ii) do not apply, but the settlor or grantor was domiciled in the US at the time of the event giving rise to the tax, credit for the US tax paid is to be given by the UK.

(*c*)   if the US imposes tax on property not referred to in specific articles and paragraph (*b*) does not apply, the US gives credit for UK tax paid.

10.29   The estate duty agreements with France and Italy provide that the country of domicile is to give credit relief for tax paid in the country in which the property is situated as determined by the agreements.

10.30   The 1982 OECD model provides two alternative methods of eliminating double taxation, one by giving relief by the 'exemption with progression' method and the other by the credit method. With both methods the country of domicile is to give the relief. In addition, relief is provided in relation to a previous gift which may, in accordance with the agreement, have been taxed in the other state. For example, where a lifetime transfer of immovable property was taxed in the state in which it was situated and, on subsequent death of the transferor, is aggregated with his estate and taxed in the country of domicile, double taxation would occur unless the country of domicile were to give relief for the tax paid on the previous lifetime transfer.

Time limit

10.31   The IHT agreements with Ireland, The Netherlands, South Africa and Sweden each contain a separate article indicating the time limit for claiming under the agreement. The US agreement has a similar time limit at the end of the 'credits' article. In the agreement with Ireland the time limit is six years from the date of the event in respect of which the claim is made. In the agreements with The Netherlands, Sweden, South Africa and the US this is extended, where later, to one year after the last date on which tax for which credit is given is due. In addition, the agreements with Sweden, South Africa and the US state that the competent authorities may extend the normal time limit in appropriate circumstances where there is a delay in final determination of taxes which are the subject of the claim. The estate duty agreements with France and Italy also contain a short article setting out the time limits available, which is five years from either the date of death or (if later) the event causing duty to be payable.

There is no reference to time limits in the 1982 OECD model.

Non-discrimination

10.32   The form of the non-discrimination articles in the IHT agreements is similar to that in the corresponding articles in the income tax agreements with the same countries. For example the 1979 agreement with The Netherlands provides that:

- the nationals of one state may not be subjected in the other state to any taxation or requirement connected with taxation which is other or more burdensome than the taxation and connected requirements to which nationals of the other state in the same circumstances are subjected;

- the taxation on a PE which an enterprise of one of the states has in the other state is not to be less favourably levied in the other state than the taxation levied on enterprises of that other state carrying on the same activities;

- where the capital of an enterprise of one of the states is owned directly or indirectly by residents of the other state, that enterprise is not to be subjected to taxation or any taxation requirement which is other or more burdensome than that to which other similar enterprises of the first state are subjected; and

- neither state is obliged to grant to a non-resident individual any personal allowance or relief which is granted to an individual who is a resident of that state.

Variations

10.33   There are a number of variations in non-discrimination articles, for example:

(*a*)   the agreement with Sweden does not contain this article;

(*b*)   the agreement with the US adds that:

   (i)   the US is not prevented from taxing a UK national who is not domiciled in the US as a non-resident alien, subject to limitations provided for in the agreement;

  (ii)   the limitation with regard to personal allowances and reliefs applies in relation to the *domicile* of an individual, not his residence — this applies also to the agreements with Ireland and South Africa; and

 (iii)   the scope of the article is limited to taxes covered by the agreement — this applies also to the agreements with Ireland, South Africa and Switzerland.

The estate duty agreements do not contain 'non-discrimination' articles.

The 1982 OECD model

10.34   The OECD model contains a 'non-discrimination' article. The first paragraph is similar to the first paragraph of the article in the IHT agreements as set out in 10.32 above. However it goes on to define 'national' as including legal persons, partnerships and associations which derive their status as such from the law in force in a contracting state. It also provides for non-discrimination against stateless persons who are domiciled in either contracting state. Finally, it indicates that the provisions of the article are to apply to taxes of every kind and description, notwithstanding the provisions of the 'taxes covered' article.

Mutual agreement procedure

10.35   The 'mutual agreement procedure' article in the UK's IHT agreements is very similar to the corresponding article in its income tax agreements (see 8.14). The 1979 agreement with The Netherlands, for example, provides as follows:

(*a*)   Where a person considers that the action of one or both states results in taxation which is not in accordance with the provisions of the agreement, he may, irrespective of remedies provided by the domestic laws of those states, present his case to the competent authorities of either state. The case must be presented within three years from the first notification of the action resulting in taxation not in accordance with the agreement.

(*b*)   The competent authority shall endeavour, if the objection appears to be justified and if it is not itself able to arrive at a satisfactory solution, to resolve the case by mutual agreement with the competent authority of the other state, with a view to the avoidance of taxation not in accordance with the provisions of the agreement.

(*c*)   The competent authorities shall endeavour to resolve by mutual agreement any difficulties or doubts arising as to the interpretation or application of the agreement.

(*d*)   The competent authorities may communicate with each other directly for the purpose of reaching an agreement in the sense of the preceding paragraphs.

There is no mutual agreement procedure in the estate duty agreements.

10.36   The 1982 OECD model has an article which is very similar to the article from The Netherlands agreement outlined above. The model also provides that the competent authorities may consult together for the elimination of double taxation not provided for in the agreement and, where it seems advisable in order to reach agreement to have an oral exchange of opinions, for the establishment of a commission of representatives of the competent authorities.

Exchange of information

10.37   The six IHT agreements all contain 'exchange of information' articles similar to those contained in the corresponding article in the UK's income tax agreements (see 8.19), although the wording in the IHT agreements is somewhat more abbreviated. The following example is from the 1993 agreement with Switzerland:

(*a*)   The competent authorities of the contracting states shall exchange such information (being information which is at their disposal under their respective taxation laws in the normal course of administration) as is necessary for carrying out the provisions of this agreement in relation to taxes which are the subject of the agreement. Any information so exchanged shall be treated as secret and shall not be disclosed to any persons other than those concerned with the assessment, determination and collection of the taxes which are the subject of the agreement. No information shall be exchanged which would disclose any trade, business, banking, industrial or professional secret or trade process.

(*b*)   In no case shall the provisions of this article be construed as imposing upon either contracting state the obligation to carry out administrative measures at variance with the regulations and practice of either contracting state or which would be contrary to its sovereignty, security, or public policy or to supply particulars which are not procurable under its own laws or those of the state making the application.

The estate duty agreements contain an 'exchange of information' article which gives each tax authority the right to exchange information to ensure the proper carrying out of the provisions of the agreement, with safeguards against the disclosure of trade secrets or processes.

The 1982 OECD model also contains an exchange of information article which has a somewhat different wording to that contained in the agreement with Switzerland, but is very much to the same effect. The article is not limited to disclosures of information concerning persons domiciled in one or both of the contracting states.

Diplomatic agents and consular officials

10.38   The wording of the article on diplomatic and consular officials in the IHT agreements is very similar to those found in some income tax agreements (see 8.21). It provides that nothing in the agreement is to affect the fiscal privileges of diplomatic or consular officials under the general rules of international law or under the provisions of special agreements. The US agreement adds a second paragraph to the effect that the agreement does not restrict in any manner any exclusion, exemption, deduction, credit or other allowance accorded by the laws of either contracting state.

No reference to these persons is contained in the estate duty agreements, but there is a brief article in the OECD model similar to that in the IHT agreements.

Transfers between spouses

10.39   The 1980 agreement with Sweden contains an important provision concerning transfers between spouses which reduces the value transferred by 50%. Under UK domestic law, property passing on the death of a UK domiciled individual to a non-domiciled spouse is exempt only on the first £55,000. Thereafter the property is fully liable to IHT. A special article headed 'spouse transfers' in the agreement with Sweden provides that property which passes to the spouse of a deceased person who was domiciled in Sweden and which may be taxed in the UK shall, where:

(*a*)   the spouse was not domiciled in the UK but the transfer would have been wholly exempt had the spouse been UK domiciled; and

(*b*)   a greater exemption is not available under UK domestic law,

be exempt from tax in the UK to the extent of 50% of all value transferred, calculated as a value on which no tax is payable after taking account of all exemptions other than those for transfers between spouses. While this wording is somewhat obscure, it is understood that this is interpreted by the Inland Revenue as meaning that relief will be given for the greater of:

* 50% of the value of the property transferred to the non-UK domiciled spouse; or

* the £55,000 exemption available under *IHTA 1984, s 18(2)*.

There is a corresponding provision with regard to Swedish tax. Where property passes to a spouse from a deceased person who was domiciled in or a national of the UK and the property rights of the spouse are not regulated by the Swedish general law regarding matrimonial property, then Swedish tax on such property shall, if the surviving spouse so requests, be assessed as if the provisions of Swedish law regulating matrimonial property rights were applicable to such property.

Entry into force

10.40   All the IHT agreements have articles concerning the entry into force of the agreement. These usually provide that the agreement comes into force 30 days after the date of exchange of the instruments of ratification and the agreement may either take effect from that date or from another date specified in the agreement. At the same time the article may provide for the termination of an earlier agreement, although in some cases, for example the 1978 agreement with the US, the provisions of the earlier agreement continue to apply for a period if they are more favourable to the taxpayer.

The 1982 OECD model agreement contains a short 'entry into force' article providing simply that the instruments of ratification shall be exchanged at an agreed venue as soon as possible. The agreement is to enter into force on exchange of those instruments and the provisions are to have effect from specified dates in each country.

Termination

10.41   Each of the IHT agreements contains a 'termination' article which enables either party to the agreement to terminate it after an agreed period of notice, following which it will cease to have effect. Usually, a minimum period of three or five years is laid down during which the agreement may not be terminated. Some agreements specify that the termination of the agreement does not have the effect of reviving any agreement terminated by the current agreement or by previous agreements between the contracting states.

The estate duty agreements require a 60-day period of notice, and the agreement is not to be effective with respect to the estates of persons dying on or after that date.

The 1982 OECD model agreement contains a short 'termination' article which provides that either contracting state may terminate the agreement, through diplomatic channels, by giving notice of termination at least six months before the end of any calendar year after a specified date. The agreement then terminates at agreed dates in each contracting state.

Appendix 1

Articles of the OECD Model Tax Convention on Income and on Capital [As they read on 29 April 2000]

Copyright OECD, 2000

Summary of the Convention

Title and preamble

Title of the Convention

Convention between (State A) and (State B) with respect to taxes on income and on capital[1]

Preamble to the Convention[2]

Chapter I   Scope of the Convention

Article 1

Persons covered

This Convention shall apply to persons who are residents of one or both of the Contracting States.

---

1. States wishing to do so may follow the widespread practice of including in the title a reference to either the avoidance of double taxation or to both the avoidance of double taxation and the prevention of fiscal evasion
2. The Preamble of the Convention shall be drafted in accordance with the constitutional procedure of both Contracting States.

Article 2

Taxes covered

1.   This Convention shall apply to taxes on income and on capital imposed on behalf of a Contracting State or of its political subdivisions or local authorities, irrespective of the manner in which they are levied.

2.   There shall be regarded as taxes on income and on capital all taxes imposed on total income, on total capital, or on elements of income or of capital, including taxes on gains from the alienation of movable or immovable property, taxes on the total amounts of wages or salaries paid by enterprises, as well as taxes on capital appreciation.

3.   The existing taxes to which the Convention shall apply are in particular:

a)   (in State A): ....

b)   (in State B): ....

4.   The Convention shall apply also to any identical or substantially similar taxes that are imposed after the date of signature of the Convention in addition to, or in place of, the existing taxes. The competent authorities of the Contracting States shall notify each other of any significant changes that have been made in their taxation laws.

Chapter II   Definitions

Article 3

General definitions

1.   For the purposes of this Convention, unless the context otherwise requires:

a)   the term 'person' includes an individual, a company and any other body of persons;

b)   the term 'company' means any body corporate or any entity that is treated as a body corporate for tax purposes;

c)   the term 'enterprise' applies to the carrying on of any business;

d)   the terms 'enterprise of a Contracting State' and 'enterprise of the other Contracting State' mean respectively an enterprise carried on by a resident of a Contracting State and an enterprise carried on by a resident of the other Contracting State;

e)   the term 'international traffic' means any transport by a ship or aircraft operated by an enterprise that has its place of effective management in a Contracting State, except when the ship or aircraft is operated solely between places in the other Contracting State;

f)   the term 'competent authority' means:

   (*i*) (in State A): ....

    (*ii*) (in State B): ....

g)   the term 'national' means:

    (*i*) any individual possessing the nationality of a Contracting State;

    (*ii*) any legal person, partnership or association deriving its status as such from the laws in force in a Contracting State;

h)   the term 'business' includes the performance of professional services and of other activities of an independent character.

2.   As regards the application of the Convention at any time by a Contracting State, any term not defined therein shall, unless the context otherwise requires, have the meaning that it has at that time under the law of that State for the purposes of the taxes to which the Convention applies, any meaning under the applicable tax laws of that State prevailing over a meaning given to the term under other laws of that State.

Article 4

Resident

1.   For the purposes of this Convention, the term 'resident of a Contracting State' means any person who, under the laws of that State, is liable to tax therein by reason of his domicile, residence, place of management or any other criterion of a similar nature, and also includes that State and any political subdivision or local authority thereof. This term, however, does not include any person who is liable to tax in that State in respect only of income from sources in that State or capital situated therein.

2.   Where by reason of the provisions of paragraph 1 an individual is a resident of both Contracting States, then his status shall be determined as follows:

a)   he shall be deemed to be a resident only of the State in which he has a permanent home available to him; if he has a permanent home available to him in both States, he shall be deemed to be a resident only of the State with which his personal and economic relations are closer (centre of vital interests);

b)   if the State in which he has his centre of vital interests cannot be determined, or if he has not a permanent home available to him in either State, he shall be deemed to be a resident only of the State in which he has an habitual abode;

c)   if he has an habitual abode in both States or in neither of them, he shall be deemed to be a resident only of the State of which he is a national;

d)   if he is a national of both States or of neither of them, the competent authorities of the Contracting States shall settle the question by mutual agreement.

3.   Where by reason of the provisions of paragraph 1 a person other than an individual is a resident of both Contracting States, then it shall be deemed to be a resident only of the State in which its place of effective management is situated.

Appendix 1

Article 5

Permanent establishment

1.   For the purposes of this Convention, the term 'permanent establishment' means a fixed place of business through which the business of an enterprise is wholly or partly carried on.

2.   The term 'permanent establishment' includes especially:

a)   a place of management;

b)   a branch;

c)   an office;

d)   a factory;

e)   a workshop, and

f)   a mine, an oil or gas well, a quarry or any other place of extraction of natural resources.

3.   A building site or construction or installation project constitutes a permanent establishment only if it lasts more than twelve months.

4.   Notwithstanding the preceding provisions of this Article, the term 'permanent establishment' shall be deemed not to include:

a)   the use of facilities solely for the purpose of storage, display or delivery of goods or merchandise belonging to the enterprise;

b)   the maintenance of a stock of goods or merchandise belonging to the enterprise solely for the purpose of storage, display or delivery;

c)   the maintenance of a stock of goods or merchandise belonging to the enterprise solely for the purpose of processing by another enterprise;

d)   the maintenance of a fixed place of business solely for the purpose of purchasing goods or merchandise or of collecting information, for the enterprise;

e)   the maintenance of a fixed place of business solely for the purpose of carrying on, for the enterprise, any other activity of a preparatory or auxiliary character;

f)   the maintenance of a fixed place of business solely for any combination of activities mentioned in subparagraphs *a)* to *e)*, provided that the overall activity of the fixed place of business resulting from this combination is of a preparatory or auxiliary character.

5.   Notwithstanding the provisions of paragraphs 1 and 2, where a person — other than an agent of an independent status to whom paragraph 6 applies — is acting on behalf of an enterprise and has, and habitually exercises, in a Contracting State an authority to conclude contracts in the name of the enterprise, that enterprise shall be deemed to have a permanent establishment in that State in respect of any activities which that person undertakes for the enterprise, unless the activities of such person are limited to those mentioned in paragraph 4 which, if exercised through a fixed place of business, would not make this fixed place of business a permanent establishment under the provisions of that paragraph.

6.   An enterprise shall not be deemed to have a permanent establishment in a Contracting State merely because it carries on business in that State through a broker, general commission agent or any other agent of an independent status, provided that such persons are acting in the ordinary course of their business.

7.   The fact that a company which is a resident of a Contracting State controls or is controlled by a company which is a resident of the other Contracting State, or which carries on business in that other State (whether through a permanent establishment or otherwise), shall not of itself constitute either company a permanent establishment of the other.

Chapter III   Taxation of income

Article 6

Income from immovable property

1.   Income derived by a resident of a Contracting State from immovable property (including income from agriculture or forestry) situated in the other Contracting State may be taxed in that other State.

2.   The term 'immovable property' shall have the meaning which it has under the law of the Contracting State in which the property in question is situated. The term shall in any case include property accessory to immovable property, livestock and equipment used in agriculture and forestry, rights to which the provisions of general law respecting landed property apply, usufruct of immovable property and rights to variable or fixed payments as consideration for the working of, or the right to work, mineral deposits, sources and other natural resources; ships, boats and aircraft shall not be regarded as immovable property.

3.   The provisions of paragraph 1 shall apply to income derived from the direct use, letting, or use in any other form of immovable property.

4.   The provisions of paragraphs 1 and 3 shall also apply to the income from immovable property of an enterprise.

Article 7

Business profits

1.   The profits of an enterprise of a Contracting State shall be taxable only in that State unless the enterprise carries on business in the other Contracting State through a permanent establishment situated therein. If the enterprise carries on business as aforesaid, the profits of the enterprise may be taxed in the other State but only so much of them as is attributable to that permanent establishment.

2.   Subject to the provisions of paragraph 3, where an enterprise of a Contracting State carries on business in the other Contracting State through a permanent establishment situated therein, there shall in each Contracting State be attributed to that permanent establishment the profits which it might be expected

to make if it were a distinct and separate enterprise engaged in the same or similar activities under the same or similar conditions and dealing wholly independently with the enterprise of which it is a permanent establishment.

3.   In determining the profits of a permanent establishment, there shall be allowed as deductions expenses which are incurred for the purposes of the permanent establishment, including executive and general administrative expenses so incurred, whether in the State in which the permanent establishment is situated or elsewhere.

4.   Insofar as it has been customary in a Contracting State to determine the profits to be attributed to a permanent establishment on the basis of an apportionment of the total profits of the enterprise to its various parts, nothing in paragraph 2 shall preclude that Contracting State from determining the profits to be taxed by such an apportionment as may be customary; the method of apportionment adopted shall, however, be such that the result shall be in accordance with the principles contained in this Article.

5.   No profits shall be attributed to a permanent establishment by reason of the mere purchase by that permanent establishment of goods or merchandise for the enterprise.

6.   For the purposes of the preceding paragraphs, the profits to be attributed to the permanent establishment shall be determined by the same method year by year unless there is good and sufficient reason to the contrary.

7.   Where profits include items of income which are dealt with separately in other Articles of this Convention, then the provisions of those Articles shall not be affected by the provisions of this Article.

Article 8

Shipping, inland waterways transport and air transport

1.   Profits from the operation of ships or aircraft in international traffic shall be taxable only in the Contracting State in which the place of effective management of the enterprise is situated.

2.   Profits from the operation of boats engaged in inland waterways transport shall be taxable only in the Contracting State in which the place of effective management of the enterprise is situated.

3.   If the place of effective management of a shipping enterprise or of an inland waterways transport enterprise is aboard a ship or boat, then it shall be deemed to be situated in the Contracting State in which the home harbour of the ship or boat is situated, or, if there is no such home harbour, in the Contracting State of which the operator of the ship or boat is a resident.

4.   The provisions of paragraph 1 shall also apply to profits from the participation in a pool, a joint business or an international operating agency.

Article 9

Associated enterprises

1.   Where:

a)   an enterprise of a Contracting State participates directly or indirectly in the management, control or capital of an enterprise of the other Contracting State, or

b)   the same persons participate directly or indirectly in the management, control or capital of an enterprise of a Contracting State and an enterprise of the other Contracting State,

and in either case conditions are made or imposed between the two enterprises in their commercial or financial relations which differ from those which would be made between independent enterprises, then any profits which would, but for those conditions, have accrued to one of the enterprises, but, by reason of those conditions, have not so accrued, may be included in the profits of that enterprise and taxed accordingly.

2.   Where a Contracting State includes in the profits of an enterprise of that State — and taxes accordingly — profits on which an enterprise of the other Contracting State has been charged to tax in that other State and the profits so included are profits which would have accrued to the enterprise of the first-mentioned State if the conditions made between the two enterprises had been those which would have been made between independent enterprises, then that other State shall make an appropriate adjustment to the amount of the tax charged therein on those profits. In determining such adjustment, due regard shall be had to the other provisions of this Convention and the competent authorities of the Contracting States shall if necessary consult each other.

Article 10

Dividends

1.   Dividends paid by a company which is a resident of a Contracting State to a resident of the other Contracting State may be taxed in that other State.

2.   However, such dividends may also be taxed in the Contracting State of which the company paying the dividends is a resident and according to the laws of that State, but if the beneficial owner of the dividends is a resident of the other Contracting State, the tax so charged shall not exceed:

a)   5 per cent of the gross amount of the dividends if the beneficial owner is a company (other than a partnership) which holds directly at least 25 per cent of the capital of the company paying the dividends;

b)   15 per cent of the gross amount of the dividends in all other cases.

The competent authorities of the Contracting States shall by mutual agreement settle the mode of application of these limitations.

Appendix 1

This paragraph shall not affect the taxation of the company in respect of the profits out of which the dividends are paid.

3.   The term 'dividends' as used in this Article means income from shares, 'jouissance' shares or 'jouissance' rights, mining shares, founders' shares or other rights, not being debt-claims, participating in profits, as well as income from other corporate rights which is subjected to the same taxation treatment as income from shares by the laws of the State of which the company making the distribution is a resident.

4.   The provisions of paragraphs 1 and 2 shall not apply if the beneficial owner of the dividends, being a resident of a Contracting State, carries on business in the other Contracting State of which the company paying the dividends is a resident through a permanent establishment situated therein and the holding in respect of which the dividends are paid is effectively connected with such permanent establishment. In such case the provisions of Article 7 shall apply.

5.   Where a company which is a resident of a Contracting State derives profits or income from the other Contracting State, that other State may not impose any tax on the dividends paid by the company, except insofar as such dividends are paid to a resident of that other State or insofar as the holding in respect of which the dividends are paid is effectively connected with a permanent establishment situated in that other State, nor subject the company's undistributed profits to a tax on the company's undistributed profits, even if the dividends paid or the undistributed profits consist wholly or partly of profits or income arising in such other State.

Article 11

Interest

1.   Interest arising in a Contracting State and paid to a resident of the other Contracting State may be taxed in that other State.

2.   However, such interest may also be taxed in the Contracting State in which it arises and according to the laws of that State, but if the beneficial owner of the interest is a resident of the other Contracting State, the tax so charged shall not exceed 10 per cent of the gross amount of the interest. The competent authorities of the Contracting States shall by mutual agreement settle the mode of application of this limitation.

3.   The term 'interest' as used in this Article means income from debt-claims of every kind, whether or not secured by mortgage and whether or not carrying a right to participate in the debtor's profits, and in particular, income from government securities and income from bonds or debentures, including premiums and prizes attaching to such securities, bonds or debentures. Penalty charges for late payment shall not be regarded as interest for the purpose of this Article.

4.   The provisions of paragraphs 1 and 2 shall not apply if the beneficial owner of the interest, being a resident of a Contracting State, carries on business in the other Contracting State in which the interest arises through a permanent

establishment situated therein and the debt-claim in respect of which the interest is paid is effectively connected with such permanent establishment. In such case the provisions of Article 7 shall apply.

5.   Interest shall be deemed to arise in a Contracting State when the payer is a resident of that State. Where, however, the person paying the interest, whether he is a resident of a Contracting State or not, has in a Contracting State a permanent establishment in connection with which the indebtedness on which the interest is paid was incurred, and such interest is borne by such permanent establishment, then such interest shall be deemed to arise in the State in which the permanent establishment is situated.

6.   Where, by reason of a special relationship between the payer and the beneficial owner or between both of them and some other person, the amount of the interest, having regard to the debt-claim for which it is paid, exceeds the amount which would have been agreed upon by the payer and the beneficial owner in the absence of such relationship, the provisions of this Article shall apply only to the last-mentioned amount. In such case, the excess part of the payments shall remain taxable according to the laws of each Contracting State, due regard being had to the other provisions of this Convention.

Article 12

Royalties

1.   Royalties arising in a Contracting State and beneficially owned by a resident of the other Contracting State shall be taxable only in that other State.

2.   The term 'royalties' as used in this Article means payments of any kind received as a consideration for the use of, or the right to use, any copyright of literary, artistic or scientific work including cinematograph films, any patent, trade mark, design or model, plan, secret formula or process, or for information concerning industrial, commercial or scientific experience.

3.   The provisions of paragraph 1 shall not apply if the beneficial owner of the royalties, being a resident of a Contracting State, carries on business in the other Contracting State in which the royalties arise through a permanent establishment situated therein and the right or property in respect of which the royalties are paid is effectively connected with such permanent establishment. In such case the provisions of Article 7 shall apply.

4.   Where, by reason of a special relationship between the payer and the beneficial owner or between both of them and some other person, the amount of the royalties, having regard to the use, right or information for which they are paid, exceeds the amount which would have been agreed upon by the payer and the beneficial owner in the absence of such relationship, the provisions of this Article shall apply only to the last-mentioned amount. In such case, the excess part of the payments shall remain taxable according to the laws of each Contracting State, due regard being had to the other provisions of this Convention.

Appendix 1

Article 13

Capital gains

1.   Gains derived by a resident of a Contracting State from the alienation of immovable property referred to in Article 6 and situated in the other Contracting State may be taxed in that other State.

2.   Gains from the alienation of movable property forming part of the business property of a permanent establishment which an enterprise of a Contracting State has in the other Contracting State, including such gains from the alienation of such a permanent establishment (alone or with the whole enterprise), may be taxed in that other State.

3.   Gains from the alienation of ships or aircraft operated in international traffic, boats engaged in inland waterways transport or movable property pertaining to the operation of such ships, aircraft or boats, shall be taxable only in the Contracting State in which the place of effective management of the enterprise is situated.

4.   Gains from the alienation of any property other than that referred to in paragraphs 1, 2 and 3, shall be taxable only in the Contracting State of which the alienator is a resident.

Article 14

Independent personal services

[Deleted]

Article 15

Income from employment

1.   Subject to the provisions of Articles 16, 18 and 19, salaries, wages and other similar remuneration derived by a resident of a Contracting State in respect of an employment shall be taxable only in that State unless the employment is exercised in the other Contracting State. If the employment is so exercised, such remuneration as is derived therefrom may be taxed in that other State.

2.   Notwithstanding the provisions of paragraph 1, remuneration derived by a resident of a Contracting State in respect of an employment exercised in the other Contracting State shall be taxable only in the first-mentioned State if:

a)   the recipient is present in the other State for a period or periods not exceeding in the aggregate 183 days in any twelve month period commencing or ending in the fiscal year concerned, and

b)   the remuneration is paid by, or on behalf of, an employer who is not a resident of the other State, and

c)   the remuneration is not borne by a permanent establishment which the employer has in the other State.

284

3.   Notwithstanding the preceding provisions of this Article, remuneration derived in respect of an employment exercised aboard a ship or aircraft operated in international traffic, or aboard a boat engaged in inland waterways transport, may be taxed in the Contracting State in which the place of effective management of the enterprise is situated.

Article 16

Directors' fees

Directors' fees and other similar payments derived by a resident of a Contracting State in his capacity as a member of the board of directors of a company which is a resident of the other Contracting State may be taxed in that other State.

Article 17

Artistes and sportsmen

1.   Notwithstanding the provisions of Articles 7 and 15, income derived by a resident of a Contracting State as an entertainer, such as a theatre, motion picture, radio or television artiste, or a musician, or as a sportsman, from his personal activities as such exercised in the other Contracting State, may be taxed in that other State.

2.   Where income in respect of personal activities exercised by an entertainer or a sportsman in his capacity as such accrues not to the entertainer or sportsman himself but to another person, that income may, notwithstanding the provisions of Articles 7 and 15, be taxed in the Contracting State in which the activities of the entertainer or sportsman are exercised.

Article 18

Pensions

Subject to the provisions of paragraph 2 of Article 19, pensions and other similar remuneration paid to a resident of a Contracting State in consideration of past employment shall be taxable only in that State.

Article 19

Government service

1.   *a)*   Salaries, wages and other similar remuneration, other than a pension, paid by a Contracting State or a political subdivision or a local authority thereof to an individual in respect of services rendered to that State or subdivision or authority shall be taxable only in that State.

    b)   However, such salaries, wages and other similar remuneration shall be taxable only in the other Contracting State if the services are rendered in that State and the individual is a resident of that State who:

(*i*) is a national of that State; or

(*ii*) did not become a resident of that State solely for the purpose of rendering the services.

2. *a)* Any pension paid by, or out of funds created by, a Contracting State or a political subdivision or a local authority thereof to an individual in respect of services rendered to that State or subdivision or authority shall be taxable only in that State.

b) However, such pension shall be taxable only in the other Contracting State if the individual is a resident of, and a national of, that State.

3. The provisions of Articles 15, 16, 17, and 18 shall apply to salaries, wages and other similar remuneration, and to pensions, in respect of services rendered in connection with a business carried on by a Contracting State or a political subdivision or a local authority thereof.

Article 20

Students

Payments which a student or business apprentice who is or was immediately before visiting a Contracting State a resident of the other Contracting State and who is present in the first-mentioned State solely for the purpose of his education or training receives for the purpose of his maintenance, education or training shall not be taxed in that State, provided that such payments arise from sources outside that State.

Article 21

Other income

1. Items of income of a resident of a Contracting State, wherever arising, not dealt with in the foregoing Articles of this Convention shall be taxable only in that State.

2. The provisions of paragraph I shall not apply to income, other than income from immovable property as defined in paragraph 2 of Article 6, if the recipient of such income, being a resident of a Contracting State, carries on business in the other Contracting State through a permanent establishment situated therein and the right or property in respect of which the income is paid is effectively connected with such permanent establishment. In such case the provisions of Article 7 shall apply.

Chapter IV   Taxation of capital

Article 22

Capital

1.   Capital represented by immovable property referred to in Article 6, owned by a resident of a Contracting State and situated in the other Contracting State, may be taxed in that other State.

2.   Capital represented by movable property forming part of the business property of a permanent establishment which an enterprise of a Contracting State has in the other Contracting State may be taxed in that other State.

3.   Capital represented by ships and aircraft operated in international traffic and by boats engaged in inland waterways transport, and by movable property pertaining to the operation of such ships, aircraft and boats, shall be taxable only in the Contracting State in which the place of effective management of the enterprise is situated.

4.   All other elements of capital of a resident of a Contracting State shall be taxable only in that State.

Chapter V   Methods for elimination of double taxation

Article 23A

Exemption method

1.   Where a resident of a Contracting State derives income or owns capital which, in accordance with the provisions of this Convention, may be taxed in the other Contracting State, the first-mentioned State shall, subject to the provisions of paragraphs 2 and 3, exempt such income or capital from tax.

2.   Where a resident of a Contracting State derives items of income which, in accordance with the provisions of Articles 10 and 11, may be taxed in the other Contracting State, the first-mentioned State shall allow as a deduction from the tax on the income of that resident an amount equal to the tax paid in that other State. Such deduction shall not, however, exceed that part of the tax, as computed before the deduction is given, which is attributable to such items of income derived from that other State.

3.   Where in accordance with any provision of the Convention income derived or capital owned by a resident of a Contracting State is exempt from tax in that State, such State may nevertheless, in calculating the amount of tax on the remaining income or capital of such resident, take into account the exempted income or capital.

4.   The provisions of paragraph 1 shall not apply to income derived or capital owned by a resident of a Contracting State where the other Contracting State applies the provisions of this Convention to exempt such income or capital from tax or applies the provisions of paragraph 2 of Article 10 or 11 to such income.

Article 23B

Credit method

1.   Where a resident of a Contracting State derives income or owns capital which, in accordance with the provisions of this Convention, may be taxed in the other Contracting State, the first-mentioned State shall allow:

a)   as a deduction from the tax on the income of that resident, an amount equal to the income tax paid in that other State;

b)   as a deduction from the tax on the capital of that resident, an amount equal to the capital tax paid in that other State.

Such deduction in either case shall not, however, exceed that part of the income tax or capital tax, as computed before the deduction is given, which is attributable, as the case may be, to the income or the capital which may be taxed in that other State.

2.   Where in accordance with any provision of the Convention income derived or capital owned by a resident of a Contracting State is exempt from tax in that State, such State may nevertheless, in calculating the amount of tax on the remaining income or capital of such resident, take into account the exempted income or capital.

Chapter VI   Special provisions

Article 24

Non-discrimination

1.   Nationals of a Contracting State shall not be subjected in the other Contracting State to any taxation or any requirement connected therewith, which is other or more burdensome than the taxation and connected requirements to which nationals of that other State in the same circumstances, in particular with respect to residence, are or may be subjected. This provision shall, notwithstanding the provisions of Article 1, also apply to persons who are not residents of one or both of the Contracting States.

2.   Stateless persons who are residents of a Contracting State shall not be subjected in either Contracting State to any taxation or any requirement connected therewith, which is other or more burdensome than the taxation and connected requirements to which nationals of the State concerned in the same circumstances, in particular with respect to residence, are or may be subjected.

3.   The taxation on a permanent establishment which an enterprise of a Contracting State has in the other Contracting State shall not be less favourably levied in that other State than the taxation levied on enterprises of that other State carrying on the same activities. This provision shall not be construed as obliging a Contracting State to grant to residents of the other Contracting State any personal allowances, reliefs and reductions for taxation purposes on account of civil status or family responsibilities which it grants to its own residents.

4.	Except where the provisions of paragraph 1 of Article 9, paragraph 6 of Article 11, or paragraph 4 of Article 12, apply, interest, royalties and other disbursements paid by an enterprise of a Contracting State to a resident of the other Contracting State shall, for the purpose of determining the taxable profits of such enterprise, be deductible under the same conditions as if they had been paid to a resident of the first-mentioned State. Similarly, any debts of an enterprise of a Contracting State to a resident of the other Contracting State shall, for the purpose of determining the taxable capital of such enterprise, be deductible under the same conditions as if they had been contracted to a resident of the first-mentioned State.

5.	Enterprises of a Contracting State, the capital of which is wholly or partly owned or controlled, directly or indirectly, by one or more residents of the other Contracting State, shall not be subjected in the first-mentioned State to any taxation or any requirement connected therewith which is other or more burdensome than the taxation and connected requirements to which other similar enterprises of the first-mentioned State are or may be subjected.

6.	The provisions of this Article shall, notwithstanding the provisions of Article 2, apply to taxes of every kind and description.

Article 25

Mutual agreement procedure

1.	Where a person considers that the actions of one or both of the Contracting States result or will result for him in taxation not in accordance with the provisions of this Convention, he may, irrespective of the remedies provided by the domestic law of those States, present his case to the competent authority of the Contracting State of which he is a resident or, if his case comes under paragraph 1 of Article 24, to that of the Contracting State of which he is a national. The case must be presented within three years from the first notification of the action resulting in taxation not in accordance with the provisions of the Convention.

2.	The competent authority shall endeavour, if the objection appears to it to be justified and if it is not itself able to arrive at a satisfactory solution, to resolve the case by mutual agreement with the competent authority of the other Contracting State, with a view to the avoidance of taxation which is not in accordance with the Convention. Any agreement reached shall be implemented notwithstanding any time limits in the domestic law of the Contracting States.

3.	The competent authorities of the Contracting States shall endeavour to resolve by mutual agreement any difficulties or doubts arising as to the interpretation or application of the Convention. They may also consult together for the elimination of double taxation in cases not provided for in the Convention.

4.	The competent authorities of the Contracting States may communicate with each other directly, including through a joint commission consisting of themselves or their representatives, for the purpose of reaching an agreement in the sense of the preceding paragraphs.

Appendix 1

Article 26

Exchange of information

1.   The competent authorities of the Contracting States shall exchange such information as is necessary for carrying out the provisions of this Convention or of the domestic laws concerning taxes of every kind and description imposed on behalf of the Contracting States, or of their political subdivisions or local authorities, insofar as the taxation thereunder is not contrary to the Convention. The exchange of information is not restricted by Articles 1 and 2. Any information received by a Contracting States shall be treated as secret in the same manner as information obtained under the domestic laws of that State and shall be disclosed only to persons or authorities (including courts and administrative bodies) concerned with the assessment or collection of, the enforcement or prosecution in respect of, or the determination of appeals in relation to the taxes referred to in the first sentence. Such persons or authorities shall use the information only for such purposes. They may disclose the information in public court proceedings or in judicial decisions.

2.   In no case shall the provisions of paragraph 1 be construed so as to impose on a Contracting State the obligation:

a)   to carry out administrative measures at variance with the laws and administrative practice of that or of the other Contracting State;

b)   to supply information which is not obtainable under the laws or in the normal course of the administration of that or of the other Contracting State;

c)   to supply information which would disclose any trade, business, industrial, commercial or professional secret or trade process, or information, the disclosure of which would be contrary to public policy (order public).

Article 27

Members of diplomatic missions and consular posts

Nothing in this Convention shall affect the fiscal privileges of members of diplomatic missions or consular posts under the general rules of international law or under the provisions of special agreements.

Article 28

Territorial extension[1]

1.   This Convention may be extended, either in its entirety or with any necessary modifications [to any part of the territory of (State A) or of (State B) which is specifically excluded from the application of the Convention or], to any

---

1. The words between brackets are of relevance when, by special provision, a part of the territory of a Contracting State is excluded from the application of the Convention.

State or territory for whose international relations (State A) or (State B) is responsible, which imposes taxes substantially similar in character to those to which the Convention applies. Any such extension shall take effect from such date and subject to such modifications and conditions, including conditions as to terminations, as may be specified and agreed between the Contracting States in notes to be exchanged through diplomatic channels or in any other manner in accordance with their constitutional procedures.

2.   Unless otherwise agreed by both Contracting States, the termination of the Convention by one of them under Article 30 shall also terminate, in the manner provided for in that Article, the application of the Convention [to any part of the territory of (State A) or of (State B) or] to any State or territory to which it has been extended under this Article.

Chapter VII   Final provisions

Article 29

Entry into force

1.   This Convention shall be ratified and the instruments of ratification shall be exchanged at .... as soon as possible.

2.   The Convention shall enter into force upon the exchange of instruments of ratification and its provisions shall have effect:

a)   (in State A): ....

b)   (in State B): ....

Article 30

Termination

This Convention shall remain in force until terminated by a Contracting State. Either Contracting State may terminate the Convention, through diplomatic channels, by giving notice of termination at least six months before the end of any calendar year after the year. . . . In such event, the Convention shall cease to have effect:

a)   (in State A): ....

b)   (in State B): ....

Terminal clause[1]

---

1. The terminal clause concerning the signing shall be drafted in accordance with the constitutional procedure of both Contracting States.

Lists of Current UK Agreements Covering Taxes on Income and Capital Gains

A. List of comprehensive agreements

Country	Date of main agreement	SI (or SR & O) No
Antigua and Barbuda	19/12/47	1947 No 2865
Argentina	3/1/96	1997 No 1777
Australia	7/12/67	1968 No 305
Austria	30/4/69	1970 No 1947
Azerbaijan	23/2/94	1995 No 762
Bangladesh	8/8/79	1980 No 708
Barbados	26/3/70	1970 No 952
Belarus (Note 1, 3)	31/07/85	1986 No 224
Belgium	1/6/87	1987 No 2053
Belize	19/12/47	1947 No 2866
Bolivia	3/11/94	1995 No 2707
Botswana	5/10/77	1978 No 183
Brunei	8/12/50	1950 No 1977
Bulgaria	16/9/87	1987 No 2054
Burma (see Myanmar)		
Canada	8/9/78	1980 No 709
China (Note 2)	26/7/84	1984 No 1826
Croatia (Note 4)	6/11/81	1981 No 1815
Cyprus	20/6/74	1975 No 425
Czech Republic	5/11/90	1991 No 2876
Denmark	11/11/80	1980 No 1960
Egypt	25/4/77	1980 No 1091
Estonia	12/5/94	1994 No 3207
Falkland Islands	25/6/97	1997 No 2985
Fiji	21/11/75	1976 No 1342
Finland	17/7/69	1970 No 153
France	22/5/68	1968 No 1869
Gambia	20/5/80	1980 No 1963
Germany	26/11/64	1967 No 25
Ghana	20/1/93	1993 No 1800
Greece	25/6/53	1954 No 142
Grenada	4/3/49	1949 No 361
Guernsey	24/6/52	1952 No 1215
Guyana	17/12/92	1992 No 3207

Hungary	28/11/77	1978 No 1056
Iceland	30/9/91	1991 No 2879
India	25/1/93	1993 No 1801
Indonesia	5/4/93	1994 No 769
Ireland (Republic of)	2/6/76	1976 No 2151
Isle of Man	29/7/55	1955 No 1205
Israel	26/9/62	1963 No 616
Italy	21/10/88	1990 No 2590
Ivory Coast	26/6/85	1987 No 169
Jamaica	16/3/73	1973 No 1329
Japan	10/2/69	1970 No 1948
Jersey	24/6/52	1952 No 1216
Kazakhstan	19/4/94	1994 No 3211
Kenya	31/7/73	1977 No 1299
Kiribati and Tuvalu	10/5/50	1950 No 750
Korea	25/10/96	1996 No 3168
Kuwait	23/2/99	1999 No 2036
Latvia	8/5/96	1996 No 3167
Lesotho	29/1/97	1997 No 2986
Luxembourg	24/5/67	1968 No 1100
Macedonia (Note 4)	6/11/81	1981 No 1815
Malawi	25/11/55	1956 No 619
Malaysia	10/12/96	1997 No 2987
Malta	12/5/94	1995 No 763
Mauritius	11/2/81	1981 No 1121
Mexico	2/6/94	1994 No 3212
Mongolia	23/4/96	1996 No 2598
Montserrat	19/12/47	1947 No 2869
Morocco	8/9/81	1991 No 2881
Myanmar (Burma)	13/3/50	1952 No 751
Namibia	28/5/62 agreement with South Africa as extended	1962 No 2352
Netherlands	7/11/80	1980 No 1961
New Zealand	4/8/83	1984 No 635
Nigeria	9/6/87	1987 No 2057
Norway	12/10/00	2000 No 3247
Pakistan	24/11/86	1987 No 2088
Papua New Guinea	17/9/91	1991 No 2882
Philippines	10/6/76	1978 No 184
Poland	16/12/76	1978 No 282
Portugal	27/3/68	1969 No 599
Romania	18/9/75	1977 No 57
Russian Federation	15/2/94	1994 No 3213
St Christopher (St Kitts) and Nevis	19/12/47	1947 No 2872
Sierra Leone	19/12/47	1947 No 2873
Singapore	12/2/97	1997 No 2988
Slovak Republic	5/11/90	1991 No 2876
Slovenia	6/11/81	1981 No 1815
Solomon Islands	10/5/50	1950 No 748
South Africa	21/11/68	1969 No 864
Spain	21/10/75	1976 No 1919

Sri Lanka	21/6/79	1980 No 713
Sudan	8/3/75	1977 No 1719
Swaziland	26/11/68	1969 No 380
Sweden	30/8/83	1984 No 366
Switzerland	8/12/77	1978 No 1408
Thailand	18/2/81	1981 No 1546
Trinidad and Tobago	31/12/82	1983 No 1903
Tunisia	15/12/82	1984 No 133
Turkey	19/2/86	1988 No 932
Uganda	23/12/92	1993 No 1802
Ukraine	10/2/93	1993 No 1803
United States	31/12/75	1980 No 568
Uzbekistan	15/10/93	1994 No 770
Venezuela	11/3/96	1996 No 2599
Vietnam	9/4/94	1994 No 3216
Yugoslavia (Federal Republic – Note 4)	6/11/81	1981 No 1815
Zambia	22/3/72	1972 No 1721
Zimbabwe	19/10/82	1982 No 1842

Many of the above conventions have been amended by Protocols, which are published separately with a new SI number. Any Protocol should be read in conjunction with the original convention.

Note 1. The UK's 1986 convention with the Soviet Union (SI 1986 No 224) is currently to be regarded as in force between the UK and the former Soviet Republic marked. The position with the former Soviet Republics not listed is less clear, but the UK will in all cases apply the provisions of the convention on the basis that it is still in force (until such time as new conventions take effect with particular countries).

Note 2. The agreement between the UK and China does not apply to the Hong Kong Special Administrative Region which came into existence on 1 July 1997.

Note 3. The 1995 convention with Belarus has not yet entered into force.

Note 4. The UK's convention with Yugoslavia (SI 1981 No 1815) is to be regarded as in force between the UK and the former Yugoslav states marked. The position with regard to the remainder of what was Yugoslavia is undetermined.

B. List of agreements covering taxes on shipping and/or air transport profits only

Country	Date of agreement	SI (or SR & O) No
Algeria (air transport)	27/5/81	1984 No 362
Brazil	29/12/67	1968 No 572
Cameroon (air transport)	22/4/82	1982 No 1841
China (air transport and employees)	10/3/81	1981 No 1119
Ethiopia (air transport)	1/2/77	1977 No 1297
Hong Kong	13/12/00	2000 No 3248
Iran (air transport)	21/12/60	1960 No 2419
Jordan	6/3/78	1979 No 300

Kuwait (air transport)	25/9/84	1984 No 1825
Lebanon	26/2/64	1984 No 278
Saudi Arabia (air transport and employees)	10/3/93	1994 No 767
USSR (air transport and employees)	3/5/74	1974 No 1269
Venezuela	8/3/78	1979 No 301
Zaire	11/10/76	1977 No 1298

List of Current UK Agreements Covering Inheritance Tax

A. Estate duty agreements

Country	Date of agreement	SI (or SR & O) No
France	21/6/63	1963 No 1319
India (Note 1)	3/4/56	1956 No 998
Italy	15/2/66	1968 No 304
Pakistan (Note 1)	8/6/57	1957 No 1522

B. Inheritance tax agreements

Irish Republic	7/12/77	1978 No 1107
Netherlands	11/12/79	1980 No 706
South Africa	31/7/78	1979 No 576
Sweden	8/10/80	1981 No 840
Switzerland	17/12/93	1994 No 3214
United States	19/10/78	1979 No 1454

Note 1. The agreements with India and Pakistan are of limited effect only following the abolition of death duties in those countries.

Appendix 4

Admissible and Inadmissible Taxes

© Crown Copyright. Reproduced with the permission of the Controller of HMSO.

(*Note:* In March 1995 the Inland Revenue published booklet IR 146 containing a list of foreign taxes which the Board had decided were inadmissible or admissible for double taxation relief. That list, as amended, is reproduced below. Changes to the list are now published in the Inland Revenue's Double Taxation Relief Manual. Booklet IR 146 has been withdrawn and will not be replaced.

It is open to the taxpayer affected to appeal against the refusal of relief for any particular tax.)

ABU DHABI
Admissible: Income tax.

AFGHANISTAN
Admissible: Company income tax.
Inadmissible: Tax on gross receipts.

ALBANIA
Admissible: Income tax.

ALGERIA
Admissible: Tax on industrial and commercial profits (*Impôt sur les bénéfices industriels et commerciaux*) (replaced from 1 January 1992) — Tax on profits of non-commercial professions (*Impôt sur les professions non-commerciales*) where charged on taxpayers having a permanent establishment in Algeria and taxed there on accounts based profits (replaced from 1 January 1992) — Complementary tax on total income (*Impôt complémentaire sur l'ensemble du revenu*) (replaced from 1 January 1992) — Petroleum tax (*Impôt pétrolier*) — Tax on income of foreign construction companies (*Impôt sur le revenu des enterprises étrangères de construction* — *IREEC*) — Tax on profits of non-commercial professions (*Impôt sur les bénéfices des professions non-commerciales*) where charged on non-Algerian taxpayers having no permanent establishment in Algeria.
Inadmissible: Sole universal tax on services (*Taxe unique globale sur les prestations de services*) (abolished from April 1992).

ANGOLA
Admissible: Industrial tax (*Contribuição industrial*) — Property tax (*contribuição predial*) — People's Resistance Tax (*Imposto de resistência popular*) (abolished from 1 January 1992).

ANTIGUA and BARBUDA
Admissible: Income tax — Land value appreciation tax.

ARGENTINA
Admissible: Income tax (*Impuesto a las ganancias*) — Tax imposed by Art. 56 of the *Hydrocarbons Law* (17,319) — Assets tax (*Impuesto sobre los activos*) —

297

Appendix 4

Personal assets tax (*Impuesto personal sobre los bienes no incorporados al proceso económico*).
Inadmissible: Real property tax (*Contribución inmobilaria*) — Tax on capital and net worth (*Impuesto sobre capitales y patrimonios*) (replaced for years beginning in 1990 and thereafter for companies) — Tax on financial services (*Gravamen sobre servicios financieros*).

AUSTRALIA
Admissible: Income tax (including the additional tax on the undistributed amount of the distributable income of a private company) — 5% additional income tax on the branch profits of non-resident companies (abolished from 1 July 1987) — Victorian taxation equivalent, to the extent that it is calculated by reference to Australian (that is, Federal) income tax.
Inadmissible: Fringe benefits tax — Petroleum resource rent tax (RRT) — Financial institutions duty (New South Wales) — New South Wales land tax.

AUSTRIA
Admissible: Income tax (*Einkommensteuer*) including wages tax (*Lohnsteuer*) — Capital yields tax (*Kapitalertragsteuer*) — Corporation tax (*Körperschaftsteuer*) — Directors' tax (*Aufsichtsratsabgabe*) (abolished from 31 December 1988) — Trade tax (*Gewerbesteuer*) on trading profits (abolished from 1 January 1994) — Tax on foreigners or non-residents (*Ausländersteuer*).
Inadmissible: Wealth tax (*Vermögensteuer*) (abolished from 1 January 1994) — Capital levy (*Vermögensabgabe*) — Substitute inheritance tax (*Erbschaftssteueräquivalent*) (abolished from 1 January 1994) — Company tax (*Gesellschaftsteuer*) (this is a capital contributions tax) — Land tax (*Grundsteuer*) — Turnover tax (*Umsatzsteuer*) — Municipal tax on commercial and industrial enterprises (*Gewerbesteuer*), so far as computed on a basis other than profits, viz tax on capital employed (*Gewerbekapital*), payroll tax (*Lohnsummensteuer*).

AZERBAIJAN
Admissible: Tax on profit and some incomes of legal persons — Income tax on physical persons — Tax on foreign subcontractors.

BANGLADESH
Admissible: Income tax — Freight tax.
Inadmissible: Jamuna multi-purpose bridge surcharge and levy (abolished from 1 April 1994).

BARBADOS
Admissible: Income tax — Corporation tax — Remittance tax on branch profits — Petroleum winnings operations tax.
Inadmissible: Hotel tax — Premium income tax levied on general insurance business — Tax on the assets of a bank *(Banks) (Tax on Assets) Act 1983-1* (not levied since 1983) — Property transfer tax.

BELARUS
Admissible: Tax on income and profits of legal persons — Income tax of individuals — Tax on immovable property.

BELGIUM
Admissible: Income tax on individuals (*Impôt des personnes physiques/personenbelasting*) — Company income tax (*Impôt des sociétés/vennootschapsbelasting*) — Income tax on legal entities (*Impôt des personnes morales/rechtspersonenbelasting*) — Income tax on non-residents (*Impôt des non-résidents/belasting der nietverblijfhouders*) — Income tax prepayments (*Précomptes/voorherffingen*) and additional prepayments (*Précomptes complémentaires/aanvullende*

voorheffingen) — Surcharges (*Centimes additionnels/opcentiemen*) on any of the above taxes including the communal supplement to the individual income tax (*Taxe communale additionnelle à l'impôt des personnes physiques/aanvullende gemeentebelasting op de personenbelasting*).
Inadmissible: Annual tax on insurance contracts (*Taxe annuelle sur les contracts d'assurance/jaarlijkse taks op de verzekeringscontracten*) — Penalty (*Majoration/ vermeerdering*).

BELIZE
Admissible: Income tax.

BENIN
Admissible: Tax on industrial and commercial profits (*Impôt sur les bénéfices industriels et commerciaux — BIC*) — Tax on distributions (*Impôt sur les revenus de valeurs mobilières — IRVM*) — Tax on profits from non-commercial occupations (*Impôt sur les bénéfices des professions non-commerciales*) — Tax on public and private salaries, allowances and emoluments, wages, pensions and life annuities (*Impôt sur les traitements publiques et privés, les indemnités et émoluments, les salaires, les pensions et les rentes viagères*) — General income tax (*Impôt général sur le revenu — IGR*) — Tax on income from movable capital (*Impôt sur le revenu des capitaux mobiliers — IRCM*).
Inadmissible: Real property tax (*Contribution foncière des propriétés bâties*) — Business licence tax (*Contribution des patentes*) — Land tax (*Contribution foncière des propriétés non-bâties*).

BOLIVIA
Admissible: The VAT complementary system (*el régimen complementario al impuesto del valor agregado*) — The tax on companies' presumed income (*el impuesto a la renta presunta de empresas*) — The tax on the presumed income of property owners (*el impuesto a la renta presunta de proprietarios de bienes*) — The tax on transactions (*el impuesto a las transacciones*) — The tax on the profits obtained from the exploitation of hydrocarbons and/or minerals (*el impuesto a las utilidades obtenidas en la explotaci ón hidrocarburos y/o minerales*). Admissible before the agreement took effect: Hydrocarbon tax (to the extent that it is not offset by a credit for royalties).

BOPHUTHATSWANA
Admissible: Normal tax — Non-resident shareholders' tax.

BOTSWANA
Admissible: Income tax.

BRAZIL
Admissible: Income tax (*Imposto de renda*) — State income taxes (*Imposto de renda — estadual*) — Corporate income tax (*Imposto de renda das pessoas jurídicas*) — Withholding tax imposed on income including tax charged on gross receipts, interest, royalties or dividends and the supplementary tax charged on dividends remitted abroad in excess of 12% registered capital — Payments to the development funds PIN and PIS (up to 1988 only) (*Programa de integração nacional/social*) and MOBRAL — (*Fundação movimento Brasileiro de Alfabetizção*) — Social contributions tax (*Contribuição social*).
Inadmissible: Federal mining tax (repealed on 1 March 1989) — Additional tax on the income tax — 8% withholding tax on net income of corporate entities (if the 8% withholding tax is offset against the 25% withholding tax payable on a dividend to a non-resident shareholder, credit is available for the net amount actually paid and the 8% set off) — Payments to the development funds for the

Appendix 4

North East (SUDENE and FINOR) and Amazon (SUDAM and FINAM) and the sectorial investment funds (SUDEPE and FISET) — Recife localisation licence tax (abolished from 31 December 1991) — 2% municipal tax on services (*Imposto sobre serviços de qualquer natureza*) — Payments to Empresa Brasileira de Aeronáutica (EMBRAER) — Tax on financial transfers (*Imposto sobre operações financiaras*) — Distribution tax — *Programa de Integração Social (PIS)* from 1989 onwards.

BRUNEI
Admissible: Income tax — Petroleum income tax.

BULGARIA
Admissible: Tax on total income (believed to have been replaced 1 January 1995) — Tax on income of single males and females, widows and widowers, divorced persons and families without children (believed to have been replaced 1 January 1995) — Tax on profits (believed to have been replaced 1 January 1995).

BURKINA
Admissible: Tax on industrial and commercial profits (*Impôt sur les bénéfices industriels et commerciaux*) — Tax on profits from non-commercial occupations (*Impôt sur les bénéfices des professions non-commerciales*) — Tax on income from movable capital (*Impôt sur le revenu des capitaux mobiliers*).
Inadmissible: Business licence tax (*Contribution des patentes*).

BURMA — see MYANMAR

BURUNDI
Admissible: Tax on income from movable capital (*impôt mobilier*) — Tax on company earnings (*Impôt professionel sur les revenus des sociétés*) where charged on profits — Tax on rental income (*Impôt sur les revenus locatifs*).

CAMEROON
Admissible: 15% special tax on non-residents.

CANADA
Admissible (Federal): Income taxes imposed by the Government of Canada — Tobacco manufacturers' surtax.
Admissible (Provincial):
ALBERTA — Provincial income tax.
BRITISH COLUMBIA — Provincial income tax — Mining tax — Logging tax — Mineral resources tax (replaced from 1 January 1990).
MANITOBA — Provincial income tax including the additional hospital services tax.
NEW BRUNSWICK — Provincial income tax — Mining tax.
NEWFOUNDLAND — Provincial income tax — Mining tax.
NOVA SCOTIA — Provincial income tax — Mining tax.
ONTARIO — Provincial corporation tax on company profits — Provincial income tax — Mining tax — Corporate minimum tax.
PRINCE EDWARD ISLAND — Provincial income tax.
QUEBEC — Provincial corporation tax on company profits — Provincial income tax on individuals — Mining tax — Logging tax.
SASKATCHEWAN — Provincial income tax — Mining royalty tax.
Inadmissible (Federal): Taxes on capital — Large corporations tax and any other taxes on capital — Petroleum and gas revenue tax — Place of business taxes — Taxes based on a percentage of premiums received by insurance companies.
Inadmissible (Provincial):
ALBERTA — Oil and gas conservation tax.

Appendix 4

CENTRAL AFRICAN REPUBLIC
Admissible: General income tax (*Impôt général sur le revenu*) — Additional taxes for the benefit of communes (*Centimes additionnels*).
Inadmissible: Business licence tax (*Contribution des patentes*) — Real property tax (*Contribution foncière des propriétés bâties*) — Land tax (*Contribution fonciére des propriétés non-bâties*).

CHAD
Admissible: Tax on industrial and commercial profits (*Impôt sur les bénéfices industriels et commerciaux*) — Tax on profits from non-commercial professions (*Impôt sur les bénéfices des professions non-commerciales*) — Tax on public and private salaries, allowances and emoluments, wages, pensions and life annuities (*Impôt sur les traitements publics et privés, les indemnités et émoluments, les pensions et les rentes viagères*) — Additional taxes for the benefit of communes (*Centimes additionnels*).
Inadmissible: Business licence tax (*Contribution des patentes*) — Real property tax (*Contribution foncière des propriétés bâties*) — Land tax (*Contribution foncière des propriétés non-bâties*).

CHILE
Admissible: Income tax (*Impuesto a la renta*) — Complementary global tax (*Impuesto global complementario*) — Additional tax (*Impuesto adicional/tasa adicional*) — Property tax (*Contribución territorial*) in so far as it is set off against first category income tax.
Inadmissible: Reinsurance premium tax.

CHINA
Admissible: Income tax levied at progressive rates on taxable income under Article 3 of the income tax law concerning foreign enterprises (replaced from 1 July 1991) – Local income tax levied on the same taxable income under Article 4 of the Income Tax law concerning foreign enterprises (replaced from 1 July 1991) — Witholding tax on dividends, interest, rents and royalties — Individual income tax — Income tax (and local income tax) on joint ventures — Income tax on foreign enterprises under the *Income Tax Law for Enterprises with Foreign Investment and Foreign Enterprises* (effective from 1 July 1991) — Local income tax levied on the same taxable income as for the *Income Tax Law for Enterprises with Foreign Investment and Foreign Enterprises*.
Inadmissible: Business tax — Urban maintenance and development tax — Consolidated industrial and commercial tax.

CISKEI
Admissible: Non-resident shareholders' tax.

COLOMBIA
Admissible: Income tax (*Impuesto sobre la renta*), including withholding on account thereof on payments made abroad — surtax on remittances (*impuesto complementario de remesas*) — Special contribution tax.
Inadmissible: Capital tax (*Impuesto sobre el patrimonio*) (abolished from 1992).

CONGO
Admissible: Tax on the income of individuals (*Impôt sur le revenu des personnes physiques*) — Complementary tax (*Impôt complémentaire*) (abolished from 1990) — Company tax (*Impôt sur les sociétés*).
Inadmissible: Business licence tax (*Contribution des patentes*).

COSTA RICA
Admissible: Income tax (*Impuesto sobre la renta*) — 2% of the normal income tax

allocated to community development (*Desarrollo de la comunidad*) (believed to have been abolished).

CYPRUS (REPUBLIC OF)
Admissible: Income tax — Special contributions under Law 55 of 1974 and subsequent annual extensions.

CZECH REPUBLIC
Admissible: Income tax (*Dan z prîjmu*) levied under the Income Tax Law 586 of 1992.

CZECHOSLOVAKIA (to 31 December 1992)
Admissible: Tax on profits — Wages tax — Tax on the income from literary and artistic activities — Agricultural tax — Tax on population income — House tax — Literary and artists' tax (*Dan z prîjmu z literarni a umelecke cinnosti*) — Taxes on profits (*Odved ze zisku a dan ze zisku*) in so far as this tax is deducted from royalty payments — Special contributions for the defence fund of the Republic.
Inadmissible: Payments to the Literary Fund.

DENMARK
Admissible: Danish state and municipality income taxes, comprising: main national income tax (*indkomstskat til staten*); special income tax (*saerlig indkomstskat*); seamen's tax (*sømandsskat*); company income tax (*indkomstskat af aktieselskaber m.v*), including the supplementary tax or surcharge (*tillaeg*); national pensions contributions (*invalidie og folkepensionsbidrag*) — Dividend tax (*Udbytteskat*) — Hydrocarbon tax (*Kulbrinteskat*) — Communal income taxes (*Kommuneskat*) including church tax (*Kirkeskat*).
Inadmissible: Payments by way of compulsory saving (*Bundenopsparing*) (these are not payments by way of taxation) — National wealth tax (*Formueskat til staten*) — Real interest rate tax.

DJIBOUTI
Admissible: Tax on profits of legal entities (*Impôt sur les bénéfices des personnes morales*).

DOMINICA
Admissible: Income tax.

DOMINICAN REPUBLIC
Admissible: Income tax (*Impuesto sobre la renta*) — Complementary tax (*Impuesto complementario*) — Withholding tax on remitted profits (abolished with effect from 1 January 1992).

DUBAI
Admissible: Income tax.

ECUADOR
Admissible: Income tax (*Impuesto a la renta*), including the tax charged on 2% of the value of goods shipped by international companies — Additional tax for the transport commission in Guayas (*Impuesto adicional al de la renta para comisión de tránsito en Guayas*) (abolished from 1 January 1990) — Additional tax for higher education (*Impuesto adicional sobre el impuesto a la renta en favor de las universidades y Escuelas Politécnicas del país*) (abolished from 1 January 1990) — Tax on international transport companies charged on 2% of gross receipts.
Inadmissible: Tax on working capital (*Impuesto sobre el capital en giro*) (replaced from 1989) — Employers' contributions to social security scheme, which are a percentage of basic wages paid.

EGYPT
Admissible: Land tax — Tax on income from movable capital — Tax on commercial and industrial profits — Tax on wages and salaries — Tax on noncommercial profits — General income tax — Tax on the profits of shareholding companies.

EL SALVADOR
Admissible: Income tax (*Impuesto sobre la renta*).

ERITREA
Admissible: Income tax — Municipality tax.
Inadmissible: Rehabilitation tax (*Mehwei Gibri*).

ESTONIA
Admissible: Income tax ('*tulumaks*').

ETHIOPIA
Admissible: Income tax chargeable under the *Income Tax Proclamation* 1961.
Inadmissible: Municipality tax.

FALKLAND ISLANDS
Admissible: Income tax, including the tax on royalties and capital gains.

FAROE ISLANDS
Admissible: Provincial income tax (*Skat til landskassen/skattur til landskassa*) — Communal income tax (*Kommunal indkomstskat/skatta til kommunu*).

FIJI
Admissible: Income tax (including basic tax and normal tax) — Non-resident dividend withholding tax — Interest withholding tax — Dividend tax — Land sales tax.

FINLAND
Admissible: State income tax (*Statlig inkomstskatt/valtion tulovero*) — Corporate income tax (*Yhteisöjen tulovero/inkomstskatten för samfund*) — Communal tax (*Kommunalskatt/kunnalisvero*) — Church tax (*Kyrkoskatt/kirkollisvero*) — State capital tax (*Valtion varallisuusvero; denstatliga förmögenhetsskatten*) (only against any similar tax which may be levied in the UK) — Tax withheld at source from non-residents' income (*Rajoitetusti verovelvollisen Lähdevero; källskatten för begränsat skattskyldig*) — Tax withheld at source from interest (*Korkotulon lähdevero/källskaten pränteinkomst*).
Inadmissible: Net asset tax (*Förmögenhetsskatt/omaisuusvero*).

FRANCE
Admissible: Income tax on the income of individuals (*Impôt sur le revenu*) — Corporation tax (*Impôt sur les sociétés*) including the surcharge (*contribution de 10%*) — Any withholding tax, prepayment (*Précompte*) or advance payment with respect to the above taxes — Property tax (*Taxe foncière sur les propriétés bâties*) — Refuse disposal tax (*Taxe d'enlèvement des ordures ménagères*).
Inadmissible: Trade tax (*Taxe professionnelle*) — Tax for the expenses of Chambers of Agriculture (*Taxe pour frais de chambres d'agriculture*) — Contribution to the supplementary fund for agricultural social benefits (*Taxe perçue au profit du budget annexe des prestations sociales agricoles*) — Special levy on financial institutions (*Contribution annuelle des institutions financières*) introduced by the finance law of 1977 — Wealth tax (*Impôt de solidarité sur la fortune*) introduced 1 January 1989 — Payments by way of annual minimum tax (*Imposition forfaitaire annuelle*) which are not set off against corporation tax.

Appendix 4

FRENCH POLYNESIA (TAHITI)
Admissible: Corporation tax (*Impôt sur les bénéfices des sociétés*) — Territorial solidarity tax (*Prélèvement territorial de solidarité*) — Extraordinary solidarity tax (*Prélèvement exceptionnel de solidarité*).

GABON
Admissible: Corporate tax (*Impôt sur les sociétés*) — Tax on income from movable capital (*Impôt sur le revenu des valeurs mobilières*).
Inadmissible: Business licence tax (*Contribution des patentes*) — Real property tax (*Contribution foncière des propriétés bâties*) — Land tax (*Contribution foncière des propriétés non-bâties*) — 10% withholding tax on royalties — Gabon investment fund levy (*Prélèvement pour le fonds gabonais d'investissement*) — Payments by way of annual minimum tax (*Impôt minimum forfaitaire*); sums paid by way of IMF are admissible for the period for which they are set against corporate tax but otherwise inadmissible — Business income tax; alternative regime for non-resident oil industry subcontractor (*Régime spécial applicable aux contracteurs pétroliers étrangers*) admitted to extent paid in respect of company tax; refused to extent paid in respect of investment fund levy or employer's liability.

THE GAMBIA
Admissible: Income tax — National development levy (abolished in 1990).

GERMAN DEMOCRATIC REPUBLIC
[All the taxes indicated were in force until reunification on 3 October 1990. However, many taxes of the GDR remained applicable until the end of 1990. The Federal (West) German tax system came into effect throughout the unified Germany on 1 January 1991.]
Admissible: Corporation tax (*Körperschaftsteuer*) — Trade tax (*Gewerbesteuer*) to the extent that it is computed by reference to trading profits — Wages tax (*Lohnsteuer*) — Composite site tax (*Betriebsstättensteuer*) to the extent that its constituent tax elements are admissible.
Inadmissible: Turnover tax (*Umsatzsteuer*) — Net worth tax — (*Betriebsvermögensteuer*) — Trade tax (*Gewerbesteuer*) to the extent that it is computed by reference to capital employed.

GERMANY (FEDERAL REPUBLIC OF)
Admissible: Income tax (*Einkommensteuer*); the *Einkommensteuer* includes wages tax (*Lohnsteuer*), capital yields tax (*Kapitalertragsteuer*) and directors' tax (*Aufsichtsratsteuer*) — Corporation tax (*Körperschaftsteuer*), including the surcharge (*Ergänzungsabgabe/Solidaritätszuschlag*) — Trade tax (*Gewerbesteuer*) to the extent that it is computed by reference to trading profits (*Gewerbeertrag*).
Inadmissible: Turnover tax (*Umsatzsteuer*) — Wealth tax or net worth tax (*Vermögensteuer*) — Trade tax on capital employed (*Gewerbekapital*) which is part of the trade tax (*Gewerbesteuer*) — Inheritance tax (*Erbschaftsteuer*) — Fire protection tax (*Feuerschutzsteuer*) — Church tax (*Kirchensteuer*).

GHANA
Admissible: Income tax — Petroleum income tax — Minerals and Mining tax — Capital gains tax.
Inadmissible: Additional profit tax — Gift tax.

GIBRALTAR
Admissible: Income tax.

GREECE
Admissible: Income tax, including schedular or analytical tax and tax charged on general public or private works' contractors on a percentage (10% or 12%) of

304

gross receipts — Capital gains tax on transfers of real property (from 1 January 1991).

GRENADA
Admissible: Income tax (abolished from 1 January 1986) — Business levy (with effect from 1 January 1989 only).

GUADELOUPE
Admissible: Company tax (*Impôt sur les sociétés*).

GUAM
Admissible: Territorial income tax.

GUATEMALA
Admissible: Income tax (*Impuesto sobre la renta*).
Inadmissible: Extraordinary and temporary tax.

GUERNSEY
Admissible: Income tax — Tax on debenture interest and on dividends.
Inadmissible: Corporation tax (abolished from 1 January 1990).

GUINEA
Admissible: Tax on industrial and commercial profits (*Impôt sur les bénéfices industriels et commerciaux*) (replaced in 1991) — Tax on profits from non-commercial occupations (*Impôt sur les bénéfices des professions non-commerciales*) (replaced in 1991) — Tax on public and private salaries, allowances and emoluments, wages, pensions and life annuities (*Impôt sur les traitements publics et privés, les indemnités et émoluments, les salaires, les pensions et les rentes viagères*) (replaced in 1991) — General income tax (*Impôt général sur le revenu*) (replaced in 1991) — Tax on income from movable capital (*Impôt sur le revenu des capitaux mobiliers*) (replaced in 1991).
Inadmissible: Real property tax (*Contribution foncière des propriétés bâties*) where charged by communes — Business licence tax (*Contribution des patentes*).

GUYANA
Admissible: Income tax, including surtax — Corporation tax — Capital gains tax.

GUYANE
Admissible: Company tax (*Impôt sur les sociétés*).

HAITI
Admissible: Income tax (*Impôt sur le revenu*) — Withholding tax on profits remitted outside Haiti (*Impôt sur dividendes devant être repartis eventuellement*).

HONDURAS
Admissible: Income tax (*Impuesto sobre la renta*).

HONG KONG
Admissible: Tax on property, earnings, profits and interest, comprising: property tax, salaries tax, profits tax (comprising corporation profits tax and business tax), interest tax (abolished from 1 April 1989).

HUNGARY
Admissible: Income tax (*Jövedelmadók*) — Profit tax (*Nyereségadók*) — Enterprises' special tax (*Vállalati különadó*) — Contribution to communal development (*Községfejlesztési hozzájárulás*) — Levy on dividends and profit distributions of commercial companies (*Kereskedelmi társaságok osztalék és nyereség kifizetései utáni illetek*) — Supplementary tax (relief only as underlying tax).

Appendix 4

ICELAND
Admissible: National income tax (*Tekjuskattur til ríkisins*) — Municipal income tax (*Tekjuútsvar til sveitarfélaga*) (not levied after 1992).

INDIA
Admissible: Income tax and any surcharge thereon imposed under *Income Tax Acts 1961*, including the alternative minimum tax on companies with effect from 1 April 1997 — Additional tax on distributed profits (relief only as underlying tax) — Income tax and super tax levied by states on agricultural income (where income is taxed partly by the state and partly by the central government, credit may be given for the total of the two taxes against the whole UK tax on the same income) (Super tax on agricultural income abolished from 1 April 1988) — Income tax ('freight tax') charged at income tax rate for non-resident companies on 7.5% of gross freight earnings — Surtax imposed under the *Companies (Profits) Surtax Act 1964* (old agreement only — suspended with effect from 1988/89 year of assessment).
Inadmissible: Wealth tax — gift tax.

INDONESIA
Admissible: Income tax (*pajak penghasilan*), including company tax (*pajak perseroan*) — (Withholding) tax on interest, dividends and royalties (*Pajak atas bunga dividen dan royalty*).
Inadmissible: Foreigners' tax (*Pajak bangsa asing — PBA*) — Capital tax (*Pajak kekayaan*) — Surcharge for the relief of poverty (Presidential Decrees No 90 of 1995 and No 92 of 1996).

IRAN
Admissible: Income tax (including surcharges levied for benefit of municipalities and Chambers of Commerce) on income of the following types: salaries, directors' remuneration, contractors' profits, including where the profits are computed on an arbitrary basis, trading profits (where charged on ascertained profits), real estate rentals, professional profits of engineers and architects, mortgage and similar interest — Tax deducted at source from gross payments made to contractors — Corporation tax.
Inadmissible: Tax on shipping (freight tax) — Tax charged under Art. 81.2 of the *Direct Taxation Act 1967* as amended on taxable income from the granting of concessions and other rights, providing technical training and assistance, etc. (repealed by the *Direct Taxation Act 1988*).

IRAQ
Admissible: Income tax.

IRELAND (REPUBLIC OF)
Admissible: Income tax — Corporation tax — Capital gains tax.

ISLE OF MAN
Admissible: Income tax — Tax on debenture interest and on dividends.

ISRAEL
Admissible: Income tax (including capital gains tax) — Company tax — Tax on gains from the sale of land under the *Land Appreciation Tax Law*.
Inadmissible: Services (Banks and Insurance Companies) tax — Profits tax when applied to financial institutions in lieu of VAT.

ITALY
Admissible: Tax on income of individuals (*Imposta sul reddito delle persone fisiche — IRPEF*) — Tax on income of corporations (*imposta sul reddito delle persone giuridiche — IRPEG*) including the equalisation tax (*imposta di conguaglio*) —

Local income tax (*imposta regionale attiva productive* — *IRAP*) — Substitute tax on reserves (*imposta sostitutiva sul riserve o fondi in sospensione di imposta* — decree law No 41/95 of 23 February 1995) — Withholding tax (*Ritenuta alla fonte*) — Local tax on income (*Imposta locale sul redditi* — *ILOR* — whether or not collected by withholding at source (*ritenuta alla fonte*) — Communal tax on capital appreciation of real property (*Imposta communale sull' incremento di valore degli immobili-INVIM*) available for relief against UK capital gains tax chargeable on the same gain (abolished from 1 January 1993 but will continue to be charged on disposals until 1 January 2003 on the increase in value to 31 December 1992).
Inadmissible: Extraordinary tax on immovable property (*Imposta straordinaria sulla proprietà immobiliare*) — Tax on the net worth of enterprises (*imposta sul patrimonio netto dele imprese*) decree law No 394 of 30 September 1992 — Mortgage tax and cadastral duty (*imposte ipotecarie e cadastrali*).

IVORY COAST (CÔTE D'IVOIRE)
Admissible: Tax on industrial and commercial profits and on agricultural profits (*Impôt sur les bénéfices industriels et commerciaux et sur les bénéfices agricoles*) — Tax on non-commercial profits (*Impôt sur les bénéfices non-commerciaux*) — Tax on salaries and wages (*Impôt sur les traitements et salaires*) — General income tax (*Impôt général sur le revenu*) — Tax on income from movable capital (*Impôt sur le revenu des capitaux mobiliers*).
Inadmissible: Real property tax (*Contribution foncière des propriétés bâties*) — Business licence tax (*Contribution des patentes*) — Land tax (*Contribution foncière des propriétés non-bâties*) — Annual levy for the National Investment Fund (*Le Fonds National d'Investissement* — *prélèvement annuel*) (discontinued after 1990).

JAMAICA
Admissible: Income tax — Transfer tax.

JAPAN
Admissible: Income tax — Corporation tax — Local inhabitant taxes — Business enterprise tax so far as payable on profits or income including the 'gross premium income' of insurance companies.
Inadmissible: Per capita elements of Japanese taxes.

JERSEY
Admissible: Income tax — Jersey tax on debenture interest and dividends.
Inadmissible: Corporation tax (not levied after 1988).

JORDAN
Admissible: Income tax — Social services tax, in so far as it is based on the income tax — Tax on buildings and land — Tax under Art. 4(a) of the additional fees law for Jordan University (a tax of 1% on net profits after other taxation).

KAZAKHSTAN
Admissible: The profits and income taxes specified in Chapters I and V of the law *On the Taxation of Enterprises, Associations, and Organisations*, as amended on 25 December 1991, 30 June 1992 and 22 December 1992 — The income tax provided under the law *On the Income Tax on Citizens of the Republic of Kazakhstan, Foreign Citizens and Stateless Persons*, as amended on 22 December 1992.
From July 1995 these taxes were replaced by the following: Corporate profits tax — Withholding taxes on income from a source in Kazakhstan — The tax on the income of physical persons.
Inadmissible: Land tax — Property tax.

Appendix 4

KENYA
Admissible: Income tax.

KIRIBATI
Admissible: Income tax.

KOREA (SOUTH)
Admissible: Income tax — Corporation tax — Inhabitant tax (resident tax) — Special tax for rural development — Temporary defence tax, but only so long as it is charged by reference to income tax, corporation tax or the inhabitant tax (not levied after 31 December 1990).
Inadmissible: Education tax.

KUWAIT
Admissible: Income tax levied under 1955 and 1957 decrees.
Inadmissible: Contributions to the Kuwait Foundation for the Advancement of Science — Zakat.

LAOS
Admissible: Profits tax (*Impôt sur les bénéfices industriels, commerciaux, non-commerciaux, agricoles et fonciers*) — Dividend tax (*Impôt sur les revenus des valeurs mobilières*) — Distribution tax (*Impôt sur les revenus des capitaux mobilières*) — Foreigners' income tax.

LATVIA
Admissible: Enterprise income tax (*Uznemumu ienakuma nodoklis*) — Personal income tax (*Iedzivotaju ienakuma nodoklis*).

LEBANON
Admissible: Income tax (*Impôt sur le revenu*) under Art. 45 as introduced by law 27 of 1980 — Additional surtax for the benefit of municipalities (*Surtaxe additionnelle*) — Tax on built-up property (*Impôt sur les immeubles bâtis*) — Tax on unbuilt-up property (where charged by reference to estimated or actual income, e.g. on worked agricultural land) (*Impôt foncier*) (suspended) — Distribution tax (Art. 72/2 as amended by law 27 of 1980).
Inadmissible: Tax on unbuilt-up property (where not charged by reference to actual or estimated income) — Municipal tax (customs duty) — Municipal surcharge on built-up property (suspended).

LESOTHO
Admissible: Income tax.

LIBERIA
Admissible: Income tax — Withholding tax — National reconstruction tax.

LIBYA
Admissible: Jihad tax (defence tax) — National income tax comprising: (a) schedular taxes, (b) general income tax, (c) company tax.
Inadmissible: Payroll tax.

LIECHTENSTEIN
Inadmissible: 4% coupon tax (*Couponsteuer*) on dividends (this is the equivalent of stamp duty).

LITHUANIA
Admissible: Tax on profits of legal persons (*Juridiniu asmenu pelno mokestis*) — Tax on income of natural persons (*Fiziniu asmenu pajamu mokestis*).

LUXEMBOURG
Admissible: Income tax on individuals (*Impôt sur le revenu des personnes physiques*) — Tax on fees of directors of companies (*Impôt sur les tantièmes*) — Corporation tax (*Impôt sur le revenu des collectivités*) — Municipal trade tax on profits and capital (*Impôt commercial communal d'après les bénéfices et capital d'exploitation*) except in so far as it is computed on a basis other than profits — Capital tax (*Impôt sur la fortune*) except when computed on a basis other than profits.

MACAU
Admissible: Complementary income tax (*Imposto complementar de rendimentos*).
Inadmissible: Stamp duty surcharge.

MADAGASCAR
Admissible: Tax on income from movable capital (*Impôt sur le revenu des capitaux mobiliers — IRCM*) — Non-residents' withholding tax (*Taxe forfaitaire sur les transferts*).

MALAWI
Admissible: Income tax — Surcharge (up to 5%) on dividends paid to a non-resident company (abolished from 1 January 1988).

MALAYSIA
Admissible: Income tax — Supplementary income tax (i.e. development tax) (abolished from 1 January 1993) — Real property gains tax — Petroleum income tax (PIT) — Excess profits tax (under the amending agreement) (abolished from 1 January 1991).
Inadmissible: Share transfer tax.

MALI
Admissible: Tax on industrial and commercial profits (*Impôt sur les bénéfices industriels et commerciaux*) — Tax on profits from non-commercial occupations (*Impôt sur les bénéfices des professions non-commerciales*) — General income tax (*Impôt général sur le revenu*) — Tax on income from movable capital (*Impôt sur le revenu des capitaux mobiliers*).
Inadmissible: Business licence tax (*Contribution des patentes*).

MALTA
Admissible: Income tax.

MARTINIQUE
Admissible: Company tax (*Impôt sur les sociétés*) — Tax on income from transferable securities (*Taxe sur le revenu des valeurs mobilières*).

MAURITANIA
Admissible: Tax on industrial and commercial profits (*Impôt sur les bénéfices industriels et commerciaux*) — Tax on profits from non-commercial occupations (*impôt sur les bénéfices des professions non-commerciales*) — Tax on public and private salaries, allowances and emoluments, wages, pensions and life annuities (*Impôt sur les traitements publics et privés et les émoluments, les salaires, les pensions et les rentes viagères*) — General income tax (*Impôt général sur le revenu*) — Tax on income from movable capital (*Impôt sur le revenu des capitaux mobiliers*).
Inadmissible: Real property tax (*Impôt foncier*); renamed in 1990 real property tax on built-up immovable property (*Contribution foncière sur les immeubles bâtis*) — Business licence tax (*Contribution des patentes*).

MAURITIUS
Admissible: Income tax — Capital gains tax (*Morcellement*).
Inadmissible: Gaming tax.

Appendix 4

MEXICO
Admissible: Income tax (*Impuesto sobre la renta*) — Tax on contractors' profits (construction companies) — Dividend withholding tax (Art. 152) — 15% gross withholding tax on technical assistance fees.
Inadmissible: Net assets tax.

MONACO
Admissible: Tax on profits (*Impôt sur les bénéfices*).

MONGOLIA
Admissible: Individual income tax — Corporate income tax.

MONTSERRAT
Admissible: Income tax.

MOROCCO
Admissible: Tax on public and private salaries, emoluments, fees, wages, pensions and life annuities (*Prélèvement sur les traitements publics et privés, indemnités et émoluments, les salaires, les pensions et les rentes viagères*) (replaced 1989) — Tax on urban real property and taxes related thereto (*Taxe urbaine et taxes qui y sont rattachées*) — Agricultural tax (*Impôt agricole*) — Complementary tax on the total income of individuals (*Contribution complémentaire sur le revenu global des personnes physiques*) (replaced 1989) — Tax on income from shares or corporate rights and assimilated income (*Taxe sur les produits des actions ou parts sociales et revenus assimilés*) — Tax on gains from real property (*Taxe sur les profits immobiliers*) — Tax on urban land (*Impôt sur les terrains urbains*) — National solidarity tax (*Participation à la solidarité nationale*).
Inadmissible: Business tax (*Impôt des patentes*) — Flat rate tax (Law of 31 December 1986) (foreign construction companies).

MOZAMBIQUE
Admissible: Complementary tax (*Imposto complementar*) — Property tax (*Contribuição predial*) but not stamp tax levied on the property tax or additional charge.

MYANMAR (formerly BURMA)
Admissible: Income tax — Business profits tax.

NAMIBIA
Admissible: Normal tax — Non-resident shareholders' tax — Undistributed profits tax (33.3% of the excess of the distributable income over dividends distributed) (abolished from 1 March 1991) — Petroleum income tax.
Inadmissible: Additional profits tax.

NEPAL
Admissible: Corporate income tax charge on construction companies (when computed by reference to net profits).

NETHERLANDS
Admissible: Income tax (*Inkomstenbelasting*) (only the income tax element is admissible in any combined levy and not the social security element) — Wages tax (*loonbelasting*) (only the income tax element is admissible in any combined levy and not the social security element) — Company tax (*Vennootschapsbelasting*) including the Government share in the net profits of the exploitation of natural resources levied pursuant to the 'Mijnwet 1810' (the *Mining Act* of 1810) with respect to concessions issued from 1967, or pursuant to the 'Mijnwet Continentaal Plat 1965' (the *Continental Shelf Mining Act* of 1965) — Dividends tax (*Dividendbelasting*) — Wealth tax (*Vermogensbelasting*), only against any UK wealth tax.

NETHERLANDS ANTILLES
Admissible: Income tax (*Inkomstenbelasting*) including the wages tax (*Loonbelasting*) — Profits tax (*Winstbelasting*) — Surcharges on the income and profits taxes.

NEW CALEDONIA
Admissible: Company tax (*Impôt sur les sociétés*) — Withholding tax on dividends, interest, etc. (*Impôt sur le revenu des valeurs mobilières*).

NEW ZEALAND
Admissible: Income tax — Excess retention tax (abolished for income derived after 1 April 1990).
Inadmissible: Approved issuer levy.

NICARAGUA
Admissible: Income tax (*Impuesto sobre la renta*).
Inadmissible: Capital tax (*Impuesto directo sobre el capital*) (replaced in 1992).

NIGER
Admissible: Tax on industrial and commercial profits (*Impôt sur les bénéfices industriels et commerciaux*) — Tax on profits from non-commercial occupations (*Impôt sur les bénéfices des professions non-commerciales*) — Tax on public and private salaries, allowances and emoluments, wages, pensions and life annuities (*Impôt sur les traitements publics et privés, les indemnités et émoluments, les salaires, les pensions et les rentes viagères*) — General income tax (*Impôt général sur le revenu*) — Tax on income from movable capital (*Impôt sur le revenu des capitaux mobiliers*).
Inadmissible: Real property tax (*Contribution foncières des propriétés bâties*) — Business licence tax (*Contribution des patentes*).

NIGERIA
Admissible: Personal income tax — Capital gains tax — Petroleum profits tax — Companies income tax, including the $2\frac{1}{2}\%$ federal tax charged on turnover of businesses in building and construction industry — Contributions to National Recovery Fund — Education tax.
Inadmissible: Special levy on excess profits of banks.

NORTHERN MARIANA ISLANDS
Admissible: Territorial income tax (NMTIT) — Business gross revenue tax (to the extent that the tax paid is used to extinguish an income tax liability).

NORWAY
Admissible: National income tax (*Inntektskatt til statskassen*) (replaced from 1988) — National contributions to the tax equalisation fund (*Inntektskatt til skattefordelingsfondet*) (*fellesskatt, 'mutual tax'*) (replaced from 1988) — National dues on remuneration to non-resident artistes (*Avgift til staten av honorarer som tilfaller kunstnere bosatt i utlandet*) — Seamen's tax (*Sjømannsskatt*) — National tax relating to income and capital from the exploration for and the exploitation of submarine petroleum resources and activities and work relating thereto including pipeline transport of petroleum produced (*Skatt til staten vedrørende inntekt og formue i forbindelse med undersøkelse etter og utnyttelse av undersjøiske petroleumsforekomster og dertil knyttet virksomhet og arbeid, herunder rørledningstransport av utvunnet petroleum*); the tax relating to capital *only* against any similar tax in the UK — Municipal capital tax (*Formueskatt til kommunen*) only against any similar tax which may be levied in the UK — County municipal income tax (*Inntektskatt til fylkeskommunen*) (replaced from 1988) — Municipal tax on income (*Inntektskatt til kommunen*) (replaced from 1988).

Appendix 4

Inadmissible: National capital tax (*Formueskatt til staten*) admissible only against any similar tax which may be levied in the UK.

OMAN
Admissible: Income tax charged under the 1971 and 1981 Income Tax decrees.
Inadmissible: Zakat.

PAKISTAN
Admissible: Income tax, including agricultural income tax levied by provinces or states but not including in the case of mineral extraction activities any royalty paid on gross production values — Supertax (abolished from 1 July 1992).
Inadmissible: 2% levy under the Workers' Welfare Ordinance 1971.

PANAMA
Admissible: Income tax (*Impuesto sobre la renta*) — Additional 10% tax on net after tax profits.

PAPUA NEW GUINEA
Admissible: Income tax including; (i) the salary or wages tax, (ii) the additional profits tax upon taxable additional profits from mining operations, (iii) the additional profits tax upon taxable additional profits from petroleum operations, (iv) the specific gains tax upon taxable specific gains, (v) the dividend withholding tax upon taxable dividend income.

PARAGUAY
Admissible: Income tax (*Impuesto sobre la renta*) — Withholding tax on remittance of branch profits.
Inadmissible: Property tax (*Impuesto immobiliario*).

PERU
Admissible: Income tax (*Impuesto sobre la renta*) except in certain cases where profits are taxed by reference to gross receipts or a fixed percentage of gross receipts — Reinsurance premium tax.
Inadmissible: 2% surtax for the food allowance fund (*Fondo de compensación nutricional*).

PHILIPPINES
Admissible: Income tax (including the corporate income tax) except the tax on gross income in respect of international carriers.
Inadmissible: Premium tax.

POLAND
Admissible: Income tax (*Podatek dochodowy*) — Tax on wages and salaries (*Podatek od wynagrodzen*) — Surcharge on the income tax and on the tax on wages and salaries (equalisation tax) (*Podatek wyrównawczy*) (abolished from 1 January 1992).

PORTUGAL
Admissible: Individual income tax (*Imposto sobre o rendimento das pessoas singulares — IRS*) — Company income tax (*Imposto sobre a rendimento das pessoas colectivas*) from 1 January 1989 — Municipal surcharge (*Derrama*) from 1 January 1989 — Property tax (*Contribuição predial*) (abolished 31 December 1988) — Agricultural tax (*Imposto sobre a industria agricola*) (abolished 31 December 1988) — Industrial tax (*Contribuição industrial*) (abolished 31 December 1988) — Tax on income from movable capital (*Imposto de capitais*) (abolished 31 December 1988) — Professional tax (*Imposto profissional*) (abolished 31 December 1988) — Complementary tax (*Imposto complementar*) (abolished 31 December 1988) — Tax on capital gains (*Imposto de mais-valias*) (abolished

31 December 1988) — Any surcharges on the preceding taxes (abolished 31 December 1988) — Other taxes charged by reference to the foregoing taxes for the benefit of local authorities and the corresponding surcharges (mostly now abolished).

Inadmissible: Unemployment fund contribution (*Imposto para o fundo de desemprego*) which was subsumed in 1986 into a single contribution which covers both social security and unemployment — Mining tax (*Imposto proporcional*) (abolished 1989) — Stamp duty (*imposto do selo*) — Tax on successions and donations (*Imposto sobre sucessões e doações*) (even where withheld from dividends) — Undocumented and confidential expenses tax (*Depesas confidenciais*) which has been subsumed within personal or company income tax from 1 January 1989 — Gaming tax (*Imposto sobre o jogo*).

PUERTO RICO
Admissible: Income tax.

QATAR
Admissible: Income tax (replaced from 1 January 1993).

RAS AL KHAIMAH
Admissible: Income tax.

RÉUNION
Admissible: Company tax (*Impôt sur les sociétés*).

ROMANIA
Admissible: Tax on incomes derived by individuals and corporate bodies (*Impozitul pe veniturile realizate de persoane fizice si juridice*) — Tax on the profits of joint companies (*Impozitul pe beneficiile societatilor mixte constituite cu participate romana si straina*) — Tax on income realised from agricultural activities (*Impozitul pe veniturile realizate din activitati agricole*).

RUSSIAN FEDERATION
Admissible: Tax on income and profits imposed under the following laws: — *On Taxes on Profits of Enterprises and Organisations* — *On Taxation of Income of Banks* — *On Taxation of Income from Insurance Activities* — *On the Income Tax of Individuals.*
Inadmissible: Wages tax.

RWANDA
Admissible: Tax on earned income (*Impôt professionel/umusoro w'umulimo*) — Tax on rental income (*Impôt sur les revenus locatifs/umusoro ku nyungu y'ubukodeshi*) — Tax on income from securities, etc. (*Impôt mobilier/umusoro ku nyungu y'ibyashowe byimukanwa*).

ST CHRISTOPHER (ST KITTS) AND NEVIS
Admissible: Income tax.

ST LUCIA
Admissible: Income tax.
Inadmissible: Foreign currency export levy.

ST VINCENT
Admissible: Income tax.
Inadmissible: Interest levy on banks charged under the *Interest Levy Act 1975*.

SAUDI ARABIA
Admissible: Income tax.

Appendix 4

SENEGAL
Admissible: Income tax on individuals (*Impôt sur le revenu des personnes physiques*) — Company tax (*Impôt sur les sociétés*) — Tax on industrial and commercial profits (*Impôt sur les bénéfices industriels et commerciaux*) (replaced 1992) — Tax on profits from non-commercial occupations (*Impôt sur les bénéfices des professions non-commerciales*) (replaced 1992) — Tax on public and private salaries, allowances and emoluments, wages, pensions and life annuities (*Impôt sur les traitements publics et privés, les indemnités et émoluments, les salaires, les pensions et les rentes viagères*) (replaced 1992) — General income tax (*Impôt général sur le revenu*) (replaced 1992) — Tax on income from movable capital (*Impôt sur le revenu des capitaux mobiliers*) (replaced 1992).
Inadmissible: Business licence tax (*Contribution des patentes*) — Real property tax (*Contribution foncière des propriétés bâties*) — Land tax (*Contribution foncière des propriétés non-bâties*).

SEYCHELLES
Admissible: Income tax — Business tax.

SHARJAH
Admissible: Income tax.

SIERRA LEONE
Admissible: Income tax — Diamond industry profits tax — Iron ore concessions tax.

SINGAPORE
Admissible: Income tax.

SOLOMON ISLANDS
Admissible: Income tax.

SOMALIA
Admissible: Income tax — Additional municipality tax.
Inadmissible: Tax on the capital of companies and corporations.

SOUTH AFRICA
Admissible: Normal tax — Non-resident shareholders' tax (NRST) (abolished from 1 October 1995) — Undistributed profits tax (UPT) (abolished with effect from the commencement of years of assessment ending on or after 1 March 1990) — Non-residents' tax on interest (abolished with effect from 16 March 1988)(CA)— Transition levy (for individuals, in the two years to 29 February 1996; for companies, to periods of account ending in the twelve months to 31 March 1995) — Secondary tax on companies (only as underlying tax).
Inadmissible: Loan levy (abolished from 1980, reintroduced in 1989, ended 31 July 1994) — Minimum tax on companies (form of loan levy) repaid in 1991.

SOVIET UNION (up to 1992)
Admissible: Income tax on foreign legal persons — Income tax on the population.

SPAIN
Admissible: Individual income tax (*Impuesto sobre la renta de las personas físicas*) — Company tax (*Impuesto sobre sociedades*) — The 'surface royalty' and tax on corporation profits regulated by the law of 27 June 1974 applicable to enterprises engaged in prospecting and exploiting oil wells (*Cánon de superficie*) but only in so far as the surface royalty is deducted from the company tax — Local taxes on income and capital generally (on capital only against any UK wealth tax) — Chamber of Commerce surcharges based on admissible taxes (*Recurso para la cámara oficial da comercio*) — Madrid levy on the increase in land values (*Arbitrio*

314

Appendix 4

sobre el incremento del valor de los terrenos) (replaced 1988) — Tax on companies' petroleum profits under the law of 27 June 1974.
Inadmissible: Wealth tax (*Impuesto extraordinario sobre el patrimonio de las personas físicas*) (replaced 1991).

SRI LANKA
Admissible: Income tax (including the 15% surcharge tax on the income tax from 1 April 1989) — Tax on remittances.
Inadmissible: Wealth tax (abolished from 1 April 1992) — Business turnover tax.

SUDAN
Admissible: Income tax — Capital gains tax — Development tax — Business profits tax — House tax — Defence tax (suspended with effect from 1 July 1990).

SURINAM
Admissible: Income tax (*Inkomstenbelasting*).

SWAZILAND
Admissible: Normal tax on income — Non-resident shareholders' tax (NRST) — Non-residents' tax on interest (NRTI).

SWEDEN
Admissible: State income tax (*Statlig Inkomstskatt*), including coupon tax (*Kupongskatt*) and sailors' tax (*Sjömansskatt*) — Tax on undistributed profits of companies (*Ersättningsskatt*) — Tax on public entertainers (*Bevillningsavgift för vissa offentliga föreställninger*) (abolished from 1 January 1993) — Communal income tax (*Kommunal inkomstskatt*) — Tax on distributed income of companies (*Utskiftningsskatt*).
Inadmissible: Special forestry care tax (*Skogsvrdsavgift*) — Profit-sharing tax (*Vinstdelningsskatt*) — Profits tax on pension funds (*lag om avkastningsskatt pa pensionsmedel*) — Real estate tax (*lag om statlig fastighetsskatt*) — (CA) Special salary tax on pension costs (*Särskild löneskatt ppensionskostneder*) — Penalty for incorrect information (*Skattetillägg*).

SWITZERLAND
Admissible: Federal and cantonal taxes on income (*Impôts fédéraux et cantonaux sur le revenu/Bundeseinkommenssteuern und Kantonseinkommenssteuern/imposte federali e cantonali sul reddito*) including the: anticipatory tax (*Impôt anticipé/ Verrechnungssteuer/imposta preventive*) — Direct federal tax (*Impôt fédéral direct/ direkte Bundessteuer/imposta federale diretta*) — Communal tax on income (*Impôt communal sur le revenu/Gemeindesteuer/imposta communale sul reddito*) — Zurich church tax (*Kirchensteuer*) where charged on a company.
Inadmissible: Geneva business tax (*Taxe professionelle*) — Geneva complemen tary property tax (*Impôt immobilier complémentaire*) — Geneva church tax (*Contribution ecclésiastique*) — Federal, cantonal and communal wealth tax (*Impôt sur la fortune/Vermögenssteuer/imposta sulla sostenza*).

SYRIA
Admissible: Income tax (*Impôt sur le revenu*) — Additional tax of 10% for the benefit of municipalities, etc. — School tax and exceptional tax in so far as they represent surcharges on the income tax.

TAHITI (See FRENCH POLYNESIA).

TAIWAN
Admissible: Profit-seeking enterprise tax — Personal income tax — Withholding tax on interest, royalties or service fees — Withholding tax at 20% or 35% on dividends (where tax is withheld at 20% from dividends paid to a 'profit seeking

315

enterprise' with a permanent establishment in Taiwan, the recipient may claim a refund of 5%: credit is restricted to the resultant 15% unless the 5% refund claim is refused) — Land value increment tax (against UK capital gains tax) — Business gross receipts tax.
Inadmissible: Stamp tax.

TANZANIA
Admissible: Income tax — Partnership tax — Tax on maritime earnings under *s 9(1)* of the *Tanzanian Income Tax Act.*

THAILAND
Admissible: Income tax (including the branch profits remittance tax) — Petroleum income tax.
Inadmissible: Business tax — Municipal surcharge.

TOGO
Admissible: Tax on industrial and commercial profits (*Impôt sur les bénéfices industriels et commerciaux*) — Tax on profits from non-commercial occupations (*Impôt sur les bénéfices des professions non-commerciales*) — Tax on public and private salaries, allowances and emoluments, wages, pensions and life annuities (*Impôts sur les traitements publics et privés, les indemnités et émoluments, les salaires, les pensions et les rentes viagères*) — General income tax (*Impôt général sur le revenu*).
Inadmissible: Levy for contributions to the national investment fund (*Fonds national d'investissement*).

TRANSKEI
Admissible: Normal tax — Non-resident shareholders' tax — General tax.

TRINIDAD AND TOBAGO
Admissible: Income tax — Corporation tax — Unemployment levy — Petroleum profits tax.
Inadmissible: Refinery throughput tax.

TUNISIA
Admissible: Company tax (*Impôt sur les sociétés*) — *Tax on industrial and commercial profits (Droit de patente)* (replaced from 1 January 1990) — Tax on income from transferable securities (*Impôt sur le revenu des valeurs mobilières*) — Tax on salaries and wages (*Impôt sur les traitements et salaires*) (replaced from 1 January 1990) — State personal levy (*Contribution personnelle d'état*) (replaced from 1 January 1990) — Trade tax (*Impôt de la patente*) — Tax on profits of non-commercial professions (*Impôt sur les bénéfices des professions non-commerciales*) (replaced from 1 January 1990) — Agricultural tax (*Impôt agricole*) — Tax on income from debts, deposits, sureties and current accounts (*Impôt sur le revenu des créances, dépots, cautionnements et comptes courants* — IRC) (replaced from 1 January 1990) — Capital gains tax on immovable property (*Impôt sur les plus-valeurs immobilières*) — Special solidarity levy (*Contribution exceptionnelle de solidarité*) (replaced from 1 January 1990).

TURKEY
Admissible: Income tax — Corporation tax — Withholding tax including withholding tax on the after-tax profits of corporations — Economic equilibrium tax.
Inadmissible: Defence industry development and support fund — Net assets tax.

TUVALU
Admissible: Income tax.

UGANDA
Admissible: Income tax (including the income tax charged on corporations).

UKRAINE
Admissible: Tax on the profits of enterprises (*Podatok na pributok (dokhody) (pidpriemstv)*) — Income tax (*Pributkovy podatok*).

UNITED ARAB EMIRATES
Admissible: Income tax levied under the Income Tax Laws of Abu Dhabi, Dubai, Ras al Khaimah and Sharjah.
Inadmissible: Zakat.

UNITED STATES OF AMERICA
Admissible (Federal): Income tax.
Inadmissible (Federal): Contributions under the *Federal Insurance Contributions Act (FICA)* — Contributions under the *Self-Employment Contributions Act* — Crude oil windfall profits tax (repealed from 23 August 1988) — Environmental insurance resolution fee (EIRF) — Environmental insurance resolution assessment (EIRA).

ALABAMA
Admissible: General income tax.
Inadmissible: Franchise tax.

ALASKA
Admissible: General income tax.
Inadmissible: Corporation tax (if 'annual corporation tax' which is a flat rate licence type levy).

ARIZONA
Admissible: General income tax.

ARKANSAS
Admissible: Income tax (on individuals and companies).
Inadmissible: Corporation franchise tax.

CALIFORNIA
Admissible: Bank and corporation franchise tax (subject to limitation) — Corporation income tax — Personal income tax — Insurance companies tax on marine insurance companies.
Inadmissible: Insurance companies tax on general insurance companies.

COLORADO
Admissible: General income tax.
Inadmissible: Insurance companies tax.

CONNECTICUT
Admissible: Corporation business tax (franchise tax) where it is charged on income — Income tax.
Inadmissible: Corporation business tax where it is charged on value or represents a minimum levy — Insurance companies tax.

DELAWARE
Admissible: Corporation income tax — Personal income tax.

DISTRICT of COLUMBIA
Admissible: Individual and corporate income tax.

FLORIDA
Admissible: Corporation franchise (income) tax — Emergency excise levy —

2.2% emergency excise tax (component of the corporate income tax).
Inadmissible: General property tax — Local tourist development taxes (charged on gross rentals) — State taxes on sales, use, rentals and admissions — Tangible personal property tax.

GEORGIA
Admissible: General income tax.

HAWAII
Admissible: General income tax.

IDAHO
Admissible: General income tax.

ILLINOIS
Admissible: Income tax — Corporate replacement income tax (personal property replacement tax).
Inadmissible: Corporation franchise tax — Personal property tax — Sales and use tax — Filing fee.

INDIANA
Admissible: Adjusted gross income tax when actually paid, i.e. to the extent that liability exceeds gross income tax — Supplemental net income tax.
Inadmissible: Gross income tax — Financial institutions tax — Insurance (foreign companies) tax — Public utilities tax.

IOWA
Admissible: General income tax.

KANSAS
Admissible: Corporation income tax (including surtax).

KENTUCKY
Admissible: General income tax — Lexington-Fayette Urban County and Louisville and Jefferson County occupational licence fee.

LOUISIANA
Admissible: General income tax.
Inadmissible: Corporation franchise tax — Sales tax — Use tax.

MAINE
Admissible: General income tax.

MARYLAND
Admissible: Corporation income tax.
Inadmissible: Insurance companies tax.

MASSACHUSETTS
Admissible: Corporate excise (income) tax, where charged on net income but not where charged on any other basis — Personal income tax.
Inadmissible: Sales and use tax — Sales and use tax registration.

MICHIGAN
Admissible: Personal income tax — Single business tax — City of Grand Rapids income tax — City of Detroit income tax.
Inadmissible: Filing fee — Intangibles tax — Sales and use tax.

MINNESOTA
Admissible: Income tax (on corporations and individuals).

MISSISSIPPI
Admissible: General income tax.
Inadmissible: Corporation franchise tax — Use tax.

MISSOURI
Admissible: Corporation income tax — Intangible personal property tax (part of property tax) — Kansas City income tax — St Louis income tax.
Inadmissible: Corporation franchise tax — Annual licence tax.

MONTANA
Admissible: Corporation licence (income) tax — Corporation income tax — Personal income tax.

NEBRASKA
Admissible: Personal income tax — Corporation income tax.
Inadmissible: Occupational tax.

NEW HAMPSHIRE
Admissible: Business profits tax.

NEW JERSEY
Admissible: Corporation franchise tax except where it represents a minimum levy or is charged on amounts other than net income — Corporation business tax on net income (not on net worth) — Insurance companies tax on marine insurance companies — Personal income tax.
Inadmissible: Bank stock tax — Excise tax — Financial business excise tax — Insurance companies tax on general and life insurance companies — Corporation business tax charged on net worth.

NEW MEXICO
Admissible: General income tax.
Inadmissible: Corporation franchise tax — Real property transfer tax — Compensating tax — Gross receipts tax.

NEW YORK CITY
Admissible: Earnings tax on non-residents where it is charged on salaries — Financial corporation income tax where it is charged on income, but not where charged on any other basis — General corporate (income) tax, where charged on net income, but not where charged on any other basis — Personal income tax on residents where it is charged on salaries — Unincorporated business tax.
Inadmissible: Gross receipts tax — Occupancy tax — Vault tax — Real estate tax.

NEW YORK STATE
Admissible: Personal income tax — Unincorporated business income tax — Corporation franchise tax except where it represents a minimum levy, is a charge based on capital, or is charged on amounts other than net income — Transfer gains tax (real property gains tax) — Metropolitan commuter transportation district surcharge.
Inadmissible: Additional charge on corporation franchise tax — Realty transfer tax — Sales and use tax.

NORTH CAROLINA
Admissible: General income tax — Financial institution excise tax except where it represents a minimum levy.
Inadmissible: Corporation franchise tax — Insurance companies tax — Intangible property tax.

Appendix 4

NORTH DAKOTA
Admissible: General income tax.

OHIO
Admissible: Corporation franchise (income) tax when charged on net income but not where charged on any other basis — City income taxes (Bexley, Brookville, Cincinatti, Cleveland, Columbus, Dayton, Dublin, Englewood, Farmersville, Grandview Heights, Grove City, Groveport, Hilliard, Huber Heights, Kettering, Marble Cliff, Oakwood, Obetz, Phillipsburg, Reynoldsburg, Riverside, Toledo, Trotwood, Upper Arlington, Vandalia, West Milton, Worthington and Yellow Springs) — Cleveland net profits tax — Village of Mariemont business earnings tax.
Inadmissible: Use tax — Excise tax.

OKLAHOMA
Admissible: General income tax.
Inadmissible: Corporation franchise tax.

OREGON
Admissible: Corporate (excise) income tax — Personal income tax.

PENNSYLVANIA
Admissible: Corporate net income tax except where it is charged on amounts other than net income — Personal income tax — Chester County income tax — School district corporate income tax (Philadelphia) — Net profit and wages tax (Philadelphia) — School district investment income tax where charged on income or, where the UK charge is to capital gains tax, where charged on capital gains — Philadelphia city income tax.
Inadmissible: Foreign corporations franchise tax — County personal property tax — Foreign corporation excise tax — Sales and use tax.

RHODE ISLAND
Admissible: Business corporate tax where charged on net income, but not where charged on any other basis.

SOUTH CAROLINA
Admissible: Corporation income tax.

TENNESSEE
Admissible: Corporation excise (income) tax.
Inadmissible: Corporation franchise tax.

TEXAS
Admissible: Corporate franchise tax (to the extent that it is charged on income).
Inadmissible: Corporation franchise tax (to the extent that it is charged on capital).

UTAH
Admissible: Corporation franchise tax when charged on net income, but not where charged on any other basis.
Inadmissible: Educational funding tax.

VERMONT
Admissible: Corporate income tax (when charged on banks, savings banks, trust companies and other financial concerns this is replaced by franchise tax) — Personal income tax.
Inadmissible: Minimum tax (represents a flat filing fee).

VIRGINIA
Admissible: Corporate income tax — Personal income tax.
Inadmissible: Insurance companies tax — Litter control tax.

WASHINGTON, STATE OF
Inadmissible: Business and occupation tax — Corporation franchise tax — Insurance companies premium tax — Litter tax — Corporation annual licence tax — Gross receipts tax — Use tax — Seattle business tax.

WEST VIRGINIA
Admissible: Corporation income tax.
Inadmissible: Licence tax.

WISCONSIN
Admissible: Corporate franchise tax — Income tax.

URUGUAY
Admissible: Tax on income from industry and commerce (*Impuesto a las rentas de la industria y comercio*); from 1983 only where the tax is levied on the basis that the taxpayer is a person domiciled in Uruguay.
Inadmissible: Property tax (*contribución inmobiliaria*) — Tax on net worth (*Impuesto al patrimonio*) — Tax on income of insurance companies (*Impuesto a los ingresos de las compañías de seguros*) — Withholding tax on fees for consultancy services — Tax on income from industry and commerce (*Impuesto a las rentas de la industria y comercio*); but see also admissible taxes.

UZBEKISTAN
Admissible (under agreement): Taxes on income and capital gains enacted in the law *On the taxation of enterprises, associations and organisations* and payable by enterprises: Tax on income — Tax on income from movable and immovable property, as part of the general income of legal entities — Tax on foreign currency income — Tax on capital gains. Taxes on income and capital gains enacted in the law *On the taxation of citizens, foreign citizens and stateless persons* and payable by individuals: Tax on income — Tax on income from movable and immovable property, as part of the general income of individuals — Tax on foreign currency income — Tax on capital gains — Payments for the issue of patent or registration certificates to engage in private entrepreneurial activity.

VENDA
Admissible: Non-resident shareholders' tax.

VENEZUELA
Admissible: Income tax (*Impuesto sobre la renta*) — Business assets tax (to the extent that the tax paid is used to extinguish an income tax liability) — Income tax on shipping companies — Reinsurance premium tax — Withholding tax on income from non-commercial professional activities charged on 90% of gross receipts — Tax charged under decree 3106 of 27 February 1979, and, as from 1 January 1980, under decrees 476 and 479 of 31 and 27 December 1979 respectively, on 30% of gross revenue from the provision of technical assistance and on 50% of gross revenue from the provision of technological services.

VIETNAM
Admissible: Income tax — Profits tax — Profits remittance tax — Foreign petroleum subcontractor tax — Foreign contractor tax.

VIRGIN ISLANDS (BRITISH)
Admissible: Income tax.

Appendix 4

VIRGIN ISLANDS (US)
Admissible: Income tax.

WESTERN SAMOA
Admissible: Income tax.

YEMEN, PEOPLE'S DEMOCRATIC REPUBLIC OF [up to 11 April 1991]
Admissible: Income tax including 5% surcharge on companies.
Inadmissible: Contractors' tax levied by cabinet resolution No 163 of 1983.

YEMEN [from 12 April 1991]
Admissible: Income tax — Tax on commercial and industrial profits.

YUGOSLAVIA
Admissible: [Note: Credit is only given for taxes ('porez' or 'davek' or 'danok') and not for contributions (doprinosi).] Tax and contributions on income of organisations of associated labour (*Porez i doprinosi iz dohotka organizacija udruzenog rada*) — Tax and contributions on personal income derived from dependent personal services (*Porez i doprinosi iz licnog dohotka iz radnog odnosa*) — Tax and contributions on personal income derived from agricultural activities (*Porez i doprinosi iz licnog dohotka od poljoprivredne delatnosti*) — Tax on personal income derived from copyrights, patents and technical improvements (*Porez iz licnog dohotka od autorskih prava, patenta i technickih unapredjenja*) — Tax and contributions on personal income derived from independent economic and non-economic activities (*Porez i doprinosi iz licnog dohotka od samostalnog obavljanja privrednih i neprivrednih delatnosti*) — Tax on income from capital and capital rights (*Porez na prihod od imovine i imovinskih prava*) — Tax on total income of citizens (*Porez iz ukupnog prihoda gradjana*) — Tax on profits of foreign persons derived from investments in a domestic organisation of associated labour for the purposes of joint business operations (*Porez na dobit stranih lica ostvarenu ulaganjem u domacu organizaciju udruznog rada za svrhe zajednickog poslovanja*) — Tax on profits of foreign persons derived from investment projects (*Porez na dobit stranih lica ostvarenu izvodjenjem investicionih radova*) — Tax on income of foreign persons derived from passenger and cargo transport (*Porez na prihod stranih lica ostvaren od prevoza putnika i robe*).

ZAIRE
Admissible: Income tax (*Impôt sur le revenu*) — Tax on dividends, interest and shares in profit (*Contribution mobilière*) — Tax on deemed distributions of a foreign company (*Forfait régime*).
Inadmissible: Turnover tax (*Contribution sur le chiffre d'affaires*).

ZAMBIA
Admissible: Income tax — Mineral tax — Personal levy.
Inadmissible: Selective employment tax.

ZIMBABWE
Admissible: Income tax — Branch profits tax — Non-resident shareholders' tax — Non-residents' tax on interest — Capital gains tax.
Inadmissible: National defence levy.

Inland Revenue Customer Service Information Leaflet: Underlying Tax — All Countries

© Crown Copyright. Reproduced with the permission of the Controller of HMSO.
Issued by Financial Intermediaries and Claims Office, Double Taxation (Rates) Section, Fitz Roy House, PO Box 46, Nottingham NG2 1BD. Contact Paul West, Tel 0115 974 2020, Fax 0115 974 1992.

Notes

This leaflet gives you general guidance on the documentation needed and on the calculation of underlying tax for the purposes of Corporation Tax, Case V. Similar leaflets about underlying tax for individual countries are available on request.

When you write to us, include 'Double Taxation (Rates) Section' in the address shown above and quote our reference.

Accounts

We are concerned with how the profits have been appropriated and with the movement in, and additions to the reserves. We need:

- the profit and loss account and the liabilities section of the balance sheet prepared under the foreign country's accounting standards (comparative figures in the following year's accounts are acceptable);

- any notes to the accounts affecting profits and reserves (for instance, the details of the accounting policy for a prior year adjustment);

- details of how the profits have been appropriated;

- details of dividends receivable if you claim underlying tax relief for them;

- in a consolidated group of companies, only the corporate (not consolidated) accounts or a breakdown of consolidated accounts by company.

We do not need:

- the cover, contents list, directors' report (where relevant details are shown elsewhere), auditors' report, detailed profit and loss account (except where details of dividends receivable are needed), changes in financial position/ source and application of funds, and details of assets.

Appendix 5

Dividend resolutions

We need a copy of the dividend resolution where the profits used for the dividend have been specified under s 799(3)(b) ICTA 1988 or where there is any doubt as to the profits used for the dividend.

Tax documents

We need:

- the notice of assessment to tax; or
- in the case of self-assessment, the first page of the tax return (which is usually sufficient).

We do not need:

- the full tax return;
- tax receipts.

Note that:

- we ask you to ensure that subsequent reductions in tax (if significant) are notified to us;
- any tax underlying pre-merger profits may not be available for credit (s 799(1) requires the tax to have been paid by the company paying the dividend).

Compliance costs

We take into account your costs in complying with the requirement for you to substantiate your claim. We try to restrict our requests to the minimum necessary consistent with our duty to ensure that the relief given is no more than is properly due. For example, we would seek a lesser degree of proof of relief for a dividend of £50,000 from a high tax rate country than for a dividend of £1m from a low tax rate country.

We are prepared to consider dispensing with the need for documentation in the case of dividends less than £50,000.

Case V computation

The gross dividend is increased by the underlying tax attributable to the dividend for the purpose of calculating the UK corporation tax on that dividend (s 795 ICTA 1988).

Example 1

Gross dividend	£200,000	
Underlying tax at 22.5%	58.065	[£200,000 × 22.5 3 (100 − 22.5)]
Case V income	£258,065	

Corporation tax × 35%		90,322
Less tax credit relief		
Underlying tax	58,065	
Withholding tax	20,000	78,065
Net corporation tax payable		£12,257

If in Example 1, the relevant profits had borne foreign tax at the rate of 40%, the equivalent Case V income would be:

$$£333,333 \quad [£200,000 \times 100 \div (100 - 40)]$$

and the total foreign tax would be £153,333 [20,000 + (333,333 − 200,000)]. However, not all of this tax could be allowed as credit since it exceeds the UK corporation tax on £333,333 (£116,666) (s 797(1)).

Where credit is claimed for spared tax, two underlying tax rates are calculated:

● the actual rate, taking into account any tax paid, for the purpose of calculating the Case V income;

● the deemed rate, including also the tax which would have been taken into account had it been payable but for the sparing provisions (s 795(3)).

Example 2a

Actual rate 5%, deemed rate 25% (including the actual rate of 5%)

Dividend	£100,000	
Underlying tax at 5%	5,263	
Case V income	£105,263	

Corporation tax × 35%	36,842
Less deemed tax credit relief	
100,000 at 25%	33,333
Net corporation tax payable	£3,509

Underlying tax

Where an overseas company pays a dividend to a UK company, the underlying tax includes tax paid on its profits:

● in the UK;

● in other foreign countries (third country taxes) (s 801(1)).

Where the overseas company receives a dividend from a third related company, then the underlying tax of that company is also taken into account. Similarly for a fourth related company (s 801(2)).

There are two limitations to this:

- where the third or any subsequent company is a UK company, the underlying tax of that company is limited to the UK corporation tax before reduction for any credit for foreign tax (s 801(4)(a)).

- where an overseas company pays a dividend to another related overseas company, the underlying tax for the former company is limited to that which could have been given under the ordinary rules if the latter company had been resident in the UK (s 801(4)(b)). For example, if the Double Taxation Convention between two overseas countries provides for credit for spared tax, that tax is only available for credit for underlying tax if the Convention with the UK also includes that tax.

A company is related to another company if one controls, directly or indirectly, not less than 10% of the voting power in the other (s 801(5)).

If the underlying tax liability is revised, the credit allowed may be consequentially adjusted within six years of the revision (s 806(2)).

If you claim underlying tax for a third company, you should reconcile the dividend paid by that company with the amount shown in the profit and loss account of the receiving company.

You should reconcile the dividend shown in the overseas company's accounts with the amount included in the Case V computation.

We suggest that you calculate the underlying tax rate to 3 decimal places for dividends over £1m.

Some corporate accounts include the equity in the profits of subsidiaries. Such profits are excluded from the underlying tax rate computation unless actually used for the dividend to the United Kingdom.

Underlying tax

Profit appropriation and prior year adjustments

General

S 799(4) ICTA 1988 provides for dividend deficiencies to be taken from earlier years' profits on a LIFO basis. The legislation is silent on the treatment of other items of appropriation and amounts deductible in arriving at relevant profits, although there is a presumption that the allocation should also be on a LIFO basis. *Bowater v Murgatroyd* (46 TC 37) decided that relevant profits meant profits available for distribution as shown in the accounts. The accounting treatment of any item is therefore of paramount importance. If the accounts show it to have been deducted from a particular part of the profits, that treatment must be followed. Where the accounting treatment is ambiguous, then any reasonable allocation, LIFO or FIFO, is acceptable.

Capitalisation of profits

The source of profits capitalised (e.g. bonus issues) is determined as above. Since the capitalisation is an appropriation of profits, not a diminution, it has no effect on the underlying tax rate computation.

Prior year adjustments/changes of accounting policy

(*a*)   Increases are regarded as relevant profit for the year in which the adjustment is made. The accounts for the period show an amount of distributable profit and it follows from Bowater that that amount is relevant profit for that period.

(*b*)   Decreases, such as losses, are deductible in arriving at relevant profit. The allocation of the decrease is determined as above. In particular, if the accounts show a loss deducted from prior years' profits in the reserves, rather than from the current year profit and loss account profits, that treatment must be followed. Prior year adjustments which are deductible may increase the underlying tax rates for earlier years but only in respect of dividends declared payable after the date of the accounting adjustment.

Double Taxation Relief (Taxes on Income) (General) Regulations 1970 (SI 1970/488) — As amended by Double Taxation Relief (Taxes on Income) (General) (Amendment) Regulations 1996 with effect from 6 April 1996

Made on 24 March 1970 by the Commissioners of Inland Revenue under s. 351 of the Income Tax Act 1952 and s. 64 of the Finance Act 1965. [ICTA 1988, s. 791].

1(1) These Regulations may be cited as the Double Taxation Relief (Taxes on Income) (General) Regulations 1970 and shall come into operation on 6 April 1970.

1(2) The Interpretation Act 1889 shall apply to these regulations as it applies to an Act of Parliament. *Note — Interpretation Act 1889 now repealed and re-enacted as Interpretation Act 1978.*

1(3) In these Regulations 'the Board' means the Commissioners of Inland Revenue; 'year' means year of assessment.

1(4) Except in relation to payments which are income of the year 1969–70 or an earlier year the Double Taxation Relief (Taxes on Income) (General) Regulations 1966 shall cease to have effect from 6 April 1970:

Provided that any notice, direction or claim given or made under Regulation 2, 9 or 11 of the said Regulations of 1966 (including any notice, direction or claim having effect as if so given or made) which was in force immediately before the coming into operation of these Regulations shall continue in force as if given or made under the corresponding provision of these Regulations and the following provisions of these Regulations shall apply accordingly.

2(1) The following provisions of these Regulations shall have effect where, under arrangements having effect under section 497 of the Income and Corporation Taxes Act 1970 [ICTA 1988, s. 788], persons resident in the territory with the government of which the arrangements are made are entitled to exemption or partial relief from United Kingdom income tax in respect of any income from which deduction of tax is authorised or required by the Income Tax Acts.

2(2) Any person who pays any such income (referred to in these Regulations as 'the United Kingdom payer') to a person in the said territory who is beneficially entitled to the income (such person being referred to in these Regulations as 'the non-resident') may be directed by a notice in writing given by or on behalf of the Board that in paying any such income specified in the notice to the non-resident he shall—

(*a*)   not deduct tax, or

(*b*)   not deduct tax at a higher rate than is specified in the notice, or

(*c*)   deduct tax at a rate specified in the notice instead of at the lower or basic rate otherwise appropriate;

and where such notice is given, any income to which the notice refers, being income for a year for which the arrangements have effect, which the United Kingdom payer pays after the date of the notice to the non-resident named therein shall, subject to the following provisions of these Regulations, be paid as directed in the notice:

Provided that income specified in a notice given under this paragraph shall not include distributions in respect of which income tax is chargeable under Schedule F.

3 Where a notice given under Regulation 2(2) directs the United Kingdom payer to deduct tax at a rate specified in the notice, the provisions of the Income Tax Acts under which he would, but for the notice, have been chargeable with or liable to account for all or part of any tax deducted at the lower or basic rate shall apply as if those Acts required him to deduct tax at the rate so specified.

4(1) Where but for a notice given under Regulation 2(2) the United Kingdom payer would have been entitled to retain any income tax deductible on making any payment, there shall be made to him against the income tax otherwise payable by him for the relevant year an allowance equal to the amount of tax which, but for the notice, he would have been entitled to retain on making the payment but in compliance with the notice has not deducted.

4(2) 'The relevant year' means the year the lower or basic rate for which would (but for the notice) have determined the amount of the deduction authorised.

5 The United Kingdom payer shall not, in respect of any payment, be charged with or liable to account for any tax which, but for a notice given under Regulation 2(2), he would have been required by the Income Tax Acts to deduct and account for on making the payment but in compliance with the notice has not deducted.

6 Where in compliance with a notice given under Regulation 2(2) a company makes the payment without deducting tax which, but for the notice, it would have been required to deduct in accordance with section 53 or 54 of the Income and Corporation Taxes Act 1970 [ICTA 1988, s. 349], the payment shall be treated for the purposes of section 248(4) of that Act [s. 338(4)] (which prohibits certain payments from being treated as charges on income for corporation tax) as if the company had deducted that tax in accordance with the said section 53 or 54 [s. 349] and had accounted for it under Part XI of that Act [ICTA 1988, Pt. VIII].

7 Where, but for a notice given under Regulation 2(2), a person would have been chargeable with tax under section 53 of the Income and Corporation Taxes Act

1970 [ICTA 1988, s. 349] in respect of any such payment as is mentioned in subsection (1) thereof, the provisions of the Income Tax Acts relating to relief for losses shall apply as if the tax which would have been so chargeable but in accordance with Regulation 5 is not so chargeable had been paid by him under an assessment under the said section 53 [s. 349].

8 Any notice given under Regulation 2(2) may be expressed to become ineffective if certain specified events happen, or, whether so expressed or not, may be cancelled by a notice of cancellation given by or on behalf of the Board, and if to the knowledge of the United Kingdom payer any of those events happens or if such notice of cancellation is given, any payment made to the non-resident by the United Kingdom payer after the happening of that event becomes known to the United Kingdom payer or after the receipt of that notice, as the case may be, shall be subject to deduction of tax in accordance with the Income Tax Acts.

9 If it is discovered after a notice has been given under Regulation 2(2) that the non-resident is not entitled to exemption or partial relief from tax in respect of income referred to in the notice, any tax which, but for the notice, would have been deductible from any payment made to the non-resident by the United Kingdom payer but in compliance with the notice has not been so deducted—

(*a*)   may be assessed on the non-resident under Case VI of Schedule D by an Inspector, or

(*b*)   shall, if a direction to that effect is given by or on behalf of the Board, be deducted by the United Kingdom payer out of so much of the first payment made to the non-resident after the date of the direction as remains after the deduction of any tax deductible therefrom under the Income Tax Acts, and any balance which cannot be deducted out of the first such payment shall be deducted, subject to the same limitation, out of the next such payment, and so on until the whole of the tax (the amount of which shall be specified in the direction) has been deducted.

Any tax which the United Kingdom payer is required to deduct under paragraph (*b*) of this Regulation shall be accounted for as if it was tax deductible under section 53 of the Income and Corporation Taxes Act 1970 [ICTA 1988, s. 349] in respect of the payment from which it is deducted.

10 A notice may be given under Regulation 2(2) where income is paid to a person authorised to receive that income on behalf of the non-resident, and in such a case the references in these Regulations to payment to the non-resident shall be treated as including references to payment to that person.

11 Regulations 2(2) and 8 shall not apply to payments in respect of coupons for any interest, but any such payments may, under arrangements approved by the Board, be made without deduction of tax or with tax deducted at a rate specified in the arrangements, if the non-resident or any person acting on his behalf makes a claim to the United Kingdom payer to that effect in such form as may be prescribed by the Board, and in the case of any payments so made Regulations 3 to 7 inclusive and Regulation 9 shall, with any necessary modifications, apply as if the claim were a notice given under Regulation 2(2).

Appendix 7

EC Parent/Subsidiary Directive 90/435/EEC

On the common system of taxation applicable in the case of parent companies and subsidiaries of different member states (23 July 1990, OJ 1990 L225/6)

[As amended by the Act of Accession of Austria, Finland and Sweden with effect from 1 January 1995.]

The Council of the European Communities,

Having regard to the treaty establishing the European Economic Community, and in particular Article 100 thereof,
Having regard to the proposal of the Commission,
Having regard to the opinion of the European Parliament,
Having regard to the opinion of the Economic and Social Committee,

[1] Whereas the grouping together of companies of different member states may be necessary in order to create within the Community conditions analogous to those of an internal market and in order thus to ensure the establishment and effective functioning of the common market; whereas such operations ought not to be hampered by restrictions, disadvantages or distortions arising in particular from the tax provisions of the member states; whereas it is therefore necessary to introduce with respect to such grouping together of companies of different member states, tax rules which are neutral from the point of view of competition, in order to allow enterprises to adapt to the requirements of the common market, to increase their productivity and to improve their competitive strength at the international level;

[2] Whereas such grouping together may result in the formation of groups of parent companies and subsidiaries;

[3] Whereas the existing tax provisions which govern the relations between parent companies and subsidiaries of different member states vary appreciably from one member state to another and are generally less advantageous than those applicable to parent companies and subsidiaries of the same member state; whereas co-operation between companies of different member states is thereby disadvantaged in comparison with co-operation between companies of the same member state; whereas it is necessary to eliminate this disadvantage by the introduction of a common system in order to facilitate the grouping together of companies;

[4] Whereas where a parent company by virtue of its association with its subsidiary receives distributed profits, the state of the parent company must:

— either refrain from taxing such profits,

— or tax such profits while authorising the parent company to deduct from the amount of tax due that fraction of the corporation tax paid by the subsidiary which relates to those profits;

[5] Whereas it is furthermore necessary, in order to ensure fiscal neutrality, that the profits which a subsidiary distributes to its parent company be exempt from withholding tax; whereas, however, the Federal Republic of Germany and the Hellenic Republic, by reason of the particular nature of their corporate tax systems, and the Portuguese Republic, for budgetary reasons, should be authorised to maintain temporarily a withholding tax,

has adopted this directive:

Art. 1 [Application]

1(1) Each member state shall apply this directive:

— to distributions of profits received by companies of that state which come from their subsidiaries of other member states,

— to distributions of profits by companies of that state to companies of other member states of which they are subsidiaries.

1(2) This directive shall not preclude the application of domestic or agreement-based provisions required for the prevention of fraud or abuse.

Art. 2 [Interpretation]

2 For the purposes of this directive 'company of a member state' shall mean any company which:

(*a*) takes one of the forms listed in the annex hereto;

(*b*) according to the tax laws of a member state is considered to be resident in that state for tax purposes and, under the terms of a double taxation agreement concluded with a third state, is not considered to be resident for tax purposes outside the Community;

(*c*) moreover, is subject to one of the following taxes, without the possibility of an option or of being exempt:

— impôt des sociétés/vennootschapsbelasting in Belgium,

— selskabsskat in Denmark,

— Körperschaftsteuer in the Federal Republic of Germany,

— φορος εἰσοδηματος υομικωυ προσωπωυ κερδοσκοπικου χαρακτηρα in Greece,

— impuesto sobre sociedades in Spain,

— impôt sur les sociétés in France,

— corporation tax in Ireland,

— imposta sul reddito delle persone giuridiche in Italy,

— impôt sur le revenu des collectivités in Luxembourg,

— vennootschapsbelasting in the Netherlands,

— imposto sobre o rendimento das pessoas colectivas in Portugal,

— corporation tax in the United Kingdom,

— Körperschaftsteuer in Austria,

— Yhteisöjen tulovero/inkomstskatten för samfund in Finland,

— Statlig inkomstskatt in Sweden,

or to any other tax which may be substituted for any of the above taxes.

Art. 3 [Interpretation]

3(1) For the purposes of applying this directive,

(*a*) the status of parent company shall be attributed at least to any company of a member state which fulfils the conditions set out in Article 2 and has a minimum holding of 25 per cent in the capital of a company of another member state fulfilling the same conditions;

(*b*) 'subsidiary' shall mean that company the capital of which includes the holding referred to in (*a*).

3(2) By way of derogation from paragraph 1, member states shall have the option of:

— replacing, by means of bilateral agreement, the criterion of a holding in the capital by that of a holding of voting rights,

— not applying this directive to companies of that member state which do not maintain for an uninterrupted period of at least two years holdings qualifying them as parent companies or to those of their companies in which a company of another member state does not maintain such a holding for an uninterrupted period of at least two years.

Art. 4 [Distribution of profits]

4(1) Where a parent company, by virtue of its association with its subsidiary, receives distributed profits, the state of the parent company shall, except when the subsidiary is liquidated, either:

— refrain from taxing such profits, or

— tax such profits while authorising the parent company to deduct from the amount of tax due that fraction of the corporation tax paid by the subsidiary which relates to those profits and, if appropriate, the amount of the withholding tax levied by the member state in which the subsidiary is resident, pursuant to the derogations provided for in Article 5, up to the limit of the amount of the corresponding domestic tax.

4(2) However, each member state shall retain the option of providing that any charges relating to the holding and any losses resulting from the distribution of the profits of the subsidiary may not be deducted from the taxable profits of the parent company. Where the management costs relating to the holding in such a case are fixed as a flat rate, the fixed amount may not exceed 5 per cent of the profits distributed by the subsidiary.

4(3) Paragraph 1 shall apply until the date of effective entry into force of a common system of company taxation.

The Council shall at the appropriate time adopt the rules to apply after the date referred to in the first subparagraph.

Art. 5 [Exemption from withholding taxes]

5(1) Profits which a subsidiary distributes to its parent company shall, at least where the latter holds a minimum of 25 per cent of the capital of the subsidiary, be exempt from withholding tax.

5(2) Notwithstanding paragraph 1, the Hellenic Republic may, for so long as it does not charge corporation tax on distributed profits, levy a withholding tax on profits distributed to parent companies of other member states. However, the rate of that withholding tax must not exceed the rate provided for in bilateral double-taxation agreements.

5(3) Notwithstanding paragraph 1, the Federal Republic of Germany may, for as long as it charges corporation tax on distributed profits at a rate at least 11 points lower than the rate applicable to retained profits, and at the latest until mid-1996, impose a compensatory withholding tax of 5 per cent on profits distributed by its subsidiary companies.

5(4) Notwithstanding paragraph 1, the Portuguese Republic may levy a with-holding tax on profits distributed by its subsidiaries to parent companies of other member states until a date not later than the end of the eighth year following the date of application of this directive.

Subject to the existing bilateral agreements concluded between Portugal and a member state, the rate of this withholding tax may not exceed 15 per cent during the first five years and 10 per cent during the last three years of that period.

Before the end of the eighth year the Council shall decide unanimously, on a proposal from the Commission, on a possible extension of the provisions of this paragraph.

Art. 6 [Prohibition of withholding taxes]

6 The member state of a parent company may not charge withholding tax on the profits which such a company receives from a subsidiary.

Art. 7 [Withholding taxes: further provisions]

7(1) The term 'withholding tax' as used in this directive shall not cover an advance payment or prepayment (précompte) of corporation tax to the member state of the subsidiary which is made in connection with a distribution of profits to its parent company.

7(2) This directive shall not affect the application of domestic or agreement-based provisions designed to eliminate or lessen economic double taxation of dividends, in particular provisions relating to the payment of tax credits to the recipients of dividends.

Art. 8 [Entry into force]

8(1) Member states shall bring into force the laws, regulations and administrative provisions necessary for them to comply with the directive before 1 January 1992. They shall forthwith inform the Commission thereof.

8(2) Member states shall ensure that the texts of the main provisions of domestic law which they adopt in the field covered by this directive are communicated to the Commission.

Art. 9 [Final provisions]

9 This directive is addressed to the member states.

Annex — List of companies referred to in Article 2(a)

(*a*)   companies under Belgian law known as: 'société anonyme'/'naamloze vennootschap', 'société en commandite par actions'/'commanditaire vennootschap op aandelen', 'société privée à responsabilité limitée'/'besloten vennootschap met beperkte aansprakelijkheid' and those public law bodies that operate under private law;

(*b*)   companies under Danish law known as: 'aktieselskab', 'anpartsselskab';

(*c*)   companies under German law known as: 'Aktiengesellschaft', 'Kommanditgesellschaft auf Aktien', 'Gesellschaft mit beschränkter Haftung', 'bergrechtliche Gewerkschaft';

(*d*)   companies under Greek law known as: 'ἀνωνυη ἑταιρεια';

(*e*)   companies under Spanish law known as: 'sociedad anónima', 'sociedad comanditaria por acciones', 'sociedad de responsabilidad limitada' and those public law bodies which operate under private law;

(*f*)   companies under French law known as: 'société anonyme', 'société en commandite par actions', 'société à responsabilité limitée' and industrial and commercial public establishments and undertakings;

(*g*)   the companies in Irish law known as public companies limited by shares or by guarantee, private companies limited by shares or by guarantee, bodies registered under the Industrial and Provident Societies Acts or building societies registered under the Building Societies Acts;

(*h*)   companies under Italian law known as: 'società per azioni', 'società in accomandati per azioni', 'società a responsabilità limitata', and public and private entities carrying on industrial and commercial activities;

(*i*)   companies under Luxembourg law known as: 'société anonyme', 'société en commandite par actions', 'société à responsabilité limitée';

(*j*)   companies under Netherlands law known as: 'naamloze vennootschap', 'besloten vennootschap met beperkte aansprakelijkheid';

(k)   commercial companies or civil law companies having a commercial form co-operatives and public undertakings incorporated in accordance with Portuguese law;

(l)   companies incorporated under the law of the United Kingdom;

(m)   companies under Austrian law known as: 'Aktiengesellschaft', 'Gesellschaft mit beschränkter Haftung';

(n)   companies under Finnish law known as: 'osakeyhtiö/aktiebolag', 'osuuskunta/andelslag', 'säästöpankki/sparbank' and 'vakuutusyhtiö/försäkringsaktiebolag';

(o)   companies under Swedish law known as: 'aktiebolag', 'bankaktiebolag', 'försäkringsaktiebolag'.

Appendix 8

Useful Addresses and Telephone Numbers

Inland Revenue Information Centre
Ground Floor
South West Wing
Bush House
Strand
London WC2B 4RD

Telephone: 020 7438 6420–5

Inland Revenue International Division
Strand Bridge House
138–142 Strand
London WC2R IHH

Financial Intermediaries and Claims Office (FICO)

FICO (International)
St John's House
Merton Road
Bootle
Merseyside L69 9BB

Telephone: 0151 472 6000

FICO (International)
Fitz Roy House
PO Box 46
Castle Meadow Road
Nottingham NG2 1BD

Telephone: 0115 974 2000

Capital Taxes Office
Inland Revenue
Ferrers House
PO Box 38
Castle Meadow Road
Nottingham NG2 1BB

Telephone: 0115 974 2400

Inland Revenue Underlying Tax Group
(as for FICO (International))

337

Entity Classification

In the Tax Bulletin, Issue 39 (February 1999) we said that we would compile and publish a list of the entities on whose classification for UK tax purposes — whether 'transparent' or 'opaque' — we have been asked for our view. That list is now set out below. A separate list of foreign entities which have been considered for Stamp Duty purposes appears in the recently published Stamp Duty manual.

It should be noted that the list only gives our general view as to the treatment of the specified foreign entity. In a particular case regard may also need to be had to:

- the specific terms of the UK taxation provision under which the matter requires to be considered;

- the provisions of any legislation, articles of association, by-laws, agreement or other document governing the entity's creation, continued existence and management; and

- the terms of any relevant Double Taxation Agreement.

It should also be borne in mind that in relation to the classifications set out on the list:

- In some instances the Revenue's view was given many years ago — as far as possible details are given in column 3. It needs to be borne in mind that since that time there may have been significant changes in the relevant foreign law which may mean that a different conclusion as to the status of that entity might now be reached. Changes in foreign law after the publication of this article may be significant for the same reason.

- Entities are described as respectively fiscally 'transparent' or 'opaque' for the purpose of deciding how a member is to be taxed on the income they derive from their interest in the entity. In the case of a 'transparent' entity the member is regarded as being entitled to a share in the underlying income of the entity as it arises. In the case of an 'opaque' entity the member generally is taxed only on the distributions made by the entity.

- The expressions 'transparent' and 'opaque' are not interchangeable with 'partnership' or 'body corporate'. For example, whilst a partnership is fiscally transparent for the purposes of UK tax on income, a fiscally transparent entity is not necessarily a partnership.

Where clarification is sought in relation to a foreign entity we will attempt to give a view in particular cases in line with Code of Practice 10. The following are the contact points:

Appendix 9

(a)   In all cases (except in relation to whether an entity may be a collective investment scheme):
Martin Brooks
Inland Revenue, International, Room 310
Victory House, 30–34 Kingsway,
London WC2B 6ES

(b)   The list does not indicate whether the particular entities constitute collective investment schemes. Where clarification is needed on this point you should contact:
Graham Turner
Inland Revenue, Business Tax
Room S3, West Wing,
Somerset House,
London WC2R ILB

Overseas Business Entitites

Country and name of entity	UK tax treatment	Date last considered
ANGUILLA Partnership	Transparent	10/1991
ARGENTINA Socieded de responsibilidad limitada	Opaque	6/1958
AUSTRIA Kommanditgesellschaft (KG)	Transparent	8/1971
BELGIUM Société de privée à responsabilité limitée (SPRL)	Opaque	8/1994
Société en nom collectif (SNC)	Transparent	5/1992
BRAZIL Sociedade por quotas de responsabilidade limitada	Opaque	1/1977
CANADA Partnership and Limited Partnership	Transparent	
CAYMAN ISLANDS Limited Partnership	Transparent	11/1993
CHILE Sociedad de responsibilidad limitada (S.R.L.)	Transparent	5/1996
FINLAND Kommandiittiyhtiö, Ky	Transparent	5/1991
FRANCE Groupement d'Intérêt economique (GIE)	Transparent	5/1988
Société en nom collectif (SNC)	Transparent	8/2000
Société civile immobiliòre (SCI)	Opaque	2/2000
Société civile agricole (SCA)	Opaque	2/1998
Société anonyme (SA)	Opaque	
Société en commandite simple	Transparent	9/1997

339

Appendix 9

Country and name of entity	UK tax treatment	Date last considered
Société en participation (SP)	Transparent	6/1992
Société à responsabilité limitée (SARL)	Opaque	
Fonds Commun de Placement à risques (FCPR)	Transparent	1/1997
GERMANY		
Stille Gesellschaft	Opaque	6/1998
Kommanditgesellschaft (KG)	Transparent	2/1997
Offene Handelsgesellschaft (OHG)	Transparent	9/1996
Gesellschaft mit Besehränkter Haftung (GmbH)	Opaque	2/1997
GMBH & Co. KG	Transparent	2/1997
Gesellschaft mit Bürgerlichen Rechts (GBR)	Transparent	4/1994
IRELAND		
Limited Partnership	Transparent	
Irish Investment Limited Partnership	Transparent	
JAPAN		
Goshi-Kaisha	Transparent	2/1997
Gomei Kaisha	Transparent	
Tokumei Kumiai (T.K.)	Transparent	8/2000
LIECHTENSTEIN		
Anstalt	Opaque	2/1987
LUXEMBOURG		
Société en commandite paractions (SCA)	Opaque	7/1992
Fonds commun de placement (FCP)	Transparent	1/1996
NETHERLANDS		
Vennootschap Onder Firma (VOF)	Transparent	2/1995
Commanditaire Vennootschap both 'open' and 'closed' (CV)	Transparent	8/2000
Naamloze Vennootschap (NV)	Opaque	10/1981
Besloten Vennootschap Met Beperkte Aansprakelijheid (BV)	Opaque	10/1981
Maatschap	Transparent	10/1993
NORWAY		
Alkjeselskap (AS)	Opaque	
Kommandittselkap (K/S)	Transparent	1/1981
POLAND		
Spolkaz ograniczonaod-powiedzialnoscia (SDP.zo.o)	Opaque	3/1996
PORTUGAL		
Sociedade por quotas (Lda)	Opaque	4/1993
Sociedade Anónima (SA)	Opaque	4/1993
RUSSIA		
Joint Venture under 'Decree No. 49'	Opaque	1/1993
SPAIN		
Sociedad Civila	Opaque	12/1980

Country and name of entity	UK tax treatment	Date last considered
SWITZERLAND Société Simple	Transparent	12/1990
USA Partnership set up under the Uniform Partnership Act	Transparent	9/1983
Limited Partnership set up under the Uniform Limited Partnership Act	Transparent	8/2000
Limited Liability Company (LLC)	Opaque	6/1997
Limited Liability Partnership (LLP)	Transparent	12/1999

[*IR Tax Bulletin*, December 2000, pp 809–812]

Index

Index

Index

348

Index

Life assurance business
periods beginning after 31 March
2000,
5.21–5.23
restriction of credit relief for overseas
business, 5.19–5.23
see also Insurance companies
Loan relationships
companies, 3.38–3.41, 3.48
Loans
interest on certain overseas loans,
5.4–5.10
Local authority taxes
unilateral relief, 2.13, 3.17
Long-term contracts
'root income' principle, 3.12
Losses
claims, 3.34
Luxembourg
holding companies, 8.3
shipping and air transport, 7.14
tax credits, payment of, 7.25

M

Maintenance payments
extra-statutory concession on source
of income, 3.11
Malaysia
directors' fees, 7.51
income not expressly mentioned, 7.65
interest, 7.33
professors and teachers, 7.64
students and apprentices, 7.62
tax sparing relief, 8.8
Malta
excluded companies, 8.3
Management fees
articles in agreements, 7.41
Mauritius
professors and teachers, 7.64
Mergers
double tax relief for foreign
mergers, 4.75
Miscellaneous rules
articles in agreements, 8.25–8.26
Model agreements, *see* OECD Model
agreement on Estates and Inheritances;
OECD Model Convention on Capital
and Income; United Nations Model
Convention
**Movable property of a permanent
establishment**
gains on sale of, 7.42
IHT agreements, 10.23
Mutual agreement
articles in agreements, 8.14–8.18
IHT agreements, 10.35–10.36
OECD and UN models, 8.16–8.18

OECD model agreement on Estates
and Inheritances, 10.36
Mutual assistance
EC Directive, 2.31
OECD/Council of Europe
Convention, 2.32
Myanmar (formerly Burma)
residence, 6.23
underlying tax relief for portfolio
shareholders, 4.26

N

Namibia
territorial extension, 8.23
Nationality
definition, 6.13
The Netherlands
artistes and athletes, 7.54
deductions, 10.25
dividends, 7.27
elimination of double taxation, 8.7
groups of companies paying tax
on a consolidated basis, 4.72–4.74
immovable property, 10.22
inheritance tax agreements, 9.10,
10.1–10.41
interest, 7.32, 7.33
movable property of a permanent
establishment, 10.23
mutual agreement, 10.35–10.36
personal allowances, 8.1
shipping and air transport, 7.14, 10.24
tax credits, payment of, 7.25
taxing rights articles, 10.16
termination of agreement, 8.33
time limit for claiming under IHT
agreements, 10.31
New Zealand
dividends, 7.27
income not expressly mentioned, 7.65
interest, 7.30
royalties, 7.35, 7.36
Nigeria
interest, 7.30
Non-discrimination
articles in agreements, 8.11–8.13
IHT agreements, 10.32–10.34
OECD and UN models, 8.13
OECD model agreement on Estates
and Inheritances, 10.34
Non-resident company, 3.6
UK branches of foreign bank, 3.7
Non-residents
UK meaning of 'resident', 3.4
Norway
tax credits, payment of, 7.25

349

Index

O

OECD/Council of Europe Convention
UK not signatory to, 2.32
OECD model agreement on Estates and Inheritances, 10.1
deductions, 10.26
diplomatic agents and consular officials, 10.38
elimination of double taxation, 10.30
exchange of information, 10.37
fiscal domicile, 10.10
general definitions, 10.5–10.6
immovable property, 10.22
mutual agreement, 10.36
non-discrimination, 10.34
other property article, 10.19
scope, 10.3
termination, 10.41
OECD Model Convention on Income and Capital
1963 Convention, 2.5
1977 Convention, 2.5
2000 Convention, Appendix 1
artistes and athletes, 7.56
associated enterprises, 7.13
business profits, 7.9
capital, 7.68
capital gains, 7.44
compared to the United Nations model, 2.5
dependent personal services, 7.50
diplomatic and consular officers, 8.21
directors' fees, 7.53
dividends, 7.28
dividends articles different in UK agreements, 2.5
elimination of double taxation, 8.9–8.10
entry into force, 8.32
exchange of information, 8.20
'general definitions' articles, 6.15
government service, 7.61
income from immovable property, 7.2–7.4
independent personal services article deleted, 7.47
interest, 7.34
mutual agreement, 8.16–8.18
non-discrimination, 8.13
pensions and annuities, 7.59
personal allowances article not included, 8.2
personal scope, 6.5–6.7
residence, 6.24
royalties, 7.40
shipping and air transport, 7.16
students and apprentices, 7.63
taxes covered, 6.9
termination, 8.34
territorial extension, 8.24

Offshore activities
articles in agreements on taxation of, 8.27–8.28
Organisation for Economic Co-operation and Development (OECD)
consultative document on permanent establishments, 7.10
electronic commerce releases, 6.39
establishment, 2.5
members, 2.5
model agreements, *see* OECD model agreement on Estates and Inheritances; OECD Model Convention on Income and Capital
report on tax sparing relief, 8.8
status of OECD commentaries in interpretation of agreements, 6.2

P

Pakistan
dividends, 7.27
estate duty agreements, 9.10, 10.1
permanent establishment, 6.27, 6.29
Parent/Subsidiary Directive, 2.7, 7.17, Appendix 7
Partnerships
definition, 6.12
France, 6.23
Germany, 6.23
personal scope, 6.5–6.6
residence, 6.23
Patent
source of income, 3.10
Paying agent
deduction of tax by, 2.22–2.23
Pension funds
residence, 6.23
Pension schemes
miscellaneous rules article, 8.25
Pensions and annuities
articles in agreements, 7.57–7.59
OECD and UN models, 7.59
Permanent establishment
articles in agreements, 6.25–6.38
definition, 6.26
movable property, 10.23
OECD consultative document, 7.10
OECD model, 6.25–6.38
transfer of assets, 3.60
UN model, 6.38
Person
definition, 6.12, 6.15
Personal allowances
article not included in OECD and UN models, 8.2
articles in agreements, 8.1–8.2
Personal scope article
articles in agreements, 3.3, 6.3–6.7

Index

Index